CASS LIBRARY OF SCIENCE CLASSICS

No. 11

General Editor: Dr. L. L. LAUDAN, University of Pittsburgh

MATHEMATICAL AND PHILOSOPHICAL

WORKS

THE

MATHEMATICAL AND PHILOSOPHICAL

WORKS

OF THE

Right Rev. John Wilkins

TWO VOLUMES IN ONE

FRANK CASS & CO. LTD.

1970

Published by
FRANK CASS AND COMPANY LIMITED
67 Great Russell Street, London WC1

First published   1708
Second edition   1802
New impression, with index,
of Second edition   1970

SBN 7146 1618 4

Printed in Great Britain by Clarke, Doble & Brendon Ltd.
Plymouth and London

Publisher's Note to the 1970 Edition

This is an exact facsimile reproduction of the 1802 edition of *The Mathematical and Philosophical Works of the Right Rev. John Wilkins*. An index, prepared by the General Editor, has been added at the end of the volume.

Editor's Note to the 1970 Edition

Bishop John Wilkins (1614–1672) occupies a prominent position in English intellectual history. As Warden of Wadham College, Oxford and (briefly) as Master of Trinity College, Cambridge, he played a major role in the revitalization of British university education in the middle of the seventeenth century; moreover, he was a prime mover in the establishment of the Royal Society of London and was its first secretary. In spite of these achievements, his works are not widely known today and are, in many cases, extremely rare. He is chiefly remembered for his *Essay towards a Real Character and a Philosophical Language* (London, 1668), a précis of which will be found at the end of this volume. During his own life-time, however, his works on astronomy, mechanics and cryptography were widely read and were the foundation for his considerable reputation. The chief of these, all of which appear in this volume, are *The Discovery of a New World* (3rd. ed., London, 1640); *A Discourse Concerning a New Planet* (London, 1640); *Mercury; or, the Secret Messenger* (London, 1641); and *Mathematical Magick* (London, 1648).

The name of the editor of the early nineteenth-century edition of Wilkins's works reprinted here is unknown. There are variations of spelling and style throughout this volume which are too numerous to document, but they should not lead to serious confusions. Generally, Wilkins's spellings have been followed in the preparation of the index.

Effigies Reverendi admodum veri
Johannis Wilkins nuper Episcopi
Cestriensis.

THE

MATHEMATICAL AND PHILOSOPHICAL

WORKS

OF THE

RIGHT REV. JOHN WILKINS,

LATE LORD BISHOP OF CHESTER,

TO WHICH IS PREFIXED

THE AUTHOR's LIFE,

AND

AN ACCOUNT OF HIS WORKS.

———

IN TWO VOLUMES.

———

VOL. I.

CONTAINING,

I. The Discovery of a New World: or, a Discourse tending to prove, that it is probable there may be another Habitable World in the Moon. With a Discourse of the Possibility of a Passage thither. II. That it is probable our Earth is one of the Planets.

———

LONDON:

PRINTED BY C. WHITTINGHAM,
Dean Street, Fetter Lane,

FOR VERNOR AND HOOD, POULTRY; CUTHELL, AND MARTIN, MIDDLE-ROW;
HOLBORN; AND J. WALKER, PATERNOSTER-ROW.

———

1802.

THE

LIFE OF THE AUTHOR:

AND AN

ACCOUNT OF HIS WRITINGS.

HE was son to Walter Wilkins, citizen and gold-
smith of Oxford; was born at Fawlsly, near
Daventry, in Northamptonshire, in the house of the
reverend and well known Mr. John Dod, who
wrote upon the commandments, he being his
grandfather by the mother's side. He was taught
his Latin and Greek by Edward Sylvester, a noted
Grecian, who kept a private school in the parish
of All Saints in Oxford: his proficiency was such,
that at thirteen years of age he entered a student in
New-Inn, in Easter-term, 1627. He made no long
stay there, but was removed to Magdalen-Hall,
under the tuition of Mr. John Tombes, and there
he took his degrees in arts. He afterwards entered into orders, and was first chaplain to William

Lord Say, and then to Charles Count Palatine of the Rhine, and Prince Elector of the Empire, with whom he continued for some time.

Upon the breaking out of the civil war, he joined with the parliament, and took the solemn league and covenant. He was afterwards made warden of Wadham College by the committee of parliament appointed for reforming the university; and being created bachelor of divinity, April 12, 1648, was the day following put in possession of his wardenship. Next year he was created doctor of divinity, and about that time took the engagement then enjoined by the powers in being.

In 1656, he married Robina, the widow of Peter French, formerly canon of Christ-Church, sister to Oliver, then Lord Protector. In 1659, he was by Richard the Protector made head of Trinity College in Cambridge, the best preferment in that university.

After king Charles the IId's restoration, he was ejected from thence, and became preacher to the honourable society of Gray's-Inn, and minister of St. Lawrence Jury, London, in the room of Dr. Ward. About this time he became a member of the royal society, was chosen one of their council, and proved one of their most eminent members, and chief benefactors. Soon after this he was

made dean of Rippon, and by the interest of the
late duke of Buckingham, he was created bishop
of Chester, and consecrated in the chapel of Ely-
house in Holborn, the 15th of November, 1668,
by Dr. Cosin, bishop of Durham; Dr. Laney,
bishop of Ely; and Dr. Ward, bishop of Salisbury;
on which occasion Dr. Tillotson, afterwards archbishop of Canterbury, preached an excellent
sermon.

He was a person of great natural endowments,
and by his indefatigable study attained to an universal insight into all, or at least most parts of useful learning. He was a great mathematician, and
very much advanced the study of astronomy, both
while he was warden of Wadham College in Oxford, and at London, when he was a member of
the royal society. He was as well seen in mechanics and experimental philosophy as any man in
his time, and was a great promoter of them. In
divinity, which was his main business, he excelled,
and was a very able critic; his talent of preaching
was admirable, and more suited to profit than to
please his hearers; he affected an apt and plain
way of speech, and expressed his conceptions in a
natural style. In his writings he was judicious
and plain, and valued not circumstances so much
as the substance. This appeared evident in whatever subject he undertook, which he always made
easier for those that came after him.

He treated sometimes on matters that did not properly belong to his profession; but always with a design to make men wiser and better; which was his chief end in promoting universal knowledge, and one of the main reasons for his entering into the royal society. His virtues and graces were very uncommon; at least as to that degree of them to which he attained : his prudence was very remarkable, and seldom failed him; but he was so openhearted and sincere himself, that he was ready (except he knew some cause to the contrary) to think other men to be so too; by which he was sometimes imposed on.

His greatness of mind was evident to all that knew any thing of him, nor was the depth of his judgment less discernible. He never was eager in pursuit of dignities; but was advanced to them by his merit. He contemned riches as much as others admired them; and spent his ecclesiastical revenues in the service of the church from which he received them; and being secured against want, he would often say, that he would be no richer: and his conduct made it evident that he was as good as his word.

He was a stranger to revenge, and yet not insensible of personal injuries, especially such as reflected on his good name, if they proceeded from such as had a good reputation of their own. The reproaches of others he despised; but frequently wished he had been better understood by the former: he bore it, however, patiently, as his misfortune; never requited them with the like measure; but always mentioned them with respect, and laid hold on all opportunities to oblige and do them good.

His conversation was profitable and pleasant; and his discourse was commonly of useful things; without occasioning trouble or weariness in those that conversed with him. He cultivated that most necessary (but too much neglected) part of friendship, to give seasonable reproof, and wholesome advice, upon occasion. This he did with a great deal of freedom; but with so much calmness and prudence, that it seldom gave offence.

He was particularly careful of the reputation of his friends; and would suffer no blot to lie upon the good name or memory of any of them, if he could help it.

His enemies, who were strangers to moderation themselves, made that virtue in which he excelled, the chief subject of their reproaches, as if he had been a person of unsteady principles, and not fixed in matters of religion; this drew severe censures upon him from archbishop Sheldon, bishop Fell, and archbishop Dolben, &c. without considering that he could not but have a great deal of charity for dissenters, by reason of his education under Mr. John Dod his grandfather, a truly pious and learned man; who dissented in many things from the church of England long before the separation which afterwards followed upon archbishop Laud's severities and new impositions.

And as his said grandfather never approved of the extremities on the other side, but continued loyal to the last, and advised others to continue in their allegiance; in like manner Doctor Wilkins, (though he had clearness when the government was dissolved, to submit to the powers then in being, by which he procured an interest and a share in the government of both universities;) was always a friend to those who were loyal, and continued well affected to the church of England, and protected several of them by the interest he had in the then government.

After the restoration he conformed himself to the church of England, and stood up for her government and liturgy; but disliked vehemence in little and unnecessary things, and freely censured it as fanatacism on both sides.

Having thus conformed to the church himself, he was very willing to bring over others: in which he was not without success, especially in his own diocese; where the extremes on both sides were as remarkable, as in most parts of the nation. Being a person of extensive charity himself, he was for an indulgence and a comprehension, in order to have brought our divisions in matters of religion to a conclusion; which drew upon him the hatred and obloquy of those who were for contrary measures.

His indefatigable pains in study brought the stone upon him; which proved incurable. He had for many days a prospect of death; which he viewed in its approaches, and gradual advances upon him: and a few days before his dissolution, he frequently said, that he found a sentence of death within himself. But in the height of his pain and apprehensions of death, he shewed no dismay or surprise, nor was ever heard to utter a word unbecoming a wise man, or a true christian. And thus he concluded his days with constancy of mind, contempt of the world, and cheerful hopes of a blessed eternity, through faith in our Lord Jesus Christ. He died in the house of his friend Dr. Tillotson, in Chancery-lane in London, on the 19th of November, 1672; and was buried on the 12th of December following, under the north wall of the chancel of the church of St. Lawrence Jewry, where he had formerly been minister. His funeral sermon was preached by Dr. William Lloyd, then dean of Bangor, (afterward Lord Bishop of Worcester) at the Guildhall chapel in London; by which, those who are curious may be satisfied, that every part of the character here given him, may be justified to advantage.

As a further proof of it, and particularly of his unwearied endeavours to promote universal knowledge, it is proper to subjoin a catalogue of his works.

The first was entitled,

1. The Discovery of a New World; or, a Discourse tending to prove, that it is probable there may be another habitable World in the Moon. Printed at London, in quarto, 1638, and had four editions, the last in 1684.

2. Discourse concerning the Possibility of a Passage to the World in the Moon. Printed with the Discovery.

3. Discourse concerning a New Planet; tending to prove, that it is probable our Earth is one of the Planets. London, 1640, in octavo.

The author's name is put to none of the three; but they were so well known to be his, that Langrenus, in his map of the moon, (dedicated to the king of Spain) calls one of the spots of his selenographic map after his name.

4. Mercury; or, the Secret Messenger: shewing how a Man may with Privacy and Speed com-

municate his Thoughts to his Friend at any Distance. London, 1641. The publication of this was occasioned by the writing of a little thing, called Nuncius Inanimatus, by Francis Goodwin.

5. Mathematical Magic; or, the Wonders that may be performed by Mechanical Geometry. In two books. Printed at London in 1648, and 1680, in octavo.

6. Ecclesiastes; or, A Discourse of the Gift of Preaching, as it falls under the Rules of Art. London, 1646, 1647, 1651, 1653, and 1675, octavo.

7. Discourse concerning the Beauty of Providence, in all the rugged Passages of it. London, 1649, in twelves; and in 1677, the fifth edition, in octavo.

8. Discourse concerning the Gift of Prayer; shewing what it is; wherein it consists; and how far it is attainable by Industry, &c. London, 1653, and 1674, octavo.

9. Of the Principles and Duties of Natural Religion. Two books. London, 1675, octavo. Published by John Tillotson, D. D.

10. Sermons preached upon several Occasions. London, 1682, octavo. They are in number fifteen, published by Dr. Tillotson.

11. Essay towards a Real Character, and a Philosophical Language.   London, 1668, folio.

12. An Alphabetical Dictionary: wherein all English Words, according to their various Significations, are either referred to their Places in the Philosophical Tables, or explained by such Words as are in those Tables. This is printed with the Essay.

CONTENTS.

VOL. I.

BOOK I.

THAT THE MOON MAY BE A WORLD.

PROPOSITION I.

BOOK II.

THAT THE EARTH MAY BE A PLANET.

PROPOSITION I.

BOOK I.

THE

DISCOVERY OF A NEW WORLD;

OR,

A DISCOURSE

TENDING TO PROVE, THAT (IT IS PROBABLE) THERE MAY BE ANOTHER

HABITABLE WORLD IN THE MOON.

WITH

A DISCOURSE CONCERNING THE POSSIBILITY OF A PASSAGE THITHER.

THE READER.

———

*I*F amongst thy leisure hours, thou canst spare any for
the perusal of this Discourse, and dost look to find somewhat in it which may serve for thy information and benefit;
let me then advise thee to come unto it with an equal mind,
not swayed by prejudice, but indifferently resolved to assent
unto that truth which upon deliberation shall seem most
probable unto thy reason; and then I doubt not, but either
thou wilt agree with me in this assertion, or at least not
think it to be as far from truth, as it is from common
opinion.

*Two cautions there are, which I would willingly admo-
nish thee of in the beginning:*

1. *That thou shouldst not here look to find an exact accurate treatise; since this discourse was but the fruit of
some lighter studies, and those too huddled up in a short
time; being first thought of and finished in the space of
some few weeks; and therefore you cannot in reason expect
that it should be so polished, as perhaps the subject would
require, or the leisure of the author might have done it.*

2. *To remember that I promise only probable arguments
for the proof of this opinion; and therefore you must not
look that every consequence should be of an undeniable dependance; or that the truth of each argument should be
measured by its necessity. I grant, that some astronomical appearances may possibly be solved otherwise than here
they are: but the thing I aim at is this: that probably
they may so be solved, as I have here set them down.
Which, if it be granted (as I think it must) then I doubt
not, but the indifferent reader will find some satisfaction in
the main thing that is to be proved.*

TO THE READER.

Many ancient philosophers of the better note have formerly defended this assertion which I have here laid down; and it were to be wished, that some of us would more apply our endeavours unto the examination of these old opinions; which, though they have for a long time lain neglected by others, yet in them you may find many truths well worthy your pains and observation. It is a false conceit, for us to think that amongst the ancient variety and search of opinions, the best hath still prevailed. Time (saith the learned Verulam) seems to be of the nature of a river or stream; which carrieth down to us that which is light, or blown up, but sinketh that which is weighty and solid.

It is my desire, that by the occasion of this discourse, I may raise up some more active spirit to a search after other hidden and unknown truths: since it must needs be a great impediment unto the growth of sciences, for men still to plod on upon beaten principles, as to be afraid of entertaining any thing that may seem to contradict them. An unwillingness to take such things into examination is one of those errors of learning, in these times observed by the judicious Verulam. Questionless there are many secret truths which the ancients have passed over, that are yet left to make some of our age famous for their discovery.

If by this occasion I may provoke any reader to an attempt of this nature, I shall think myself happy, and this Work successful.

Farewell.

BOOK I.

THAT THE MOON MAY BE A WORLD.

PROP. I.

BY WAY OF PREFACE.

*That the strangeness of this opinion is no sufficient reason
why it should be rejected; because other certain truths
have been formerly esteemed ridiculous, and great absurdities entertained by common consent.*

THERE is an earnestness and hungering after novelty,
which doth still adhere unto all our natures; and it
is part of that primitive image, that wide extent and infinite
capacity at first created in the heart of man. For this,
since its depravation in Adam, perceiving itself altogether
emptied of any good, doth now catch after every new thing,
conceiving that possibly it may find satisfaction among
some of its fellow creatures. But our enemy the devil
(who strives still to pervert our gifts, and beat us with our
own weapons) hath so contrived it, that any truth doth
now seem distasteful for that very reason, for which error
is entertained; novelty. For let but some upstart heresy
be set abroach, and presently there are some out of a
curious humour; others, as if they watched an occasion of
singularity, will take it up for canonical, and make it part
of their creed and profession; whereas solitary truth cannot anywhere find so ready entertainment; but the same
novelty which is esteemed the commendation of error, and
makes that acceptable, is counted the fault of truth, and
causes that to be rejected.

How did the incredulous world gaze at Columbus, when he promised to discover another part of the earth? And he could not for a long time, by his confidence or arguments, induce any of the christian princes, either to assent unto his opinion, or go to the charges of an experiment. Now if he, who had such good grounds for his assertion, could find no better entertainment among the wiser sort, and upper end of the world; it is not likely then that this opinion which I now deliver, shall receive any thing from the men of these days; especially our vulgar wits, but misbelief or derision.

It hath always been the unhappiness of new truths in philosophy, to be derided by those that are ignorant of the causes of things; and rejected by others, whose perverseness ties them to the contrary opinion; men whose envious pride will not allow any new thing for truth, which they themselves were not the first inventors of. So that I may justly expect to be accused of a pragmatical ignorance, and bold ostentation; especially, since for this opinion Xenophanes, a man whose authority was able to add some credit to his assertion, could not escape the like censure from others. For Natales Comes*, speaking of that philosopher, and this his opinion, saith thus: *Nonnulli ne nihil scisse videantur, aliqua nova monstra in philosophiam introducunt, ut alicujus rei inventores fuisse appareant.* " Some there " are who lest they might seem to know nothing, will " bring up monstrous absurdities in philosophy, that so " afterward they may be famed for the invention of some- " what." The same author doth also in another place† accuse Anaxagoras of folly for the same opinion. *Est enim non ignobilis gradus stultitiæ, vel si nescias quid dicas, tamen velle de rebus propositis hanc vel illam partem stabilire.* " 'Tis none of the worst kinds of folly, boldly " to affirm one side or other, when a man knows not what " to say."

If these men were thus censured, I may justly then expect

---

* Mythol. lib. 3. c. 17.   † Lib. 7. c. 1.

to be derided by most, and to be believed by few or none; especially since this opinion seems to carry in it so much strangeness, and contradiction to the general consent of others. But however, I am resolved that this shall not be any discouragement, since I know that it is not common opinion that can either add or detract from the truth. For,

1. Other truths have been formerly esteemed altogether as ridiculous as this can be.

2. Gross absurdities have been entertained by general opinion.

I shall give an instance of each, that so I may the better prepare the reader to consider things without a prejudice; when he shall see that the common opposition against this which I affirm, cannot anyway derogate from its truth.

1. Other truths have been formerly accounted as ridiculous as this. I shall specify that of the Antipodes, which have been denied, and laughed at by many wise men and great scholars; such as were Herodotus, Chrysostom, Austin, Lactantius, the venerable Bede, Lucretius the poet, Procopius, and the voluminous Abulensis, together with all those fathers or other authors who denied the roundness of the heavens*. Herodotus counted it so horrible an absurdity, that he could not forbear laughing to think of it. Γελω δε ορων γης περιοδας γραψαντας, πολλας ηδη και αδενα νοον εχοντας εξηγησαμενον οι Ωκεανοντε ρεοντα γραφασι, περιξ την τε γην εασαν κυκλο τερεα ως απο τορνα. "I cannot chuse but "laugh, (saith he) to see so many men venture to describe "the earth's compass, relating those things that are without "all sense: as that the sea flows about the world, and that "the earth itself is round as an orb." But this great ignorance is not so much to be admired in him, as in those learned men of later times, when all sciences began to flourish in the world. Such were St. Chrysostom, who in his 14th homily upon the Epistle to the Hebrews, does make a challenge to any man that shall dare to defend that the heavens are round, and not rather as a tent. Thus

* Vid. Josep. Acosta, de nat. novi orbis, l. 1. cap. 1.

likewise St. Austin*, who censures that relation of the
Antipodes to be an incredible fable; and with him agrees
the eloquent Lactantius†. *Quid illi qui esse contrarios
vestigiis nostris Antipodes putant? num aliquid loquuntur?
aut est quispiam tam ineptus, qui credat esse homines, quorum
vestigia sunt superiora quam capita? aut ibi quæ apud nos
jacent inversa pendere? fruges & arbores deorsum versus
crescere, pluvias & nives, & grandinem sursum versus cadere
in terram? & miratur aliquis hortos pensiles inter septem
mira narrari, quum philosophi, & agros, & maria, & urbes,
& montes pensiles faciunt, &c.* " What (saith he) are they
" that think there are Antipodes, such as walk with their
" feet against ours? do they speak any likelihood; or is
" there any one so foolish as to believe that there are men
" whose heels are higher than their heads? that things
" which with us do lie on the ground, do hang there?
" that the plants and trees grow downwards, that the hail,
" and rain, and snow fall upwards to the earth? and do we
" admire the hanging orchards amongst the seven wonders,
" whereas here the philosophers have made the fields and
" seas, the cities and mountains hanging?" What shall we
think (saith he in Plut.) that men do cling to that place
like worms, or hang by their claws as cats? or if we suppose a man a little beyond the centre, to be digging with a
spade, is it likely (as it must be according to this opinion)
that the earth which he loosened, should of itself ascend
upwards? Or else suppose two men with their middles
about the centre, the feet of the one being placed where
the head of the other is, and so two other men cross them;
yet all these men thus situated, according to this opinion
should stand upright, and many other such gross consequences would follow (saith he) which a false imagination
is not able to fancy as possible. Upon which considerations, *Bede* also denies the being of any Antipodes, *Neque
enim Antipodarum ullatenus est fabulis accommodandus*

* De civit. Dei, l. 16. cap. 9.   † Institut. l. 3. cap. 24.

assensus *.   " Nor should we any longer assent to the fable
" of Antipodes."   So also Lucretius the poet speaking of
the same subject, says,

Sed vanus stolidis hæc omnia finxerit error †.

That some idle fancy feigned these for fools to believe.
Of this opinion was Procopius Gazæus ‡; but he was persuaded to it by another kind of reason; for he thought that
all the earth under us was sunk in the water, according to
the saying of the Psalmist, *He hath founded the earth upon
the seas* §; and therefore he accounted it not inhabited by
any.   Nay, Tostatus, a man of later years and general
learning, doth also confidently deny that there are any
such Antipodes, though the reason which he urges for it be
not so absurd as the former; for the apostles, saith he,
travelled through the whole habitable world, but they never
passed the equinoctial ‖ : and if you answer, that they are
said to go through all the earth, because they went through
all the known world; he replies, That this is not sufficient,
since Christ would have all men to be saved, and come to
the knowledge of his truth ¶, and therefore it is requisite
that they should have travelled thither also, if there had
been any inhabitants; especially since he did expressly
command them to go and teach all nations, and preach the
gospel through the whole world **: and therefore he thinks,
that as there are no men, so neither are there seas, or
rivers, or any other conveniency for habitation ††.   It is commonly related of one Virgilius, that he was excommunicated and condemned for a heretic by Zachary bishop of
Rome, because he was not of the same opinion.   But
Baronius says ‡‡, it was because he thought there was another habitable world within ours.   However, you may well
enough discern in these examples, how confident many of
these great scholars were in so gross an error; how un-

---

* De ratione temporum, cap. 32.   † De nat. rerum, lib. 1.
‡ Comment. in 1 cap. Gen.   § Psalm xxiv. 2.
‖ Comment. in 1 Gen.   ¶ 1 Tim. ii. 4.   ** Matt. xxviii. 19.
†† Aventinus Annal. Boiorum, lib. 3.   ‡‡ Annal. Eccles. A.D. 748.

likely, what an incredible thing it seemed to them, that there should be any Antipodes; and yet now this truth is as certain and plain, as sense or demonstration can make it. This then which I now deliver, is not to be rejected, though it may seem to contradict the common opinion.

2. Gross absurdities have been entertained by general consent. I might instance in many remarkable examples, but I will only speak of the supposed labour of the moon in her eclipses, because this is nearest to the chief matter in hand, and was received as a common opinion amongst many of the ancients; insomuch, that from hence they stiled eclipses by the name of παϑη, passions, or in the phrase of the poets,

Solis lunæque labores.

And therefore Plutarch speaking of a lunary eclipse, relates, that at such times it was a custom amongst the Romans, (the most civil and learned people in the world) to sound brass instruments, and hold great torches toward the heaven*. Των δε Ρωμαιων (ωσπερ εςιν ενομισμενον) χαλκε τε παταγοις ανακαλεμενων το Φως αυτης και πυρα πολλα δαλοις και δασσιν ανεχοντων προς τον ερανον. For by this means they supposed the moon was much eased in her labours; and therefore Ovid calls such loud instruments, the auxiliaries or helps of the moon,

Cum frustra resonant æra auxiliaria lunæ†.

And therefore the satyrist too, describing a loud scold, says, She was able to make noise enough to deliver the labouring moon.

Una laboranti poterit succurrere lunæ‡.

Now the reason of all this their ceremony, was, because they feared the world would fall asleep, when one of its eyes began to wink, and therefore they would do what they could by loud sounds to rouse it from its drowsiness, and keep it awake, by bright torches, to bestow that light upon it which it began to lose.

In vita Paul Æmil.   † Metam. lib. 4.   ‡ Juven. Sat. 6.

Some of them thought hereby to keep the moon in her orb, whereas otherwise she would have fallen down upon the earth, and the world would have lost one of its lights; for the credulous people believed that inchanters and witches could bring the moon down; which made Virgil say,

Cantus & è cælo possunt deducere lunam.

And those wizards knowing the times of her eclipses, would then threaten to shew their skill, by pulling her out of her orb. So that when the silly multitude saw that she began to look red, they presently feared they should lose the benefit of her light, and therefore made a great noise that she might not hear the sound of those charms, which would otherwise bring her down; and this is rendered for a reason of this custom by Pliny and Propertius * :

Cantus & è curru lunam deducere tentant,
Et facerent, si non æra repulsa sonent.

Plutarch gives another reason of it; and he says, it is because they would hasten the moon out of the dark shade wherein she was involved, that so she might bring away the souls of those saints that inhabit within her, which cry out by reason they are then deprived of their wonted happiness, and cannot hear the music of the spheres; but are forced to behold the torments and wailings of those damned souls which are represented to them as they are tortured in the region of the air. But whether this, or whatever else was the meaning of this superstition, yet certainly it was a very ridiculous custom, and bewrayed a great igno-rance of those ancient times; especially since it was not only received by the vulgar, such as were men of less note and learning, but believed also by the more famous and wiser sort; such as were those great poets, Stesichorus and Pindar: and not only amongst the more sottish heathens, who might account that planet to be one of their gods, but the primitive christians also were in this kind guilty; which made St. Ambrose so tartly to rebuke those of his

* Nat, Hist. lib, 2. cap, 12.

time, when he said, *Tum turbatur carminibus globus lunæ,
quando calicibus turbantur & oculi.* " When your heads
" are troubled with cups, then you think the moon to be
" troubled with charms."

And for this reason also did Maximus *, a bishop, write a
homily against it, wherein he shewed the absurdity of that
foolish superstition. I remember that Ludovicus Vives
relates a more ridiculous story of a people that imprisoned
an ass for drinking up the moon, whose image appearing
in the water, was covered with a cloud as the ass was drinking; for which the poor beast was afterward brought to the
bar, to receive a sentence according to his deserts ; where
the grave senate being set to examine the matter, one of
the counsel (perhaps wiser than the rest) rises up, and out
of his deep judgment, thinks it not fit that their town should
lose its moon, but that rather the ass should be cut up, and
that taken out of him ; which sentence being approved by
the rest of those politicians, as the subtilest way for the
conclusion of the matter, was accordingly performed. But
whether this tale were true or no, I will not question;
however, there is absurdity enough in that former custom
of the ancients, that may confirm the truth to be proved,
and plainly declare the insufficiency of common opinion to
add true worth or estimation unto any thing. So that from
that which I have said, may be gathered thus much.

1. That a new truth may seem absurd and impossible,
not only to the vulgar, but to those also who are otherwise
wise men and excellent scholars : and hence it will follow,
that every new thing which seems to oppose common
principles, is not presently to be rejected, but rather to be
pryed into with a diligent enquiry, since there are many
things which are yet hid from us, and reserved for future
discovery.

2. That it is not the commonness of an opinion that can
privilege it for a truth; the wrong way is sometimes a well
beaten path, whereas the right way (especially to hidden
truths) may be less trodden and more obscure.

* Turinens. Episc.

True indeed, the strangeness of this opinion will detract much from its credit; but yet we should know that nothing is in itself strange, since every natural effect has an equal dependance upon its cause, and with the like necessity doth follow from it; so that it is our ignorance which makes things appear so: and hence it comes to pass, that many more evident truths seem incredible, to such who know not the causes of things.   You may as soon persuade some country peasants that the moon is made of green cheese, (as we say) as that it is bigger than his cart-wheel, since both seem equally to contradict his sight, and he has not reason enough to lead him farther than his senses.   Nay, suppose (saith Plutarch) a philosopher should be educated in such a secret place, where he might not see either sea or river, and afterwards should be brought out where one might shew him the great ocean, telling him the quality of that water, that it is brackish, salt, and not portable, and yet there were many vast creatures of all forms living in it, which make use of the water as we do of the air; questionless he would laugh at all this, as being monstrous lies and fables, without any colour of truth.   Just so will this truth which I now deliver appear unto others, because we never dreamt of any such matter as a world in the moon; because the state of that place hath as yet been veiled from our knowledge, therefore we can scarcely assent to any such matter.   Things are very hardly received, which are altogether strange to our thoughts and our senses.   The soul may with less difficulty be brought to believe any absurdity, when as it has formerly been acquainted with some colours and probabilities for it; but when a new, and an unheard of truth shall come before it, though it have good grounds and reasons, yet the understanding is afraid of it as a stranger, and dares not admit it into his belief, without a great deal of reluctancy and trial.   And besides, things that are not manifested to the senses, are not assented unto without some labour of mind, some travel and discourse of the understanding; and many lazy souls had rather quietly repose themselves in an easy error, than take pains to search out the truth. The strangeness then of this opinion which I now deliver, will be a great hindrance to its belief; but this is not to be respected, by reason it cannot be helped. I have stood the longer in the Preface, because that prejudice which the mere title of the book may beget, cannot easily be removed without a great deal of preparation: and I could not tell otherwise how to rectify the thoughts of the reader, for an impartial survey of the following discourse.

I must needs confess, though I had often thought with myself that it was possible there might be a world in the moon, yet it seemed such an uncouth opinion, that I never durst discover it, for fear of being counted singular and ridiculous; but afterward, having read Plutarch, Galileus, Keplar, with some others, and finding many of mine own thoughts confirmed by such strong authority, I then concluded that it was not only possible there might be, but probable that there was another habitable world in that planet. In the prosecuting of this assertion, I shall first endeavour to clear the way from such doubts as may hinder the speed or ease of farther progress. And because the suppositions implied in this opinion, may seem to contradict the principles of reason or faith, it will be requisite that I first remove this scruple, shewing the conformity of them to both these, and proving those truths that may make way for the rest; which I shall labour to perform in the second, third, fourth, and fifth chapters, and then proceed to confirm such propositions which do more directly belong to the main point in hand.

PROP. II.

That a plurality of worlds doth not contradict any principle of reason or faith.

IT is reported of Aristotle, that when he saw the books of Moses, he commended them for such a majestic stile as might become a god; but withal, he censured that manner of writing to be very unfitting for a philosopher; because there was nothing proved in them, but matters were delivered as if they would rather command than persuade belief. And it is observed, that he sets down nothing himself, but he confirms it by the strongest reasons that may be found, there being scarce an argument of force for any subject in philosophy, which may not be picked out of his writings; and therefore it is likely if there were in reason a necessity of one only world, that he would have found out some such necessary proof as might confirm it; especially since he labours for it so much in two whole chapters. But now all the arguments which he himself urges in this subject, are very weak, and far enough from having in them any convincing power*. Therefore it is likely that a plurality of worlds doth not contradict any principle of reason. However, I will set down the two chief of his arguments from his own works, and from them you may guess the force of the other.

The first is this †: Since every heavy body doth naturally tend downwards, and every light body upwards, what a huddling and confusion must there be, if there were two places for gravity, and two places for lightness? For it is probable that the earth of that other world would fall down to this centre, and so mutually the air and fire here ascend to those regions in the other; which must needs much derogate from the providence of nature, and cause a great disorder in his works. But *ratio hæc est minimè firma,*

---

* De Cælo, l. 1. cap. 8, 9.　　　　　† Ibid.

(saith Zanchy*.)   And if you well consider the nature of
gravity, you will plainly see there is no ground to fear any
such confusion; for heaviness is nothing else but such a
quality as causes a propension in its subject to tend downwards towards its own centre : so that for some of that earth
to come hither, would not be said a fall, but an ascension,
since it is moved from its own place; and this would be
impossible (saith Ruvio †) because against nature, and therefore no more to be feared than the falling of the heavens.

If you reply, that then according to this, there must be
more centres of gravity than one; I answer, it is very probable there are; nor can we well conceive what any piece
of the moon would do, being severed from the rest in the
free and open air, but only return unto it again.

Another argument he had from his master Plato ‡, That
there is but one world, because there is but one first mover,
God.

Infirma etiam est hæc ratio (saith Zanchy); and we
may justly deny the consequence, since a plurality of
worlds doth not take away the unity of the first Mover, *Ut
enim forma substantialis, sic primum efficiens apparentem
solummodo multiplicitatem induit per signatam materiam*
(saith a countryman of ours §.) As the substantial form, so
the efficient cause hath only an appearing multiplicity from
its particular matter. You may see this point more largely
handled, and these arguments more fully answered by Plutarch in his book, " Why Oracles are silent," and Jacob
Carpentarius in his comment on Alcinous.

But our opposites, the interpreters themselves, (who too
often do *jurare in verba magistri)* will grant that there is
not any strength in these consequences; and certainly then
such weak arguments could not convince that wise philosopher, who in his other opinions was wont to be swayed by
the strength and power of reason; wherefore I should
rather think that he had some by-respect, which made him

* De operibus Dei, par.2. lib.2. cap. 2.   † De Cælo, l. 1.c.9.q. i.
‡ Metaphys. l. 12. c. 8. Diog. Laert. lib. 3.
§ Nic. Hill. de Philosoph. Epic. partic. 379.

first assent to this opinion, and afterwards strive to prove it.
Perhaps it was because he feared to displease his scholar
Alexander*; of whom it is related, that he wept to hear a
disputation of another world, since he had not then attained
the monarchy of this ; his restless wide heart would have
esteemed this globe of earth not big enough for him, if
there had been another ; which made the satyrist say of
him,

Æstuat infœlix angusto limite mundi †.

" That he did vex himself, and sweat in his desires, as
" being penned up in a narrow room, when he was con-
" fined but to one world." Before, he thought to seat
himself next the gods, but now, when he had done his
best, he must be content with some equal, or perhaps
superior kings.

It may be, that Aristotle was moved to this opinion, that
he might thereby take from Alexander the occasion of this
fear and discontent ; or else, perhaps, Aristotle himself was
as loth to hold the possibility of a world which he could not
discover, as Alexander was to hear of one which he could
not conquer. It is likely that some such by-respect moved
him to this opinion, since the arguments he urges for it are
confessed by his zealous followers and commentators, to
be very slight and frivolous ; and they themselves grant,
what I am now to prove, that there is not any evidence in
the light of natural reason, which can sufficiently manifest
that there is but one world.

But however some may object, would it not be inconvenient and dangerous to admit of such opinions that do
destroy those principles of Aristotle which all the world
hath so long followed ?

This question is much controverted by some of the
Romish divines ‡ : Campanella hath writ a treatise in defence of it, in whom you may see many things worth the
reading and notice.

To it I answer, That this position in philosophy doth

* Plutarch. de tranq. anim. † Juvenal. ‡ Apologia pro Galileo.

not bring any inconveniency to the rest, since it is not Aristotle, but truth, that should be the rule of our opinions, and if they be not both found together, we may say to him, as he said to his master Plato *,

" Though Plato were his friend, yet he would rather " adhere to truth than him."

I must needs grant, that we are all much beholden to the industry of the ancient philosophers, and more especially to Aristotle, for the greater part of our learning; but yet it is not ingratitude to speak against him, when he opposeth truth; for then many of the fathers would be very guilty, especially Justin, who hath writ a treatise purposely against him. But suppose this opinion were false, yet it is not against the faith, and so it may serve for the better confirmation of that which is true; the sparks of error being forced out by opposition, as the sparks of fire by the striking of the flint and steel. But suppose too that it were heretical, and against the faith, yet may it be admitted with the same privilege as Aristotle, from whom many more dangerous opinions have proceeded: as that the world is eternal; that God cannot have while to look after these inferior things; that after death there is no reward or punishment, and such like blasphemies; which strike directly at the fundamentals of our religion.

So that it is justly to be wondered, why some should be so superstitious in these days, as to stick closer unto him, than unto scripture, as if his philosophy were the only foundation of all divine truths.

Upon these grounds, both St. Vincentius and Serafinus de Firmo (as I have seen them quoted) think that Aristotle was the viol of God's wrath, which was poured out upon the waters of wisdom by the third angel †: but for my part, I think the world is much beholden to him for all his sciences. But yet it were a shame for these later ages, to rest ourselves merely upon the labours of our forefathers, as if they had informed us of all things to be known; and

* Ethic. l. 1. c. 6.   † Rev. xvi. 4.

when we are set upon their shoulders, not to see further than they themselves did. It were a superstitious, a lazy opinion, to think Aristotle's works the bounds and limits of all human invention, beyond which there could be no possibility of reaching. Certainly there are yet many things left to discovery, and it cannot be any inconveniency for us to maintain a new truth, or rectify an ancient error.

But the position (say some) is directly against scripture; for,

1. Moses tells us but of one world, and his history of the creation had been very imperfect, if God had made another.

2. St. John, speaking of God's works, says, he made the world, in the singular number, and therefore there is but one. It is the argument of Aquinas*, and he thinks that none will oppose it, but such who with Democritus esteem some blind chance, and not any wise Providence, to be the framer of all things.

3. The opinion of more worlds has in ancient times been accounted a heresy; and Baronius affirms that for this very reason Virgilius was cast out of his bishoprick †, and excommunicated from the church.

4. A fourth argument there is urged by Aquinas: if there be more worlds than one, then they must either be of the same, or of a diverse nature; but they are not of the same kind; for this were needless, and would argue an improvidence, since one would have no more perfection than the other ‡: not of divers kinds; for then one of them could not be called the world or universe, since it did not contain universal perfection. I have cited this argument, because it is so much stood upon by Julius Cæsar la Galla §, one that has purposely writ a treatise against this opinion which I now deliver; but the dilemma is so blunt, that it cannot cut on either side, and the consequences so weak, that I dare trust them without an answer: and (by the way) you

---

* Part 1. Q. 47. Art. 3.   † Annal. Eccl. A.D. 748.   ‡ Ibid.
§ De Phenom. in Orbe Lunæ.

may see this later author in that place, where he endeavours to prove a necessity of one world, doth leave the chief
matter in hand, and take much needless pains to dispute
against Democritus, who thought that the world was made
by the casual concourse of atoms in a great vacuum. It
should seem that either his cause or his skill was weak, or
else he would have ventured upon a stronger adversary.
These arguments which I have set down are the chiefest
which I have met with against this subject; and yet the
best of these hath not force enough to endanger the truth
that I have delivered.

Unto the two first it may be answered, that the negative
authority of scripture is not prevalent in those things which
are not the fundamentals of religion.

But you will reply, though it do not necessarily conclude,
yet it is probable if there had been another world, we
should have had some notice of it in scripture.

I answer, it is as probable that the scripture should have
informed us of the planets, they being very remarkable parts
of the creation; and yet neither Moses, nor Job, nor the
Psalms (the places most frequent in astronomical observations) nor any other scripture mention any of them but the
sun and moon. Because the difference betwixt them and
the other stars, was known only to those who were learned
men, and had skill in astronomy. As for that expression
in Job *, כוכבי בקר, the stars of the morning, it is in the
plural number, and therefore cannot properly be applied to
Venus. And for that in Isaiah, הילל, it is confessed to be a
word of obscure interpretation, and therefore is but by
guess translated in that sense. It being a true and common
rule, that *Hebræi rei sideralis minime curiosi cœlestium
nominum penuriâ laborant.* The Jews being but little skilled in astronomy, their language does want proper expressions for the heavenly bodies; and therefore they are fain

---

* Job xxxviii. 7. Isa. xiv. 12. Fromond. Vesta, t. 3. cap. 2. So 2 Reg.
xxiii. 5. מזלות, which is interpreted both for the planets and for the
twelve signs.

THAT THE MOON MAY BE A WORLD. 19

sometimes to attribute the same name unto divers constellations.

Now if the Holy Ghost had intended to reveal unto us any natural secrets, certainly he would never have omitted the mention of the planets, *Quorum motu nihil est quod de conditoris sapientiâ testatur evidentius apud eos qui capiunt* *. Which do so evidently set forth the wisdom of the Creator. And therefore you must know that it is besides the scope of the Old Testament or the New, to discover anything unto us concerning the secrets of philosophy. It is not his intent in the New Testament, since we cannot conceive how it might anyway belong either to the historical, exegetical, or prophetical parts of it: nor is it his intent in the Old Testament, as is well observed by our countryman Master Wright †. *Non Mosis aut prophetarum institutum fuisse videtur mathematicas aliquas aut phisicas subtiltates promulgare, sed ad vulgi captum & loquendi morem, quemadmodum nutrices infantulis solent, sese accommodare.* " It is not the endeavour of Moses or the " prophets to discover any mathematical or philosophical " subtilties; but rather to accommodate themselves to " vulgar capacities, and ordinary speech, as nurses are wont " to use their infants." True indeed, Moses is there to handle the history of the creation. But it is certain (saith Calvin ‡) that his purpose is to treat only of the visible form of the world, and those parts of it which might be most easily understood by the ignorant and ruder sort of people, and therefore we are not thence to expect the discovery of any natural secret. *Artes reconditas aliunde discat qui volet; hic spiritus dei omnes simul sine exceptione docere voluit.* As for more hidden arts, they must be looked for elsewhere; the Holy Ghost did here intend to instruct all without exception. And therefore it is observed, that Moses does not anywhere meddle with such matters as were very hard to be conceived; for being to inform the

---

* Keplar. introduct. in Mart. † In Epist. ad Gilbert.
‡ Calvin in 1 Gen,

common people as well as others, he does it after a vulgar
way, as it is commonly noted, declaring the original chiefly
of those things which are obvious to the sense; and being
silent of other things which then could not well be apprehended. And therefore Pererius * proposing the question,
why the creation of plants and herbs is mentioned, but not
of metals and minerals?

Answers: *Quia istarum rerum generatio est vulgo occulta & ignota :* Because these things are not so commonly
known as the other; and he adds, *Moses non omnia, sed
manifesta omnibus enarranda suscepit.* Moses did not intend to relate unto us the beginnings of all things, but those
only which were most evident unto all men. And therefore too, Aquinas observes †, that he writes nothing of the
air; because that being invisible, the people knew not
whether there were any such body or no. And for this
very reason St. Jerom ‡ also thinks that there is nothing
exprest concerning the creation of angels; because the rude
and ignorant vulgar were not so capable of apprehending
their natures. And yet notwithstanding, these are as remarkable parts of the creation, and as fit to be known as
another world. And therefore the Holy Ghost too, uses
such vulgar expressions, which set things forth rather as
they appear than as they are, as when he calls the moon
one of the greater lights §, whereas it is the least that we can
see in the whole heavens. So afterwards speaking of the
great rain which drowned the world, he says, the windows of heaven were opened ‖, because it seemed to come
with that violence, as if it were poured out from windows
in the firmament ¶.

And in reference to this, a drowth is described in sundry
other places ** by the heavens being shut up. So that the
phrases which the Holy Ghost uses concerning these things,
are not to be understood in a literal sense; but rather as

* Com. in 1 Gen. 11. † Part 1. Q. 68. Art. 3.
‡ Epist. 139. ad Cypri. So Pererius in 2 Gen. § Gen. i. 16.
‖ Gen. xi. Mal. iii. 10. ¶ Sir Walter Rawl. cap. 7. sect. 6.
** Deut. xi. 17. 1 Reg. iii. 55. Luke iv. 25.

vulgar expressions; and this rule is set down by St. Austin*, where speaking concerning that in the psalm, who stretched the earth upon the waters, he notes, that when the words of scripture shall seem to contradict common sense or experience, there are they to be understood in a qualified sense, and not according to the letter. And it is observed, that for want of this rule †, some of the ancients have fastened strange absurdities upon the words of the scripture. So St. Ambrose esteemed it a heresy to think that the sun and stars were not very hot, as being against the words of scripture, Psalm xix. 6. where the Psalmist says, that there is nothing that is hid from the heat of the sun. So others there are that would prove the heavens not to be round, out of that place, Psalm civ. 2. *He stretched out the heavens like a curtain.* So Procopius also was of opinion, that the earth was founded upon the waters; nay, he made it part of his faith, proving it out of Psalm xxiv. 2. *He hath founded the earth upon the seas, and established it upon the floods.* These and such like absurdities have followed, when men look for the grounds of philosophy in the words of scripture. So that, from what hath been said, I may conclude that the silence of scripture concerning any other world, is not sufficient argument to prove that there is none. Thus for the two first arguments.

Unto the third, I may answer, that this very example is quoted by others, to shew the ignorance of those primitive times, who did sometimes condemn what they did not understand ; and have often censured the lawful and undoubted parts of mathematics for heretical, because they themselves could not perceive a reason of it. And therefore their practice in this particular is no sufficient testimony against us.

But lastly, I answer to all the above-named objections, that the term (world) may be taken in a double sense, more generally for the whole universe, as it implies in it

---

* L. 2. in Gen.   Ps. cxxxvi. 6.

† Hexamer lib. 2. Item Basil. Hom. 3. in Gen. Wisd. ii. 4. xvii. 5. Ecclus. xliii. 3, 4. Com. in c. 1 Gen.

the elementary and æthereal bodies, the stars and the earth. Secondly, more particularly for an inferior world, consisting of elements.

Now the main drift of all these arguments, is to confute a plurality of worlds in the first sense; and if there were any such, it might (perhaps) seem strange, that Moses or St. John should either not know, or not mention its creation. And Virgilius was condemned for this opinion, because he held *quod sit alius mundus sub terra, aliusque sol & luna,* (as Baronius) that within our globe of earth, there was another world, another sun and moon, and so he might seem to exclude this from the number of the other creatures.

But now there is no such danger in this opinion, which is here delivered; since this world is said to be in the moon, whose creation is particularly expressed.

So that in the first sense, I yield that there is but one world, which is all that the arguments do prove; but understand it in the second sense, and so I affirm there may be more, nor do any of the above-named objections prove the contrary.

Neither can this opinion derogate from the divine wisdom (as Aquinas thinks) but rather advance it, shewing a compendium of Providence, that could make the same body a world, and a moon; a world for habitation, and a moon for the use of others, and the ornament of the whole frame of nature. For as the members of the body serve not only for the preservation of themselves, but for the use and conveniency of the whole, as the hand protects the head as well as saves itself*; so is it in the parts of the universe, where each one may serve as well for the conservation of that which is within it, as the help of others without it.

Mersennus a late jesuit †, proposing the question whether or no the opinion of more worlds than one, be heretical and

---

* Cusanus de Doct. Ignor. l. 2. c. 12.
† Comment. in Gen. Qu. 19. Art. 2.

against the faith ? He answers it negatively ; because it does not contradict any express place of scripture, or determination of the church. And though (saith he) it seems to be a rash opinion, as being against the consent of the fathers; yet if this controversy be chiefly philosophical, then their authorities are not of such weight. Unto this it may be added, that the consent of the fathers is prevalent only in such points as were first controverted amongst them, and then generally decided one way, and not in such other particulars as never fell under their examination and dispute.

I have now in some measure shewed that a plurality of worlds does not contradict any principle of reason or place of scripture ; and so cleared the first part of that supposition which is implied in the opinion.

It may next be enquired, whether it is possible there may be a globe of elements in that which we call the æthereal parts of the universe ; for if this (as it is according to the common opinion) be privileged from any change or corruption, it will be in vain then to imagine any element there ; and if we will have another world, we must then seek out some other place for its situation. The third proposition therefore shall be this.

PROP. III.

That the heavens do not consist of any such pure matter, which can privilege them from the like change and corruption as these inferior bodies are liable unto.

IT hath been often questioned amongst the ancient fathers and philosophers, what kind of matter that should be of which the heavens are framed. Some think that they consist of a fifth substance distinct from the four elements, as Aristotle holds *, and with him

* De Cælo, lib. 1. cap. 2.

some of the late schoolmen; whose subtil brains could
not be content to attribute to those vast glorious bodies,
but common materials, and therefore they themselves had
rather take pains to prefer them to some extraordinary
nature; whereas notwithstanding, all the arguments they
could invent, were not able to convince a necessity of
any such matter, as is confessed by their own side *.   It
were much to be desired, that these men had not in other
cases, as well as this, multiplied things without necessity ;
and, as if there had not been enough to be known in the
secrets of nature, have spun out new subjects from their
own brains, to find more work for future ages.   I shall
not mention their arguments, since it is already confessed,
that they are none of them of any necessary consequence ;
and besides, you may see them set down in any of the
books *de Cælo.*

But it is the general consent of the fathers, and the opinion of Lombard, that the heavens consist of the same
matter with these sublunary bodies.   St. Ambrose is so
confident of it, that he esteems the contrary a heresy †.
True indeed, they differ much among themselves, some
thinking them to be made of fire, others of water, and
others of both : but herein they generally agree, that they
are all framed of some element or other; which Dionysius Carthusianus ‡ collects from that place in Genesis,
where the heavens are mentioned in their creation, as divided only in distance from the elementary bodies, and
not as being made of any new matter.   To this purpose
others cite the derivation of the Hebrew word שמים,
quasi שם *ibi* & מים *aquæ* or *quasi* אש *ignis* & מים *aquæ*,
because they are framed out of these elements.   But concerning this, you may see sundry discourses more at large
in Ludovicus Molina, Eusebius Nirembergius, with divers others.   The venerable Bede thought the planets to
consist of all the four elements §; and it is likely that the

* Colleg. Conimb. de cælo. l. 1. c. 2. q. 6. art. 3.   † In Hexam. lib 4.
‡ Enarrat. in Genes. art. 10.   § In operc. 6 dierum disput. 5.

other parts of it are of an aereous substance, as will be shewed afterwards* : however, I cannot now stand to recite the arguments for either; I have only urged these authorities to countervail Aristotle and the schoolmen, and the better to make way for a proof of their corruptibility.

The next thing then to be enquired after, is, Whether they be of a corruptible nature † ; not whether they can be destroyed by God; for this scripture puts out of doubt.

Nor whether or no in a long time they would wear away and grow worse, for from any such fear they have been lately privileged ‡. But whether they are capable of such changes and vicissitudes, as this inferior world is liable unto.

The two chief opinions concerning this, have both erred in some extremity, the one side going so far from the other, that they have both gone beyond the right ; whilst Aristotle hath opposed the truth as well as the Stoics.

Some of the ancients have thought, that the heavenly bodies have stood in need of nourishment from the elements, by which they were continually fed, and so had divers alterations by reason of their food. This is fathered on Heraclitus, followed by that great naturalist Pliny, and in general attributed to all the Stoicks §. You may see Seneca expressly to this purpose in these words. *Ex illa alimenta omnibus animalibus, omnibus satis, omnibus stellis dividuntur; hinc profertur quo sustineantur tot sidera tam exercitata, tam avida, per diem, noctemque, ut in opera, ita in pastu.* Speaking of the earth, he says, from thence it is that nourishment is divided to all the living creatures, the planets and the stars ; hence were sustained so many constellations, so laborious, so greedy,

---

* In lib. de Mundi constit.   † 2 Pet. iii. 12.
  ‡ By Doctor Hakewill. Apol. lib. 2.   § Plutarch de plac. Philos. l. 2. c. 17.   Nat. Hist. l. 2. c. 9.   Nat. quest. lib. 2. cap. 5.

both day and night, as well in their feeding as working.
Thus also Lucan sings,

Necnon oceano pasci Phœbumque polumque credimus.

Unto these, Ptolomy also[*], that learned Egyptian,
seemed to agree, when he affirms that the body of the
moon is moister and cooler than any of the other planets,
by reason of the earthly vapours that are exhaled unto
it. You see these ancients thought the heavens to be so
far from this imagined incorruptibility, that rather like the
weakest bodies they stood in need of some continual nourishment, without which they could not subsist.

But Aristotle and his followers were so far from this[†],
that they thought those glorious bodies could not contain
in them any such principles as might make them liable to
the least change or corruption ; and their chief reason was,
because we could not in so long a space discern any alteration amongst them. But unto this I answer :

1. Supposing we could not, yet would it not hence follow
that there were none, as he himself in effect doth confess
in another place ; for speaking concerning our knowledge
of the heavens, he says [‡], it is very imperfect and difficult,
by reason of the vast distance of those bodies from us, and
because the changes which may happen unto them, are
not either big enough, or frequent enough to fall within
the apprehension and observation of our senses ; no wonder then, if he himself be deceived in his assertions concerning these particulars. But yet, in this he implies, that
if a man were nearer to these heavenly bodies, he would
be a fitter judge to decide this controversy than himself.
Now it is our advantage, that by the help of Galileus's
glass, we are advanced nearer unto them, and the heavens
are made more present to us than they were before.
However, as it is with us, where there be many vicissitudes
and successions of things, though the earth abideth for

[*] 1 Apostol.   [†] De Cælo, l. 1. c. 3.
[‡] De cælo, l. 2. cap. 5.

ever; so likewise may it be amongst the planets; in which, though there should be divers alterations, yet they themselves may still continue of the same quantity and light.

2. Though we could not by our senses see such alterations, yet our reason might perhaps sufficiently convince us of them. Nor can we well conceive how the sun should reflect against the moon, and yet not produce some alteration of heat. Diogenes the philosopher was hence persuaded, that those scorching heats had burnt the moon into the form of a pumice-stone.

3. I answer, That there have been some alterations observed there; witness those comets which have been seen above the moon; as also those spots or clouds that encompass the body of the sun; amongst which, there is a frequent succession by a corruption of the old, and a generation of new. So that though Aristotle's consequence were sufficient, when he proved that the heavens were not corruptible, because there have not any changes been discovered in it; yet this by the same reason must be as prevalent, that the heavens are corruptible, because there have been so many alterations observed there. But of these, together with a farther confirmation of this proposition, I shall have occasion to speak afterwards: in the mean space, I will refer the reader to that work of Scheiner, a late jesuit, which he titles his *Rosa Ursina* *, where he may see this point concerning the corruptibility of the heavens largely handled, and sufficiently confirmed.

There are some other things, on which I might here take an occasion to enlarge myself; but because they are directly handled by many others, and do not immediately belong to the chief matter in hand, I shall therefore refer the reader to their authors, and omit any large proof of them myself, as desiring all possible brevity.

1. The first is this: That there are no solid orbs. If there be a habitable world in the moon, (which I now af-

* Lib. 4. par. 2. cap. 24. 35.

firm) it must follow, that her orb is not solid, as Aristotle
supposed ; and if not hers, why any of the other ? I rather think that they are all of a fluid (perhaps aereous)
substance. St. Ambrose and St. Basil did endeavour to
prove this out of that place in Isaiah *, where they are
compared to smoke, as they are both quoted by Rhodiginus. Eusebius Nierembergus doth likewise from that
place †, confute the solidity and incorruptibility of the
heavens, and cites for the same interpretation the authority of Eustachius, of Antioch ; and St. Austin ‡, I am sure,
in one place seems to assent unto this opinion, though he
does often in his other works contradict it.

If you esteem the testimony of the ancient fathers, to be
of any great force or consequence in a philosophical dispute, you may see them to this purpose in Sixtus Senensis,
lib. 5. Biblioth. annot. 14. The chief reasons that are
commonly urged for the confirmation of it, are briefly
these three.

1. From the altitude of divers comets, which have been
observed to be above the planets ; through whose orbs (if
they had been solid) there would not have been any passage. To these may be added those lesser planets lately
discovered about Jupiter and Saturn, for which astronomers had not yet framed any orbs.

2. From that uncertainty of all astronomical observations, which will follow upon the supposition of such solid
spheres. For then we should never discern any star, but
by a multitude of refractions, and so consequently we
could not possibly find their true situations, either in respect of us, or in regard of one another : since whatever
the eye discerns by a refracted beam, it apprehends to be
in some other place than wherein it is. But ·now this
would be such an inconvenience, as would quite subvert
the grounds and whole art of astronomy, and therefore is
by no means to be admitted.

---

* Isa. li. 1. 6.   Ant. lect. l. 1. c. 4.
† Hist. nat. l. 2. c. 11. 13.   ‡ In lib. sup. Gen. ad. lit.

Unto this it is commonly answered, That all those orbs are equally diaphanous, though not of a continued quantity. We reply, That supposing they were, yet this cannot hinder them from being the causes of refraction, which is produced as well by the diversity of superficies, as the different perspicuity of bodies. Two glasses put together, will cause a diverse refraction from another single one, that is but of equal thickness and perspicuity.

3. From the different height of the same planet at several times. For, if according to the usual hypothesis, there should be such distinct, solid orbs, then it would be impossible that the planets should intrench upon one another's orbs, or that two of them at several times should be above one another, which notwithstanding hath been proved to be so by later experience. Tycho hath observed, that Venus is sometimes nearer to us than the Sun or Mercury, and sometimes farther off than both: which appearances Regiomontanus himself does acknowledge, and withal, does confess that they cannot be reconciled to the common hypothesis.

But for your better satisfaction herein, I shall refer you to the above-named Scheiner, in his *Rosa Ursina**, in whom you may see both authorities and reason very largely and distinctly set down for this opinion. For the better confirmation of which, he adjoins also some authentical epistles of Fredericus Cæsius Lynceus, a noble prince, written to Bellarmine, containing divers reasons to the same purpose. You may also see the same truth set down by Johannes Pena, in his preface to Euclid's Opticks, and Christoph. Rothmannus, both who thought the firmament to be only air; and though the noble Tycho do dispute against them †, yet he himself holds, *Quod propius ad veritatis penetralia accedit hæc opinio, quam Aristotelica vulgariter approbata, quæ cælum pluribus realibus atque imperviis orbibus citra rem replevit.* " That this opinion " comes nearer to the truth, than that common one of

---

* Lib. 4. p. 11. 2. c. 7. 26. 30.   † De stell. 1, 15, 72, l. 1. c. 9.

" Aristotle, which hath to no purpose filled the heavens
" with such real and impervious orbs.

2. There is no element of fire, which must be held with
this opinion here delivered ; for if we suppose a world in
the moon, then it will follow, that the sphere of fire either
is not there, where it is usually placed in the concavity of
his orb, or else that there is no such thing at all ; which is
most probable, since there are not any such solid orbs,
that by their swift motion might heat and enkindle the adjoining air, which is imagined to be the reason of that element.   The arguments that are commonly urged to this
purpose, are these.

1. That which was before alleged concerning the refractions which will be caused by a different medium.
For if the matter of the heavens be of one thickness, and
the element of fire another, and the upper region of air
distinct from both these, and the lower region several
from all the rest; there will then be such a multiplicity of
refractions, as must necessarily destroy the certainty of
all astronomical observations.   All which inconveniences
might be avoided, by supposing (as we do) that there is
only one orb of vaporous air which encompasses our earth,
all the rest being æthereal, and of the same perspicuity.

2. The situation of this element does no way agree with
Aristotle's own principles, or that common Providence of
nature, which we may discern in ordinary matters.   For
if the heavens be without all elementary qualities, as is
usually supposed, then it would be a very incongruous
thing for the element of fire to be placed immediately
next unto it; since the heat of this is the most powerful
and vigorous quality that is among all the rest: and nature in her works, does not join extremes, but by something of a middle disposition.   So in the very frame of
our bodies, the bones which are of a hard substance, and
the flesh of a soft, are not joined together but by the in-
tercession of membranes and gristles, such as being of a
middle nature may fitly come betwixt.

3. It is not conceiveable for what use or benefit there should be any such element in that place ; and certain it is, that nature does not do any thing in vain.

4. Betwixt two extremes there can be but one medium ; and therefore between those two opposite elements of earth and water, it may seem more convenient to place only the air, which shall partake of middle qualities different from both.

5. Fire does not seem so properly and directly to be opposed to any thing as ice ; and if the one be not an element, why should the other ?

If you object, that the fire which we commonly use does always tend upwards; I answer, This cannot prove that there is a natural place for such an element, since our adversaries themselves do grant, that culinary and elementary fire are of different kinds. The one does burn, shine, and corrupt its subject ; the other disagrees from it in all these respects. And therefore from the ascent of the one, we cannot properly infer the being or the situation of the other.

But for your farther satisfaction herein, you may peruse Cardan, Johannes Pena, that learned Frenchman the noble Tycho, with divers others who have purposely handled this proposition.

3. I might add a third, viz. That there is no music of the spheres ; for if they be not solid, how can their motion cause any such sound as is conceived? I do the rather meddle with this, because Plutarch speaks as if a man might very conveniently hear that harmony, if he were an inhabitant in the moon. But I guess that he said this out of incogitancy, and did not well consider those necessary consequences which depend upon his opinion. However, the world would have no great loss in being deprived of this music, unless at some times we had the privilege to hear it* : then indeed Philo the Jew thinks it would save us the charges of diet, and we might live at

---

* De somniis.

an easy rate by feeding at the ear only, and receiving no other nourishment; and for this very reason, says he, was Moses enabled to tarry forty days and forty nights in the mount without eating any thing, because he there heard the melody of the heavens.—*Risum teneatis.* I know this music hath had great patrons, both sacred and profane authors, such as Ambrose, Bede, Boetius, Anselm, Plato, Cicero, and others; but because it is not now, I think, affirmed by any, I shall not therefore bestow either pains or time in arguing against it.

It may suffice that I have only named these three last, and for the two more necessary, have referred the reader to others for satisfaction. I shall in the next place proceed to the nature of the moon's body, to know whether that be capable of any such conditions, as may make it possible to be inhabited, and what those qualities are wherein it more nearly agrees with our earth.

PROP. IV.

That the Moon is a solid, compacted, opacous body.

I Shall not need to stand long in the proof of this proposition, since it is a truth already agreed on by the general consent of the most and the best philosophers.

It is solid, in opposition to fluid, as is the air; for how otherwise could it beat back the light which it receives from the sun?

But here it may be questioned, whether or no the moon bestow her light upon us by the reflection of the sun-beams from the superficies of her body, or else by her own illumination? Some there are who affirm this latter part. So Averroes[*], Cælius Rhodiginus[†], Julius Cæsar[‡], &c. And their reason is, because this light is discerned in many

---

[*] De cœlo l. 2. com. 49.　　　　　[†] Ant. lection. l. 20. c. 4.
[‡] De phænom. lunæ. c. 11.

places, whereas those bodies which give light by reflexion, can there only be perceived where the angle of reflexion is equal to the angle of incidence, and this is only in one place ; as in a looking-glass, those beams which are reflected from it, cannot be perceived in every place where you may see the glass, but only there where your eye is placed on the same line whereon the beams are reflected.

But to this I answer, That the argument will not hold of such bodies whose superficies is full of unequal parts and gibbosities, as the moon is. Wherefore it is as well the more probable as the more common opinion, that her light proceeds from both these causes, from reflexion and illumination ; nor doth it herein differ from our earth, since that also hath some light by illumination . For how otherwise would the parts about us in a sun-shine -day appear so bright, when as the rays of reflexion cannot enter into our eye ?

For the better illustration of this, we may consider the several ways whereby divers bodies are enlightened. Either as water by admitting the beams into its substance ; or as air and thin clouds, by transmitting the rays quite through their bodies ; or as those things that are of an opacous nature, and smooth superficies, which reflect the light only in one place ; or else as those things which are of an opacous nature, and rugged superficies, which by a kind of circumfluous reflexion, are at the same time discernible in many places, as our earth and the moon.

2. It is compact, and not a spungy and porous substance. But this is denied by Diogenes*, Vitellio†, and Reinoldus‡, and some others, who held the moon to be of the same kind of nature as a pumice-stone ; and this, say they, is the reason why in the sun's eclipses, there appears within her a duskish ruddy colour, because the sun-beams being refracted in passing through the pores of her body, must necessarily be represented under such a colour.

* Plut. de pla. Phil. 1. 2. c. 13.   † Opt. l. 4.
‡ Com. Purbac. Theo. p. 164.

But I reply, if this be the cause of her redness, then why doth she not appear under the same form when she is about a sextile aspect, and the darkened part of her body is discernible? for then also do the same rays pass through her, and therefore in all likelihood should produce the same effect; and notwithstanding those beams are then diverted from us, that they cannot enter into our eyes by a straight line, yet must the colour still remain visible in her body. And besides, according to this opinion, the spots would not always be the same, but diverse as the various distance of the sun requires. Again, if the sun-beams did pass through her, why then hath she not a tail (saith Scaliger*) as the comets? Why doth she appear in such an exact round? and not rather attended with a long flame, since it is merely this penetration of the sun-beams that is usually attributed to be the cause of beards in blazing stars.

3. It is opacous, not transparent or diaphanous like crystal or glass, as Empedocles thought†, who held the moon to be a globe of pure congealed air, like hail inclosed in a sphere of fire; for then,

1. Why does she not always appear in the full? since the light is dispersed through all her body?

2. How can the interposition of her body so darken the sun‡, or cause such great eclipses as have turned day into night; that have discovered the stars, and frightened the birds with such a sudden darkness, that they fell down upon the earth? as it is related in divers histories. And therefore Herodotus telling of an eclipse which fell in Xerxes's time, describes it thus: ὁ ἥλιΘ- εκλιπην την εκ τε ερανε ἑδρην αφανης ην §. The sun leaving his wonted seat in the heavens, vanished away: all which argues such a great darkness as could not have been, if her body had been perspicuous. Yet some there are who interpret all these relations to be hyperbolical expressions; and the noble Tycho thinks it naturally impossible that any eclipse should

---

* Scaliger Exercit. 80. sect. 13.   † Plut. de facie lunæ.
‡ Thucid. Livii. Plut. de facie lunæ.   § Herodot. l. 7. c. 37.

cause such darkness, because the body of the moon can never totally cover the sun. However, in this he is singular, all other astronomers (if I may believe Keplar) being on the contrary opinion, by reason the diameter of the moon does for the most part appear bigger to us than the diameter of the sun.

But here Julius Cæsar once more puts in to hinder our passage. The moon (saith he*) is not altogether opacous, because it is still of the same nature with the heavens, which are incapable of total opacity: and his reason is, because perspicuity is an inseparable accident of those purer bodies; and this he thinks must necessarily be granted; for he stops there, and proves no further; but to this I shall defer an answer till he hath made up his argument.

We may frequently see, that her body does so eclipse the sun, as our earth doth the moon. And besides, the mountains that are observed there, do cast a dark shadow behind them, as shall be shewed afterwards †. Since then the like interposition of them both, doth produce the like effect, they must necessarily be of the like natures, that is, alike opacous, which is the thing to be shewed; and this was the reason (as the interpreters guess) why Aristotle ‡ affirmed the moon to be of the earth's nature, because of their agreement in opacity; whereas all the other elements, save that, are in some measure perspicuous.

But the greatest difference which may seem to make our earth altogether unlike the moon, is, because the one is a bright body, and hath light of its own, and the other a gross dark body which cannot shine at all. It is requisite therefore that in the next place I clear this doubt, and shew that the moon hath no more light of her own than our earth.

* De phænom. lunæ, c. 11.   † Prop. 9.   ‡ In lib. de animalib.

PROP V.

That the Moon hath not any light of her own.

IT was the fancy of some of the Jews, and more especially of Rabbi Simeon*, that the moon was nothing
else but a contracted sun; and that both those planets,
at their first creation, were equal both in light and quantity.   For, because God did then call them both great
lights, therefore they inferred that they must be both
equal in bigness.   But a while after (as the tradition goes)
the ambitious moon put up her complaint to God against
the sun, shewing that it was not fit there should be
two such great lights in the heavens ; a monarchy would
best become the place of order and harmony.   Upon this,
God commanded her to contract herself into a narrower
compass ; but she being much discontented hereat, replies,
What! because I have spoken that which is reason and
equity, must I therefore be diminished? This sentence
could not chuse but much trouble her ; and for this reason
was she in great distress and grief for a long space ; but
that her sorrow might be some way pacified, God bid her
be of good cheer, because her privileges and charter should
be greater than the sun's; he should appear in the day
time only, she both in the day and night ; but her melancholy being not satisfied with this, she replied again, That
that alas was no benefit ; for in the day time she should be
either not seen, or not noted.   Wherefore, God to comfort her up, promised, that his people the Israelites should
celebrate all their feasts and holidays by a computation of
her months; but this being not able to content her, she
has looked very melancholy ever since; however, she hath
still reserved much light of her own.

Others there were, that did think the moon to be a
round globe ; the one half of whose body was of a bright
substance, the other half being dark; and the divers con-

* Tostatus in 1 Gen. Hyeron. de sancta fide Hebræomast. l. 2. c. 4.

versions of those sides towards our eyes, caused the variety of her appearances. Of this opinion was Berosus, as he is cited by Vitruvius*; and St. Austin † thought it was probable enough. But this fancy is almost equally absurd with the former, and both of them sound rather like fables, than philosophical truths. You may commonly see how this latter does contradict frequent and easy experience; for it is observed, that that spot which is perceived about her middle when she is in the increase, may be discerned in the same place when she is in the full: whence it must follow, that the same part which was before darkened, is after enlightened, and that the one part is not always dark, and the other light of itself. But enough of this; I would be loth to make an enemy, that I may afterwards overcome him, or bestow time in proving that which is already granted; I suppose now, that neither of them hath any patrons, and therefore need no confutation.

It is agreed upon by all sides, that this planet receives most of her light from the sun; but the chief controversy is, whether or no she hath any of her own? The greater multitude affirm this. Cardan ‡ amongst the rest, is very confident of it; and he thinks that if any of us were in the moon at the time of her greatest eclipse, *lunam aspiceremus non secus ac innumeris cereis splendidissimis accensis, atque in eas oculis defixis cæcutiremus*; " we should per-" ceive so great a brightness of her own, that would blind " us with the mere sight, and when she is enlightened by " the sun, then no eagle's eye (if there were any there) is " able to look upon her." This Cardan says, and he doth but say it, without bringing any proof for its confirmation. However, I will set down the arguments that are usually urged for this opinion, and they are taken either from scripture or reason; from scripture is urged that place, 1 Cor. xv. where it is said, There is one glory of the sun, and another glory of the moon. Ulysses Albergettus urges

---

* Lib. 9. Architect.　　　† Narrat. Psalm. item ep. 119.
‡ De subtil. l. 3.

that in Matth. xxiv. 29. ἡ σεληνην ȣ δωσει το Φεγγῶ αυτης, the moon shall not give her light: therefore (says he) she hath some of her own.

But to these we may easily answer, that the glory and light there spoken of, may be said to be hers, though it be derived, as you may see in many other instances.

The arguments from reason are taken either,

1. From that light which is discerned in her, when there is a total eclipse of her own body, or of the sun.

2. From the light which is discerned in the darker part of her body, when she is but a little distant from the sun.

1. For when there are any total eclipses, there appears in her body a great redness, and many times light enough to cause a remarkable shade, as common experience doth sufficiently manifest: but this cannot come from the sun, since at such times either the earth or her own body shades her from the sun-beams; therefore it must proceed from her own light.

2. Two or three days after the new moon, we may perceive light in her whole body, whereas the rays of the sun reflect but upon a small part of that which is visible; therefore it is likely that there is some light of her own.

In answering to these objections, I shall first shew, that this light cannot be her own; and then declare that which is the true reason of it.

That it is not her own, appears,

1. Because then she would always retain it; but she has been sometimes altogether invisible, when as notwithstanding some of the fixed stars of the fourth or fifth magnitude might easily have been discerned close by her: as it was in the year 1620 *

2. This may appear likewise from the variety of it at divers times; for it is commonly observed that sometimes it is of a brighter, sometimes of a darker appearance; now redder, and at another time of a more duskish colour. The observation of this variety in divers eclipses, you may

* Keplar ep. Astron. cop. l. 6. p. 5. sect. 2,

see set down by Keplar and many others*. But now this could not be, if that light were her own, that being constantly the same, and without any reason of such an alteration : so that thus I may argue.

If there were any light proper to the moon, then would that planet appear brightest when she is eclipsed in her perige, being nearest to the earth ; and so consequently more obscure and duskish when she is in her apoge or farthest from it ; the reason is, because the nearer any enlightened body comes to the sight, by so much the more strong are the species, and the better perceived. This sequel is granted by some of our adversaries, and they are the very words of noble Tycho ; *Si luna genuino gauderet lumine, utique cum in umbra terræ esset, illud non amitteret, sed eo evidentius exerceret; omne enim lumen in tenebris, plus splendet cum alio majore fulgore non præpeditur* †. If the moon had any light of her own, then would she not lose it in the earth's shadow, but rather shine more clearly ; since every light appears greater in the dark, when it is not hindered by a more conspicuous brightness.

But now the event falls out clean contrary, (as observation doth manifest, and our opposites themselves do grant) the moon appearing with a more reddish and clear light when she is eclipsed, being in her apoge or farthest distance, and a more blackish iron colour when she is in her perige or nearest to us, therefore she hath not any light of her own. Nor may we think that the earth's shadow can cloud the proper light of the moon from appearing, or take away any thing from her inherent brightness ‡ ; for this were to think a shadow to be a body, an opinion altogether misbecoming a philosopher, as Tycho grants in the fore-cited place, *Nec umbra terræ corporeum quid est, aut densa aliqua substantia, ut lunæ lumen obtenebrare possit, atque id visui nostro præripere, sed est quædam privatio luminis solaris, ob interpositum opacum corpus terræ.*

---

* Opt. astron. c. 7. num. 3.   † De nova stella. l. 1. c. 10.
‡ Reinold Comment. in Purb. Theor. p. 164.

Nor is the earth's shadow any corporeal thing, or thick substance, that it can cloud the moon's brightness, or take it away from our sight; but it is a mere privation of the sun's light by reason of the interposition of the earth's opacous body.

3. If she had any light of her own, then that would itself be either such a ruddy brightness as appears in the eclipses, or else such a leaden duskish light, as we see in the darker parts of her body, when she is a little past the conjunction. (That it must be one of these, may follow from the opposite arguments;) but it is neither of these, therefore she hath none of her own.

1. It is not such a ruddy light as appears in eclipses; for then why can we not see the like redness, when we may discern the obscurer parts of the moon?

You will say, perhaps, that then the nearness of that greater light takes away that appearance.

I reply, This cannot be. For then, why does Mars shine with his wonted redness, when he is near the moon? Or why cannot her greater brightness make him appear white, as the other planets? Nor can there be any reason given, why that greater light should represent her body under a false colour.

2. It is not such a duskish leaden light, as we see in the darker part of her body, when she is about a sextile aspect distant from the sun; for then, why does she appear red in the eclipses; since mere shade cannot cause such a variety? For it is the nature of darkness, by its opposition, rather to make things appear of a more white and clear brightness, than they are in themselves. Or, if it be the shade, yet those parts of the moon are then in the shade of her body, and therefore in reason should have the like redness. Since, then, neither of these lights are hers; it follows, that she hath none of her own. Nor is this a singular opinion, but it hath had many learned patrons: such was Macrobius*, who being for this quoted of Rho-

* Somn. Scip. l. 1. c. 20.   Lect. antiq. l. 1. c. 15.

diginus, he calls him, *vir reconditissimæ scientiæ*, a man who knew more than ordinary philosophers; thus commending the opinion in the credit of the author. To him assents the venerable Bede[*], upon whom the gloss hath this comparison: As the looking-glass represents not any image within itself, unless it receive some from without; so the moon hath not any light, but what is bestowed by the sun. To these agreed Albertus Magnus[†], Scaliger[‡], Mæslin[§], Keplar, and more especially Mulapertius[||]; whose words are more pat to the purpose than others, and therefore I shall set them down as you may find them in his preface to his treatise concerning the Austriaca Sydera: *Luna, Venus, et Mercurius, terrestris et humidæ sunt substantiæ; ideoque de suo non lucere, sicut nec terra.* The Moon, Venus, and Mercury (saith he), are of an earthly and moist substance; and therefore have no more light of their own, than the earth hath. Nay, some there are who think (though without ground), that all the other stars do receive that light whereby they appear visible to us, from the sun. So Ptolomy, Isidore Hispalensis[¶], Albertus Magnus[**], and Bede[††]: much more then, must the moon shine with a borrowed light.

But enough of this. I have now sufficiently shewed what at the first I promised; that this light is not proper to the moon. It remains in the next place, that I tell you the true reason of it. And here, I think it is probable, that the light which appears in the moon at the eclipses, is nothing else but the second species of the sun's rays, which pass through the shadow unto her body: and from a mixture of this second light with the shadow, arises that redness which at such times appears unto us. I may call it *lumen crepusculinum*, the Aurora of the moon, or such a kind of blushing light that the sun causes when he is near

---

[*] In lib. de nat. rer. [†] De 4 Coævis. Q. 4. Art. 21. [‡] Exercit. 62.
[§] Epitom Astron. l. 4. p. 2. [||] Epit. Astron. Cop. l. 6. part 2. sect. 2.
[¶] Origin. l. 3. c. 60. [**] De Cælo, l. 2.
[††] De ratione temp. c. 4. Item Plin. l. 2. c. 6. Hugo de Sancto Victore. Annot in Gen. vi.

his rising, when he bestows some small light upon the thicker vapours. Thus we see commonly the sun being in the horizon, and the reflection growing weak, how his beams make the waters appear very red.

The Moabites, in Jehoram's time, when they rose early in the morning, and beheld the waters afar off, mistook them for blood *. *Et causa hujus est, quia radius solaris in aurora contrahit quondam rubedinem, propter vapores combustos manentes circa superficiem terræ, per quos radii transeunt ; & ideo cum repercutiantur in aqua ad oculos nostros, trahunt secum eundem ruborem, & faciunt apparere locum aquarum, in quo est repercussio, esse rubrum* ; saith Tostatus. The reason is, because of his rays ; which being in the lower vapours, those do convey an imperfect mixed light upon the waters. Thus the moon being in the earth's shadow, and the sun-beams which are round about it not being able to come directly unto her body ; yet some second rays there are, which passing through the shadow, make her appear in that ruddy colour : so that she must appear brightest, when she is eclipsed, being in her apoge or greatest distance from us ; because then the cone of the earth's shadow is less, and the refraction is made through a narrower medium. So on the contrary, she must be represented under a more dark and obscure form when she is eclipsed, being in her perige, or nearest to the earth ; because then she is involved in a greater shadow, or bigger part of the cone ; and so the refraction passing through a greater medium, the light must needs be weaker which doth proceed from it. If you ask now, What the reason may be of that light which we discern in the darker part of the new moon? I answer; it is reflected from our earth; which returns as great a brightness to that planet, as it receives from it. This I shall have occasion to prove afterward.

I have now done with these propositions, which were set down to clear the passage, and confirm the suppositions

---

* 2 Kings iii. 22.   2 Quæst. in hoc cap.

implied in the opinion. I shall in the next place proceed to a more direct treating of the chief matter in hand.

PROP. VI.

That there is a world in the Moon, hath been the direct opinion of many ancient, with some modern mathematicians; and may probably be deduced from the tenets of others.

SINCE this opinion may be suspected of singularity, I shall therefore first confirm it by sufficient authority of divers authors, both ancient and modern; that so I may the better clear it from the prejudice either of an upstart fancy, or an obsolete error. This is by some attributed to Orpheus, one of the most ancient Greek poets[*], who speaking of the moon, says thus; ἡ πολλ᾽ ϋρεα εχει, πολλ᾽ αστεα, πολλα μελαθρα, that it hath many mountains, and cities, and houses in it. To him assented Anaxagoras, Democritus, and Heraclides[†]; all who thought it to have firm solid ground, like to our earth; containing in it many large fields, champion grounds, and divers inhabitants.

Of this opinion likewise was Xenophanes[‡], as he is cited for it by Lactantius[§]; though that father (perhaps) did mistake his meaning, whilst he relates it thus: *Dixit Xenophanes, intra concavum lunæ esse aliam terram, et ibi aliud genus hominum, simili modo vivere sicut nos in hac terra, &c.* As if he had conceived the moon to be a great hollow body, in the midst of whose concavity, there should be another globe of sea and land, inhabited by men, as our earth is; whereas, it seems to be more likely by the relation of others, that this philosopher's opinion is to be understood in the same sense as it is here to be proved. True indeed, the father condemns this assertion, as an equal

[*] Plut. de plac. phil. l. 2. c. 13. [†] Ibid. c. 25.
[‡] Diog. Laert. l. 2. & l. 9. [§] Div. Inst. l. 3. c. 13.

absurdity to that of Anaxagoras, who affirmed the snow to
be black: but no wonder; for in the very next chapter it
is, that he does so much deride the opinion of those who
thought there were antipodes. So that his ignorance in
that particular, may perhaps disable him from being a
competent judge in any other the like point of philosophy.
Unto these agreed Pythagoras, who thought that our earth
was but one of the planets which moved round about the
sun, (as Aristotle relates it of him *;) and the Pythagoreans
in general did affirm that the moon also was terrestrial, and
that she was inhabited as this lower world: that those living creatures and plants which are in her, exceed any of
the like kind with us in the same proportion, as their days
are longer than ours, viz. by fifteen times. This Pythagoras † was esteemed by all, of a most divine wit, as appears
especially by his valuation amongst the Romans; who
being commanded by the oracle to erect a statue to the
wisest Grecian ‡, the senate determined Pythagoras to be
meant; preferring him in their judgments before the divine Socrates, whom their gods pronounced the wisest.
Some think him a Jew by birth; but most agree that he
was much conversant amongst the learneder sort and
priests of that nation, by whom he was informed of many
secrets; and (perhaps) this opinion which he vented afterwards in Greece, where he was much opposed by Aristotle
in some worded disputations, but never confuted by any
solid reason.

To this opinion of Pythagoras did Plato also assent,
when he considered that there was the like eclipse made
by the earth; and this, that it had no light of its own, that
it was so full of spots §. And therefore we may often read
in him and his followers, of an *ætherea terra*, and *lunares
populi*, an æthereal earth, and inhabiters in the moon; but
afterwards this was mixed with many ridiculous fancies:
for some of them considering the mysteries implied in the

* De Cœlo, l. 2. c. 13.   † Plut. ibid. cap. 30.
‡ Plin. Nat. Hist. l. 34. cap. 6.
§ Plat de conviviis.   Macrob. Somn. Scip. l. 1. c. 11.

number three, concluded that there must necessarily be a trinity of worlds, whereof the first is this of ours; the second in the moon, whose element of water is represented by the sphere of Mercury, the air by Venus, and the fire by the sun. And that the whole universe might the better end in earth as it began; they have contrived it, that Mars shall be a sphere of the fire, Jupiter of air, Saturn of water; and above all these, the Elysian fields, spacious and pleasant places appointed for the habitation of those unspotted souls, that either never were imprisoned in, or else now have freed themselves from any commerce with the body. Scaliger * speaking of this Platonic fancy, *quæ in tres trientes mundum quasi assem divisit,* thinks it is confutation enough to say, it is Plato's. However, for the first part of this assertion, it was assented unto by many others, and by reason of the grossness and inequality of this planet, it was frequently called *quasi terra cœlestis* †, as being esteemed the sediment and more imperfect part of those purer bodies; you may see this proved by Plutarch, in that delightful work which he properly made for the confirmation of this particular. With him agreed Alcinous and Plotinus, later writers ‡.

Thus Lucian also in his discourse of a journey to the moon, where though he does speak many things out of mirth and in a jesting manner; yet in the beginning of it he does intimate that it did contain some serious truths concerning the real frame of the universe.

The cardinal Cusanus and Jornandus Brunus §, held a particular world in every star; and therefore one of them defining our earth, he says, it is *stella quædam nobilis, quæ lunam et calorem et influentiam habet aliam, et diversam ab omnibus aliis stellis;* " a noble star, having a distinct " light, heat, and influence from all the rest." Unto this " Nicholas Hill ‖, a countryman of ours, was inclined,

---

* Exerc. 62.   † De facie Lunæ.
‡ Instit. ad discip. plat.   Cal. Rhodig. l. 1. c. 4.
§ Cusa de doct. ign. l. 2. cap. 12.   ‖ Philos. Epicur. par. 434.

when he said, *astrea terræ natura probabilis est:* " That
" it is probable the earth hath a starry nature."

But the opinion which I have here delivered, was more
directly proved by Mæslin[*], Keplar[†], and Galilæus[‡]; each
of them late writers, and famous men for their singular
skill in astronomy. Keplar calls this world by the name of
Levania, from the Hebrew word לבנה which signifies the
moon, and our earth by the name of *volva, a volvendo;*
because it does by reason of its diurnal revolution appear
unto them constantly to turn round; and therefore he stiles
those who live in that hemisphere which is towards us, by
the title of Subvolvani, because they enjoy the sight of this
earth; and the others Privolvani, *quia sunt privati conspectu*
volvæ, because they are deprived of this privilege. But Julius
Cæsar, whom I have above quoted, speaking of their testimony whom I cite for this opinion, viz. Keplar and Galilæus [§], affirms that to his knowledge they did but jest in
those things which they write concerning this; and as for
any such world, he assuredly knows they never so much as
dreamt of it. But I had rather believe their own words,
than his pretended knowledge.

It is true indeed, in some things they do but trifle, but
for the main scope of those discourses, it is as manifest
they seriously meant it, as any indifferent reader may easily
discern: as for Galilæus, it is evident that he did set
down his own judgment and opinion in these things;
otherwise sure Campanella (a man as well acquainted with
his opinion, and perhaps his person, as Cæsar was) would
never have writ an apology for him. And besides, it is
very likely if it had been but a jest, Galilæus would never
have suffered so much for it, as report saith afterwards he
did.

And as for Keplar, I will only refer the reader to his
own words, as they are set down in the preface to the
fourth book of his Epitom; where his purpose is to make

---

* In Thesibus.   † Dissertatio cum Nunc.
‡ Nuncius Sydereus. Somn. Astr.   § De phænom. Lunæ, c. 4.

an apology for the strangeness of those truths that he was
there to deliver, amongst which there are divers things to
this purpose concerning the nature of the moon. He professes that he did not publish them either out of a humour
of contradiction, or a desire of vain-glory, or in a jesting
way to make himself or others merry, but after a consi-
derate and solemn manner for the discovery of the truth.

Now as for the knowledge which Cæsar pretends to the
contrary, you may guess what it was by his strange confidence in other assertions, and his boldness in them may
well derogate from his credit in this. For speaking of
Ptolemy's Hypothesis *, he pronounces this verdict, *Impossibile est excentricorum et epicyclorum positio, nec aliquis
est ex mathematicis adeo stultus qui veram illam existimet.*
" The position of excentrics and epicycles is altogether im-
" possible, nor is there any mathematician such a fool as
" to think it true." I should guess he could not have
knowledge enough to maintain any other hypothesis, who
was so ignorant in mathematics as to deny that any good
author held this. For I would fain know whether there
were never any that thought the heavens to be solid bodies, and that there were such kinds of motion as is by
those feigned orbs supplied ; if so, Cæsar la Galla was
much mistaken. I think his assertions are equally true,
that Galilæus and Keplar did not hold this ; and that there
were none which ever held that other. Thus much for the
testimony of those who were directly of this opinion.

But, in my following discourse, I shall most insist on the
observation of Galilæus, the inventor of that famous perspective, whereby we may discern the heavens hard by us ;
whereby those things which others have formerly guessed
at, are manifested to the eye, and plainly discovered beyond exception or doubt ; of which admirable invention,
these latter ages of the world may justly boast, and for this
expect to be celebrated by posterity. It is related of Eudoxus, that he wished himself burnt with Phaeton, so he

* Cap. 7.

might stand over the sun to contemplate its nature; had he lived in these days, he might have enjoyed his wish at an easier rate; and scaling the heavens by this glass, might plainly have discerned what he so much desired. Keplar considering those strange discoveries which this perspective had made, could not choose but cry out in a προσοπο- τεια and rapture of admiration, *O multiscium et quovis scep- tro pretiosius perspicillum! an qui te dextrâ tenet, ille non dominus constituatur operum Dei?* And Johannes Fabri- cius*, an elegant writer, speaking of the same glass, and for this invention preferring our age before those former times of greater ignorance, says thus: *Adeo sumus superi- ores veteribus, ut quam illi carminis magici pronunciatu de- missam representasse putantur, nos non tantum innocenter demittamus, sed etiam familiari quodam intuitu ejus quasi conditionem intueamur.* " So much are we above the an-
" cients, that whereas they were fain by their magical
" charms to represent the moon's approach, we cannot
" only bring her lower with a greater innocence, but may
" also with a more familiar view behold her condition."
And because you shall have no occasion to question the truth of those experiments which I shall afterwards urge from it, I will therefore set down the testimony of an enemy; and such a witness hath always been accounted prevalent: you may see it in the above-named Cæsar la Galla †, whose words are these. *Mercurium caduceum gestantem, cælestia nunciare, et mortuorum animas ab in- feris revocare sapiens finxit antiquitas. Galilæum vero no- vum Jovis interpretem telescopio caduceo instructum sydera aperire, et veterum philosophorum manes ad superos revo- care solers nostra ætas vidçt et admiratur.* " Wise anti-
" quity fabled Mercury carrying a rod in his hand to re-
" late news from heaven, and call back the souls of the
" dead; but it hath been the happiness of our industrious
" age, to see and admire Galilæus (the new ambassador of
" the gods), furnished with his perspective to unfold the

* De macula in sol. obser.   † De phænom. cap. 1.

" nature of the stars, and awaken the ghosts of the ancient
" philosophers." So worthily and highly did these men
esteem of this excellent invention.

Now if you would know what might be done by this
glass, in the sight of such things as were nearer at hand,
the same author will tell you, when he says *, That by it
those things which could scarce at all be discerned by the
eye, at the distance of a mile and a half, might plainly and
distinctly be perceived for sixteen Italian miles, and that as
they were really in themselves, without any transposition
or falsifying at all. So.that what the ancient poets were
fain to put in a fable, our more happy age hath found out
in a truth; and we may discern as far with these eyes
which Galilæus hath bestowed upon us, as Lynceus could
with those which the poets attributed unto him. But if
you yet doubt whether all these observations were true, the
same author may confirm you, when he says they were
shewed, *Non uni aut alteri, sed quamplurimis, neque gre-
gariis hominibus, sed præcipuis atque disciplinis omnibus,
necnon mathematicis et opticis præceptis optime instructis
sedulà ac diligenti inspectione**. "Not to one or two, but
" to very many, and those not ordinary men, but to those
" who were well versed in mathematics and optics; and
" that not with a mere glance, but with a sedulous and di-
" ligent inspection." And lest any scruple might remain
unanswered, or you might think the men who beheld al
this, though they might be skilful, yet they came with credulous minds, and so were more easy to be deluded: He
adds that it was shewed, *Viris qui ad experimenta hæc
contradicendi animo accesserant†*. "To such as were
" come with a great deal of prejudice, and an intent of
" contradiction." Thus you may see the certainty of
those experiments which were taken by this glass. I have
spoken the more concerning it, because I shall borrow
many things in my further discourse, from those discoveries which were made by it.

* De phænom. c. 6.　　† Cap. 1.　　‡ Cap. 5.

I have now cited such authors, both ancient and modern, who have directly maintained the same opinion. I told you likewise in the proposition, that it might probably be deduced from the tenets of others* : such were Aristarchus, Philolaus, and Copernicus, with many other later writers, who assented to their hypothesis; so Joach. Rhelicus, David Origanus Lansbergius, Guil. Gilbert; and, (if I may believe Campanella) *innumeri alii Angli et Galli;* very many others, both English and French, all who affirmed our earth to be one of the planets, and the sun to be the centre of all, about which the heavenly bodies did move. And how horrid soever this may seem at the first, yet it is likely enough to be true, nor is there any maxim or observation in optics (saith Pena) that can disprove it.

Now if our earth were one of the planets (as it is according to them) then why may not another of the planets be an earth?

Thus have I shewed you the truth of this proposition. Before I proceed farther, it is requisite that I inform the reader what method I shall follow in the proving of this assertion, That there is a world in the moon.

The order by which I shall be guided, will be that which Aristotle uses in his book *De Mundo* (if that book were his).

First, περι των εν αυτη, of those chief parts which are in it; not the elementary and ethereal (as he doth there), since this does not belong to the present question, but of the sea and land, &c. Secondly, περι αυτην παθων, of those things which are extrinsical to it, as the seasons, meteors, and inhabitants.

* See the second book, 1 prop.   † Apologia pro Galilæo.

PROP. VII.

That those spots and brighter parts, which by our sight
may be distinguished in the Moon, do shew the difference
betwixt the sea and land in that other world.

FOR the clear proof of this proposition, I shall firs
reckon up and refute the opinions of others concern
ing the matter and form of those spots, and then shew the
greater probability of this present assertion, and how agreeable it is to that truth which is most commonly received
As for the opinions of others concerning these, they have
been very many : I will only reckon up those which are
common and remarkable.

Some there are that think those spots do not arise from
any deformity of the parts, but a deceit of the eye, which
cannot at such a distance discern an equal light in that
planet : but these do but only say it, and shew not any
reason for the proof of their opinion. Others think that
there are some bodies betwixt the sun and moon, which
keeping off the light in some parts, do by their shadow
produce these spots which we there discern*.

Others would have them to be the figure of the seas or
mountains here below, represented there as in a looking-
glass. But none of those fancies can be true, because the
spots are still the same, and not varied according to the
difference of places ; and besides, Cardan † thinks it is impossible that any image should be conveyed so far, as there
to be represented unto us at such at a distance. But it is
commonly related of Pythagoras, that he by writing wha
he pleased in a glass, by the reflexion of the same species
would make those letters to appear in the circle of the
moon, where they should be legible by any other, who

* So Bede in l. de Mund. constit.   † De subtil. lib. 3.

might at that time be some miles distant from him.
Agrippa * affirms this to be possible, and the way of performing it not unknown to himself, with some others in
his time. It may be, that bishop Godwin did by the like
means perform those strange conclusions, which he professes in his Nuncius Inanimatus; where he pretends, that
he can inform his friends of what he pleases, though they
be an hundred miles distant, *forte etiam, vel milliare mil-
lesimum* (they are his own words), and perhaps a thousand; and all this in a little space, quicker than the sun can
move.

Now, what conveyance there should be for so speedy a
passage, I cannot conceive, unless it be carried with the
light, than which we know not any thing quicker. But of
this only by the way. However, whether those images
can be represented so or not, yet certain it is, those spots
are not such representations. Some think that when God
had at first created too much earth to make a perfect globe,
not knowing well where to bestow the rest, he placed it in
the moon, which ever since hath so darkened it in some
parts: but the impiety of this is sufficient confutation, since
it so much detracts from the divine power and wisdom.

The stoics † held that planet to be mixed of fire and air;
and in their opinion, the variety of its composition caused
her spots: being not ashamed to stile the same body a
goddess, calling it Diana, Minerva, &c. and yet affirm it to
be an impure mixture of flame and smoke, and fuliginous
air.——But this planet cannot consist of fire, saith Plutarch,
because there is not any fuel to maintain it. And the poets
have therefore feigned Vulcan to be lame, because he can
no more subsist without wood or other fuel, than a lame
man without a staff.

Anaxagoras thought all the stars to be of an earthly nature, mixed with some fire; and as for the sun, he affirmed
it to be nothing else but a fiery stone: for which latter opi-

---

* Occulta Philos. l. 1. cap. 6.   † Plut. de placit. phil. l. 2. c. 25.

nion, the Athenians sentenced him to death*; those zealous idolaters counting it a great blasphemy to make their
god a stone; whereas notwithstanding, they were so senseless in their adoration of idols, as to make a stone their
god.   This Anaxagoras affirmed the moon to be more terrestrial than the other planets, but of a greater purity than
any thing here below; and the spots he thought were nothing else but some cloudy parts intermingled with the
light which belonged to that planet; but I have above destroyed the supposition on which this fancy is grounded.
Pliny † thinks they arise from some drossy stuff, mixed
with that moisture which the moon attracts unto herself;
but he was of their opinion who thought the stars were nourished by some earthly vapours; which you may commonly see refuted in the Commentators on the books De
Cœlo.

Vitellio and Reinoldus ‡ affirm the spots to be the
thicker parts of the moon, into which the sun cannot infuse
much light; and this (say they) is the reason why in the
sun's eclipses the spots and brighter parts are still in some
measure distinguished, because the sun-beams are not able
so well to penetrate through those thicker, as they may
through the thinner parts of that planet.   Of this opinion
also was Cæsar la Galla, whose words are these §; " The
" moon doth there appear clearest, where she is transpi-
" cuous, not only through the superficies, but the substance
" also; and there she seems spotted, where her body is
" most opacous."   The ground of this his assertion was,
because he thought the moon did receive and bestow her
light by illumination only, and not at all by reflection; but
this, together with the supposed penetration of the sun-
beams, and the perspicuity of the moon's body I have
above answered and refuted.

* Josephus l. 2. con. App. August. de Civit. Dei, l. 18. c. 41.
† Nat. Hist. l. 2. c. 9.   ‡ Opt. lib. 9. Comment. in Purb. p. 164.

§ Ex qua parte luna est transpicua non solum secundum superficiem,
sed etiam secundum substantiam, eatenus clara, ex qua autem parte
opaca est, eatenus obscura videtur.   De Phænom. cap. 11.

The more common and general opinion is, that the spots are the thinner parts of the moon, which are less able to reflect the beams that they receive from the sun, and this is most agreeable to reason; for if the stars are therefore brightest, because they are thicker and more solid than their orbs, then it will follow, that those parts of the moon which have less light, have also less thickness *. It was the providence of nature (say some) that so contrived that planet to have these spots within it; for since that is nearest to those lower bodies which are so full of deformity, it is requisite that it should in some measure agree with them; and as in this inferior world, the higher bodies are the most complete, so also in the heavens, perfection is ascended unto by degrees, and the moon being the lowest, must be the least pure; and therefore Philo the Jew interpreting Jacob's dream concerning the ladder †, doth in an allegory shew how that in the fabric of the world, all things grow perfecter as they grow higher; and this is the reason (saith he) why the moon doth not consist of any pure simple matter, but is mixed with air, which shews so darkly within her body.

But this cannot be a sufficient reason; for though it were true that nature did frame every thing perfecter as it was higher, yet is it as true that nature frames every thing fully perfect for that office to which she intends it. Now had she intended the moon merely to reflect the sun-beams, and give light, the spots then had not so much argued her providence, as her unskilfulness and oversight, as if in the haste of her work she could not tell how to make that body exactly fit for that office to which she intended it ‡.

It is likely then that she had some other end which moved her to produce this variety; and this, in all probability, was her intent, to make it a fit body for habitation, with the same conveniences of sea and land, as this inferior world doth partake of. For since the moon is such a

* Albert. mag. de Coævis. Q. 4. Art. 21. Colleg. Con.
† De somniis.   ‡ Scalig. exercit. 62.

vast, such a solid and opacous body, like our earth (as was
above proved) why may it not be probable that those thinner
and thicker parts appearing in her, do shew the difference
betwixt the sea and land in that other world? And Galilæus doubts not, but that if our earth were visible at the
same distance, there would be the like appearance of it.

If we consider the moon as another habitable earth, then
the appearances of it will be altogether exact and beauti-
ful, and may argue unto us that it is fully accomplished for
all those ends to which Providence did appoint it. But
consider it barely as a star or light, and then there will appear in it much imperfection and deformity, as being of an
impure dark substance, and so unfit for the office of that
nature.

As for the form of those spots, some of the vulgar think
they represent a man, and the poets guess it is the boy
Endymion, whose company she loves so well, that she carries him with her: others will have it only to be the face
of a man, as the moon is usually pictured; but Albertus
thinks rather, that it represents a lion with his tail towards
the east, and his head the west; and some others * have
thought it to be very much like a fox; and certainly it is
as much like a lion as that in the zodiac, or as ursa major
is like a bear.

I should guess that it represents one of these as well as
another, and any thing else as well as any of these, since
it is but a strong imagination which fancies such images, as
school-boys usually do in the marks of a wall, whereas
there is not any similitude in the spots themselves, which
rather like our sea, in respect of the land, appears under a
rugged and confused figure, and doth not represent any
distinct image: so that both in respect of the matter and
the form, it may be probable enough that those spots and
brighter parts may shew the distinction betwixt the sea and
land in that other world.

* Eusebius Nieremb. Hist. Nat. l. 8. c. 15.

PROP. VIII.

The spots represent the sea, and the brighter parts the land.

WHEN I first compared the nature of our earth and water with those appearances in the moon, I concluded contrary to the proposition, that the brighter parts represented the water, and the spots the land. Of this opinion likewise was Keplar at the first [*]. But my second thoughts, and the reading of others, have now convinced me (as after he was) of the truth of that proposition which I have now set down. Before I come to the confirmation of it, I shall mention those scruples which at first made me doubt the truth of this opinion.

1. It may be objected, it is probable, if there be any such sea and land as ours, that it bears some proportion and similitude with ours: but now this proposition takes away all likeness betwixt them. For whereas the superficies of our earth is but the third part of the whole surface in the globe, two parts being overspread with the water (as Scaliger observes [†]), yet here, according to this opinion, the sea should be less than the land, since there is not so much of the bespotted as there is of the enlightened parts; wherefore it is probable that there is no such thing at all, or else that the brighter parts are the sea.

2. The water, by reason of the smoothness of its superficies, seems better able to reflect the sun-beams than the earth, which in most places is so full of ruggedness, of grass and trees, and such like impediments of reflection ; and besides, common experience shews that the water shines with a greater and more glorious brightness than the earth ; therefore it should seem that the spots are the earth, and

[*] Opt. Astro. c. 6. num. 9. Dissert. cum nuncio Gal.
[†] Exercit. 38.

the brighter parts the water. But to the first it may be answered.

1. There is no great probability in this consequence, that because it is so with us, therefore it must be so with the parts of the moon; for since there is such a difference betwixt them in divers other respects, they may not perhaps agree in this.

2. That assertion of Scaliger * is not by all granted for a truth. Fromondus with others think that the superficies of the sea and land, in so much of the world as is already discovered, is equal and of the same extension.

3. The orb of thick and vaporous air which encompasses the moon, makes the brighter parts of that planet appear bigger than in themselves they are; as I shall shew afterwards.

To the second it may be answered, That though the water be of a smooth superficies, and so may seem most fit to reverberate the light, yet because it is of a perspicuous nature, therefore the beams must sink into it, and cannot so strongly and clearly be reflected. *Sicut in speculo ubi plumbum abrasum fuerit* (saith Cardan), as in looking-glasses, where part of the lead is razed off, and nothing left behind to reverberate the image, the species must there pass through, and not back again: so it is where the beams penetrate and sink into the substance of the body, there cannot be such an immediate and strong reflection, as when they are beat back from the superficies; and therefore the sun causes a greater heat by far upon the land, than upon the water. Now as for that experiment, where it is said, that the waters have a greater brightness than the land; I answer, It is true only there where they represent the image of the sun, or some bright cloud, and not in other places; especially if we look upon them at any great distance, as is very plain by common observation.

And it is certain, that from any high mountain the land does appear a great deal brighter than any lake or river.

* De Meteoris, l. 5. c. 1. Art. 1.

This may yet be farther illustrated by the similitude of a
looking-glass hanging upon a wall in the sun-shine; where,
if the eye be not placed in the just line of reflection from
the glass, it is manifest that the wall will be of a brighter
appearance than the glass.   True indeed, in the line of reflection, the light of the glass is equal almost unto that
which comes immediately from the sun itself; but now
this is only in one particular place, and so is not like that
brightness which we discern in the moon; because this
does appear equally in several situations, like that of the
wall, which does seem bright as well from every place, as
from any one.   And therefore the roughness of the wall,
or (as it is in the objection) the ruggedness of our earth, is
so far from being an hindrance of such a reflection as there
is from the moon, that it is rather required as a necessary
condition unto it.   We may conceive that in every rough
body, there are, as it were, innumerable superficies, disposed unto an innumerable diversity of inclinations. *Ita
ut nullus sit locus, ad quem non pertingant plurimi radii
reflexi a plurimis superficieculis, per omnem corporis scabri
radiis luminosis percussi superficiem dispersis**.   " So that
" there is not any place unto which there are not some
" beams reflected from these diverse superficies, in the
" several parts of such a rugged body."   But yet (as I
said before) the earth does receive a great part of its light
by illumination, as well as by reflection.

So that notwithstanding those doubts, yet this proposition may remain true, That the spots may be the sea, and
the brighter parts the land.   Of this opinion was Plu-
tarch†: unto him assented Keplar and Galilæus, whose words
are these: *Si quis veterum Pythagoreorum sententiam ex-
suscitare velit, lunam scilicet esse quasi tellurem alteram ejus
pars lucidior terrenam superficiem, obscurior vero aqueam
magis congruè repræsentet.   Mihi autem dubium fuit nunquam terrestris globi à longe conspecti, atque a radiis sola-*

---

* Galilæus System. Coll. 1.

† De facie Lun. Dissertatio Nunc. Syd.

*ribus perfusi, terream superficiem clariorem, obscuriorem
vero aqueam sese in conspectum daturam.* " If any man
" have a mind to renew the opinion of the Pythagoreans,
" That the moon is another earth ; then her brighter parts
" may fitly represent the earth's superficies, and the darker
" part the water : and for my part, I never doubted but
" that our earthly globe being shined upon by the sun, and
" beheld at a great distance, the land would appear bright-
" est, and the sea more obscurely." The reasons may
be,

1. That which I urged about the foregoing chapter ;
because the water is the thinner part, and therefore must
give less light.

Since the stars and planets, by reason of their brightness,
are usually concluded to be the thicker parts of their orb.

2. Water is in itself of a blacker colour (saith Aristotle*),
and therefore more remote from light than the earth. Any
part of the ground being moistened with rain, does look
much more darkly than when it is dry.

6. It is observed that the secondary light of the moon
(which afterwards is proved to proceed from our earth) is
sensibly brighter unto us, for two or three days before the
conjunction, in the morning when she appears eastward,
than about the same time after the conjunction, when she
is seen in the west. The reason of which must be this,
because that part of the earth which is opposite to the
moon in the east, has more land in it than sea. Whereas
on the contrary, the moon when she is in the west, is
shined upon by that part of our earth where there is more
sea than land ; from whence it will follow with good probability, that the earth does cast a greater light than the
water.

4. Because observation tells us, that the spotted parts are
always smooth and equal, having everywhere an equality
of light, when once they are enlightened by the sun ;
whereas the brighter parts are full of rugged gibbosities

* In lib. de coloribus.

and mountains, having many shades in them, as I shall shew more at large afterwards.

That in this planet there must be seas, Campanella * endeavours to prove out of Scripture, interpreting the waters above the firmament, spoken in Genesis, to be meant of the sea in this world. For (saith he) it is not likely that there are any such waters above the orbs to moderate that heat which they receive from their swift motion (as some of the fathers think). Nor did Moses mean the angels, which may be called spiritual waters, as Origen and Austin‡ would have it, for both these are rejected by the general consent: nor could he mean any waters in the second region, as most commentators interpret it. For first there is nothing but vapours, which though they are afterwards turned into water, yet while they remain there, they are only the matter of that element, which may as well be fire, or earth, or air. 2. Those vapours are not above the expansum, but in it. So that he thinks there is no other way to salve all, but by making the planets several worlds with sea and land, with such rivers and springs as we have here below: especially since Esdras speaks of the springs above the firmament †. But I cannot agree with him in this, nor do I think that any such thing can be proved out of scripture.

Before I proceed to the next position, I shall first answer some doubts which might be made against the generality of this truth, whereby it may seem impossible that there should be either sea or land in the moon: for since she moves so swiftly as astronomers observe, why then does there nothing fall from her, or why doth she not shake something out by the celerity of her revolution? I answer, You must know that the inclination of every heavy body to its proper centre, doth sufficiently tie it unto its place; so that suppose any thing were separated, yet must it ne-

* Apologia pro Galilæo.

† Vide Ieron. Epist. ad Pammachium.   Confession. l. 13. c. 32.
Retracted lib. 2. Retr. cap. 6.

‡ 2 Esdr. iv. 7.

cessarily return again. And there is no more danger of their falling into our world, than there is fear of our falling into the moon.

But yet there are many fabulous relations of such things as have dropped thence *. There is a tale of the Nemean lion that Hercules slew, which first rushing among the herds out of his unknown den in the mountain of Cytheron in Bœotia, the credulous people thought he was sent from their goddess the moon And if a whirlwind did chance to snatch any thing up, and afterwards rain it down again, the ignorant multitude were apt to believe that it dropt from heaven. Thus Avicenna relates the story of a calf which fell down in a storm, the beholders thinking it a moon-calf, and that it fell thence. So Cardan travelling upon the Apennine mountains, a sudden blast took off his hat, which if it had been carried far, he thinks the peasants, who had perceived it to fall, would have sworn it had rained hats. After some such manner many of our prodigies come to pass, and the people are willing to believe any thing which they may relate to others as a very strange and wonderful event. I doubt not but the Trojan Palladium, the Roman Minerva, and our lady's church at Loretto, with many sacred relics preserved by the papists, might drop from the moon as well as any of these.

But it may be again objected, Suppose there were a bullet shot up in that world, would not the moon run away from it before it could fall down, since the motion of her body (being every day round our earth) is far swifter than the other, and so the bullet must be left behind, and at length fall down to us? To this I answer,

1. If a bullet could be shot so far till it came to the circumference of those things which belong to our centre, then it would fall down to us.

2. Though there were some heavy body a great height in that air, yet would the motion of that magnetical globe to which it did belong, by an attractive virtue still hold it within its convenient distance, so that whether their earth

---

* Vide Guli. Nubrigers. de rebus Anglica. lib. 1.

moved or stood still, yet would the same violence cast a body from it equally far. That I may the plainer express my meaning, I will set down this diagram.

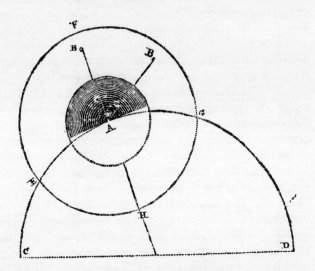

Suppose this earth were A, which was to move in the circle C, D, and let the bullet be supposed at B, within its proper verge; I say, whether this earth did stand still, or move swiftly towards D, yet the bullet would still keep at the same distance, by reason of that magnetic virtue of the centre (if I may so speak) whereby all things within its sphere are attracted with it. So that the violence to the bullet, being nothing else but that whereby it is removed from its centre, therefore an equal violence can carry a body from its proper place but at an equal distance, whether or no this earth where its centre is, does stand still or move.

The impartial reader may find sufficient satisfaction for this and such other arguments as may be urged against the motion of that earth, in the writings of Copernicus and his followers; unto whom, for brevity sake, I will refer them.

PROP. IX.

That there are high mountains, deep vallies, and spacious plains in the body of the Moon.

THOUGH there are some who think mountains to be a deformity to the earth, as if they were either beat up by the flood, or else cast up like so many heaps of rubbish left at the creation ; yet if well considered, they will be found as much to conduce to the beauty and conveniency of the universe, as any of the other parts. Nature (saith Pliny *) purposely framed them for many excellent uses; partly to tame the violence of greater rivers, to strengthen certain joints within the veins and bowels of the earth, to break the force of the sea's inundation, and for the safety of the earth's inhabitants, whether beasts or men. That they make much for the protection of beasts, the Psalmist testifies † ; The highest hills are a refuge for the wild goats, and the rocks for conies. The kingly prophet had likewise learned the safety of these by his own experience, when he also was fain to make a mountain his refuge from the fury of his master Saul, who persecuted him in the wilderness.

True indeed, such places as these keep their neighbours poor, as being most barren, but yet they preserve them safe, as being most strong; witness our unconquered Wales and Scotland, whose greatest protection hath been the natural strength of their country; so fortified with mountains, that these have always been unto them sure retreats from the violence and oppression of others. Wherefore a good author doth rightly call them nature's bulwarks, cast up at God Almighty's own charges, the scorns and curbs of victorious armies. Which made the Barbarians in Curtius so confident of their own safety, when they

---

* Nat. Hist. l. 36. c. 5.   † Psal. civ. ver. 18.

were once retired to an inaccessible mountain; that when Alexander's legate had brought them to a parley, and persuading them to yield, told them of his master's victories, what seas and wildernesses he had passed; they replied, that all that might be, but could Alexander fly too? Over the seas he might have ships, and over the land horses, but he must have wings before he could get up thither. Such safety did those barbarous nations conceive in the mountains whereunto they were retired. Certainly then such useful parts were not the effect of man's sin, or produced by the world's curse, the flood; but rather at the first created by the goodness and providence of the Almighty.

This truth is usually concluded from these and the like arguments.

1. Because the scripture itself, in the description of that general deluge, tells us, it overflowed the highest mountains.

2. Because Moses who writ long after the flood, does yet give the same description of places and rivers, as they had before; which could not well have been if this had made so strange an alteration.

3. It is evident that the trees did stand as before. For otherwise, Noah could not so well have concluded, that the waters were abated, from this reason, because the dove brought an olive leaf in her mouth, when she was sent forth a second time: whereas had the trees been rooted up, she might have taken it the first time, from one of them as it was floating on the top of the waters. Now if the motion of the water was not so violent as to subvert the trees, much less was it able to cast up such vast heaps as the mountains.

4. When the scripture doth set forth unto us the power and immensity of God by the variety or usefulness of the creatures which he hath made; amongst the rest it doth often mention the mountains. Psal. civ. 8. item, cviii. 9 Isa. xl. 12. And therefore it is probable they were created at the first. Unto this I might add that in other places,

divine wisdom in shewing of its own antiquity; saith that
he was from the beginning, before the earth or the mountains were brought forth*.

5. If we may trust the relations of antiquity †, there
were many monuments left undefaced after the flood.

So that if I intend to prove that the moon is such a habitable world as this is; it is requisite that I shew it to
have the same conveniences of habitation as this hath.
And here if some Rabbi or Chymic were to handle the
point, they would first prove it out of scripture, from that
place in Moses his blessing, where he speaks of the ancient mountains and lasting hills, Deut. 33. תררי קרם וגבעות
עולם for having immediately before mentioned those
blessings which should happen unto Joseph by the influence of the moon, he does presently exegetically ite-
rate them, in blessing him with the chief things of the
ancient mountains and lasting hills; you may also see the
same expression used in Jacob's blessing of Joseph ‡.

But however we may deal *pro* or *con* in philosophy, yet
we must not be too bold with divine truths, or bring scripture to patronize any fancy of our own; though, (perhaps)
it be a truth. I am not of their mind, who think it a
good course to confirm philosophical secrets from the letter of the scripture, or by abusing some obscure text in
it. Methinks it favours too much of that melancholy humour of the chymics, who, aiming in all their studies at the
making of gold, do persuade themselves, that the most
learned and subtile of the ancient authors, in all their obscure places do mean some such sense as may make to
their purpose. And hence it is that they derive such
strange mysteries from the fables of the poets; and can
tell you what great secret it was, that antiquity did hide
under the fiction of Jupiter being turned into a shower of
gold: of Mercury's being made the interpreter of the
Gods: of the Moon's descending to the earth for the love

* Prov. viii. 25.   Psal. xc. 2.   † Joseph. Ant. l. 1. cap. 3.
‡ Gen. xlix. 26.

of Endymion : with such ridiculous interpretations of these
and the like fables, which any reasonable considering man
cannot conceive to proceed from any but such as are dis-
tracted.   No less fantastical in this kind are the Jewish
Rabbies ; amongst whom, is not any opinion, whether in
nature or policy, whether true or false, but some of them,
by a cabalistical interpretation can father it upon a dark
place of scripture, or (if need be) upon a text that is clean
contrary.   There being not any absurdity so gross and incredible, for which these abusers of the text, will not find
out an argument.   Whereas, it is the more natural way,
and should be observed in all controversies, to apply unto
every thing the proper proofs of it ; and when we deal
with philosophical truths, to keep ourselves within the
bounds of human reason and authority.

But this by the way.   For the better proof of this proposition, I might here cite the testimony of Diodorus, who
thought the moon to be full of rugged places, *velut terres-
tribus tumulis superciliosam;* but he erred much in some
circumstances of this opinion, especially where he says,
there is an island amongst the Hyperboreans, wherein
those hills may to the eye be plainly discovered ; and for
this reason Cælius * calls him a fabulous writer.   But you
may see more express authority for the proof of this in
the opinions of Anaxagoras and Democritus †, who held
that this planet was full of champion grounds, mountains
and vallies.   And this seemed likewise probable unto Au-
gustinus Nisus ‡, whose words are these: *Forsitan non est
remotum dicere lunæ partes esse diversas, veluti sunt partes terræ, quarum aliæ sunt vallosæ, aliæ montosæ, ex quarum differentia effici potest facies illa lunæ, nec est rationi
dissonum, nam luna est corpus imperfecte sphæricum, cum
sit corpus ab ultimo cælo elongatum, ut supra dixit Aristoteles.*   " Perhaps, it would not be amiss to say that the
" parts of the moon were divers, as the parts of this

---

* Lect. aut. l. 1. c. 15.   † Plut. de plac. l. 2. c. 25.
‡ De Cœlo. l. 2. part. 49.

" earth, whereof some are vallies, and some mountains;
" from the difference of which, some spots in the moon
" may proceed ; nor is this against reason ; for that pla-
" net cannot be perfectly spherical, since it is so remote a
" body from the first orb, as Aristotle had said before."
You may see this truth assented unto by Blancanus the
Jesuit *, and by him confirmed with divers reasons. Keplar hath observed in the moon's eclipses, that the division
of her enlightened part from the shaded, was made by a
crooked unequal line †, of which there cannot be any probable cause conceived, unless it did arise from the ruggedness of that planet ; for it cannot at all be produced from
the shade of any mountains here upon earth ; because
these would be so lessened before they could reach so
high in a conical shadow, that they would not be at all
sensible unto us (as might easily be demonstrated) ; nor
can it be conceived what reason of this difference there
should be in the sun. Wherefore there being no other
body that hath any thing to do in eclipses, we must necessarily conclude, that it is caused by a variety of parts in
the moon itself; and what can these be but its gibbosities ?
now if you should ask a reason why there should be such
a multitude of these in that planet, the same Keplar shall
jest you out an answer. Supposing (saith he) that those
inhabitants are bigger than any of us, in the same proportion as their days are longer than ours, viz. by fifteen
times ; it may be, for want of stones to erect such vast
houses as were requisite for their bodies, they are fain to
dig great and round hollows in the earth ‡. where they may
both procure water for their thirst, and turning about with
the shade, may avoid those great heats which otherwise
they would be liable unto. Or if you will give Cæsar la
Galla leave to guess in the same manner, he would rather
think that those thirsty nations cast up so many and so

* De Mundi fab. par. 3. c. 4.   † Astron. Opt. c. 6. num. 9.
‡ Kep. appen. Selenogra.

great heaps of earth in digging of their wine cellars; but this only by the way.

I shall next produce the eye-witness of Galilæus *, on which I most of all depend for the proof of this proposition; when he beheld the new moon through his perspective, it appeared to him under a rugged and spotted figure, seeming to have the darker and enlightened parts divided by a tortuous line, having some parcels of light at a good distance from the other; and this difference is so remarkable, that you may easily perceive it through one of those ordinary perspectives, which are commonly sold amongst us; but for your better apprehending of what I deliver, I will set down the figure as I find it in Galilæus.

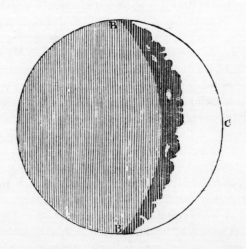

Suppose *B C B* to represent the appearance of the Moon's body being in a sextile, you may see some brighter parts separated at a pretty distance from the other, which can be nothing else but a reflection of the sun-beams upon some parts that are higher than the rest; and those obscure gibbosities which stand out towards the enlightened parts,

* Nuncius Sydereus.

must be such hollow and deep places whereto the rays cannot reach. But when the moon is got farther off from the sun, and come to that fulness as this line $B\ B$ doth represent her under; then do these parts also receive an equal light, excepting only that difference which doth appear betwixt their sea and land. And if you do consider how any rugged body would appear being enlightened, you would easily conceive that it must necessarily seem under some such gibbous unequal form, as the moon is here represented. Now for the infallibility of these appearances, I shall refer the reader to that which hath been said in the sixth proposition.

But Cæsar la Galla affirms, that all these appearances may consist with a plain superficies, if we suppose the parts of the body to be some of them diaphanous, and some opacous; and if you object that the light which is conveyed to any diaphanous part in a plain superficies, must be by a continued line; whereas here there appear many brighter parts among the obscure at some distance from the rest: to this he answers, it may rise from some secret conveyances and channels within her body, that do consist of a more diaphanous matter; which being covered over with an opacous superficies, the light passing through them may break out a great way off; whereas the other parts betwixt, may still remain dark. Just as the river Arethusa in Sicily, which runs under ground for a great way, and afterwards breaks out again. But, because this is one of the chiefest fancies, whereby he thinks he hath fully answered the argument of this opinion, I will therefore set down his answer in his own words, lest the reader might suspect more in them than I have expressed*. *Non est impossibile cæcos ductus diaphani & perspicui corporis, sed opaca superficie protendi, usque in diaphanam aliquam ex profundo in superficiem emergentem partem, per quos ductus lumen longo postmodum interstitio erumpat, &c.* But I reply, if the superficies betwixt these two

* Cap. 11.

two enlightened parts remain dark because of its opacity ;
then would it always be dark, and the sun could not make
it partake of light more than it could of perspicuity.   But
this contradicts all experience, as you may see in Galilæus, who affirms that when the sun comes nearer to his
opposition, then that which is betwixt them both, is enlightened as well as either.   Nay, this opposes his own
eye-witness; for he confesses himself that he saw this by
the glass.   He had said before, that he came to see those
strange sights discovered by Galilæus his glass, with an
intent of contradiction ; and you may read that confirmed
in the weakness of this answer, which rather bewrays an
obstinate, than a persuaded will; for otherwise sure he
would never have undertook to have destroyed such certain proof with so groundless a fancy.

That instance of Galilæus *, would have been a better
evasion, had this author been acquainted with it; who
might then have compared the moon to that which we
call mother of pearl, which though it be most exactly polished in the superficies of it, yet will seem unto the eye
as if there were divers swellings and risings in its several
parts.   But yet, this neither would not well have shifted
the experiment of the perspective.   For these rugged parts
do not only appear upon one side of the moon, but as the
sun does turn about in divers places, so do they also cast
their shadow.   When the moon is in her increase, then
do they cast their shadows to the east.   When she is in
the decrease, and the sun on the other side of her, then
likewise may we discover these brighter parts casting their
shadows westward.   Whereas in the full moon there are
none of all these to be seen.

But it may be objected, that it is almost impossible, and
altogether unlikely, that in the moon there should be any
mountains so high as those observations make them.   For
do but suppose, according to the common principles, that
the moon's diameter unto the earth's, is very near to the

* Syst. mund. col. 1.

proportion of two to seven. Suppose withal that the
earth's diameter contains about 7000 Italian miles, and the
moon's 2000 (as is commonly granted.) Now Galilæus
hath observed, that some parts have been enlightened, when
they were the twentieth part of the diameter distant from
the common term of illumination. From whence it must
necessarily follow, that there may be some mountains
in the moon so high, that they are able to cast a shadow a hundred miles off. An opinion that sounds like a
prodigy or a fiction ; wherefore it is likely that either those
appearances are caused by somewhat else besides mountains, or else those are fallible observations; from whence
may follow such improbable, inconceivable consequences.

But to this I answer ;

1. You must consider the height of the mountains is
but very little, if you compare them to the length of their
shadows. Sir Walter Rawleigh* observes that the mount
Athos, now called Lacas, casts its shadow 300 furlongs,
which is above 37 miles ; and yet that mount is none of the
highest. Nay Solinus † (whom I should rather believe in
this kind) affirms that this mountain gives his shadow
quite over the sea, from Macedon to the isle of Lemnos,
which is 700 furlongs, or 84 miles, and yet according to
the common reckoning it doth scarce reach 4 miles upwards in its perpendicular height.

2. I affirm that there are very high mountains in the
moon. Keplar and Galilæus think that they are higher
than any which are upon our earth. But I am not of
their opinion in this, because I suppose they go upon a
false ground, whilst they conceive that the highest mountain upon the earth is not above a mile perpendicular.

Whereas it is the common opinion, and found true
enough by observation, that Olympus, Atlas, Taurus and
Emus, with many others, are much above this height.
Tenariffa, in the Canary islands, is commonly related to be
above 8 miles perpendicular, and about this height (say

---

* Hist. l. 1. cap. 7. sect. 11.   † Poly. Hist. c. 21.

some) is the mount Perjacaca in America. Sir Walter Rawleigh* seems to think that the highest of these is near 30 miles upright: nay Aristotle, speaking of Caucasus in Asia, affirms it to be visible for 560 miles, as some interpreters find by computation ; from which it will follow, that it was 78 miles perpendicularly high ; as you may see confirmed by Jacobus Mazonius †, and out of him in Blancanus the Jesuit. But this deviates from the truth more in excess than the other doth in defect. However, though these in the moon are not so high as some amongst us ; yet certain it is they are of a great height, and some of them at the least four miles perpendicular. This I shall prove from the observation of Galilæus, whose glass can shew to the senses a proof beyond exception; and certainly that man must needs be of a most timorous faith, who dares not believe his own eye.

By that perspective you may plainly discern some enlightened parts (which are the mountains) to be distant from the other about the twentieth part of the diameter. From whence it will follow, that those mountains must necessarily be at the least four Italian miles in height.

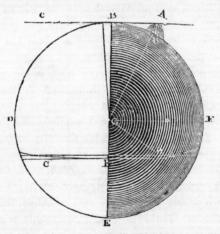

† Comparatio Arist. cum. Platone, sect. 3. c. 5. Expost. in loc. Matth. Arlis loc. 148.

For let B D E F be the body of the moon, A B C will
be a ray or beam of the sun, which enlightens a mountain
at A, and B is the point of contingency; the distance betwixt
A and B must be supposed to be the twentieth part of the
ciameter, which is an 100 miles, for so far are some enlightened parts severed from the common term of illumination. Now the aggregate of the quadrate from A B a
hundred, and B G 1000 will be 1010000; unto which the
quadrate arising from A G must be equal; according to
the 47th proposition in the first book of elements. Therefore the whole line A G is somewhat more than 104, and
the distance betwixt H A must be above 4 miles, which
was the thing to be proved.

But it may be again objected, if there be such rugged
parts, and so high mountains, why then cannot we discern them at this distance? Why doth the moon appear
unto us so exactly round, and not rather as a wheel with
teeth?

I answer, by reason of too great a distance; for if the
whole body appears to our eye so little, then those parts
which bear so small a proportion to the whole, will not at
all be sensible.

But it may be replied, if there were any such remarkable
hills, why does not the limb of the moon appear like a
wheel with teeth, to those who look upon it through the
great perspective, on whose witness you so much depend?
Or what reason is there that she appears as exactly round
through it, as she doth to the bare eye? certainly then
either there is no such thing as you imagine, or else the
glass fails much in this discovery.

To this I shall answer out of Galilæus.

1. You must know, that there is not merely one rank
of mountains above the edge of the moon, but divers orders, one mountain behind another, and so there is somewhat to hinder those void spaces which otherwise, perhaps, might appear.

Now where there be many hills, the ground seems even
to a man that can see the tops of all. Thus when the sea

rages, and many vast waves are lifted up, yet all may appear plain enough to one that stands at the shore. So where there are so many hills, the inequality will be less remarkable if it be discerned at a distance.

2. Though there be mountains in that part which appears unto us to be the limb of the moon, as well as in any other place, yet the bright vapours hide their appearance; for there is an orb of thick vaporous air that doth immediately compass the body of the moon; which though it have not so great opacity, as to terminate the sight, yet being once enlightened by the sun, it doth represent the body of the moon under a greater form, and hinders our sight from a distinct view of her true circumference. But of this in the next chapter.

3. Keplar hath observed*, that in the solary eclipses, when the rays may pass through this vaporous air, there are some gibbosities to be discerned in the limb of the moon.

I have now sufficiently proved, that there are hills in the moon; and hence it may seem likely that there is also a world: for since providence hath some special end in all its works, certainly then these mountains were not produced in vain; and what more probable meaning can we conceive there should be, than to make that place convenient for habitation.

* Somn. Astr. not. 207.

PROP. X.

That there is an Atmo-sphæra, or an orb of gross, vapo-rous air immediately encompassing the body of the Moon.

AS that part of our air which is nearest to the earth is of a thicker substance than the other, by reason it is always mixed with some vapours which are continually ex-haled into it: so is it equally requisite, that if there be a world in the moon, that the air about that should be alike qualified with ours. Now that there is such an orb of gross air, was first of all (for ought I can read) observed by Meslin*, afterwards assented unto by Keplar and Galilæus, and since by Baptista Cittacus, Scheiner, with others, all of them confirming it by the same arguments; which I shall only cite, and then leave this proposition.

1. It is not improbable that there should be a sphere of grosser air about the moon; because it is observed that there are such kind of evaporations which proceed from the sun itself. For there are discovered divers moveable spots, like clouds, that do encompass his body; which those authors who have been most frequently versed in these kind of experiments and studies, do conclude to be nothing else but evaporations from it. The probability and truth of which observations may also be inferred from some other appearances. As,

1. It hath been observed that the sun hath sometimes for the space of four days together†, appeared as dull and ruddy almost as the moon in her eclipses, insomuch that the stars have been seen at mid-day. Nay, he hath been constantly darkened for almost a whole year, and never shined but with a kind of heavy and duskish light, so that

---

* Vide Euseb. Nicrem. de Nat. Hist. l. 2. c. 11.
† So A. D. 1547, April 24th to the 28th.

there was scarce heat enough to ripen the fruits. As it was about the time when Cæsar was killed. Which was recorded by some of the poets. Thus Virgil speaking of the sun.

> *Ille etiam extincto miseratus Cæsare Romam,*
> *Cum caput obscura nitidum ferrugine texit,*
> *Impiaque æternam timuerunt sæcula noctem* *

> He pitying Rome when as great Cæsar dy'd,
> His head within a mourning vail did hide.
> And thus the wicked guilty world did fright
> With doubtful fears of an eternal night.

Ovid likewise, speaking of his death,

> ——————— *Solis quoque tristis imago*
> *Lurida sollicitis præbebat lumina terris.* †

> ——————— The sun's sad image then
> Did yield a lowering light to fearful men.

Now these appearances could not arise from any lower vapour : for then, 1. They would not have been so universal as they were, being seen through all Europe : or else, 2. That vapour must have covered the stars as well as the sun, which yet notwithstanding were then plainly discerned in the day-time. You may see this argument illustrated in another the like case, chap. 12. Hence then it will follow, that this fuliginous matter, which did thus obscure the sun, must needs be very near his body ; and if so, then what can we more probably guess it to be than evaporations from it ?

2. It is observed, that in the sun's total eclipses, when there is no part of his body discernible, yet there does not always follow so great a darkness as might be expected from his total absence. Now it is probable that the reason is, because these thicker vapours being enlightened by his beams, do convey some light unto us, notwithstanding the interposition of the moon betwixt his body and our earth.

* Virgil, Georg. l. 1.   † Metam. lib. 15.

3. This likewise is by some guessed to be the reason of the *crepusculum*, or that light which we have before the sun's rising.

Now if there be such evaporations from the sun, much more then from the moon, which does consist of a more gross and impure substance. The other arguments are taken from several observations in the moon herself, and do more directly tend to the proof of this proposition.

2. It is observed, that so much of the moon as is enlightened, is always part of a bigger circle than that which is darker. The frequent experience of others hath proved this, and an easy observation may quickly confirm it. But now this cannot proceed from any other cause so probable as from this orb of air; especially when we consider how that planet shining with a borrowed light, doth not send forth any such rays as may make her appearance bigger than her body.

3. When the moon being half enlightened, begins to cover any star, if the star be towards the obscurer part, then may it by the perspective be discerned to be nearer unto the center of the moon than the outward circumference of the enlightened part. But the moon being in the full, then does it seem to receive these stars without its limb.

4. Though the moon do sometime appear the first day of her change, when so much as appears enlightened cannot be above the 80th part of her diameter, yet then will the horns seem at least to be of a finger's breadth in extension; which could not be, unless the air about it were illuminated.

5. It is observed in the solary eclipses, that there is sometimes a great trepidation about the body of the moon, from which we may likewise argue an atmosphæra, since we cannot well conceive what so probable a cause there should be of such an appearance as this, *Quod radii solares a vaporibus lunam ambientibus fuerint intercisi*[*], that the

---

[*] Scheiner Ros. Urs. l. 4. part. 2. c. 27.

sun-beams were broken and refracted by the vapours that
encompassed the moon.

6. I may add the like argument taken from another observation which will be easily tried and granted. When
the sun is eclipsed, we discern the moon as she is in her
own natural bigness ; but then she appears somewhat less
than when she is in the full, though she be in the same
place of her supposed excentrick and epicycle ; and therefore Tycho hath calculated a table for the diameter of the
divers new moons. But now there is no reason so probable to solve this appearance, as to place an orb of thicker
air near the body of that planet, which may be enlightened
by the reflected beams, and through which the direct rays
may easily penetrate.

But some may object, that this will not consist with that
which was before delivered, where I said, that the thinnest
parts had least light.

If this were true, how comes it to pass then that this
air should be as light as any of the other parts, when as it
is the thinnest of all ?

I answer, if the light be received by reflection only, then
the thickest body hath most, because it is best able to beat
back the rays ; but if the light be received by illumination
(especially if there be an opacous body behind, which may
double the beams by reflexion) as it is here, then I deny
not but a thin body may retain much light ; and perhaps
some of those appearances which we take for fiery comets,
are nothing else but a bright cloud enlightened ; so that
probable it is there may be such air without the moon :
and hence it comes to pass, that the greater spots are only
visible towards her middle parts, and none near the circumference ; not but that there are some as well in those
parts as elsewhere, but they are not there perceiveable,
by reason of those brighter vapours which hide them.

PROP. XI.

That as their World is our Moon, so our World is their Moon.

I Have already handled the first thing that I promised, according to the method which Aristotle uses in his book De Mundo; and shewed you the necessary parts that belong to this world in the moon. In the next place it is requisite that I proceed to those things which are extrinsical unto it, as the seasons, the meteors, and the inhabitants.

1. Of the seasons;

And if there be such a world in the moon, it is requisite then that their seasons should be some way correspondent unto ours, that they should have winter and summer, night and day, as we have.

Now that in this planet there is some similitude of winter and summer, is affirmed by Aristotle himself*; since there is one hemisphere that hath always heat and light and the other that hath darkness and cold. True indeed, their days and years are always of one and the same length; (unless we make one of their years to be 19 † of ours, in which space all the stars do arise after the same order.) But it is so with us also under the poles, and therefore that great difference is not sufficient to make it altogether unlike ours; nor can we expect that every thing there should be in the same manner as it is here below, as if nature had no way but one to bring about her purposes. We have no reason then to think it necessary that both these worlds should be altogether alike; but it may suffice if they be correspondent in something only. However, it may be questioned whether it doth not seem to be against the wisdom of Providence, to make the night of so

* Degen. anima. 1. 4. 12.   † Golden number.

great a length, when they have such a long time unfit for
work? I answer, no; since it is so, and more with us also
under the poles; and besides, the general length of their
night is somewhat abated in the bigness of their moon,
which is our earth. For this returns as great a light unto
that planet, as it receives from it. But for the better proof
of this, I shall first free the way from such opinions as
might otherwise hinder the speed of a clearer progress.

Plutarch, one of the chief patrons of this world in the
moon*, doth directly contradict this proposition; affirming, that those who live there, may discern our world, as
the dregs and sediment of all other creatures; appearing
to them through clouds and foggy mists, and that altogether devoid of light, being base and unmoveable; so
that they might well imagine the dark place of damnation
to be here situate, and that they only were the inhabiters
of the world, as being in the midst betwixt heaven and
hell.

To this I may answer, it is probable that Plutarch spake
this inconsiderately and without a reason; which makes
him likewise fall into another absurdity, when he says our
earth would appear immoveable; whereas questionless,
though it did not, yet would it seem to move, and theirs
to stand still, as the land doth to a man in a ship; according to that of the poet:

Provehimur portu, terræque, urbesque recedunt.

And I doubt not but that an ingenious author would easily
have recanted, if he had been but acquainted with those
experiences which men of later times have found out, for
the confirmation of this truth.

2. Unto him assents Macrobius, whose words are these;
*Terra accepto solis lumine clarescit tantummodo, non re-
lucet†.* "The earth is by the sun-beams made bright,
" but not able to enlighten any thing so far." And his
reason is, because this being of a thick and gross matter,

---

* Plut. de fac. lunæ.   † Somm. Scip. l. 1. c. 19.

the light is terminated in its superficies, and cannot penetrate into the substance ; whereas the moon doth therefore seem so bright to us, because it receives the beams
within itself. But the weakness of this assertion may be
easily manifest by a common experience; for polished
steel (whose opacity will not give any admittance to the
rays) reflects a stronger heat than glass, and so consequently a greater light.

3. It is the general consent of philosophers, that the reflection of the sun-beams from the earth doth not reach
much above half a mile high, where they terminate the
first region ; so that to affirm they might ascend to the
moon, were to say, there were but one region of air,
which contradicts the proved and received opinion.

Unto this it may be answered :

That it is indeed the common consent, that the reflection of the sun-beams reach only to the second region ;
but yet some there are, and those too, philosophers of
good note, who thought otherwise. Thus Plotinus is
cited by Cælius, *Si concipias te in sublime quopiam mundi
loco, unde oculis subjiciatur terræ moles aquis circumfusa,
& solis syderumque radiis illustrata, non aliam profecto
visam iri probabile est, quam qualis modo visatur lunaris
globi species* *. " If you conceive yourself to be in some
" such high place, where you might discern the whole
" globe of the earth and water, when it was enlightened
" by the sun's rays, it is probable it would then appear to
" you in the same shape as the moon doth now unto us."
So Paulus Foscarinus. *Terra nihil aliud est quam altera
luna, vel stella, talisque nobis appareret, si ex convenienti
elongatione eminus conspiciretur, in ipsaque observari pos-
sent eadem aspectuum varietates, quæ in Luna apparent* †.
" The earth is nothing else but another moon or star, and
" would appear so unto us if it were beheld at a conve-
" nient distance, with the same changes and varieties as
" there are in the moon." Thus also Carolus Malaper-

tius, whose words are these: *Terra hæc nostra, si in lunâ constituti essemus, splendida prorsus quasi non ignobilis planeta, nobis appareret**. " If we were placed in the moon, " and from thence beheld this our earth, it would appear " unto us very bright, like one of the nobler planets." Unto these doth Fromondus assent, when he says, *Credo equidem quod si oculus quispiam in orbe lunari foret, globum terræ & aquæ instar ingentis syderis à sole illustrem conspiceret†*. " I believe that this globe of earth and water " would appear like some great star to any one, who " should look upon it from the moon." Now this could not be, nor could it shine so remarkably, unless the beams of light were reflected from it. And therefore the same *Fromondus* expressly holds, that the first region of air is there terminated, where the heat caused by reflection begins to languish, whereas the beams themselves do pass a great way further. The chief argument which doth most plainly manifest this truth, is taken from a common observation which may be easily tried.

If you behold the moon a little before or after the conjunction, when she is in a sextile with the sun, you may discern not only the part which is enlightened, but the rest also to have in it a kind of a duskish light; but if you chuse out such a situation, where some house or chimney (being some seventy or eighty paces distant from you) may hide from your eye the enlightened horns, you may then discern a greater and more remarkable shining in those parts unto which the sun-beams cannot reach ; nay, there is so great a light, that by the help of a good perspective you may discern its spots. In so much that Blancanus the Jesuit speaking of it, says, *Hæc experientia ita me aliquando fefellit, ut in hunc fulgorem casu ac repente incidens, existimarim novo quodam miraculo tempore adolescentis lunæ factum esse plenilunium ‡*. " This experiment " did once so deceive me, that happening upon the sight

* Præfat. ad Austriaca Syd.   † Meteor. l. 1. c. 2. art. 2.
‡ De mundi fab. p. 3. c. 3.

" of this brightness upon a sudden, I thought that by some
" new miracle the moon had been got into her full a little
" after her change."

But now this light is not proper to the moon; it doth
not proceed from the rays of the sun which doth penetrate her body, nor is it caused by any other of the planets
and stars. Therefore it must necessarily follow, that it
comes from the earth. The two first of these I have already proved, and as for the last, it is confidently affirmed
by Cœlius, *Quod si in disquisitionem evocet quis, an lunari
syderi lucem fœnerent planetæ item alii, asseverantur as-
truendum non fœnerare* *. " If any should ask whether the
" other planets lend any light to the moon? I answer,
" they do not." True indeed, the noble Tycho discussing the reason of this light, attributes it to the planet Venus † ; and I grant that this may convey some light, to
the moon; but that it is not the cause of this whereof
we now discourse, is of itself sufficiently plain; because
Venus is sometimes over the moon, when as she cannot
convey any light to that part which is turned from her.

It doth not proceed from the fixed stars; for then it
would retain the same light in eclipses, whereas the light
at such times is more ruddy and dull. Then also the light
of the moon would not be greater or lesser, according to
its distance from the edge of the earth's shadow, since it
did at all times equally participate this light of the stars.

In brief, this is neither proper to the moon, nor does it
proceed from any penetration of the sun's rays, or the
shining of Venus, or the other planets, or the fixed stars.
Now because there is no other body in the whole universe,
save the earth, it remains that this light must necessarily
be caused by that, which with a just gratitude repays to
the moon such illumination as it receives from her.

And as loving friends equally participate of the same
joy and grief, so do these mutually partake of the same
light from the sun, and the same darkness from the eclipses,

* Ant Lect. l. 20. c. 5.   † Progym. 1.

being also severally helped by one another in their greatest wants: for when the moon is in conjunction with the sun, and her upper part receives all the light, then her lower hemisphere (which would otherwise be altogether dark) is enlightened by the reflection of the sun-beams from the earth. When these two planets are in opposition, then that part of the earth which could not receive any light from the sun-beams, is most enlightened by the moon, being then in her full; and as she doth most illuminate the earth when the sun-beams cannot, so the grateful earth returns to her as great (nay greater) light when she most wants it; so that always that visible part of the moon which receives nothing from the sun, is enlightened by the earth, as is proved by Galilæus, with many more arguments, in that treatise which he calls Systema Mundi. True indeed, when the moon comes to a quartile, then you can neither discern this light; nor yet the darker part of her body; and that for a double reason;

1. Because the nearer it comes to the full, the less light does it receive from the earth, whose illumination does always decrease in the same proportion as the moon does increase.

2. Because of the exuberancy of the light in the other parts. *Quippe illustratum medium speciem recipit valentiorem* *. The clearer brightness involves the weaker; it being with the species of sight, as it is with those of sound; and as the greater noise drowns the less, so the brighter object hides that which is more obscure. But as they do always in their mutual vicissitudes participate of one another's light: so also do they partake of the same defects and darkenings; for when our moon is eclipsed, then is their sun darkened; and when our sun is eclipsed, then is their moon deprived of its light, as you may see affirmed by Meslin †. *Quod si terram nobis ex alto liceret intueri, quemadmodum deficientem lunam ex longinquo spectare possumus, videremus tempore eclipsis solis terræ aliquam*

* Scal. exerc. 62.   † Epit. Astr. l. 4. part 2.

partem lumine solis deficere, eodem plane mode sicut ex
opposito luna deficit. " If we might behold this globe of
" earth at the same distance as we do the moon in her
" defect, we might discern some part of it darkened in
" the sun's eclipses, just so as the moon is in hers."
For as our moon is eclipsed by the interposition of our
earth, so is their moon eclipsed by the interposition of
theirs. The manner of this mutual illumination betwixt
these two you may plainly discern in this figure following.

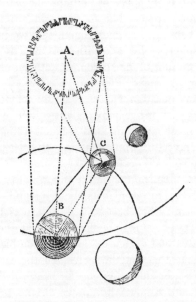

Where *A* represents the sun, *B* the earth, and *C* the
moon : Now suppose the moon *C* to be in a sextile of increase, when there is only one small part of her body enlightened, then the earth *B* will have such a part of its visible hemisphere darkened, as is proportionable to that part
of the moon which is enlightened ; and as for so much of
the moon, as the sun-beams cannot reach unto, it re-

ceives light from a proportionable part of the earth which shines upon it, as you may plainly perceive by the figure.

You see then that agreement and similitude which there is betwixt our earth and the moon. Now the greatest difference which makes them unlike, is this, that the moon enlightens our earth round about, whereas our earth gives light only to that hemisphere of the moon which is visible unto us; as may be certainly gathered from the constant appearance of the same spots, which could not thus come to pass, if the moon had such a diurnal motion about its own axis as perhaps our earth hath. And though some suppose her to move in an epicycle, yet this doth not so turn her body round, that we may discern both hemispheres; for according to that hypothesis (say they) the motion of her eccentric doth turn her face towards us, as much as the other doth from us.

But now, if any question what they do for a moon, who live in the upper part of her body? I answer, The solving of this, is the most uncertain and difficult thing that I know of, concerning this whole matter. But yet unto me this seems a probable conjecture.

That the upper hemisphere of the moon doth receive a sufficient light from those planets about it; and amongst these, Venus (it may be) bestows a more especial brightness, since Galilæus hath plainly discerned that she suffers the same increases and decreases, as the moon hath; and it is probable that this may be perceived there, without the help of a glass, because they are far nearer it than we. When Venus (saith Keplar) lies down in the perige or lower part of her supposed epicycle, then is she in conjunction with her husband the sun; from whom, after she hath departed for the space of ten months, she gets *plenum uterum*, and is in the full.

But you will reply, though Venus may bestow some light when she is over the moon, and in conjunction, yet being in opposition, she is not visible to them, and what shall they then do for light?

I answer; then they have none; nor doth this make so great a difference betwixt those two hemispheres, as there is with us betwixt the places under the poles and the line. And besides, it is considerable that there are two kind of planets.

1. Primary; such whose proper circle do encompass the body of the Sun, whereof there are six; Saturn, Jupiter, Mars, Ceres or the Earth, Venus, Mercury. As in the frontispiece.

2. Secondary; such whose proper circles are not about the sun, but some of the other primary planets. Thus are there two about Saturn, four about Jupiter, and thus likewise does the moon encompass our earth. Now it is probable that these lesser secondary planets, are not so accommodated with all conveniencies of habitation, as the others that are more principal.

But it may seem a very difficult thing to conceive, how so gross and dark a body as our earth, should yield such a clear light as proceeds from the moon; and therefore the Cardinal de Cusa* (who thinks every star to be a several world) is of opinion, that the light of the sun is not able to make them appear so bright; but the reason of their shining is, because we behold them at a great distance through their regions of fire, which do set a shining lustre upon those bodies that of themselves are dark. *Unde si quis esset extra regionem ignis, terra ista in circumferentia suæ regionis per medium ignis lucida stella appareret.* " So that if a man were beyond the region of fire, this " earth would appear through that as a bright star." But if this were the only reason, then would the moon be freed from such increases and decreases, as she is now liable unto.

Keplar thinks that our earth receives that light whereby it shines, from the sun; but this (saith he) is not such an intended clear brightness as the moon is capable of, and therefore he guesses that the earth there is of a more

* De doct. ig. l. 2, c. 12.

choaky soil, like the isle of Crete, and so is better able to
reflect a stronger light; whereas our earth must supply
this intention with the quantity of its body.   But this I
conceive to be a needless conjecture, since our earth (if all
things were well considered) will be found able enough to
reflect as great a light.   For,

1. Consider its opacity; if you mark these sublunary
things, you shall perceive that amongst them, those that
are most perspicuous, are not so well able to reverberate
the sun-beams, as the thicker bodies.   The rays pass singly
through a diaphanous matter, but in an opacous substance
they are doubled in their return, and multiplied by reflection.   Now if the moon and the other planets can shine
so clearly by beating back the sun-beams, why may not
the earth also shine as well, which agrees with them in
the cause of this brightness, their opacity?

2. Consider what a clear light we may discern reflected
from the earth in the midst of summer; and withal, conceive how much greater that must be which is under the
line, where the rays are more directly and strongly rever-
berated.

3. It is considerable, that though the moon does in
the night-time seem to be of so clear a brightness, yet
when we look upon it in the day, it appears like some
little whitish cloud: not but that at both times, she is of
an equal light in herself.   The reason of this difference
is, because in the night we look upon it through a dark
and obscure medium, there being no other enlightened
body, whose brightness may abate from this: whereas in
the day-time, the whole heavens round about it are of an
equal clearness, and so make it to appear with a weaker
light.   Now because we cannot see how the enlightened
parts of our earth do look in the night, therefore in com-
paring it with the moon, we must not consider her, as
she is beheld through the advantage of a dark medium,
but as she seems in the day-time.   Now in any clear sun-
shine day, our earth does appear as bright as the moon,
which at the same time does seem like some duskish cloud

(as any little observation may easily manifest.) Therefore we need not doubt but that the earth is as well able to
give light as the moon. To this it may be added, that
those very clouds, which in the day-time seem to be of an
equal light to the moon, do in the evening become as dark
as our earth; and as for those of them which are looked
upon at any great distance, they are often mistaken for
the mountains.

4. It is considerable, that though the moon seem to be
of so great a brightness in the night, by reason of its nearness unto those several shadows which it casts, yet is it of
itself weaker than that part of twilight, which usually we
have for half an hour after sun-set, because we cannot till
after that time discern any shadow to be made by it.

5. Consider the great distance at which we behold the
planets, for this must needs add much to their shining; and
therefore Cusanus (in the above-cited place) thinks that if
a man were in the sun, that planet would not appear so
bright to him, as now it doth to us, because then his eye
could discern but little; whereas here, we may comprehend the beams as they are contracted in a narrow body.
Keplar beholding the earth from a high mountain, when it
was enlightened by the sun, confesses that it appeared unto him of an incredible brightness, whereas then he could
only see some small parts of it; but how much brighter
would it have appeared, if he might in a direct line behold
the whole globe of earth and these rays gathered together?
So that if we consider that great light which the earth receives from the sun in the summer, and then suppose we
were in the moon, where we might see the whole earth
hanging in those vast spaces, where there is nothing to
terminate the sight, but those beams which are there contracted into a little compass; I say, if we do well consider this, we may easily conceive that our earth appears
as bright to those other inhabitants in the moon, as theirs
doth to us.

But here it may be objected, that with us for many
days in the year, the heavens are so overclouded, that we

cannot see the sun at all; and for the most part, in our
brightest days, there are many scattered clouds which
shade the earth in sundry places: so that in this respect, it
must needs be unlike the moon, and will not be able to
yield so clear, unintermitted a light, as it receives from
that planet.

To this I answer.

1. As for those lesser brighter clouds, which for the
most part are scattered up and down in the clearest days,
these can be no reason why our earth should be of a darker
appearance, because these clouds being near unto the
earth, and so not distinguishable at so great a distance from
it ; and likewise being illuminated on their back parts by
the sun that shines upon them, must seem as bright to
those in the moon, as if the beams were immediately reflected from our earth.

2. When these clouds that are interposed, are of any
large extension, or great opacity, as it is in extraordinary
lasting and great rains, then there must be some discernible alteration in the light of our earth: but yet this
does not make it to differ from the moon, since it is so
also with that planet, as is shewed in the latter part of the
next chapter.

PROP. XII.

*That it is probable there may be such meteors belonging
to that world in the Moon, as there are with us.*

PLUTARCH discussing on this point, affirms that it is
not necessary there should be the same means of
growth and fructifying in both these worlds, since nature
might in her policy find out more ways than one how to
bring about the same effect. But however, he thinks it is
probable that the moon herself sendeth forth warm winds;
and by the swiftness of her motion, there should breathe

out a sweet and comfortable air, pleasant dews, and gentle moisture, which might serve for refreshing and nourishment of the inhabitants and plants in that other world.

But since they have all things alike with us, as sea and land, and vaporous air encompassing both; I should rather therefore think, that nature there should use the same way of producing meteors as she doth with us; and not by a motion, (as Plutarch supposes) because she doth not love to vary from her usual operations without some extraordinary impediment, but still keeps her beaten path, unless she be driven thence.

One argument whereby I shall manifest this truth, may be taken from those new stars which have appeared in divers ages of the world, and by their paralax have been discerned to have been above the moon; such as was that in Cassiopeia, that in Sagittarius, with many others betwixt the planets. Hipparchus* in his time took especial notice of such as these, and therefore fancied out such constellations in which to place the stars, shewing how many there were in every asterism; that so afterwards, posterity might know whether there were any new star produced, or any old one missing. Now the nature of these comets may probably manifest, that in this other world there are other meteors also; for these in all likelihood, are nothing else but such evaporations caused by the sun from the bodies of the planets. I shall prove this by shewing the improbabilities and inconveniences of any other opinion.

For the better pursuit of this, it is in the first place requisite, that I deal with our chief adversary, Cæsar la Galla, who doth most directly oppose that truth which is here to be proved. He endeavouring to confirm the incorruptibility of the heavens, and being there to satisfy the argument which is taken from these comets; he answers it thus: *Aut argumentum desumptum ex paralaxi, non est efficax, aut si est efficax, eorum instrumentorum usum decipere, vel ratione astri, vel medii, vel distantiæ, aut ergo*

* Plin. Nat. Hist. l. 2. c. 26.

*erat in suprema parte aeris, aut si in cœlo, tum forsan fac-
tum erat ex reflexione radiorum Saturni & Jovis, qui tunc
in conjunctione fuerant.* " Either the argument from the
" paralax is not efficacious, or if it be, yet the use of the
" instruments might deceive, either in regard of the star,
" or the medium, or the distance, and so this comet
" might be in the upper regions of the air ; or if it were
" in the heavens, there it might be produced by the re-
" flection of the rays from Saturn and Jupiter, who were
" then in conjunction." You see what shifts he is driven
to, how he runs up and down to many starting holes that
he may find some shelter ; and instead of the strength of
reason, he answers with a multitude of words, thinking (as
the proverb is) that he may use hail when he hath no
thunder. *Nihil turpius* (saith Seneca *) *dubio & incerto,
pedem modo referente, modo producente.* " What can
" there be more unseemly in one that should be a fair
" disputant, than to be now here, now there, and so un-
" certain, that one cannot tell where to find him ?" He
thinks that there are not comets in the heavens, because
there may be many other reasons of such appearances ;
but what he knows not : perhaps (he says†) that argument from the paralax is not sufficient ; or if it be, then
there may be some deceit in the observation. To this I
may safely say, that he may justly be accounted a weak
mathematician, who mistrusts the strength of this argument ; not can he know much in astronomy, who understands not the paralax, which is a foundation of that
science : and I am sure that he is a timorous man, who
dares not believe the frequent experience of his senses, or
trust to a demonstration.

True indeed, I grant it is possible that the eye, the medium, and the distance, may all deceive the beholder, but
I would have him shew which of all these was likely to
cause an error in this observation ? Merely to say they
might be deceived, is no sufficient answer ; for by this I

* Epist. 95.   † Vide Galilæum Syst. Mundi, Colloq. 3.

might confute the positions of all astronomers, and affirm
the stars are hard by us, because it is possible they might
be deceived in their observing distance. But I forbear any
further reply : my opinion is of that treatise, that either it
was set forth purposely to tempt a confutation, that he
might see the opinion of Galilæus confirmed by others;
or else it was invented with as much haste and negligence
as it was printed, there being in it almost as many faults
as lines.

Others think that these are not any new comets, but
some ancient stars that were there before, which now
shine with that unusual brightness, by reason of the interposition of such vapours, which do multiply their light ;
and so the alteration will be here only, and not in the
heavens. Thus Aristotle thought the appearance of the
milky way was produced : for he held that there were
many little stars, which by their influence did constantly
attract such a vapour towards that place of heaven, so
that it always appeared white. Now by the same reason
may a brighter vapour be the cause of these appearances.

But how probable soever this opinion may seem, yet if
well considered, you shall find it to be altogether absurd
and impossible : for,

1. These stars were never seen there before ; and it is
not likely that a vapour being hard by us, can so multiply
that light which could not before be at all discerned.

2. This supposed vapour cannot be either contracted
into a narrow compass, or dilated into a broad. 1. It
could not be within a little space, for then that star would
not appear with the same multiplied light to those in other
climates. 2. It cannot be a dilated vapour, for then other
stars which were discerned through the same vapour, would
seem as big as that. This argument is the same in effect
with that of the paralax, as you may see in this figure.

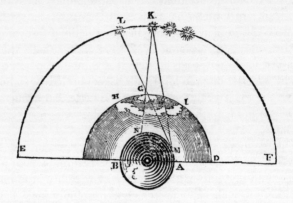

Suppose *A B* to be a hemisphere of one earth, *G D* to be the upper part of the highest region, in which there might be either a contracted vapour, as *G*, or else a dilated one, as *H I*. Suppose *E F* likewise to represent half the heavens, wherein was this appearing comet at *K*. Now I say, that a contracted vapour, as *G*, could not cause this appearance, because an inhabitant at *M* could not discern the same star with this brightness, but perhaps another at *L*, betwixt which the vapour is directly interposed. Nor could it be caused by a dilated vapour, as *H I*, because then all the stars that were discerned through it, would be perceived with the same brightness.

It is necessary therefore that the cause of this appearance should be in the heavens. And this is granted by the most and best astronomers. But, say some, this doth not argue any natural alteration in those purer bodies, since it is probable that the concourse of many little vagabond stars, by the union of their beams may cause so great a light. Of this opinion were Anaxagoras and Zeno amongst the ancient, and Baptista Cisatus, Blancanus, with others amongst our modern astronomers. For, say they, when there happens to be a concourse of some few stars, then do many other fly unto them from all the parts of heaven like so many bees unto their king. But 1. It is not likely that amongst those which we count the fixed stars, there should be any such uncertain motions, that they can wander from all parts of the heavens, as if nature had neglected them, or forgot to appoint them a determinate course. 2. If there be such a conflux of these, as of bees to their king, then what reason is there that they do not still tarry with it, that so the comet may not be dissolved? But enough of this. You may commonly see it confuted by many other arguments. Others there are, who affirm these to be some new created stars, produced by an extraordinary supernatural power *. I answer, true indeed, it is possible they might be so, but however it is not likely they were so, since such appearances may be solved some other way ; wherefore to fly unto a miracle for such things, were a great injury to nature, and to derogate from her skill; an indignity much misbecoming a man who professes himself to be a philosopher. *Miraculum* (saith one) *est ignorantiæ asylum;* a miracle often serves for the receptacle of a lazy ignorance ; which any industrious spirit would be ashamed of ; it being but an idle way to shift off the labour of any further search. But here is the misery of it, we first tie ourselves unto Aristotle's principles, and then conclude that nothing could contradict them but a miracle ; whereas it would be much better for the commonwealth of learning, if we would ground our principles rather upon the frequent experiences of our own, than the bare authority of others.

Some there are who think that these comets are nothing else but exhalations from our earth †, carried up into the higher parts of the heaven. So Peno, Rothmannus and Galilæus. But this is not possible, since by computation it is found, that one of them is above 300 times bigger than the whole globe of land and water. Others therefore have thought that they did proceed from the body of the sun, and that that planet only is *cometarum officina, unde tanquam emissarii & exploratores emitterentur, brevi ad solem redituri,* the shop or forge of comets, from

---

* Clavius in sphæram, cap. 1.　　　† Tycho Progym. l. c. 9.

whence they were sent, like so many spies, that they
might in some short space return again. But this cannot
be, since if so much matter had proceeded from him alone,
it would have made a sensible diminution in his body.
The noble Tycho therefore thinks that they consist of
some such fluider parts of the heaven, as the milky way is
framed of, which being condensed together, yet not attaining to the consistency of a star, is in some space of time
rarified again into its wonted nature. But this is not likely,
because the appearance of the milky way does not arise
from some fluider parts of the heaven (as he supposes)
but from the light of many lesser stars which are there-
abouts*. And therefore it is usually thus described: *Via
lactea nihil aliud est quam innumerabilis stellarum fixarum
greges, qui confuso & pallenti lumine tractum illum inal-
bant.* The milky way is nothing else but the pale and
confused light of many lesser stars, whereby some parts
of the heaven are made to appear white.

And beside, what likely cause can we conceive of this
condensation, unless there be such qualities there, as there
are in our air, and then why may not the planets have the
like qualities as our earth? And if so, then it is more probable that they are made by the ordinary way of nature,
as they are with us, and consist of such exhalations from
the bodies of the planets, as being very much rarified,
may be drawn up through the orb of gross vaporous air
that encompasses them. Nor is this a singular opinion ;
but it seemed most likely to Camillus Gloriosus, Th. Campanella, Fromondus, with some others†. But if you ask,
whither shall all these exhalations return? I answer, every
one into his own planet. If it be again objected, that then
there will be so many centers of gravity, and each several
planet will be a distinct world : I reply, we have not like
probability concerning the rest; but yet perhaps all of
them are so, except the sun, though Cusanus and some

---

* Promond. Meteor. l. 2. c. 5. art. 2.   Item Vesta, tract. 5. c. 2.
† De Comet. l. 5. c. 4. Apol. pro, Galil. Meteor. l. 3. c. 2. art. 6.

others, think there is one also ; and later times have discovered some lesser clouds moving round about him*. But
as for Saturn, he hath two moons on each side. Jupiter
hath four, that encircle him with their motion ; which are
likewise eclipsed by the interposition of his body, as the
moon is by our earth. Venus is observed to increase and
decrease as the moon. And this perhaps hath been noted
by former ages, as may be guessed by that relation of St.
Austin out of Varro†. Mars, and all the rest, derive their
light from the sun. Concerning Mercury, there hath been
little or no observation, because, for the most part, he lies
hid under the sun-beams, and seldom appears by himself.
But when he does, yet the compass of his body is so little,
and his light of so clear a brightness, by reason of his
nearness to the sun, that the perspective cannot make the
same discoveries upon him, as from the rest.

So that if you consider their quantity, their opacity, or these
other discoveries, you shall find it probable enough, that
each of them may be a several world. Especially since
every one of them is allotted to a several orb, and not altogether in one, as the fixed stars seem to be. But this
would be too much for to vent at the first : the chief thing
at which I now aim in this discourse, is to prove that there
may be one in the moon.

It hath been before confirmed, that there was a sphere
of thick vaporous air encompassing the moon, as the first
and second regions do this earth. I have now shewed,
that thence such exhalations may proceed as do produce
the comets : now from hence it may probably follow,
that there may be wind also and rain, with such other meteors as are common amongst us. This consequence is so
dependant, that Fromondus dares not deny it, though he
would (as he confesses himself ‡ ;) for if the sun be able to
exhale from them such fumes as may cause comets, why
not then such as may cause winds, and why not such also

---

* Lactant. Inst. l. 3. c. 23.   † De Civit. Dei, l. 21. c. 8.
‡ De Meteor. l. 3. c. 2. art. 6.

as may cause rain, since I have above shewed, that there is sea and land, as with us? Now rain seems to be more especially requisite for them, since it may allay the heat and scorchings of the sun when he is over their heads. And nature hath thus provided for those in Peru, with the other inhabitants under the line.

But if there be such great and frequent alterations in the heavens, why cannot we discern them?

I answer:

1. There may be such, and we not able to perceive them, because of the weakness of our eye, and the distance of those places from us; they are the words of Fienus (as they are quoted by Fromondus in the above-cited place) *Possunt maximæ permutationes in cælo fieri, etiamsi a nobis non conspiciantur; hoc visus nostri debilitas & immensa cæli distantia faciunt.* And unto him assents Fromondus himself, when a little after he says, *Si in sphæris planetarum degeremus, plurima forsan cælestium nebularum vellera toto æthere passim dispersa videremus, quorum species jam evanescit nimia spatii intercapedine.* " If we " did live in the spheres of the planets, we might there " perhaps discern many great clouds dispersed through " the whole heavens, which are not now visible by reason " of this great distance.

2. Mæslin and Keplar affirm, that they have seen some of these alterations. The words of Mæslin are these (as I find them cited.) *In eclipsi lunari vespere dominicæ palmarum anni* 1605, *in corpore lunæ versus boream, nigricans quædam macula conspecta fuit, obscurior cætero toto corpore, quod candentis ferri figuram repræsentabat; dixisses nubila in multam regionem extensa pluviis & tempestuosis imbribus gravida, cujusmodi ab excelsorum montium jugis in humiliora convallium loca videre non raro contingit**. " In that lunary eclipse which happened in " the even of Palm-Sunday, in the year 1605, there was a " certain blackish spot discerned in the northerly part of

---

* Dissert. 2. cum nunc. Galil. item Somn. Astron. nota ultima.

" the moon, being darker than any other place of her
" body, and representing the colour of red hot iron ; you
" might conjecture that it was some dilated cloud, being
" pregnant with showers ; for thus do such lower clouds
" appear from the tops of high mountains."

And a little before this passage, the same author speaking of that vaporous air about the moon, tells us ; *Quod
circumfluus ille splendor diversis temporibus apparet lim-
pidior plus minusve.* That it does at divers times appear
of a different clearness, sometimes more, and sometimes
less : which he guesses to arise from the clouds and vapours that are in it.

Unto this I may add another testimony of Bapt. Cisatus,
as he is quoted by Nierembergius, grounded upon an observation taken 23 years after this of Mæslin, and writ to
this Euseb. Nieremberg. in a letter by that diligent and
judicious astronomer. The words of it run thus ; *Et quidem in eclipsi nupera solari, quæ fuit ipso die natali Christi,
observavi clare in luna soli supposita, quidpiam quod valde
probat id ipsum quod cometæ quoque & maculæ solares urgent, nempe cælum non esse a tenuitate & variationibus
aeris exemptum ; nam circa lunam adverti esse sphæram
seu orbem quendam vaporosum, non secus atque circum terram, adeoque sicut ex terra in aliquam usque sphæram vapores & exhalationes expirant, ita quoque ex luna**.   " In
" that late solary eclipse which happened on Christmas-
" day, when the moon was just under the sun, I plainly
" discerned that in her which may clearly confirm what
" the comet's and sun's spots do seem to prove, viz. That
" the heavens are not so solid, nor freed from those
" changes which our air is liable unto; for about the
" moon I perceived such an orb, or vaporous air as that is
" which doth encompass our earth ; and as vapours and
" exhalations are raised from our earth into this air, so are
" they also from the moon."

* Histor. nat. l. 2. c. 11.

You see what probable grounds, and plain testimonies I have brought for the confirmation of this proposition: many other things in this behalf might be spoken, which for brevity sake I now omit, and pass unto the next.

PROP. XIII.

That it is probable there may be inhabitants in this other world; but of what kind they are, is uncertain.

I Have already handled the seasons, and meteors belonging to this new world: it is requisite that in the next place I should come unto the third thing which I promised, and say somewhat of the inhabitants: concerning whom there might be many difficult questions raised; as, whether that place be more inconvenient for habitation than our world (as Keplar thinks); whether they are the seed of Adam; whether they are there in a blessed estate, or else what means there may be for their salvation? With many other such uncertain enquiries, which I shall willingly omit; leaving it to their examination who have more leisure and learning for the search of such particulars.

Being for mine own part content only to set down such notes belonging unto these, which I have observed in other writers. *Cum tota illa regio nobis ignota sit, remanent inhabitatores illi ignoti penitus* (saith Cusanus *;) since we know not the regions of that place, we must be altogether ignorant of the inhabitants. There hath not yet been any such discovery concerning these, upon which we may build a certainty, or good probability: well may we

* De doct. ignorantia, l. 2. c. 12.

guess at them, and that too very doubtfully, but we can know nothing; for, if we do hardly guess aright at things which be upon earth, if with labour we do find the things that are at hand, how then can we search out those things that are in heaven*? What a little is that which we know, in respect of those many matters contained within this great universe? This whole globe of earth and water, though it seem to us to be of a large extent, yet it bears not so great a proportion unto the whole frame of nature, as a small sand doth unto it; and what can such little creatures as we discern, who are tied to this point of earth? or what can they in the moon know of us? If we understand any thing (saith Esdras †) it is nothing but that which is upon the earth; and he that dwelleth above in the heavens, may only understand the things that are above in the height of the heavens.

So that it were a very needless thing for us to search after any particulars; however, we may guess in the general that there are some inhabitants in that planet: for why else did providence furnish that place with all such conveniences of habitation as have been above declared?

But you will say, perhaps, is there not too great and intolerable a heat, since the sun is in their zenith every month, and doth tarry there so long before he leaves it?

I answer, 1. This may, perhaps, be remedied (as it is under the line (by the frequency of mid-day showers, which may cloud their sun, and cool their earth.

2. The equality of their nights doth much temper the scorching of the day; and the extreme cold that comes from the one, requires some space before it can be dispelled by the other; so that the heat spending a great while before it can have the victory, hath not afterwards much time to rage in. Wherefore notwithstanding this doubt, yet that place may remain habitable. And this was the opinion of the Cardinal de Cusa, when speaking of this planet, he says, *Hic locus mundi est habitatio ho-*

* Wisd. ix. 16.   † 2 Esd. iv. 21.

minum & animalium atque vegetabilium*.   " This part of
" the world is inhabited by men, and beast, and plants."
To him assented Campanella ; but he cannot determine
whether they were men or rather some other kind of
creatures.   If they were men, then he thinks they could
not be infected with Adam's sin ; yet, perhaps, they had
some of their own, which might make them liable to the
same misery with us ; out of which, it may be, they were
delivered by the same means as we, the death of Christ ;
and thus he thinks that place of the Ephesians may be interpreted, where the Apostle says, God gathered all things
together in Christ, both which are in earth, and which are
in the heavens †.   So also that of the same Apostle to the
Colossians, where he says, that it pleased the father to reconcile all things unto himself by Christ, whether they be
things in earth, or things in heaven ‡.

But I dare not jest with divine truths, or apply these
places according as fancy directs.   As I think this opinion
doth not any where contradict scripture ; so I think likewise, that it cannot be proved from it.   Wherefore Campanella's second conjecture may be more probable, that
the inhabitants of that world are not men as we are ; but
some other kind of creatures which bear some proportion
and likeness to our natures.   Or it may be, they are of a
quite different nature from any thing here below, such as
no imagination can describe ; our understandings being capable only of such things as have entered by our senses,
or else such mixed natures as may be composed from them.
Now, there may be many other species of creatures beside those that are already known in the world ; there is a
great chasm betwixt the nature of men and angels : it may
be the inhabitants of the planets are of a middle nature between both these.   It is not improbable that God might
create some of all kinds, that so he might more completely glorify himself in the works of his power and
wisdom.

---

* De doct. ign. l. 2, cap. 12.   † Ephes. i. 10.   ‡ Col. i. 20.

Cusanus too, thinks they differ from us in many respects; I will set down his words as they may be found in the above-cited place, *Suspicamur in regione solis magis esse solares, claros & illuminatos intellectuales habitatores, spiritualiores etiam quam in luna, ubi magis lunatici, & in terra magis materiales & crassi, ut illi intellectualis naturæ solares sint multum in actu & parum in potentia, terreni vero magis in potentia, & parum in actu, lunares in medio fluctuantes. Hoc quidem opinamur ex influentia ignili solis, aquatica simul & aerea lunæ & gravedine materiali terræ, & consimiliter de aliis stellarum regionibus, suspicantes nullam habitationibus carere, quasi tot sint partes particulares mundiales unius universi, quot sunt stellæ quarum non est numerus, nisi apud eum qui omnia in numero creavit.*

" We may conjecture (saith he) the inhabitants of the
" sun are like to the nature of that planet, more clear and
" bright, more intellectual than those in the moon, where
" they are nearer to the nature of that duller planet, and
" those of the earth being more gross and material than
" either; so that these intellectual natures in the sun, are
" more form than matter, those in the earth more matter
" than form, and those in the moon betwixt both. This
" we may guess from the fiery influence of the sun, the
" watery and aereous influence of the moon, as also the
" material heaviness of the earth. In some such manner
" likewise is it with the regions of the other stars; for
" we conjecture that none of them are without inhabi-
" tants, but that there are so many particular worlds and
" parts of this one universe, as there are stars, which are
" innumerable, unless it be to him who created all things
" in number."

For he held that the stars were not all in one equal orb as we commonly suppose; but that some were far higher than others, which made them appear less; and that many others were so far above any of these, that they were altogether invisible unto us. An opinion which (as I conceive) hath not any great probability for it, nor certainty against it.

The priest of Saturn relating to Plutarch (as he feigns it) the nature of these Selenites, told him they were of divers dispositions, some desiring to live in the lower parts of the moon, where they might look downwards upon us, while others were more surely mounted aloft, all of them shining like the rays of the sun, and as being victorious, are crowned with garlands made with the wings of Eustathia or Constancy.

It hath been the opinion amongst some of the ancients, that their heavens and Elysian fields were in the moon, where the air is most quiet and pure. Thus Socrates, thus Plato*, with his followers, did esteem this to be the place where those purer souls inhabit, who are freed from the sepulchre, and contagion of the body. And by the fable of Ceres, continually wandering in search of her daughter Proserpina, is meant nothing else but the longing desire of men, who live upon Ceres, earth, to attain a place in Proserpina, the moon or heaven.

Plutarch also seems to assent unto this; but he thinks moreover, that there are two places of happiness answerable to two parts, which he fancies to remain of a man when he is dead, the soul and the understanding; the soul he thinks is made of the moon; and as our bodies do so proceed from the dust of this earth, that they shall return to it hereafter; so our souls were generated out of that planet, and shall be resolved into it again; whereas the understanding shall ascend unto the sun, out of which it was made; where it shall possess an eternity of well-being, and far greater happiness than that which is enjoyed in the moon. So that when a man dies, if his soul be much polluted, then must it wander up and down in the middle region of the air where hell is, and there suffer unspeakable torments for those sins whereof it is guilty. Whereas the souls of better men, when they have in some space of time

* Nat. Com. l. 3. c. 19.

been purged from that impurity which they did derive from the body, then do they return into the moon, where they are possest with such joy, as those men feel who profess holy mysteries; from which place (saith he) some are sent down to have the superintendance of oracles, being diligent either in the preservation of the good, either from, or in, all perils, and the prevention or punishment of all wicked actions; but if in these employments they misbehave themselves, then are they again to be imprisoned in a body, otherwise they remain in the moon, till their souls be resolved into it, and the understanding being cleared from all impediments, ascends to the sun, which is its proper place. But this requires a diverse space of time, according to the divers affections of the soul. As for those who have been retired and honest, addicting themselves to a studious and quiet life, these are quickly preferred to a higher happiness. But as for such who have busied themselves in many broils, or have been vehement in the prosecution of any lust, as the ambitious, the amorous, the wrathful man, these still retain the glimpses and dreams of such things as they have performed in their bodies, which make them either altogether unfit to remain there, where they are, or else keeps them long ere they can put off their souls. Thus you see Plutarch's opinion concerning the inhabitants and neighbours of the moon, which (according to the manner of the Academics) he delivers in a third person; you see he makes that planet an inferior kind of heaven; and though he differs in many circumstances, yet doth he describe it to be some such place, as we suppose Paradise to be. You see likewise his opinion concerning the place of the damned spirits, that it is in the middle region of the air; and in neither of these is he singular, but some more late and orthodox writers have agreed with him. As for the place of hell, many think it may be in the air, as well as any where else.

True indeed, St. Austin affirms*, that this place cannot be discovered; but others there are who can shew the si-

* De Civit. Dei, l. 22. c. 16.

tuation of it out of scripture ; some holding it to be in another world without this, because our Saviour calls it σκοτος εξωτερον *, outward darkness. But the most will have it placed towards the center of our earth, because it is said, Christ descended into the lower parts of the earth : and some of these are so confident that this is its situation, that they can describe you its bigness also, and of what capacity it is. Francis Ribera in his comment on the Revelations, speaking of those words, where it is said, that the blood went out of the wine-press, even unto the horses bridles, by the space of one thousand and six hundred furlongs †, interprets them to be meant of hell, and that that number expresses the diameter of its concavity, which is 200 Italian miles. But Lessius ‡ thinks that this opinion gives them too much room in hell, and therefore he guesses that it is not so wide ; for, saith he, the diameter of one league being cubically multiplied, will make a sphere capable of 800000 millions of damned bodies, allowing to each six foot in the square ; whereas, says he, it is certain, that there shall not be one hundred thousand millions in all that shall be damned. You see the bold Jesuit was careful that every one should have but room enough in hell ; and by the strangeness of the conjecture, you may guess that he had rather be absurd, than seem either uncharitable or ignorant. I remember there is a relation in Pliny, how that Dionysiodorus a mathematician, being dead, did send a letter from this place to some of his friends upon earth, to certify them what distance there was betwixt the center and superficies : he might have done well to have prevented this controversy, and informed them the utmost capacity of that place. However, certain it is, that that number cannot be known ; and probable it is, that the place is not yet determined, but that hell is there where there is any tormented soul, which may be in the regions of the air, as well as in the center ; and

---

* Mat. xxv. 30.   Eph. iv. 9.   † Rev. xiv. 20.
‡ De morib. div. l. 13. c 24.

therefore perhaps it is, that the devil is stiled the prince of
the air. But of this only occasionally, and by reason of
Plutarch's opinion concerning those that are round about
the moon. As for the moon itself, he esteems it to be a
lower kind of heaven; and therefore in another place he
calls it a terrestrial star, and an olympian or cælestial
earth; answerable, as I conceive, to the paradise of the
schoolmen *. And that paradise was either in, or near the
moon, is the opinion of some late writers, who derived it
(in all likelihood) from the assertion of Plato, and perhaps, this of Plutarch. Tostatus lays this opinion upon
Isiodor. Hispalensis, and the venerable Bede, and Perius,
father it upon Strabus and Rabanus his master †. Some
would have it to be situated in such a place as could not be
discovered; which caused the penman of Esdras to make
it a harder matter to know the out-goings of paradise, than
to weigh the weight of the fire, or measure the blasts of
wind, or call again a day that is past ‡. But notwithstanding this, there be some others, who think that it is on the
top of some high mountain under the line; and these interpreted the torrid zone to be the flaming sword whereby
paradise was guarded. It is the consent of divers others,
that paradise is situated in some high and eminent place.
So Tostatus: *Est etiam paradisus situ altissima, supra
omnem terræ altitudinem* §. " Paradise is situated in some
" high place above the earth." And therefore in his
comment upon the 49th of Genesis, he understands the
blessing of Jacob concerning the everlasting hills, to be
meant of paradise, and the blessing itself to be nothing else
but a promise of Christ's coming, by whose passion the
gates of paradise should be opened. Unto him assented
Rupertus, Scotus, and most of the other schoolmen, as I
find them cited by Pererius, and out of him in Sir Walter
Rawleigh ¶. Their reason was this; because in probabi-

---

* Cur silent oracula.   † Sir W. Raw. 1. 1. c. 3. sect. 7. In Genes.
‡ 2 Esdr. iv. 7.   § In Genes.
¶ Comment. in 2 Gen. v. 8. 1. 1. c. 3. sect. 6, 7.

lity, this place was not overflowed by the flood, since there were no sinners there, which might draw that curse upon it. Nay, Tostatus thinks that the body of Enoch was kept there; and some of the fathers, as Tertullian and Austin have affirmed, that the blessed souls were reserved in that place till the day of judgment; and therefore it is likely that it was not overflowed by the flood. It were easy to produce the unanimous consent of the fathers, to prove that paradise is yet really existent. Any diligent peruser of them, may easily observe how they do generally interpret the paradise whereto St. Paul* was wrapt, and that wherein our Saviour promised the thief should be with him, to be locally the same from whence our first parents were banished. Now there cannot be any place on earth designed where this should be; and therefore it is not altogether improbable that it was in this other world.

And besides, since all men should have went naked if Adam had not fell, it is requisite therefore that it should be situated in some such place where it might be privileged from the extremities of heat and cold. But now this could not be (they thought) so conveniently in any lower, as it might in some higher air. For these and such like considerations, have so many affirmed that paradise was in a high elevated place: which some have conceived could be no where but in the moon: for it could not be in the top of any mountain; nor can we think of any other body separated from this earth, which can be a more convenient place for habitation than this planet; therefore they concluded that it was there.

It could not be on the top of any mountain:

1. Because we have express scripture, that the highest of them was overflowed †.

2. Because it must be of a greater extension, and not some small patch of ground, since it is likely all men should have lived there, if Adam had not fell. But for a satisfaction of the arguments, together with a farther dis-

---

* 2 Cor. xii. 4. Luke xxiii. 43.   † Gen. vii. 19.

course of paradise, I shall refer you to those who have written purposely upon this subject.   Being content for my own part to have spoken so much of it, as may conduce to shew the opinion of others concerning the inhabitants of the moon; I dare not myself affirm any thing of these Selenites, because I know not any ground whereon to build any probable opinion.   But I think that future ages will discover more; and our posterity, perhaps, may invent some means for our better acquaintance with these inhabitants.

PROP. XIV.

That it is possible for some of our posterity to find out a conveyance to this other world; and if there be inhabitants there, to have commerce with them.

ALL that hath been said concerning the people of the new world, is but conjectural, and full of uncertainties; nor can we ever look for any evident or more probable discoveries in this kind, unless there be some hopes of inventing means for our conveyance thither.   The possibility of which shall be the subject of our enquiry in this last proposition.

And, if we do but consider by what steps and leisure, all arts do usually rise to their growth, we shall have no cause to doubt why this also may not hereafter be found out amongst other secrets.   It hath constantly yet been the method of providence, not presently to shew us all, but to lead us on by degrees, from the knowledge of one thing to another.

It was a great while ere the planets were distinguished from the fixed stars; and some time after that, ere the morning and evening star were found to be the same;

and in greater space (I doubt not) but this also, and other as excellent mysteries will be discovered. Time, who hath always been the father of new truths, and hath revealed unto us many things which our ancestors were ignorant of, will also manifest to our posterity that which we now desire, but cannot know. *Veniet tempus* (saith Seneca *) *quo ista quæ nunc latent, in lucem dies extrahet, & longioris ævi diligentia.* Time will come, when the endeavours of after-ages shall bring such things to light, as now lie hid in obscurity. Arts are not yet come to their solstice; but the industry of future times, assisted with the labours of their forefathers, may reach that height which we could not attain to. *Veniet tempus quo posteri nostri nos tam aperta nescisse mirentur.* As we now wonder at the blindness of our ancestors, who were not able to discern such things as seem plain and obvious unto us; so will our posterity admire our ignorance in as perspicuous matters.

In the first ages of the world, the inlanders thought themselves either to be the only dwellers upon earth, or else if there were any other, they could not possibly conceive how they might have any commerce with them, being severed by the deep and broad sea. But after-times found out the invention of ships; in which notwithstanding, none but some bold daring men durst venture, according to that of the tragedian:

> *Audax nimium qui freta primus*
> *Rate tam fragili perfida rupit †.*

Too bold was he, who in a ship so frail,
First ventured on the treacherous waves to sail.

And yet now, how easy a thing is this even to a timorous and cowardly nature? And questionless, the invention of some other means for our conveyance to the moon, cannot seem more incredible to us, than this did at first

---

* Nat. Qu. l. 7. c. 25.   † Sen. Med. act. 1. Vide Hor. Od. 3. Juvenal. sat. 12. Claud. præf. ad. 1 lib. de rap. Proser.

to them; and therefore we have no just reason to be discouraged in our hopes of the like success.

Yea, but (you will say) there can be no sailing thither, unless that were true which the poet does but feign, that she made her bed in the sea. We have not now any Drake, or Columbus, to undertake this voyage, or any Dædalus to invent a conveyance through the air.

I answer, though we have not, yet why may not succeeding times raise up some spirits as eminent for new attempts, and strange inventions, as any that were before them? It is the opinion of Keplar*, that as soon as the art of flying is found out, some of their nation will make one of the first colonies that shall transplant into that other world. I suppose his appropriating this preheminence to his own countrymen, may arise from an over-partial affection to them. But yet thus far I agree with him, that whenever that art is invented, or any other, whereby a man may be conveyed some twenty miles high, or thereabouts, then it is not altogether improbable that some or other may be successful in this attempt.

For the better clearing of which I shall first lay down, and then answer those doubts that may make it seem utterly impossible.

These are chiefly three.

The first, taken from the natural heaviness of a man's body, whereby it is made unfit for the motion of ascent, together with the vast distance of that place from us.

2. From the extreme coldness of the æthereal air.

3. The extreme thinness of it.

Both which must needs make it impassible, though it were but as many single miles thither as it is thousands.

For the first. Though it were supposed that a man could fly, yet we may well think he would be very slow in it, since he hath so heavy a body, and such a one too, as nature did not principally intend for that kind of motion. It is usually observed, that amongst the variety of birds,

* Dissert. cum Nun. Syder.

those which do most converse upon the earth, and are swiftest in their running, as a pheasant, partridge, &c. together with all domestical fowl, are less able for flight than others which are for the most part upon the wing, as a swallow, swift, &c. And therefore we may well think, that man being not naturally endowed with any such condition as may enable him for this motion; and being necessarily tied to a more especial residence on the earth, must needs be slower than any fowl, or less able to hold out. Thus it is also in swimming; which art, though it be grown to a good eminence, yet he that is best skilled in it, is not able either for continuance, or swiftness, to equal a fish; because he is not naturally appointed to it. So that though a man could fly, yet he would be so slow in it, and so quickly weary, that he could never think to reach so great a journey as it is to the moon.

But suppose withal that he could fly as fast and long as the swiftest bird, yet it cannot possibly be conceived how he should ever be able to pass through so vast a distance as there is betwixt the moon and our earth. For this planet, according to the common grounds, is usually granted to be at the least 52 semidiameters of the earth from us; reckoning for each semidiameter 3456 English miles, of which the whole space will be about 179712.

So that though a man could constantly keep on in his journey thither by a strait line, though he could fly a thousand miles in a day, yet he would not arrive thither under 180 days, or half a year.

And how were it possible for any to tarry so long without diet or sleep?

1. For diet. I suppose there could be no trusting to that fancy of Philo the Jew (mentioned before *,) who thinks that the music of the spheres should supply the strength of food.

* Prop. 3.

Nor can we well conceive how a man should be able to carry so much luggage with him, as might serve for his *viaticum* in so tedious a journey.

2. But if he could, yet he must have some time to rest and sleep in. And I believe he shall scarce find any lodgings by the way. No inns to entertain passengers, nor any castles in the air (unless they be enchanted ones) to receive poor pilgrims, or errant knights. And so consequently he cannot have any possible hopes of reaching thither.

Notwithstanding all which doubts, I shall lay down this position.

That supposing a man could fly, or by any other means raise himself twenty miles upwards, or thereabouts, it were possible for him to come unto the moon.

As for those arguments of the first kind, that seem to overthrow the truth of this, they proceed upon a wrong ground ; whilst they suppose that a condensed body, in any place of the air, would always retain in it a strong inclination of tending downwards towards the centre of this earth. Whereas 'tis more probable, that if it were but somewhat above this orb of vaporous air, it might there rest immovable, and would not have in it any propension to this motion of descent.

For the better illustration of this, you must know, that the heaviness of a body, or (as *Aristotle* defines it *) the proneness of it to tend down unto some centre, is not any absolute quality intrinsical unto it, as if where-ever the body did retain its essence, it must also retain this quality ; or as if nature had implanted in every condensed body *appetitionem centri, & fugam extremitatis*, such a love to the centre, and hatred to the extremities. Because one of these being less than a quantity, and the other no more, cannot have any power of attraction or depulsion in them. According to that common principle, *quantitatis nulla est efficacia.*

* De cælo, lib. 4. c. 1.

But now the true nature of gravity is this. 'Tis such a respective mutual desire of union, whereby condensed bodies, when they come within the sphere of their own vigour, do naturally apply themselves one to another by attraction or coition.   But being both without the reach of either's virtue, they then cease to move, and though they have general aptitude, yet they have not any present inclination or proneness to one another.   And so consequently cannot be styled heavy *.

The meaning of this will be more clearly illustrated by a similitude. As any light body (suppose the sun) does send forth its beams in an orbicular form ; so likewise any magnetical body, for instance a round loadstone, does cast abroad his magnetical vigour in a sphere †.   Thus

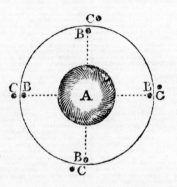

Where suppose the inward circle at A to represent the loadstone, and the outward one betwixt B, C, the orb that does determinate its virtue.

Now any other body that is like affected coming within this sphere, as B, will presently descend towards the centre of it, and in that respect may be styled heavy. But place it without this sphere as C, and then the desire of union ceaseth, and so consequently the motion also.

* So Keplar, Somn. Astron. N. 66. Coper. l. 1. cap. 26. Foscarin in epist. ad Sebast. Fantonum.

† Gilbert. de Magnet. l. 2. cap. 7.

THAT THE MOON MAY BE A WORLD. 115

To apply then what hath been said. This great globe of earth and water hath been proved by many observations, to participate of magnetical properties. And as the loadstone does cast forth its own vigour round about its body, in a magnetical compass, so likewise does our earth. The difference is, that it is another kind of affection which causes the union betwixt the iron and loadstone, from that which makes bodies move unto the earth. The former is some kind of nearness and similitude in their natures, for which philosophy, as yet, has not found a particular name. The latter does arise from that peculiar quality whereby the earth is properly distinguished from the other elements, which is its condensity. Of which the more any thing does participate, by so much the stronger will be the desire of union to it. So gold and other metals which are most close in their composition, are likewise most swift in their motion of descent.

And though this may seem to be contradicted by the instance of metals which are of the same weight, when they are melted, and when they are hard : as also of water, which does not differ in respect of gravity, when it is frozen, and when it is fluid: yet we must know that metals are not rarified by melting, but mollified. And so too for frozen waters, they are not properly condensed, but congealed into a harder substance, the parts being not contracted closer together, but still possessing the same extension. But yet (I say) 'tis very probable that there is such a sphere about the earth, which does terminate its power of attracting other things unto it. So that suppose a body to be placed within the limits of this sphere, and then it must needs tend downwards towards the centre of it. But on the contrary, if it be beyond this compass, then there can be no such mutual attraction ; and so consequently it must rest immovable from any such motion.

For the farther confirmation of this, I shall propose two pertinent observations.

The first taken in the presence of many physicians, and

related by an eminent man in that profession, *Hieron.*
Fracastorius*. There being divers needles provided of
several kinds, like those of a mariner's chart ; they found
that there was an attractive power not only in the magnet, but that iron also, and steel, and silver did each of
them draw its own metal. Whence he concludes, *omne*
trahit quod sibi simile est. And as these peculiar like-
nesses have such a mutual efficacy, so it is probable that
this more general qualification of condensity may be the
cause why things so affected desire union to the earth †.
And though 'tis likely that this would appear betwixt two
lesser condensed bodies, (as suppose two pieces of earth)
if they were both placed at liberty in their æthereal air,
yet being near the earth, the stronger species of this great
globe does, as it were, drown the less.

'Tis a common experiment, that such a lump of ore or
stone, as being on the ground, cannot be moved by less
than six men, being in the bottom of a deep mine, may
be stirred by two. The reason is, because then 'tis com-
passed with attractive beams, there being many above it
as well as below it. Whence we may probably infer
(saith the learned *Verulam* ‡), " That the nature of gravity
" does work but weakly also far from the earth ; because
" the appetite of union in dense bodies must be more dull
" in respect of distance." As we may also conclude from
the motion of birds, which rise from the ground but
heavily, though with much labour ; whereas being on high,
they can keep themselves up, and soar about by the meer
extension of their wings. Now the reason of this difference is not (as some falsely conceive) the depth of air
under them. For a bird is not heavier when there is but a
foot of air under him, than where there is a furlong. As
appears by a ship in the water, (an instance of the same
nature) which does not sink deeper, and so consequently is
not heavier, when it has but five fathom depth, than when

---

* Lib. de Sympath. & Antip. c. 7.

† Vid. Bapt. Masul. exer. Acad. de attract. exer. 4.

‡ Nat. Hist. Cent. 1. exper. 33.

it has fifty. But the true reason is, the weakness of the desire of union in dense bodies at a distance.

So that from hence, there might be just occasion to tax *Aristotle* and his followers, for teaching that heaviness is an absolute quality of itself, and really distinct from condensity : whereas it is only a modification of it, or rather another name given to a condensed body in reference to its motion.

For if it were absolute, then it should always be inherent in its subject, and not have its essence depend upon the bodies being here or there. But it is not so. For,

1. Nothing is heavy in its proper place, according to his own principle, *Nihil grave est in suo loco*. And then,

2. Nothing is heavy, which is so far distant from that proper orb to which it does belong, that it is not within the reach of its virtue. As was before confirmed.

But unto this it may be objected ; though a body being so placed, be not heavy *in actu secundo*; yet it is *in actu primo :* because it retains in it an inward proneness to move downwards, being once severed from its proper place. And this were reason enough why the quality of heaviness should have an absolute being.

I answer, this distinction is only applicable to such natural powers as can suspend their acts; and will not hold in elementary qualities, whose very essence does necessarily require an exercise of the second act, as you may easily discern by an induction of all the rest. I cannot say, that body has in it the quality of heat, coldness, dryness, moisture, hardness, softness, &c. which for the present has not the second act of these qualities. And if you mean by the essence of them, a power unto them : why, there is not any natural body but has a power to them all.

From that which hath been said concerning the nature of gravity, it will follow, That if a man were above the sphere of this magnetical virtue which proceeds from the earth, he might there stand as firmly in the open air, as he can now upon the ground : and not only so, but he may also move with a far greater swiftness, than any living creatures here below; because then he is without all gravity, being not attracted any way; and so consequently will not be liable to such impediments as may in the least manner resist that kind of motion which he shall apply himself unto.

If you yet enquire, how we may conceive it possible, that a condensed body should not be heavy in such a place?

I answer, by the same reason as a body is not heavy in its proper place. Of this I will set down two instances.

1. When a man is in the bottom of a deep river, though he have over him a multitude of heavy waters, yet he is not burdened with the weight of them. And though another body, that should be but of an equal gravity with these waters, when they are taken out, would be heavy enough to press him to death; yet notwithstanding whilst they are in the channel, they do not in the least manner crush him with their load. The reason is, because they are both in their right places; and it is proper for the man, being the more condensed body, to be lower than the waters. Or rather thus, Because the body of the man does more nearly agree with the earth, in this affection, which is the ground of its attraction, and therefore doth that more strongly attract it, than the waters that are over it. Now, as in such a case, a body may lose the operation of its gravity, which is, to move, or to press downwards: so may it likewise, when it is so far out of its place, that this attractive power cannot reach unto it.

It is a pretty notion to this purpose, mentioned by Albertus de Saxonia *, and out of him by Francis Mendoca †, that the air is in some part of it navigable. And that upon this static principle, any brass or iron vessel (suppose a kettle) whose substance is much heavier than that of the water; yet being filled with the lighter air, it will swim upon it, and not sink ‡. So suppose a cup, or wooden vessel, upon

* Phys. l. 3. Q. art. 2. 6.   † Viridar. l. 4. prob. 47.
‡ Vid. Arch. l. de insidentibus humido.

the outward borders of this elementary air, the cavity of it being filled with fire, or rather æthereal air, it must necessarily upon the same ground remain swimming there, and of itself can no more fall, than an empty ship can sink.

2. It is commonly granted, that if there were a hole quite through the centre of the earth, though any heavy body (as suppose a millstone) were let fall into it; yet when it came unto the place of the centre, it would there rest immoveable in the air. Now, as in this case, its own condensity cannot hinder, but that it may rest in the open air, when there is no other place to which it should be attracted; so neither could it be any impediment unto it, if it were placed without the sphere of the earth's magnetical vigor, where there should be no attraction at all.

From hence then (I say) you may conceive, that if a man were beyond this sphere, he might there stand as firmly in the open air, as now upon the earth. And if he might stand there, why might he not also go there? And if so; then there is a possibility likewise of having other conveniences for travelling.

And here it is considerable, that since our bodies will then be devoid of gravity, and other impediments of motion; we shall not at all spend ourselves in any labour, and so consequently not much need the reparation of diet: but may perhaps live altogether without it, as those creatures have done, who by reason of their sleeping for many days together, have not spent any spirits, and so not wanted any food: which is commonly related of serpents, crocodiles, bears, cuckoos, swallows, and such like. To this purpose, Mendoca * reckons up divers strange relations. As that of Epimenides, who is storied to have slept 75 years. And another of a rustic in Germany, who being accidentally covered with a hay-rick slept there for all autumn, and the winter following, without any nourishment.

Or, if this will not serve; yet why may not a papist fast

* Viridar. l. 4. prob. 24.

so long, as well as Ignatius or Xaverius? Or if there be
such a strange efficacy in the bread of the eucharist, as
their miraculous relations do attribute to it: why then,
that may serve well enough, for their *viaticum.*

Or, if we must needs feed upon something else, why
may not smells nourish us? Plutarch * and Pliny † and
divers other ancients, tell us of a nation in *India* that lived
only upon pleasing odours.   And it is the common opinion
of physicians, that these do strangely both strengthen and
repair the spirits.   Hence was it that Democritus was able,
for divers days together, to feed himself with the meer
smell of hot bread ‡.

Or if it be necessary that our stomachs must receive the
food: why then it is not impossible that the purity of the
æthereal air, being not mixed with any improper vapours,
may be so agreeable to our bodies, as to yield us sufficient
nourishment; according to that of the Poet § :

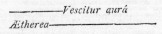

It was an old Platonic principle, that there is in some
part of the world such a place where men might be plen-
tifully nourished by the air they breathe : which cannot
more properly be assigned to any one particular, than to
the æthereal air above this.

I know it is the common opinion, that no element can
prove aliment, because it is not proportionate to the bodies
of living creatures which are compounded ‖.   But,

1. The æthereal air is not an element ; and though it be
purer, yet it is perhaps of a greater agreeableness to man's
nature and constitution.

2. If we consult experience and the credible relations of
others, we shall find it probable enough that many things
receive nourishment from meet elements.

First, for the earth ; Aristotle ** and Pliny ††, those two

* De facie in Luna.   † Nat. Hist. l. 7. c. 2.   ‡ Diog. Laer. l. 1. c. 9.
§ Virgil.   ‖ Arist. de Sens. c. 5.   ** Hist. Animal. l. 8. c. 5,
†† Hist. l. 10. c. 72.

great naturalists, tell us of some creatures, that are fed only
with this.   And it was the curse of the serpent, Gen. iii.
14.   Upon thy belly shalt thou go, and dust shalt thou eat
all the days of thy life.

So likewise for the water.   Albertus Magnus * speaks
of a man who lived seven weeks together by the meer
drinking of water.   Rondoletius † (to whose diligence these
later times are much beholden for sundry observations
concerning the nature of aquatils;) affirms that his wife
did keep a fish in a glass of water, without any other food,
for three years; in which space it was constantly augmented, till at first it could not come out of the place at
which it was put in, and at length was too big for the glass
itself, though that were of a large capacity.   Cardan tells us
of some worms, that are bred and nourished by the snow,
from which being once separated, they die ‡.

Thus also is it with the air, which we may well conceive
does chiefly concur to the nourishing of all vegetables.   For
if their food were all sucked out from the earth, there must
needs be then some sensible decay in the ground by them;
especially since they do every year renew their leaves
and fruits: which being so many, and so often, could not be
produced without abundance of nourishment.   To this purpose is the experiment of trees cut down which will of
themselves put forth sprouts.   As also that of onions, and
the semper-vive, which will strangely shoot forth, and grow
as they hang in the open air.   Thus likewise is it with
some sensible creatures; the camelion (saith Pliny‖ and
Solinus §) meerly nourished by this: and so are the birds of
paradise, treated of by many, which reside constantly in the
air, nature having not bestowed upon them any legs, and
therefore they are never seen upon the ground but being
dead ¶.   If you ask how they multiply? It is answered, they

---

* De Animal. l. 7.   † De Pisc. l. 1. c. 12.   ‡ Subtil. l. 9.

‖ Hist. l. 8. cap. 33. Polyhistor. cap. 53.

§ Lop. hist. Ind. Occid. cap. 96. Maiolus, Colloq. 3.

¶ Tis likely that these birds do chiefly reside in the æthereal air,
where they are nourished and upheld.

lay their eggs on the backs of one another, upon which they sit till their young ones be fledged.   Rhondoletius*, from the history of Hermolaus Barbarus, tells us of a priest (of whom one of the popes had the custody) that lived forty years upon meer air.   As also of a maid in France, and another in Germany, that for divers years together did feed on nothing but this: nay, he affirms that he himself had seen one, who lived till ten years of age without any other nourishment.   You may find most of these, and some other examples to this purpose, gathered together by Mendoca, Viridar. lib. 4. prob. 23, 24.   Now, if this elementary air, which is mixed with such improper vapours, may accidentally nourish some persons; perhaps then, that pure æthereal air may of itself be more natural to our tempers.

But if none of these conjectures may satisfy; yet there may haply be some possible means for the conveyance of other food, as shall be shewed afterwards.

Again, seeing we do not then spend ourselves in any labour, we shall not, it may be, need the refreshment of sleep. But if we do, we cannot desire a softer bed than the air, where we may repose ourselves firmly and safely as in our chambers.

But here you may ask, whether there be any means for us to know, how far this sphere of the earth's virtue does extend itself?

I answer, 'tis probable that it does not reach much farther than that orb of thick vaporous air, that encompasseth the earth; because 'tis likely the sun may exhale some earthly vapours, near unto the utmost bounds of the sphere allotted to them.

Now there are divers ways used by astronomers, to take the altitude of this vaporous air.   As,

1. By observing the height of that air which causeth the crepusculum, or twilight; for the finding of which, the ancients used this means: as soon as ever they could discern the air in the east to be altered with the least light, they

* De Piscibus, l. 1. cap. 13.

would by the situation of the stars find out how many degrees the sun was below the horizon, which was usually about eighteen.　From whence they would easily conclude, how high that air must be above us, which the sun could shine upon, when he was 18 degrees below us.　And from this observation, it was concluded to be about 52 miles high*.

But in this conclusion, the ancients were much deceived, because they proceeded upon a wrong ground, whilst they supposed that the shining of the sun's direct rays upon the air, was the only reason of the crepusculum; whereas it is certain that there are many other things which may also concur to the causing of it†.　As,

1. Some bright clouds below the horizon, which being illuminated by the sun, may be the means of conveying some light to our air, before the direct rays can touch it.

2. The often refraction of the rays, which suffer a frequent repercussion from the cavity of this sphere, may likewise yield us some light.

3. And so may the orb of enlightened air compassing the sun, part of which must rise before his body.

2. The second way whereby we may more surely find the altitude of this grosser air, is by taking the heighth of the highest cloud: which may be done,　1. Either as they use to measure the altitude of things that cannot be approached unto, viz. by two stations, when two persons shall at the same time, in several places, observe the declination of any cloud from the vertical point.　Or, 2. which is the more easy way, when a man shall chuse such a station, where he may at some distance discern the place on which the cloud does cast its shadow, and withal does observe, how much both the cloud and the sun decline from the vertical point ‡.　From which he may easily conclude the true altitude of it, as you may more plainly conceive by this following diagram.

* Vitel. l. 10. Theo. 7.　　† Keplar Ep. Coper. l. 1. part 3.
‡ Stevinius, Geog. l. 3. prop. 3.

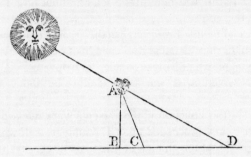

Where A B is a perpendicular from the cloud, C the station of him that measures, D the place where the shadow of the cloud does fall.

The instrument being directed from the station C, to the cloud at A, the perpendicular will shew the angle B A C. Then letting the sun shine through the sights of your instrument, the perpendicular of it will give the angle B A D. Afterwards having measured the distance C D by paces, you may according to the common rules, find the heighth B A*.

But if without making the observation, you would know of what altitude the highest of these are found by observation; Cardan† answers, not above two miles; Keplar‡ not above 16000 paces or thereabouts.

3. Another way to find the height of this vaporous air, is, by knowing the difference of altitude which it causeth in refracting the beams of any star near the horizon. And from this observation also, it is usually concluded to be about two or three miles high.

But now you must not conceive, as if the orb of magnetical vigour were bounded in an exact superficies, or as if it did equally hold out just to such a determinate line, and no farther. But, as it hath been said of the first region, which is there terminated where the heat of reflexion does begin to languish; so likewise is it probable, that this magnetical vigour does remit of its degrees proportionally to its distance from the earth, which is the cause of it: and therefore

* Pitisc. Trigon.   † Subt. l. 17.   ‡ Epit. Cop. l. 1. p. 3.

though the thicker clouds may be elevated no higher, yet this orb may be continued in weaker degrees a little beyond them. We will suppose it (which in all likelihood is the most) to be about twenty miles high. So that you see the former thesis remains probable; that if a man could but fly, or by any other means get twenty miles upwards, it were possible for him to reach unto the moon.

But it may be again objected; though all this were true; though there were such an orb of air which did terminate the earth's vigor: and though the heaviness of our bodies could not hinder our passage through the vast spaces of the æthereal air; yet those two other impediments may seem to deny the possibility of any such voyage.

1. The extreme coldness of that air. If some of our higher mountains for this reason be not habitable, much more then will those places be so, which are farther from any cause of heat.

2. The extreme thinness of it, which may make it unfit for expiration. For, if in some mountains (as Aristotle tells us of Olympus, and out of him St. Austin*) the air be so thin, that men cannot draw their breath, unless it were through some moistened spunges; much more then must that air be thin, which is more remotely situated from the causes of impurity and mixture. And then beside, the refraction that is made by the vaporous air encompassing our earth, may sufficiently prove that there is a great difference betwixt the æthereal air and this, in respect of rarity.

To the first of these I answer, that though the second region be naturally endowed with so much coldness, as may make it fit for the production of meteors; yet it will not hence follow, that all that air above it, which is not appointed for the like purpose, should partake of the same condition: but it may seem more probable, that this æthereal air is freed from having any quality in the extremes. And this may be confirmed from those common arguments,

* In Gen. ad literam, l. 3. cap. 2.

which are usually brought to prove the warmness of the
third region; as you may see in Fromundus*, and others
who treat of that subject.

'Tis the assertion of Pererius†, that the second region is
not cold merely for this reason, because it is distant from
the ordinary causes of heat, but because it was actually
made so at the first, for the condensing of the clouds, and
the production of other meteors that were there to be generated; which (as I conceive) might be sufficiently confirmed
from that order of the creation observed by Moses, who
tells us that the waters above the firmament (by which,
in the greatest probability, we are to understand the clouds
in the second region) were made the second day, Gen. i.
7, 8. whereas the sun itself (whose reflection is the cause
of heat) was not created till the fourth day, ver. 16, 19.

To the other objection I answer, that though the air in
the second region (where by reason of its coldness there are
many thick vapours) do cause a great refraction; yet it is
probable that the air which is next the earth, is sometimes,
and in some places, of a far greater thinness; nay, as thin
as the æthereal air itself; since sometimes there is such a
special heat of the sun, as may rarify it in an eminent degree: and in some dry places, there are no gross impure
exhalations to mix with it.

But here it may be objected: if the air in the second
region were more condensed and heavy than this wherein
we breath, then that must necessarily tend downwards, and
possess the lower place.

To this some answer, that the hanging of the clouds in
the open air, is no less than a miracle.   They are the words
of Pliny‡: *quid mirabilius aquis in cælo stantibus?* what
more wonderful thing is there, than that the waters should
stand in the heavens? Others prove this from the derivation
of the word שמים from שאה *stupescere* and מים *aquæ*; because the waters do hang there after such a stupendous in-

* Meteor. lib. 1. ca. 2. art. 1.   † Comment. in Gen. i. 8.
‡ Hist. l. 3. cap. 1.

conceivable manner: which seems likewise to be favoured by scripture, where it is mentioned as a great argument of God's omnipotency, that he holds up the clouds from falling. He binds up the waters in his thick clouds, and the cloud is not rent under them*.

But that which unto me seems full satisfaction against this doubt, is this consideration; that the natural vigour whereby the earth does attract dense bodies unto it, is less efficacious at a distance; and therefore a body of less density, which is near unto it, as suppose this thin air wherein we breathe, may naturally be lower in its situation, than another of a greater condensity that is farther off; as suppose the clouds in the second region. And though the one be absolutely, and in itself more fit for this motion of descent; yet by reason of its distance, the earth's magnetical virtue cannot so powerfully work upon it.

As for that relation of Aristotle, if it were true, yet it does not prove this air to be altogether impassible, since moistened sponges might help us against its thinness: but it is more likely that he took it upon trust, as he did some other relations concerning the height of the mountains, wherein it is evident that he was grosly mistaken: as where he tells us of Caucasus, that it casts its shadow 560 miles†. And this relation being of the same nature, we cannot safely trust unto him for the truth of it.

If it be here enquired, what means there may be conjectured, for our ascending beyond the sphere of the earth's magnetical vigour.

I answer. 1. It is not perhaps impossible that a man may be able to fly by the application of wings to his own body: as angels are pictured, as Mercury and Dædalus are feigned, and as hath been attempted by divers; particularly by a Turk in Constantinople, as Busbequius relates.

2. If there be such a great ruck in Madagascar, as Marcus Polus‡ the Venetian mentions, the feathers in whose wings

---

* Job xxvi. 8.   † Meteor. l. 1. c. 11.   ‡ Lib. 3. c. 40.

are twelve foot long, which can soop up a horse and his
rider, or an elephant, as our kites do a mouse; why then
it is but teaching one of these to carry a man, and he may
ride up thither, as Ganymede does, upon an eagle.

3. Or if neither of these ways will serve : yet I do seriously, and upon good grounds affirm it possible to make a
flying-chariot; in which a man may sit, and give such a
motion unto it, as shall convey him through the air.   And
this perhaps might be made large enough to carry divers
men at the same time, together with food for their *viaticum*,
and commodities for traffic.   It is not the bigness of any
thing in this kind, that can hinder its motion, if the motive
faculty be answerable thereunto.   We see a great ship
swims as well as a small cork, and an eagle flies in the air
as well as a little gnat.

This engine may be contrived from the same principles
by which Archytas made a wooden dove, and Regiomontanus a wooden eagle.

I conceive it were no difficult matter (if a man had leisure)
to shew more particularly the means of composing it.

The perfecting of such an invention, would be of such
excellent use, that it were enough, not only to make a man
famous, but the age also wherein he lives.   For besides the
strange discoveries that it might occasion in this other
world, it would be also of inconceivable advantage for travelling, above any other conveyance that is now in use.

So that notwithstanding all these seeming impossibilities,
it is likely enough, that there may be a means invented of
journeying to the moon; and how happy shall they be, that
are first successful in this attempt ?

> ——— *Felicesque animæ, quas nubila supra,*
> *Et turpes fumos, plenumque vaporibus orbem,*
> *Inseruit cælo sancti scintilla Promethei.*

Having thus finished this discourse, I chanced upon a
late fancy to this purpose, under the feigned name of Domingo Gonsales, written by a late reverend and learned

bishop: in which (besides sundry particulars wherein this latter chapter did unwittingly agree with it) there is delivered a very pleasant and well-contrived fancy concerning a voyage to this other world.

He supposeth that there is a natural and usual passage for many creatures betwixt our earth and this planet. Thus he says, those great multitudes of locusts, wherewith divers countries have been destroyed, do proceed from thence. And if we peruse the authors who treat of them, we shall find that many times they fly in numberless troops, or swarms, and for sundry days together before they fall, are seen over those places in great high clouds, such as coming nearer, are of extension enough to obscure the day, and hinder the light of the sun. From which, together with divers other such relations, he concludes that it is not altogether improbable they should proceed from the moon. Thus likewise he supposeth the swallows, cuckoos, nightingales, with divers other fowl, which are with us only half the year, to fly up thither, when they go from us. Amongst which kind, there is a wild-swan in the East Indies, which at certain seasons of the year do constantly take their flight thither. Now this bird being of great strength, able to continue for a long flight, as also going usually in flocks, like our wild-geese; he supposeth that many of them together, might be taught to carry the weight of a man; especially if an engine were so contrived (as he thinks it might) that each of them should bear an equal share in the burthen. So that by this means it is easily conceivable, how once every year a man might finish such a voyage; going along with these birds at the beginning of winter, and again returning with them at the spring.

And here, one that had a strong fancy, were better able to set forth the great benefit and pleasure to be had by such a journey. And that whether you consider the strangeness of the persons, language, arts, policy, religion of those inhabitants, together with the new traffic that might be brought thence. In brief, do but consider the pleasure and profit of those later discoveries in America, and we must needs conclude this to be inconceivably beyond it.

But such imaginations as these, I shall leave to the fancy of the reader.

———————————— *Sic itur ad astra.*
Reptet humi quicunque velit ————————

Cœlo restat iter, cœlo tentabimus ire.

BOOK II.

A

DISCOURSE

CONCERNING A

NEW PLANET,

TENDING TO PROVE, THAT (IT IS PROBABLE)

OUR EARTH IS ONE OF THE PLANETS.

Digna res est contemplatione, ut sciamus in quo rerum statu scimus : pigeri‑
mam sortiti, an velocissimam sedem : circa nos deus omnia, an nos agat.

Sen. Nat. Quæst. lib. 7. cap. 2.

TO THE READER.

NOT to trouble you with an invective against those multitudes of pamphlets which are every day pressed into the world; or an apology, why this was published amongst the rest (the usual matter for such kind of epistles:) let me in brief premonish you something concerning the

CHIEF SCOPE
  and   } *of this following Discourse.*
MANNER

1. It is not the purpose of it to set down an exact treatise of this kind of astronomy, but rather to remove those common prejudices which usually deter men from taking any argument, tending this way, into their considerations. For we may observe, that in those points which are cried down by the more general opinion, men do for the most part rest themselves in the superficial knowledge of things, as they seem at their first appearances, thinking they can say enough to any paradox, against which they can urge the most obvious and easy objections; and therefore seldom or never search into the depth of these points, or enter into any serious impartial examination of those grounds on which they are bottomed. Which as it must needs be a great hindrance to the proficiency of all kind of learning, so more especially is it in this particular. We might discern a greater comeliness and order in this great fabrick of the world, and more easily understand the appearances in astronomy, if we could with indifferency attend to what might be said for that opinion of Copernicus, which is here defended.

2. For the manner. It is not maintained with such heat and religion, as if every one that reads it were presently bound to yield up his assent: but as it is in other wars where victory cannot be had, men must be content with peace: so likewise is it in this, and should be in all other philosophical contentions. *If there be nothing able to convince and satisfy the indifferent reader, he may still enjoy his own opinion. All men have not the same way of apprehending things; but according to the variety of their temper, custom, and abilities, their understandings are severally fashioned to different assents: which had it been but well considered by some of our hot adversaries*, they would not have shewed more violence in opposing the persons against whom they write, than strength in confuting the cause.*

It is an excellent rule to be observed in all disputes, that men should give soft words and hard arguments; that they would not so much strive to vex, as to convince an enemy. If this were but diligently practised in all cases, and on all sides, we might in a good measure be freed from those vexations in the search of truth, which the wise Solomon, by his own experience did so much complain of, Ecclesiastes i. 18. In much wisdom there is much grief; and he that increaseth knowledge, increaseth sorrow.

To conclude: though there should be nothing in this discourse conducible to your information and benefit; yet it may serve in the perusal, as it did in the composure, for the recreation of such leisure hours as may conveniently be spared from more weighty employments.

Farewell.

* Fromond. Al. Ross

BOOK II.

THAT THE EARTH MAY BE A PLANET.

PROP. I

That the seeming novelty and singularity of this opinion,
can be no sufficient reason to prove it erroneous.

IN the search of theological truths, it is the safest method,
first of all to look unto divine authority; because that
carries with it as clear an evidence to our faith, as any thing
else can be to our reason. But on the contrary, in the examination of philosophical points, it were a preposterous
course to begin at the testimony and opinion of others, and
then afterwards to descend unto the reasons that may be
drawn from the nature and essence of the things themselves:
because these inartificial arguments (as the logicians call
them) do not carry with them any clear and convincing
evidence; and therefore should come after those that are
of more necessary dependance, as serving rather to confirm,
than resolve the judgment.

But yet, so it is, that in those points which are besides
the common opinion, men are carried away at the first by
the general cry, and seldom or never come so far, as to
examine the reasons that may be urged for them. And
therefore, since it is the purpose of this discourse, to remove those prejudices which may hinder our judgment in
the like case, it is requisite that in the first place there be
some satisfaction given to those arguments that may be
taken from the authority of others.

Which arguments are insisted on by our adversaries
with much heat and violence.

†

What (say they) shall an upstart novelty thrust out
such a truth as hath passed by successive tradition through
all ages of the world; and hath been generally entertained, not only in the opinion of the vulgar, but also
of the greatest philosophers, and most learned men*?
Shall we think that amongst the multitude of those who
in several times have been eminent for new inventions,
and strange discoveries, there was none able to find out
such a secret as this, besides some fabulous Pythagoreans, and of late Copernicus? Is it probable that the
world should last for above five thousand years together,
and yet the inhabitants of it be so dull and stupid, as to be
unacquainted with its motion? Nay, shall we think that
those excellent men whom the Holy Ghost made use of
in the penning of scripture, who were extraordinarily inspired with supernatural truths, should notwithstanding be
so grossly ignorant of so common a matter as this? Can we
believe, if there were any such thing, that Joshua, and
Job, and David, and Solomon, &c. should know nothing of
it? Certainly it must needs argue a strong affectation of
singularity, for a man to take up any groundless fancy
against such ancient and general authority.

I answer: as we should not be so fondly conceited of
ourselves, and the extraordinary abilities of these present
ages, as to think every thing that is ancient to be obsolete:
or, as if it must needs be with opinions as it is with
clothes, where the newest is for the most part best. So
neither should we be so superstitiously devoted to antiquity, as to take up every thing for canonical, which drops
from the pen of a father, or was approved by the consent
of the ancients. It is an excellent saying, Δει ελευθεριον ειναι
τη γνωμη τον μελλοντα Φιλοσοφειν. It behoves every one in
the search of truth, always to preserve a philosophical
liberty; not to be so enslaved to the opinion of any man,
as to think whatever he says to be infallible. We must

---

* Alex. Ross de terræ motu, contra Lansb. l. 1. sect. 1. cap. 10.

† Alcinous.

labour to find out what things are in themselves, by our own experience, and a thorough examination of their natures, not what another says of them. And if in such an impartial enquiry, we chance to light upon a new way, and that which is besides the common road, this is neither our fault, nor our unhappiness.

Not our fault, because it did not arise from singularity or affectation. Not our unhappiness, because it is rather a privilege to be the first in finding out such truths as are not discernible to every common eye. If novelty should always be rejected, neither would arts have arrived to that perfection wherein now we enjoy them, nor could we ever hope for any future reformation : though all truth be in itself eternal, yet in respect of men's opinions, there is scarce any so ancient but had a beginning, and was once counted a novelty ; and if for this reason it had been condemned as an error, what a general darkness and ignorance would then have been in the world, in comparison of that light which now abounds ; according to that of the poet :

> *Quod si tam antiquis novitas invisa fuisset,*
> *Quam nobis, quid nunc esse vetus aut quid haberet,*
> *Quod legeret tereretque viritim publicus usus** ?*

> If our forefathers had but hated thus,
> All that were new ; what had been old to us ?
> Or, how might any thing confirmed be,
> For public use by its antiquity ?

But for more full satisfaction of all those scruples that may arise from the seeming novelty or singularity of this opinion, I shall propose these following considerations.

1. Suppose it were a novelty, yet it is in philosophy, and that is made up of nothing else; but receives addition from every day's experiment. True indeed, for divinity we have an infallible rule that does plainly inform us of all necessary truths ; and therefore the primitive times are of greater

---

* Horat. lib. 2. ep. 1.

authority, because they were nearer to those holy men who were the penmen of scripture. But now for philosophy, there is no such reason: whatever the schoolmen may talk, yet Aristotle's works are not necessarily true, and he himself hath by sufficient arguments proved himself to be liable unto error   Now in this case, if we should speak properly, antiquity does consist in the old age of the world, not in the youth of it.   In such learning as may be increased by fresh experiments and new discoveries; it is we are the fathers, and of more authority than former ages ; because we have the advantage of more time than they had, and truth (we say) is the daughter of time.   However, there is nothing in this opinion so magisterially proposed, but the reader may use his own liberty; and if all the reasons considered together do not seem convincing unto him, he may freely reject it.

In those natural points which carry with them any doubt or obscurity, it is the safest way to suspend our assents; and though we may dispute *pro* or *con*, yet not to settle our opinion on either side.

2. In weighing the authority of others, it is not their multitude that should prevail, or their skill in some things that should make them of credit in every thing ; but we should examine what particular insight and experience they had in those things for which they are cited. Now it is plain, that common people judge by their senses, and therefore their voices are altogether unfit to decide any philosophical doubt, which cannot well be examined or explained without discourse and reason.   And as for the ancient fathers, though they were men very eminent for their holy lives, and extraordinary skill in divinity, yet they were most of them very ignorant in that part of learning which concerns this opinion; as appears by many of their gross mistakes in this kind ; as that concerning the antipodes, &c. and therefore it is not their opinion neither, in this business, that to an indifferent seeker of truth will be of any strong authority.

But against this it is objected*.   That the instance of the antipodes does not argue any special ignorance in these learned men; or that they had less skill in such human arts than others; since Aristotle himself, and Pliny, did deny this as well as they.

I answer:

1. If they did, yet this does make more to the present purpose : for if such great scholars, who were so eminent for their knowledge in natural things, might yet notwithstanding be grossly mistaken in such matters as are now evident and certain, why then we have no reason to depend upon their assertions or authorities, as if they were infallible.

2. Though these great naturalists, for want of some experience, were mistaken in that opinion, whilst they thought no place was habitable but the temperate zones: yet it cannot be from hence inferred that they denied the possibility of antipodes; since these are such inhabitants as live opposite unto us in the other temperate zone: and it were an absurd thing to imagine that those who lived in different zones, can be antipodes to one another; and argues that a man did not understand, or else had forgotten that common distinction in geography, wherein the relation of the world's inhabitants unto one another are reckoned up under these three heads; *antaci, periæci,* and *antipodes.* But to let this pass : it is certain, that some of the fathers did deny the being of any such, upon other more absurd grounds.   Now if such as Chrysostom, Lactantius, &c. who were noted for great scholars; and such too as flourished in these latter times, when all human learning was more generally professed, should notwithstanding be so much mistaken in so obvious a matter: why then may we not think that those primitive saints, who were the penmen of scripture, and eminent above others in their time for holiness and knowledge; might yet be utterly ignorant of many philosophical truths, which are commonly known in these

* Alex. Ross. l. 1. sect. c. 8.

days? It is probable, that the Holy Ghost did inform them only with the knowledge of those things whereof they were to be the penmen, and that they were not better skilled in points of philosophy than others.   There were indeed some of them who were supernaturally endowed with human learning; yet this was, because they might thereby be fitted for some particular ends, which all the rest were not appointed unto: thus Solomon was strangely gifted with all kind of knowledge, in a great measure; because he was to teach us by his own experience the extreme vanity of it, that we might not so settle our desires upon it, as if it were able to yield us contentment*.   So too the apostles were extraordinarily inspired with the knowledge of languages, because they were to preach unto all nations.   But it will not hence follow, that therefore the other holy penmen were greater scholars than others.   It is likely that Job had as much human learning as most of them, because his book is more especially remarkable for lofty expressions, and discourses of nature; and yet it is not likely that he was acquainted with all those mysteries which later ages have discovered; because when God would convince him of his own folly and ignorance, he proposes to him such questions, as being altogether unanswerable; which notwithstanding, any ordinary philosopher in these days might have resolved. As you may see at large in the thirty-eighth chapter of that book.

The occasion was this: Job† having before desired that he might dispute with the Almighty concerning the uprightness of his own ways, and the unreasonableness of those afflictions which he underwent, does at length obtain his desire in this kind; and God vouchsafes, in this thirty-eighth chapter, to argue the case with him.   Where he does shew Job how unfit he was to judge of the ways of providence, in disposing of blessings and afflictions; when as he was so ignorant in ordinary matters, being not able to discern the reason of natural and common events.   As why

* Eccl. i. 18.   † Cap. xiii. 3.

the sea should be so bounded from overflowing the land* ?
What is the breadth of the earth† ? What is the reason of
the snow or hail‡ ? What was the cause of the rain or dew,
of ice and frost, and the like ‖ ? By which questions, it
seems, Job was so utterly puzzled, that he is fain afterwards
to humble himself in this acknowledgment: I have uttered
that I understood not, things too wonderful for me, which
I knew not.   Wherefore I abhor myself, and repent in dust
and ashes §.

So that it is likely these holy men had not these human
arts by any special inspiration, but by instruction and study,
and other ordinary means; and therefore Moses his skill
in this kind is called the learning of the Egyptians¶. Now,
because in those times all sciences were taught only in a rude
and imperfect manner; therefore it is likely that they also
had but a dark and confused apprehension of things, and
were liable to the common errors.   And for this reason is
it, why Tostatus** (speaking of Joshua's bidding the moon
stand still as well as the sun) says, *Quod forte erat impe-
ritus circa astrorum doctrinam, sentiens ut vulgares senti-
unt:* that perhaps he was unskilful in astronomy, having
the same gross conceit of the heavens, as the vulgar had.
From all which it may be inferred, that the ignorance of
such good men and great scholars concerning these philosophical points, can be no sufficient reason, why after examination we should deny them, or doubt of their truth.

3. It is considerable, that in the rudiments and first beginnings of astronomy, and so in several ages after, this
opinion hath found many patrons, and those too men of
eminent note and learning.   Such was more especially Pythagoras, who was generally and highly esteemed for his
divine wit, and rare inventions; under whose mysterious
sayings, there be many excellent truths to be discovered.
But against his testimony, it is again objected††; if Pytha-

---

* Ver. 8, 10, 11.   † Ver. 18.   ‡ Ver. 22.   ‖ Ver. 28, 29.
§ Cap. xlii. ver. 3, 6.   ¶ Acts vii. 22.
** Josh. c. 10. Quæst. 19.   †† Alex. Ros. l. 2. sect. 2. c. 10.

goras were of this opinion, yet his authority should not be of any credit, because he was the author of many other monstrous absurdities.

To this I answer; if a man's error in some particulars should take away his credit for every thing else, this would abolish the force of all human authority ; for *humanum est errare*. Secondly, it is probable that many of Pythagoras's sayings which seem so absurd, are not to be understood according to their letter, but in a mystical sense.

2. But he objects again, that Pythagoras was not of this opinion; and that for two reasons; first, because no ancient author that he had read ascribes it unto him. Secondly, it is contradictory to his other opinions, concerning the harmony that was made by the motion of the heavens; which could not consist with this other of the earth's motion.

To the first I answer; the objector could not chuse but know that this assertion is by many ancient authors ascribed to that sect whereof Pythagoras was the chief. He might have seen it expressly in Aristotle* himself. Οι δε Πυθαγορειοι λεγουσιν επι μεν του μεσω πυρ ειναι, την τε γην εν τον αστραν ουσαν κυηλω Φερομενην ωερι μεσιν, νυκτα τε και ἱμεραν ωοιειν.

In which the philosopher does compendiously reckon up the three chief particulars implied in the opinion of the Pythagoreans. First, the sun's being in the centre of the world. Secondly, the earth's annual motion about it, as being one of the planets. Thirdly, its diurnal revolution, whereby it caused day and night.

To his second reason I answer; first, that Pythagoras thought the earth to be one of the planets (as appears by Aristotle's testimony concerning him) and to move amongst the rest. So that his opinion concerning the motion of the heavens is not inconsistent with that of the earth. Secondly, but as for the celestial harmony, he might perhaps under this mystical expression, according to his usual custom, shadow forth unto us that mutual proportion and harmonical consent, which he did conceive in the several big-

* De Cælo, l. 2. c. 13

ness, distance, motions of the orbs.   So that notwithstanding these objections, it is evident that Pythagoras was of
this opinion, and that his authority may add somewhat for
the confirmation of it.   Unto him assented Aristarchus
Samius*, who flourished about 280 years before the birth of
our Saviour; and was by reason of this opinion, arraigned
for profaneness and sacrilege by the Areopagites; because
he had blasphemed the deity of Vesta, affirming the earth
to move.   To them agreed Philolaus, Heraclides, Pontius,
Nicetas, Syracusanus, Ecphantus, Lucippus, and Plato himself (as some think.)   So likewise Numa Pompilius, as
Plutarch relates it in his life; who in reference to this opinion, built the temple of Vesta round, like the universe; in
the middle of it was placed the perpetual vestal fire ; by
which he did represent the sun in the centre of the world.
All these men were in their several times of special note, as
well for their extraordinary learning, as for this opinion.

4. It is considerable, that since this science of astronomy
hath been raised to any perfection, there have been many
of the best skill in it, that have assented unto that assertion
which is here defended.   Amongst whom was the cardinal
Cusanus†, but more especially Copernicus, who was a man
very exact and diligent in these studies for above thirty
years together, from the year 1500 to 1530, and upwards;
and since him, most of the best astronomers have been of
this side.   So that now there is scarce any of note and
skill, who are not Copernicus's followers; and if we should
go to most voices, this opinion would carry it from any
other.   It would be too tedious to reckon up the names of
those that may be cited for it; I will only mention some of
the chief; such were Joachinus Rheticus, an elegant writer;
Christopherus Rothman; Mestlin, a man very eminent for
his singular skill in this science; who though at the first he
were a follower of Ptolemy, yet upon his second and more
exact thoughts, he concluded Copernicus to be in the right;
and that the usual hypothesis, *præscriptione potius quam*

---

* Archimedes de aræne numero.   † De doct. ignor. l. 2. cap. 12.

ratione valet*, does prevail more by prescription than reason. So likewise Erasmus Reinoldus, who was the man that calculated the prutenical tables from Copernicus his Observations, and did intend to write a commentary upon his other works, but that he was taken out of this life before he could finish those resolutions. Unto these also I might add the names of Gilbert, Keplar, Galilæus, with sundry others, who have much beautified and confirmed this hypothesis, with their new inventions†. Nay I may safely affirm, that amongst the variety of those opinions that are in astronomy, there are more (of those which have skill in it) that are of this opinion, not only than any other side, but than all the rest put together. So that now it is a greater argument of singularity to oppose it.

5. It is probable, that many other of the ancients would have assented unto this opinion, if they had been acquainted with those experiments which later times have found out for the confirmation of it : and therefore Rheticus‡ and Keplar‖ do so often wish that Aristotle were now alive again. Questionless, he was so rational and ingenious a man, (not half so obstinate as many of his followers) that upon such probabilities as these, he would quickly have renounced his own principles, and have come over to this side : for in one place, having proposed some questions about the heavens§, which were not easy to be resolved, he sets down this rule; that in difficulties, a man may take a liberty to speak that which seems most likely to him; and in such cases, an aptness to guess at some resolution, for the satisfying of our philosophical thirst, does deserve rather to be stiled by the name of modesty, than boldness. And in another place¶, he refers the reader to the different opinions of astronomers, advising him to examine their several tenets, as well Eudoxus as Calippus; and to entertain that (not which is most ancient, but) which is most exact and

* Præf. ad Narrat. Rhetici.   † Ibid.   ‡ In narratione,
‖ Myst. Cosmogr. c. 1. item Præf. ad 4. l. Astr. Copern.
§ De Cœl. l. 2. c. 12.   ¶ Met. lib. 12. cap. 8.

agreeable to reason. And as for Ptolomy, it is his counsel*, that we should endeavour to frame such suppositions of the heavens, as might be more simple, being void of all super- fluities: and he confesses, that his hypothesis had many implications in it, together with sundry intricate and un- likely turnings; and therefore in the same place, he seems to admonish us, that we should not be too confident the heavens were really in the same form wherein astronomers did suppose them. So that it is likely, it was his chief in- tent to propose unto us such a frame of the celestial bodies, from which we might, in some measure, conceive of their different appearances; and according to which, we might be able to calculate their motions. But now it is Coperni- cus's endeavour, to propound unto us the true natural causes of these several motions and appearances : it was the in- tent of the one, to settle the imagination; and of the other, to satisfy the judgment. So that we have no reason to doubt of his assent unto this opinion, if he had but clearly understood all the grounds of it.

It is reported of Clavius, that when lying upon his death- bed, he heard the first news of those discoveries which were made by Galilæus's glass, he brake forth into these words: *videre astronomos, quo pacto constituendi sunt orbes cœlestes, ut hæc phænomena salvari possint*; that it did be- hove astronomers to consider of some other hypothesis, beside that of Ptolomy, whereby they might solve all those new appearances. Intimating that this old one, which for- merly he had defended, would not now serve the turn : and doubtless, if he had been informed how congruous all these might have been unto the opinion of Copernicus, he would quickly have turned on that side. It is considerable, that amongst the followers of Copernicus, there are scarce any who were not formerly against him; and such, as at first had been thoroughly seasoned with the principles of Ari- stotle ; in which, for the most part, they have no less skill than those who are so violent in the defence of them.

* Alm. l. 13. cap. 2.

Whereas on the contrary, there are very few to be found amongst the followers of Aristotle and Ptolomy, that have read any thing in Copernicus, or do fully understand the grounds of his opinion; and I think, not any, who having been once settled with any strong assent on this side, that have afterwards revolted from it. Now if we do but seriously weigh with ourselves, that so many ingenious, considering men, should reject that opinion which they were nursed up in, and which is generally approved as the truth; and that for the embracing of such a paradox as is condemned in schools, and commonly cried down, as being absurd and ridiculous; I say, if a man do but well consider all this, he must needs conclude, that there is some strong evidence for it to be found out by examination; and that in all probability, this is the righter side.

7. It is probable, that most of those authors who have opposed this opinion, since it hath been confirmed by new discoveries, were stirred up thereunto by some of these three insufficient grounds.

1. An over-fond and partial conceit of their proper inventions. Every man is naturally more affected to his own brood, than to that of which another is the author; though perhaps it may be more agreeable to reason. It is very difficult for any one, in the search of truth, to find in himself such an indifferency, as that his judgment is not at all swayed by an over-weaning affection unto that which is proper unto himself. And this perhaps might be the first reason that moved the noble Tycho with so much heat to oppose Copernicus, that so he might the better make way for the spreading of that hypothesis which was of his own invention. To this I might likewise refer that opinion of Origanus and Mr. Carpenter, who attribute to the earth only a diurnal revolution. It does more especially concern those men that are leaders of several sides, to beat down any that should oppose them.

2. A servile and superstitious fear of derogating from the authority of the ancients, or opposing that meaning of scripture-phrases, wherein the supposed infallible church hath

for a long time understood them. It is made part of the
new creed, set forth by Pius the Fourth, 1564. That no
man should assent unto any interpretation of scripture,
which is not approved of by the authority of the fathers.
And this is the reason why the jesuits, who are otherwise
the greatest affectors of those opinions which seem to be
new and subtil, do yet forbear to say any thing in defence
of this; but rather take all occasions to inveigh against it.
One of them* does expressly condemn it for a heresy.
And since him, it hath been called in by two sessions of the
cardinals†, as being an opinion both absurd and dangerous.
And therefore likewise do they punish it, by casting the
defenders of it into the pope's truest purgatory, the inquisition: but yet neither these councils, nor any (that I know
of) since them, have proceeded to such a peremptory censure of it, as to conclude it a heresy; fearing perhaps, lest
a more exact examination, and the discovery of future
times, finding it to be an undeniable truth, it might redound
to the prejudice of their church, and its infallibility.   And
therefore he that is most bitter against it, in the heat and
violence of opposition, will not call it a heresy: the worst
that he dares say of it, is, that it is *opinio temeraria quæ
altero saltem pede intravit hæresios limen*‡: a rash opinion,
and bordering upon heresy. Though unto this likewise he
was incited by the eagerness of disputation, and a desire of
victory; for it seems many eminent men of that church
before him, were a great deal more mild and moderate in
their censures of it.

Paul the Third was not so much offended at Copernicus,
when he dedicated his work unto him.

The cardinal of Cusa does expressly maintain this opinion.

Schonbergius, the cardinal of Capua, did with much im-
portunity and great approbation, beg of Copernicus the
commentaries that he writ in this kind: and it seems the

---

* Serrarius Commen. in Jos. cap. 10. quæst. 14. So Lipsius, Physiol. l. 2.
† Ann. Dom. 1616. item 1633.   ‡ Fromondus, Antarist. cap .6.

fathers of the council of Trent were not such confident defenders of Ptolomy's hypothesis against Copernicus, as many now are. For, speaking of those intricate subtilties which the fancies of men had framed to maintain the practice of the church, they compared them to astronomers, who, say they, do feign excentrics and epicicles, and such engines of orbs, to save the phænomena; though they know there are no such things. But now, because this opinion of Copernicus in later times hath been so strictly forbidden and punished, it will concern those of that religion, to take heed of meddling in the defence of it, but rather to submit the liberty of their reason under the command of their superiors, and (which is very absurd) even in natural questions, not to assent unto any thing but what authority shall allow of.

3. A judging of things by sense rather than by discourse and reason: a tying of the meaning of scripture to the letter of it, and from thence concluding philosophical points, together with an ignorance of all those grounds and probabilities in astronomy, upon which this opinion is bottomed. And this, in all likelihood, is the reason why some men, who in other things perhaps are able scholars, do write so vehemently against it; and why the common people in general do cry it down, as being absurd and ridiculous. Under this head I might refer the opposition of Mr. Fuller, Al. Ross. &c.

But now, no prejudice that may arise from the bare authority of such enemies as these, will be liable to sway the judgment of an indifferent considering man; and I doubt not but that he who will thoroughly weigh with himself these particulars that are here propounded, may find some satisfaction for these arguments, which are taken from the seeming novelty and singularity of this opinion.

PROP. II.

That there is not any place in scriptures, from which (being rightly understood) we may infer the diurnal motion of the sun or heavens.

IT were happy for us, if we could exempt scripture from philosophical controversies: if we could be content to let it be perfect for that end unto which it was intended, for a rule of our faith and obedience; and not stretch it also to be a judge of such natural truths as are to be found out by our own industry and experience. Though the Holy Ghost could easily have given us a full resolution of all such particulars; yet he hath left this travel to the sons of men to be exercised therewith*: *mundum reliquit disputationibus hominum*: that being busied for the most part in an inquisition after the creatures, we might find the less leisure to wait upon our lusts, or serve our more sinful inclinations.

But however, because our adversaries generally do so much insult in those arguments that may be drawn from hence; and more especially, because Pineda† doth for this reason with so many bitter and empty reproaches, revile our learned countryman, Dr. Gilbert; in that renewing of this opinion, he omitted an answer to the scripture expressions: therefore it is requisite, that in the prosecution of this discourse, we should lay down such satisfaction as may clear all doubts that may be taken thence: especially since the prejudice that may arise from the misapprehension of those scripture phrases, may much disable the reader from looking on any other argument with an equal and indifferent mind.

The places that seem to oppose this, are of two kinds. First, such as imply a motion in the heavens: or, secondly, such as seem to express a rest and immobility in the earth.

---

* Eccles. iii. 10, 11.   † Comment. in Eccles. ch. i. ver. 4.

Those of the first kind seem to bear in them the clearest evidence, and therefore are more insisted on by our adversaries. They may be referred unto these three heads.

1. All those scriptures where there is any mention made of the rising or setting of the sun or stars.

2. That story in Joshua, where the sun standing still is reckoned for a miracle.

3. That other wonder in the days of Hezekiah, when the sun went back ten degrees in the dial of Ahaz. All which places do seem to conclude, that the diurnal motion is caused by the heavens.

To this I answer in general;

That the Holy Ghost in these scripture expressions, is pleased to accommodate himself unto the conceit of the vulgar, and the usual opinion: whereas, if in the more proper phrase it had been said, that the earth did rise and set; or, that the earth stood still, &c. the people who had been unacquainted with that secret in philosophy, would not have understood the meaning of it; and therefore it was convenient that they should be spoken unto in their own language.

Ay, but you will reply, it should seem more likely, if there had been any such thing, that the Holy Ghost should use the truest expressions: for then he would at the same time have informed them of the thing, and reformed them in an error: since his authority alone had been sufficient to have rectified the mistake.

I answer:

1. Though it were, yet it is beside the chief scope of those places, to instruct us in any philosophical points, as hath been proved in the former book; especially when these things are neither necessary in themselves, nor do necessarily induce to a more full understanding of that which is the main business of those scriptures. But now the people might better conceive the meaning of the Holy Ghost, when he does conform himself unto their capacities and opinions, than when he talks exactly of things in such a proper phrase as is beyond their reach: and therefore it

is said in Isaiah, I am the Lord which teacheth thee *utilia*,
profitable things: where the Gloss has it, *non subtilia*, not
such curiosities of nature as are not easily apprehended.

2. It is not only besides that which is the chief purpose
of those places, but it might happen also to be somewhat
opposite unto it. For men being naturally unapt to believe
any thing that seems contrary to their senses, might upon
this begin to question the authority of that book which affirmed it, or at least to retch scripture some wrong way, to
force it to some other sense, which might be more agreeable to their own false imagination. Tertullian* tells us
of some heretics, who when they were plainly confuted
out of any scripture, would presently accuse those texts or
books to be fallible, and of no authority ; and rather yield
scripture to be erroneous, than forego those tenets for which
they thought there was so good reason. So likewise might
it have been in these points which seem to bear in them so
much contradiction to the senses and common opinion :
and therefore it is excellent advice set down by St. Austin†,
*Quod nihil credere de re obscurâ temere debemus, ne forte
quod postea veritas patefecerit, quamvis libris sanctis sive
testamenti veteris, sive novi, nullo modo esse possit adversum,
tamen propter amorem nostri erroris oderimus:* that we
should not hastily settle our opinions concerning any obscure matter, lest afterwards, the truth being discovered,
(which, however it may seem, cannot be repugnant to any
thing in scripture) we should hate that, out of love to the
error that we have before entertained. A little reading
may inform us how those texts have been abused to strange
and unmeant allegories, which have mentioned any natural
truth in such a manner as was not agreeable to men's conceits. And besides, if the Holy Ghost had propounded unto
us any secrets in philosophy, we should have been apt to
be so busied about them, as to neglect other matters of
greater importance. And therefore St. Austin‡ proposing
the question, what should be the reason, why the scripture

* Præscript. c. 17.   † In Genes. ad lit. l. 2. in fine.   ‡ Ibid. cap. ix.

does not clearly set down any thing concerning the nature, figure, magnitude and motion of the heavenly orbs; he answers it thus: the Holy Ghost being to deliver more necessary truths, would not insert these, lest men, according to the pravity of their dispositions, should neglect the more weighty matters, and bestow their thoughts about the speculative natural points, which were less needful. So that it might seem more convenient that the scripture should not meddle with the revealing of these unlikely secrets, especially when it is to deliver unto us many other mysteries of greater necessity, which seem to be directly opposite to our sense and reason. And therefore, I say, the Holy Ghost might purposely omit the treating of these philosophical secrets, till time and future discovery might with leisure settle them in the opinion of others: as he is pleased in other things of a higher kind, to apply himself unto the infirmity of our apprehensions, by being represented, as if he were a human nature, with the parts and passions of a man. So in these things likewise, that he might descend to our capacities, does he vouchsafe to conform his expressions unto the error and mistake of our judgments.

But before we come to a further illustration, let us a little examine those particular scriptures which are commonly urged to prove the motion of the sun or heavens. These (as was said) might be distributed under these three heads.

1. Those places which mention the rising or setting of the sun; as that in the psalm*, *The sun like a bridegroom cometh out of his chamber, and rejoiceth as a giant to run his race: his going forth is from the end of heaven, and his circuit unto the end of it, and there is nothing hid from the heat thereof*. And that in Ecclesiastes†, *The sun ariseth, and the sun goeth down,* &c.

In which scriptures we may observe divers phrases that are evidently spoken in reference to the appearance of things, and the false opinion of the vulgar. And therefore it is not altogether unlikely, that this, which they seem to

* Psal. xix. 5, 6.   † Eccles. i, 5.

affirm concerning the motion of the heavens, should also be understood in the same sense.

The sun like a bridegroom cometh out of his chamber; alluding perhaps unto the conceit of ignorant people: as if it took rest all the while it was absent from us, and came out of its chamber when it arose.

And rejoiceth as a giant to run his race; because in the morning it appears bigger than at other times; and therefore in reference to this appearance, may then be compared unto a giant.

His going forth is from the end of heaven, and his circuit unto the ends of it. Alluding again unto the opinion of the vulgar: who not apprehending the roundness of the heavens, do conceive it to have two ends, one where the sun riseth, the other where it setteth.

And there is nothing hid from the heat thereof; speaking still in reference to the common mistake, as if the sun were actually hot in itself; and as if the heat of the weather were not generated by reflection, but did immediately proceed from the body of the sun.

So likewise, for that in Ecclesiastes, where it is said, *the sun riseth, and the sun goeth down,* &c. which phrases being properly understood, do import that he is sometimes in a higher place than at others: whereas, in a circumference, there is no place higher or lower, each part being at the same distance from the centre, which is the bottom. But now understand the phrase in reference to the sun's appearance, and then we grant that he does seem sometimes to rise, and sometimes to go down, because in reference to the horizon, (which common people apprehend to be the bottom, and in the utmost bounds of it to join with the heavens,) the sun does appear in the morning to rise up from it, and in the evening to go down unto it. Now, I say, because the Holy Ghost, in the manner of these expressions, does so plainly allude unto vulgar errors, and the false appearance of things; therefore it is not without probability, that he should be interpreted in the same sense, when he seems to imply a motion in the sun or heavens.

2. The second place was that relation in Joshua; where it is mentioned as a miracle, that the sun did stand still. And Joshua said*, *Sun, stand thou still upon Gibeon, and thou moon in the valley of Ajalon. So the sun stood still in the midst of heaven, and hasted not to go down about a whole day. And there was no day like that, before it, or after it.* In which place likewise there are divers phrases wherein the Holy Ghost does not express things according to their true nature, and as they are in themselves; but according to their appearances, and as they are conceived in common opinion. As,

1. When he says, *Sun, stand thou still upon Gibeon,* or *over Gibeon.* Now the whole earth being so little in comparison to the body of the sun, and but as a point, in respect of that orb wherein the sun is supposed to move; and Gibeon being, as it were, but a point of this globe of earth; therefore the words cannot be understood properly, but according to appearance. It is probable that Joshua was then at Azecha, a little east from Gibeon, and the sun being somewhat beyond the meridian, did seem unto him as he was in that place, to be over against Gibeon; and in reference to this appearance, and vulgar conceit, does he command it to stand still upon that place†.

2. And so secondly for that other expression; *and thou moon in the valley of Ajalon.* This planet was now a little east from the sun, it being about three or four days old (as commentators‡ guess.) Ajalon was three miles from Gibeon eastward, and Joshua commanded the moon to stand still there; because unto him it did then seem to be over against that valley; whereas, it is certain, if he had been there himself, it would still have seemed to be as much distant from him. Just as men commonly speak in shewing another the stars: we point to a star over such a chimney, or such a tree, because to us it appears so;

* Jos. x. 12, 14. Galilæus maintains the literal sense of this place, towards the end of that treatise, which he calls, Nov. Antiq. pat. doctrina.

† Tostat. in locum, quæst. 16, 17.   Arius Montanus in locum.

‡ Tostat. ib. quæst. 18.   Serrarius in Josh. 10. quæst. 21, 22.

whereas the star in itself is not sensibly more over them, than it is over us. So that in this phrase likewise the Holy Ghost doth conform himself unto the appearance of things, and our grosser conceit.

3. *And the sun stood still in the midst of heaven.* Now to speak properly, and as the thing is in itself, heaven has no midst but the centre; and therefore this also must be interpreted in reference to the opinion of the vulgar; and by the midst of heaven, we are to understand such a place as was not very near to either of the ends, the east or west.

4. *And there was no day like that, before it, or after it :* which words are not to be understood absolutely, for there are always longer days under the poles; but in respect to the opinion of the vulgar; that is, there was never any day so long which these ignorant people knew of.

3. As for this last place concerning the sun's returning ten degrees in the dial of Ahaz* : I think it may probably be affirmed, that it is to be understood only concerning the shadow: which though it do necessarily happen in all horizontal dials, for any latitude betwixt the tropics: and so consequently in all declining dials, the elevation of whose pole is less than the sun's greatest declination; as Clavius de Horol. cap. 21. observes: yet the circumstances of this relation in scripture, make the event to differ from that other which is common and natural: which against its nature did seem to go backwards, when as the sun itself was not in the least manner altered from its usual course. Of this opinion were Abarbinel, Arius Montanus, Burgensis, Vatablas Sanctius, &c.

The reasons for it may be these;

1. The miracle is proposed only concerning the shadow; Wilt thou that the shadow shall ascend or return by ten degrees? there being not in the offer of this wonder, any the least mention made concerning the sun's going backwards.

2. It is likely we should have had some intimation concerning the extraordinary length of the day, as it is in that

---

* 2 Kings xx. 11. Isa. xxxviii. 8.

of Joshua; but in this relation, the chief matter that the
story takes notice of, is the alteration of the shadow.

3. Had it been by the supposed return of the sun's body,
this had been a greater miracle than those which were performed upon more solemn occasions; it had been more
wonderful than its seeming rest in Joshua's time; than the
supernatural eclipse at our Saviour's death, when the moon
was in the full.   And then it is not likely, that the Holy
Ghost in relating of this miracle, should chiefly insist in expressing how the shadow returned, and that only in the dial
of Ahaz.

4. This sign did not appear in the sun itself; because in
the 2 Chron. xxxii. 31. it is said, that the ambassadors of
the king of Babylon did come unto Hezekiah, to enquire of
the wonder that was done in the Lord; and therefore it
seems the miracle did not consist in any change of the
heavens.

5. If it had been in the sun, it would have been as well
discerned in other parts of the world, as in the land of Judea.
And then,

1. What need the king of Babylon send thither to enquire after it? If you reply, because it was occasioned by
Hezekiah's recovery; I answer, it is not likely that the
heathens would ever believe so great a miracle should be
wrought merely for a sign of one man's recovery from a
disease: but would rather be apt to think that it was done
for some more remarkable purpose, and that by some of
their own gods, unto whom they attributed a far greater
power than unto any other.   It is more probable, they
might hear some flying rumour of a miracle that was seen
in Judea: which because it happened only in Hezekiah's
house and dial, and that too upon his recovery from a dangerous sickness, they might be more apt to believe that it
was a sign of it.

2. Why have we no mention made of it in the writings
of the ancients? It is no way likely, that so great a miracle
as this was (if it were in the sun) should have been passed
over in silence; especially, since it happened in those later

times, when there were many heathen writers that flourished in the world; Hesiod, Archilochus, Symonides;
and not long after, Homer, with divers others; and yet
none of them have the least mention of any such prodigy.
We have many relations of matters that were less observable, which were done about that time; the history of
Numa Pompilius, Gyges; the fight betwixt the three bre-
thren, with divers such stories.   And it is scarce credible,
that this should have been omitted amongst the rest.

Nay, we have (as many guess) some hints from profane
antiquity, of the miracle wrought by Joshua.   Unto which,
it is thought the ancients did allude in the fable of Phaeton;
when the sun was so irregular in his course, that he burnt
some part of the world.   And questionless then, this which
happened in later times, would not have been so wholly
forgotten.   It is an argument urged by Origen*, that the
eclipse at our Saviour's passion was not universal, because
no profane author of those times mentions it.   Which
consequence is the very same with that which is urged in
this other case; but by the way, his antecedent was false,
since Tertullian † affirms, that it was recorded amongst the
Roman annals.

Now as for that story in Herodotus ‡, where after he had
related the flight of Senacherib, he tells us, how the sun did
four times in the space of 10340 years invert his course, and
rise in the west; which would seem so unto other nations,
if he had only returned, as many conclude, from this scripture: as for this story, (I say) it cannot well be urged as
pertinent to the present business, because it seems to have
reference unto times that never were.

So that all these things being well considered, we shall
find it more probable, that this miracle doth consist in the
return of the shadow.

If you object, that the scripture does expressly say, the
sun itself returned ten degrees ‖ ; I answer, it is a frequent

* Tractat. 35. in Mat.   † Apologet. c. 21.
‡ Lib. 2.   ‖ Isa. xxxviii. 8.

manner of speech in scripture, to put the cause for the effect; as that in Jonas*, where it is said, that the sun did beat upon the head of Jonas; that is, the beams of the sun. So that of the Psalmist†, the sun shall not smite thee by day, that is, the heat which proceeds from the sun's reflection. In the same sense may the phrase be understood in this place; and the sun may be said to return back, because the light, which is the effect of it, did seem to do so; or rather, because the shadow, which is the effect of that, did change its course.

This later scripture then, will not at all make to the present purpose: as for those of the two former kinds, I have already answered, that they are spoken in reference to the appearance of things, and vulgar opinion. For the further illustration of which, I shall endeavour to confirm these two particulars.

1. That the Holy Ghost in many other places of scripture, does accommodate his expressions unto the error of our conceits: and does not speak of divers things as they are in themselves, but as they appear unto us. Therefore it is not unlikely, that these phrases also may be liable unto the same interpretation.

2. That divers men have fallen into great absurdities, whilst they have looked for the grounds of philosophy from the words of scripture ; and therefore it may be dangerous in this point also, to adhere so closely unto the letter of the text.

* Jonah iv. 8.   † Psalm cxxi. 6.

PROP. III.

That the Holy Ghost, in many places of scripture, does plainly conform his expressions unto the errors of our conceits; and does not speak of divers things as they are in themselves, but as they appear unto us.

THERE is not any particular by which philosophy hath been more endamaged, than the ignorant superstition of some men: who in stating the controversies of it, do so closely adhere unto the mere words of scripture. *Quam plurima occurrunt in libris sacris ad naturam pertinentia,* &c. They are the words of Vallesius* " There are sun-
" dry things in holy writ concerning natural points, which
" most men think are not so to be understood, as if the
" Holy Ghost did intend to unfold unto us any thing in
" that kind: but referring all to the salvation of our souls,
" does speak of other matters according to common opi-
" nion." And a little after, *Ego, divina hæc eloquia,* &c.
" I for my part am persuaded, that these divine treatises
" were not written by the holy and inspired penmen, for
" the interpretation of philosophy, because God left such
" things to be found out by men's labour and industry.
" But yet whatsoever is in them concerning nature is most
" true: as proceeding from the God of nature, from whom
" nothing could be hid." And questionless, all those things which the scripture does deliver concerning any natural point, cannot be but certain and infallible, being understood in that sense, wherein they were first intended; but now that it does speak sometimes according to common opinion, rather than the true nature of the things themselves, was intimated before; wherefore (by the way) Fromondus † his triumph upon the latter part of this quotation, is but vain, and to no purpose. It is a good rule set down

---

* Proœm. ad Phil. sacram.   † Vest. tract. 3. c. 2.

by a learned commentator *, to be observed in the interpretation of scripture: *scriptura sacra sæpe non tam ad
veritatem ipsam, quam ad hominum opinionem, sermonem
accommodat*; that it does many times accommodate its expressions, not so much to the truth itself, as to men's opinions.   And in this sense is that speech of Gregory concerning images and pictures, attributed by Calvin † unto the
history of the creation; viz. *librum esse ideotarum*, that it is
a book for the simpler and ignorant people.   For it being
written to inform them, as well as others, it is requisite that
it should use the most plain and easy expressions.   To this
purpose likewise is that of Mersennus ‡, *mille sunt scriptura
loca* &c.   " There are very many places of scripture, which
" are not to be interpreted according to the letter; and
" that for this reason, because God would apply himself
" unto our capacity and sense ‖ :" *presertim in iis, quæ ad
res naturales, oculisque subjectas pertinent*; more especially
in those things which concern nature, and are subject to
our eyes.   And therefore in the very same place, though
he be eager enough against Copernicus, yet he concludes
that opinion not to be a heresy; b'ecause (saith he) those
scriptures which seem to oppose it, are not so evident, but
that they may be capable of another interpretation: intimating, that it was not unlikely they should be understood
in reference to outward appearance and common opinion;
and that this manner of speech is frequently used in many
other places of scripture, may be easily manifest from these
following examples.

Thus though the moon may be proved by infallible observations, to be less than any of the visible stars; yet because of its appearance, and vulgar opinion, therefore doth
the scripture in comparison to them, call it one of the great
lights.   Of which place, saith Calvin §, *Moses populariter
scripsit, nos potius respexit quam sydera.*   Moses did not

---

* Sanctius in Isa. xiii. 5.   Item in Zachar. l. 9. n. 45.
† Comment. in Gen. c. i.   ‡ In Gen. cap. i. ver. 10. art. 6.
‖ Vid. Hiero. in Jer. 28. Aquinas in Job xxvi. 7.
§ Gen. i. 16. Psal. cxxxvi. 7.

so much regard the nature of the thing, as our capacity;
and therefore uses a popular phrase: so as ordinary people
without the help of arts and learning, might easily understand him; and in another place, *non fuit spiritus sancti
concilium astrologiam docere* *: "It was not the purpose
" of the Holy Ghost to teach us astronomy: but being to
" propound a doctrine that concerns the most rude and
" simple people, he does (both by Moses and the prophets)
" conform himself unto their phrases and conceits: lest
" any should think to excuse his own ignorance with the
" pretence of difficulty: as men commonly do in those
" things which are delivered after a learned and sublime
" manner." Thus Zanchy † likewise, *Moses majorem ra-
tionem habuit nostri humanique judicii,* &c. "When Moses
" calls the moon a great light, he had a more especial refe-
" rence to men's opinions of it, than to the truth of the
" thing itself; because he was to deal with such, who do
" usually judge rather by their sense than by their reason."
Nor will that distinction of Fromondus and others avoid
this interpretation, when he tells us of *magnum materiale,*
which refers to the bulk and quantity of the body; and
magnum formale, which imports the greatness of its light.
For we grant, that it is really unto us a greater light than
any of the stars, or than all of them together: yet there is
not one of them, but is in itself a bigger light than this:
and therefore when we say this speech is to be understood
according to its appearance, we do not oppose this to reality: but it is implied, that this reality is not absolute, and
in the nature of the thing itself; but only relative, and in
reference to us. I may say a candle is a bigger light than a
star, or the moon, because it is really so to me. However
any one will think this to be spoken, only in relation to its
appearance, and not to be understood as if the thing were
so in itself. But (by the way) it does concern Fromondus ‡
to maintain the scripture's authority, in revealing of natural

* Comment. in Psal. cxxxvi.   † De Oper. Dei. par. 2. l. 6. c. 1.
‡ De Meteor. l. 4. c. 2. art. 5.

secrets; because, from thence it is that he fetches the chief
argument for that strange assertion of his, concerning the
heaviness of the wind; where Job says*, that God makes
the weight for the wind.   Thus likewise, because the common people usually think the rain to proceed from some
waters in the expansum, therefore doth Moses in reference
to this erroneous conceit, tell us of waters above the firmament, and the windows of heaven: of which saith Calvin †,
nimis serviliter literæ se astringunt, &c.   " Such men too
" servilely tie themselves unto the letter of the text, who
" hence conclude, that there is a sea in the heavens: when
" as we know that Moses and the prophets, to accommo-
" date themselves unto the capacity of ruder people, do
" use a vulgar expression; and therefore it would be a
" preposterous course, to reduce their phrases unto the
" exact rules of philosophy."   Let me add, that from this
mistake, it is likely did arise that groundless observation of
the ancient Jews, who would not admit any to read the beginning of Genesis, till he was arrived to thirty years of age.
The true reason of which was this: not because that book
was harder than any other, but because Moses conforming
his expression to vulgar conceits, and they examining of
them by more exact rules of philosophy, were fain to force
upon them many strange allegories, and unnatural mysteries.

Thus also, because for the most part we conceive the
stars to be innumerable, therefore doth the Holy Ghost
often speak of them in reference to this opinion.   So Jere-
my ‡, as the host of heaven cannot be numbered, neither
the sand of the sea measured, so will I multiply the seed of
David.   So likewise, when God would comfort Abraham
with the promise of a numberless posterity, he bids him
look up to heaven, and tells him, that his seed should be
like those stars for number ‖; which, saith Clavius §, *intel-
ligendum est secundum communem sententiam vulgi, existi-*

* Job xxviii. 25.   † Comment. in Ps. cxlviii. 4.   ‡ Jer. xxxv. 22.
‖ Gen. xv. 5.   § In 1 cap. Sphæræ.

*mantis infinitam esse multitudinem stellarum dum eas nocte
serena confuse intuetur,* is to be understood according to
the common opinion of the vulgar, who think the stars to
be of an infinite multitude, whilst they behold them all (as
they seem confused) in a clear night. And though many
of our divines do commonly interpret this speech to be a
hyperbole; yet being well considered, we shall find that
Abraham's posterity, in some few generations, were far
more than there are visible stars in the firmament; and of
such only does God speak, because he bids Abraham look
up to the heavens.

Now all these, even unto six differences of magnitude, are
reckoned to be but 1022. True indeed, at the first viewing
of the heavens, it may seem an incredible thing that they
should be of no greater a number; but the reason of this
is, because they appear scattered and confused, so that the
eye cannot place them in any such order, as to reckon them
up, or take any distinct survey of them. Now it is a known
truth, *quod fortius operatur pluralitas partium, ubi ordo
abest; nam inducit similitudinem infiniti, et impedit com-
prehensionem* *; that a plurality of parts without order, has
a more strong operation, because it has a kind of seeming
infinity, and so hinders comprehension. And then besides,
there are more appearances of stars many times, than there
are bodies of them: for the eye, by reason of its weakness
and disability to discern any thing at so great a distance; as
also, because of those beams which proceed from such remote bodies in a twinkling and wavering manner, and so
mix and confound themselves at their entrance into that
organ; it must needs receive more representations than
there are true bodies. But now, if a man do but leisurely
and distinctly compare the stars of the heaven with those
of this number that are noted in a celestial globe, he shall
scarce find any in the sky which are not marked with the
globe; nay, he may observe many in the globe, which he
can scarce at all discern in the heavens.

* Sir Fr. Bac. Table of Colours, No. 5.

Now this number of the stars is commonly distributed into 48 constellations; in each of which, though we should suppose ten thousand stars, (which can scarce be conceived) yet would not all this number equal that of the children of *Israel*. Nay, it is the assertion of Clavius*, that Abraham's posterity in some few generations were far more than there could be stars in the firmament, though they stuck so close that they touched one another. And he proves it thus: a great circle in the firmament does contain the diameter of a star of the first magnitude 14960 times. In the diameter of the firmament, there are contained 4760 diameters of such a star: now if we multiply this circumference by this diameter, the product will be 71209600, which is the full number of stars, that the eighth sphere (according to Ptolemy's grounds) would contain, if they stood so close that they touched one another.

The children of *Israel* were reckoned at their going out of Egypt 603550†, of such as were one and twenty years old and upwards, and were able to go to war; besides children, and women, and youths, and old men, and the Levites; which in probability, did always treble the other number. Now if they were so many at one time, we may well conceive that in all those several generations, both before and since, the number was much augmented; and long before this time, did far exceed this supposed multitude of the stars. From all which, we may infer, that the scripture expressions in this kind, are to be understood according to appearance and common opinion.

Another place usually cited for the same purpose, to shew that the Holy Ghost does not speak exactly concerning natural secrets, is that in the Kings and Chronicles‡, which relates unto us the measure of Solomon's brazen sea, whose diameter was ten cubits, and its circumference thirty; whereas to speak geometrically, the more exact proportion betwixt the diameter and the circumference, is not as ten to thirty, but rather as seven to twenty-two.

---

* In prim. ca. Sphæræ.　　† Num. i. 46.
‡ 1 King. vii. 23.　2 Chr. iv. 2

THAT THE EARTH MAY BE A PLANET.   165

But against this it is objected by our adversaries,

1. This sea was not perfectly round, but rather inclining to a semicircular form, as Josephus[2] affirms.

I reply: if it were so, yet this is so much from helping the matter, that it makes it much worse; for then the disproportion will be far greater.

But secondly, scripture, which is to be believed before Josephus, does tell us in express terms, that it was round all about, 1 Kings vii. 23.

2. The proportion of the diameter to the circumference, is not exactly the same as seven to two and twenty, but rather less[3]. I answer, though it be, yet it is nearer unto that, than any other number.

3. The scripture does but, according to its usual custom, suppress the less number, and mention only that which is bigger and more full[4]. So in some places[5], Abraham's posterity is said to remain in the land of Egypt for four hundred years; when as notwithstanding, other scriptures tell us[6], that they tarried there thirty years longer. Thus likewise in one place[7], the number of Jacob's house who came into Egypt, is reckoned to be seventy; whereas elsewhere[8] they are said to be seventy-five.

I answer: all this is so far from destroying the force of the present argument, that it does rather confirm it, and more clearly evidence unto us, that the scripture does not only, not speak exactly in these subtle and more secret points of philosophy; but also, in the ordinary obvious numbering of things, does conform unto common custom, and often use the round number for the whole.

4. It is yet objected by another adversary[9], that we have no reason to expect the Holy Ghost should reveal unto us this secret in nature; because neither Archimedes, nor any other, had then found it out. I reply, and why then should we think that the scripture must needs inform

---

[1] Ross. l. 1. sect. 1. c. 8.   [2] Antiq. Jud. lib. 8. cap. 2.
[3] Ross. ibid.   [4] Ibid.   [5] Gen. xv. 13. Acts. vii. 6.
[6] Exod. xii. 41. Gal. iii. 17.   [7] Gen. xlvi. 27.
[8] Acts. vii. 4.   [9] Fromond. Vesta 4. tract. 3. c. 2.

us of the earth's motion ; when as neither Pythagoras, nor
Copernicus, nor any else, had then discovered it ?

5. In taking the compass of this vessel, they measured
somewhat below the brim, where it was narrower than at
the top, and so the circumference there might be exactly
but thirty cubits : whereof its diameter was ten*.

I answer : it is evident this is a mere shift, there being
not the least ground for it in the text. And then besides,
why might not we affirm, that the diameter was measured
from that place, as well as the circumference? since it is
very probable that the Holy Ghost did speak *ad idem*, and
not tell us the breadth of one place, and the compass of
another. So that all our adversaries evasions cannot well
avoid the force of the argument that is taken from this
scripture.

Again, common people usually conceive the earth to be
such a plain, as in its utmost parts is terminated by the
heavens, so that if a man were in the farthermost coasts of
it, he might touch the sky. And hence also, they think
that the reason why some countries are hotter than others,
is, because they lie nearer unto the sun. Nay, Strabo tells
us of some philosophers too, who in this point have grossly
erred ; affirming, that there was a place towards the utmost coasts of Lusitania, where a man might hear the
noise that the sun made, as he quenched his beams in his
descent to the ocean ; which, though it be an absurd mistake, yet we may note, that the Holy Ghost in the expression of these things, is pleased to conform himself unto
such kind of vulgar and false conceits ; and therefore often
speaks of the ends of heaven †, and the ends of the
world ‡. In this sense, they that come from any far country
are said to come from the end of heaven, Isaiah xiii. 5.
And in another place, from the side of the heavens, Deut.
iv. 32. All which phrases do plainly allude unto the error
of vulgar capacities (saith Sanctius §) which hereby is better
instructed, than it would be by more proper expressions.

---

* Fromond. Vesta. 4. tract. 3. c. 2.   † Ps. xix. 6.   Mat. xxiv. 31.
‡ Ps. xxii. xxvii. &c.   § Comment. in Isa. xiii. 5.

Thus likewise, because ignorant people cannot well apprehend how so great a weight as the sea and land should hang alone in the open air, without being founded upon some basis to uphold it; therefore in this respect also does scripture apply itself unto their conceits, where it often mentions the foundations of the earth *. Which phrase, in the letter of it, does manifestly allude unto men's imaginations in this kind.

Thus also the common people usually conceive the earth to be upon the water; because, when they have travelled any way as far as they can, they are at length stopped by the sea. Therefore doth scripture in reference to this, affirm†, that God stretched the earth upon the waters, founded the earth upon the seas, and established it upon the floods. Of which places saith Calvin, *Non disputat philosophice David, de terræ situ; sed populariter loquens, ad rudium captum se accommodat :* It was not David's intent to speak philosophically concerning the earth's situation; but rather by using a popular phrase, to accommodate his speech unto the capacities of the ruder people.

In this sense likewise, are we to understand all those places of scripture, wherein the coasts of heaven are denominated from the relations of before, behind, the right hand, or the left. Which do not imply, saith Scaliger ‡, any absolute difference in such places, but are spoken merely in reference to men's estimations, and the common opinion of those people for whom the scriptures were first penned. Thus because it was the opinion of the Jewish rabbies, that man was created with his face to the east, therefore the Hebrew word קדם signifies *ante*, or the east; אחור *post*, or the west; ימין *dextra*, or the south; שמאל *sinistra*, or the north. You may see all of them put together in that place of Job § : Behold I go forward, and he is not there, and backward, but I cannot perceive him ; on the left hand, where he doth work, but I cannot

* Job. xxxviii. 4.　Ps. cii. 25.　　† Ps. cxxxvi. 6.　xxiv. 2.
‡ Subtil. Exercit. 67.　　　§ Job xxiii. 8. 9.

behold him. He hideth himself on the right hand, that I
cannot see him. Which expressions are by some interpreters referred unto the four coasts of heaven, according
to the common use of those original words. From hence
it is, that many of the ancients have concluded hell to be
in the north, which is signified by the left hand: unto
which side our Saviour tells us, that the goats shall be divided *. Which opinion likewise seems to be favoured
by that place in Job †, where it is said, hell is naked before God, and destruction hath no covering. And presently is added, he stretched out the north over the empty
place.

Upon these grounds, St. Jerom interprets that speech of
the preacher, Eccles. xi. 3. If the tree falls towards the
south, or towards the north, in the place where the tree
falleth, there shall it be. Concerning those who shall go
either to heaven or hell. And in this sense also do some
expound that of Zachary, xiv. 4, where it is said, that
the Mount of Olives shall cleave in the midst; half of it
shall remove towards the north, and half of it towards the
south. By which is intimated, that amongst those Gen-
tiles who shall take upon them the profession of Christ,
there are two sorts; some that go to the north, that is, to
hell, and others to the south, that is to heaven. And
therefore it is (say they) that God so often threatens evil
out of the north; and upon this ground it is (saith Besol-
dus§) that there is no religion that worships that way. We
read of the Mahometans, that they adore towards the
south; the Jews towards the west; Christians towards the
east, but none to the north.

But of this only by the way. However, certain it is
that the Holy Ghost does frequently in scripture set forth
the several coasts of heaven, by those relative terms of
right hand and left hand, &c. which expressions do not denote any real intrinsical difference betwixt those places,

---

* Mat. xxv. 33.   † Job xxxvi. 6, 7.
‡ Jer. i. 14, 15.   Item cap. iv. 6. vi. 1.   § L. de nat. pop. e. 4.

but are rather fitted for the apprehension of those men, from whose fancy it is that they have such denominations. And though Aristotle * concludes these several positions to be natural unto the heavens; yet his authority in this particular is not available, because he delivers it upon a wrong ground, supposing the orbs to be living creatures, and assisted with intelligences. We may observe, that the meaning of these coasts by the relations of right hand and left hand, &c. is so far from having any ground in the nature of those several places, that these relations are not only variously applied unto them by divers religions (as was said before,) but also by divers arts and professions. Thus because astronomers make their observations toward the south parts of the horizon, where there be most stars that rise and set; therefore do they account the west to be at their right hand, and the east at their left. The cosmographers in taking the latitude of places, and reckoning their several climates must look towards the north pole; and therefore in their phrase, by the right hand is meant the east, and by the left hand, the west: and thus (saith Plutarch †) a e we to understand these expressions in Pythagoras, Plato, Aristotle. The poets count the south to be towards the left, and the north the right hand. Thus Lucan ‡ speaking of the Arabians coming unto Thessaly says:

> *Ignotum vobis Arabes venistis in orbem:*
> *Umbras mirati nemorum, non ire sinistras.*

The augurs taking their observations at the east, count the south to be at their right hand, and the north their left: so that these denominations have not any real ground in the nature of the things, but are imposed upon them by the scripture phrase, in reference to the account and opinion of the Jews.

Thus also, because heretofore it was generally received, that the heart was the principal seat of the faculties§; there-

---

* De Cœl. l. 2. c. 2.   † De plac. Philosoph. l. 2. c. 10.
‡ Lib. 3.   § D. Hakwel, Apol. l. 1. c. 1. sect. 2.

fore doth the spirit apply himself unto this common tenent; and in many places, attributes wisdom and understanding to the heart *. Whereas, to speak properly, the
reason and discursive faculties have their principal residence in the head (saith Galen and Hippocrates, together
with the generality of our later physicians,) because they
are hindered in their operations by the distempers of that
part, and recovered by medicines applied unto it.

So likewise are we to understand those other places, Isa.
lix. 5. where some translations read it, *ova aspidum rupe-
runt*, they have broken the vipers eggs; alluding to that
common but fabulous story of the viper, who breaks his
passage through the bowels of the female. So Psal. lviii.
4, 5. where the prophet speaks of the deaf adder, that stops
her ears against the voice of the charmer. Both which relations (if we may believe many naturalists) are as false as
they are common; and yet because they were entertained
with the general opinion of those days, therefore doth the
Holy Ghost vouchsafe to allude unto them in holy writ. It
is a plain mistake of Fromondus †, when in answer to these
places, he is fain to say, that they are used proverbially
only, and do not positively conclude any thing. For when
David writes these words, that they are like the deaf adder
which stoppeth her ears, &c. this affirmation is manifestly
implied, that the deaf adder does stop her ears against the
voice of the charmer: which because it is not true in the
letter of it, (as was said before) therefore it is very probable
that it should be interpreted in the same sense wherein here
it is cited.

In reference to this also, we are to conceive of those
other expressions; Cold cometh out of the north; Job
xxxvii. 9. and again, Fair weather comes out of the north,
ver. 22. So ver. 17. Thy garments are quieted when he
warmeth the earth by the south wind. And Prov. xxv. 23.
The north wind driveth away rain. Which phrases do not

---

* Prov. viii. 5. x. 8. Eccles. i. 13, 16, 17. and viii. 5.
† Vesta Trac. 3. cap. 3.

THAT THE EARTH MAY BE A PLANET.

contain in them any absolute general truth, but can so far only be verified, as they referred to several climates: and though unto us who live on this side of the line, the north wind be coldest and driest; and on the contrary, the south wind moist and warm, by reason that in one of these places there is a stronger heat of the sun to exhale moist vapours, than in the other; yet it is clean otherwise with the inhabitants beyond the other tropic; for there the north wind is the hottest, and moist, and the south the coldest, and dry: so that with them, these scriptures cannot properly be affirmed, that cold or that fair weather cometh out of the north; but rather on the contrary. All which notwithstanding, does not in the least manner derogate from the truth of these speeches, or the omnisciency of the speaker, but do rather shew the wisdom and goodness of the blessed spirit, in vouchsafing thus to conform his language unto the capacity of those people unto whom these speeches were first directed: in the same sense are we to understand all those places where the lights of heaven are said to be darkened, and the constellations not to give their light, Isa. xiii. 10*. Not as if they were absolutely in themselves deprived of their light, and did not shine at all; but because of their appearance to us; and therefore in another place answerable to these, God says, he will cover the heavens, and so make the stars thereof dark, Ezek. xxxvii. 2. Which argues, that they themselves were not deprived of this light (as those other speeches seem to imply) but we.

In reference to this likewise are we to conceive of those other expressions, that the moon shall blush, and the sun be ashamed, Isa. xxiv. 23. That they shall be turned into blood, Matth. xxiv. 29. Not that these things shall be so in themselves (saith St. Jerom†,) but because they shall appear so unto us. Thus also Mark xiii. 25. The stars shall fall from heaven; that is, they shall be so wholly covered from our sight, as if they were quite fallen from their wonted places. Or if this be understood of their real fall, as it

---

* Joel ii. 31. item iii. 15.   † Comment. in Joel, c. 3.

may seem probable by that place in the Revelations, vi. 13. And the stars of heaven fell unto the earth, even as a fig-tree casteth her untimely figs, when she is shaken by a mighty wind: then is it to be interpreted not of them that are truly stars, but them that appear so: alluding unto the opinion of the unskilful vulgar (saith Sanctius[1]) that think the meteors to be stars. And Mersennus[2] speaking of the same scripture, says, *hoc de veris stellis minime volunt interpretes intelligi, sed de cometis et aliis ignitis meteoris:* interpreters do by no means understand this of true stars, but of the comets and other fiery meteors. Though the falling of these be a natural event, yet may it be accounted a strange prodigy, as well as an earthquake, and the dark-ening of the sun and moon, which are mentioned in the verse before.

In reference to this, doth the scripture speak of some common natural effects, as if their true causes were altoge-ther inscrutable, and not to be found out, because they were generally so esteemed by the vulgar. Thus of the wind it is said[3], that none know whence it cometh, nor whither it goeth. In another place[4] God is said to bring it out of his treasures; and elsewhere[5] it is called the breath of God[6]; and so likewise of the thunder: concerning which, Job[7] proposes this question, the thunder of his power who can understand? and therefore too David[8] does so often stile it, the voice of God. All which places seem to imply, that the cause of these things was not to be discovered, which yet later philosophers pretend to know: so that according to their construction, these phrases are to be understood in relation unto their ignorance unto whom these speeches were immediately directed[9].

For this reason is it; why, though there be in nature many other causes of springs and rivers than the sea, yet Solomon (who was a great philosopher, and perhaps not

---

[1] Commen. in Isa. c. xiii. 5

[2] Comment. in Gen. c. iii. v. 10. ar. 6.   [3] Joh. iii. 8.

[4] Jer. x. 13. item li. 16.   [5] נשם   [6] Job xxxvii. 10.

[7] Jo. xxvi. 14.   [8] Psal. ii. 9. iii. 4, &c.   [9] Eccles. i. 7.

ignorant of them) does mention only this; because most obvious, and easily apprehended by the vulgar *. Unto all these scriptures, I might add that in Amos v. 8. which speaks of the constellation commonly called the seven stars; whereas later discoveries have found that there are but six of them discernible to the bare eye, as appears by Galilæus his glass †: the seventh of them being but a deceit of the eye, arising from their too great nearness, and if a man try in a clear night to number them distinctly, he shall find that there will sometimes appear but six, and sometimes more.

True indeed, the original word of this scripture כימה, does not necessarily imply any such number in its signification, but yet our English translation renders it the seven stars; and if it had been expressly so in the original too, it might have spoken true enough, because they are usually esteemed of that number. And when it had been said, he made the seven stars and Orion, we might have easily understood the words thus: he made those constellations that are commonly known unto us under such names.

From all these scriptures it is clearly manifest, that it is a frequent custom for the Holy Ghost to speak of natural things, rather according to their appearance and common opinion, than the truth itself. Now it is very plain, and our enemies themselves do grant it, that if the world had been framed according to the system of Copernicus ‡, *futurum esset ut vulgus, de solis motu et terræ statu proinde ut nunc loqueretur*. The vulgar phrase would have been the same as now it is, when it speaks of the sun's motion, and the earth's standing still.

Wherefore it is not improbable, that such kind of scripture-expressions are to be understood only in relation to outward appearances, and vulgar opinion.

---

* Job ix. 9. item. xxxviii. 31.
† Vide Fromond. Met. l. 3. c. 1. art. 1.   ‡ Fromond. Ant. c. 6.

PROP. IV.

*That divers learned men have fallen into great absurdities,
whilst they have looked for the sects of philosophy from
the words of scripture.*

IT has been an ancient and common opinion amongst the
Jews, that the law of Moses did contain in it, not only
those things which concern our religion and obedience, but
every secret also that may possibly be known in any art or
science*; so that there is not a demonstration in geometry,
or rule in arithmetic; not a mystery in any trade, but it
may be found out in the Pentateuch.   Hence it was (say
they) that Solomon had all his wisdom and policy : hence
it was that he did fetch his knowledge concerning the nature of vegetables, from the cedar of Lebanon, to the hyssop
that grows upon the wall.   Nay from hence, they thought
a man might learn the art of miracles, to remove a mountain, or recover the dead.   So strangely have the learneder
sort of that nation been befooled, since their own curse hath
lighted upon them.

Not much unlike this foolish superstition of theirs, is
that custom of many artists amongst us; who upon the invention of any new secret, will presently find out some obscure text or other to father it upon, as if the Holy Ghost
must needs take notice of every particular which their partial fancies did over-value.

Nor are they altogether guiltless of this fault, who look
for any secrets of nature from the words of scripture; or
will examine all its expressions by the exact rules of philosophy.

Unto what strange absurdities this false imagination of
the learneder Jews hath exposed them, may be manifest by
a great multitude of examples.   I will mention only some
few of them.   Hence it is that they prove the shin-bone of

* Schickard. Bechin. Hapern. Disp. 5. Num. 8.

Og the giant to be above three leagues long*; or (which is a more modest relation) that Moses being fourteen cubits in stature, having a spear ten ells in length, and leaping up ten cubits, could touch this giant but on the ancle. All which they can confirm unto you by a cabalistical interpretation of this story, as it is set down in scripture. Hence it is that they tell us of all those strange beasts which shall be seen at the coming of the Messias †: as first, the ox, which Job calls Behemoth, that every day devours the grass on a thousand mountains, as you may see it in the psalm ‡, where David mentions the cattle, or בהמות upon a thousand hills. If you ask how this beast does to find pasture enough, they answer, that he remains constantly in one place, and where there is as much grass grows up in the night, as was eaten in the day.

They tell us also of a bird, which was of that quantity, that having upon a time cast an egg out of her nest, there were beaten down by the fall of it three hundred of the tallest cedars, and no less than threescore villages drowned. As also of a frog as big as a town capable of sixty houses; which frog, notwithstanding his greatness, was devoured by a serpent, and that serpent by a crow; which crow, as she was flying up to a tree, eclipsed the sun, and darkened the world; by which you may guess what a pretty twig that tree was. If you would know the proper name of this bird, you may find it in Psal. l. 11. where it is called זיז, or in our translation, the fowl of the mountains ‖. It seems it was somewhat of kin to that other bird they tell us of, whose legs were so long, that they reached unto the bottom of that sea, where there had been an axe-head falling for seven years together, before it could come to the bottom.

Many other relations there are, which contain such horrible absurdities, that a man cannot well conceive how they should proceed from reasonable creatures. And all this arising from that wrong principle of theirs, that scripture

---

* Schickard. ib. Disp. 6. num. 2.   † Buxtor. Synag. Juda. c. 36.
‡ Psal. l. 10.   ‖ Vide Parap. Chald.

did exactly contain in it all kind of truths; and that every meaning was true, which by the letter of it, or by cabalistical interpretations might be found out.

Now as it hath been with them, so likewise hath it happened in proportion unto others, who by a superstitious adhering unto the bare words of scripture, have exposed themselves unto many strange errors. Thus St. Basil[1] holds, that next to the sun, the moon is bigger than any of the stars, because Moses does call them only two great lights.

Thus others maintain, that there are waters properly so called, above the starry firmament, because of these vulgar expressions in scripture, which in their literal sense do mention them. Of this opinion were many of the ancients, Philo, Josephus, and since them the fathers Justin Martyr[2], Theodoret[3], Austin[4], Ambrose[5], Basil[6], and almost all the rest. Since them sundry other learned men, as Beda, Strabo, Damascen, Tho. Aquinas, &c. If you ask for what purpose they were placed here, Justin Martyr tells us, for these two ends: first, to cool the heat that might otherwise arise from the motion of the solid orbs; and hence it is, say they, that Saturn is colder than any of the other planets, because though he move faster, yet he is nearer to these waters. Secondly, to press and keep down the heavens, lest the frequency and violence of winds might break and scatter them asunder: which opinion, together with both its reasons, are now accounted absurd and ridiculous.

St. Austin[7] concludes the visible stars to be innumerable, because scripture phrases seem to imply as much.

That the heavens are not round, was the opinion of Justin Martyr[8], Ambrose[9], Chrysostom[10], Theodoret[11], Theophilact[12], doubted of by St. Austin[13], and divers others. Nay, St. Chrysostom was so confident of it, that he pro-

---

[1] Enarrat. in Gen.   [2] Respons. ad Ques. 93. Orthod.
[3] Que. 11. sup. Gen.   [4] De Civ. Dei, lib. 11. cap. ult.
[5] Hexam. l. 2. c. 2.   [6] Homil. 3. in Gen.   [7] Civ. Dei, l. 16. c. 23.
[8] Respon. ad Quest. 93.   [9] Hexam. l. 1. c. 6.
[10] Homil. 14. in Ep. ad Hebr.   [11] In c. 8. Hebr.
[12] In id. c.   [13] In Gen. ad lit. l. 1. c. 9. item. l. 2. c. 6.

poses the question in a triumphant manner: Πε ειϭιν ϲϊ
ϭφαιροειδη ϭϱανον ειναι απoφαινoμενoι ;   Where are those men
that can prove the heavens to have a spherical form? The
reason of which was this, because it is said in one scripture,
that God stretched forth the heavens as a curtain, Psal. civ.
2. and spreadeth them as a tent to dwell in, Isa. xl. 22. and
so in that place of the epistle to the Hebrews, viii. 2. they
are called, a tent or tabernacle: which because it is not
spherical, therefore they conclude also, that the heavens
are not of that form; whereas now, the contrary is as evident as demonstration can make a thing.   And therefore,
St. Jerom[1] in his time, speaking of the same error, gives it
this plain censure: *est in ecclesia stultiloquium, si quis cælum putet fornicis modo curvatum, Esaiæ quem non intelligit
sermone deceptus.*   It is foolish speaking in the church, if
any through misapprehension of those words in Isaiah, shall
affirm the heavens not to be round.

  That the seas not overflowing the land is a miracle, was
the opinion of Basil[2], Chrysostom[3], Theodoret[4], Ambrose[5],
Nazianzen[6], and since them, Aquinas[7], Luther[8], Calvin,
Marlorate, with sundry others: which they proved from
these scripture expressions: that in Job xxxviii. 8, 11. who
hath shut up the sea with doors, when it brake forth, as if
it had issued out of the womb; when I did break up for it
my decreed place; and set bars, and doors, and said, hi-
therto shalt thou come, and no further, and here shall the
pride of the waves be staid.   So likewise, Prov. viii. 29.
God gave to the sea his decree, that the waters should not
pass his commandment.   And Jerem. v. 22. I have placed
the sand for a bound of the sea by a perpetual decree, that
they cannot pass it; and though the waves thereof toss
themselves, yet can they not prevail; though they roar, yet
can they not pass over, that they turn not again to cover
the earth.   In all which places, say they, it is implied, that

[1] Lib. 3. Comment. in Galat. c. 5.   [2] Homil. 4. Hexam.
[3] Comment. in Job.   [4] In Psal. ciii.   [5] Hexam. l. 3. c. 2, 3 ,
[6] Orat. 34.   [7] Aquinas, part 1. quest. 69. art. 1.
[8] Comment. in Psal. xxiv. item in Psal. cxxxvi. 6.

the water of itself, were it not withheld from its own natural inclination by a more special power of God, would overflow the land.

Others infer the same conclusion from that in Ecclesiastes, where the rivers are said to come from the sea, which they could not do, unless that were higher. I answer: they should as well consider the latter part of that scripture, which says, that the rivers return to that place from whence they came, and then the force of this consequence will vanish. To this purpose some urge that speech of our Saviour, where he bids Simeon to launch forth into the deep*; the Latin word is, *in altum*; from whence they gather, that the sea is higher than the land. But this savours so much of monkish ignorance, that it deserves rather to be laughed at, than to be answered.

But now if we consider the true properties of this element, according to the rules of philosophy, we shall find, that its not overflowing the land is so far from being a miracle, that it is a necessary consequence of its nature; and it would rather be a miracle, if it should be otherwise, as it was in the general deluge. The reason is, because the water of itself must necessarily descend to the lowest place; which it cannot do, unless it be collected in a spherical form, as you may plainly discern in this figure.

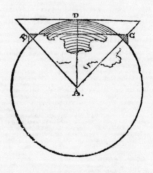

---

* Luke v. 4. Εις το βαθος

Where the sea at D, may seem to be higher than a mountain at B, or C, because the rising of it in the midst, does so intercept our sight from either of those places, that we cannot look in a strait line, from the one to the other. So that it may seem to be no less than a miracle, by which the sea (being a heavy body) was withheld from flowing down to those lower places of B, or C. But now, if you consider that the ascending of a body is its motion from the centre, and descent is its approaching unto it; you shall find, that for the sea to move from D, to B or C, is a motion of ascent, which is contrary to its nature, because the mountains at B, or C, are farther off from the centre, than the sea at D; the lines A B, and A C, being longer than the other A D. So that for the sea to keep always in its channel, is but agreeable to its nature, as being a heavy body. But the meaning of those scriptures is, to set forth the power and wisdom of God; who hath appointed these channels for it, and beset it with such strong banks to withstand the fury of its waves. Or if these men do so much rely in natural points, upon the bare words of scripture, they might easily be confuted from those other places, where God is said to have founded the earth upon the seas, and established it upon the floods. From the literal interpretation of which, many of the ancients have fallen into another error; affirming the water to be in the lower place; and as a basis, whereon the weight of the earth was borne up. Of this opinion were Clemens Alexandrinus *, Athanasius †, Hillary ‡, Eusebius ‖, and others. So that it seems, if a man should resolutely adhere to the bare words of the scripture, he might find contradiction in it; of which the natural meaning is altogether incapable. St. Jerom § tells us of some who would prove stars to have understanding, from that place in Isaiah, xlv. 12. My hands have stretched out the heavens, and all their host have I commanded. Now (say they) none but intelligent creatures are capable

---

* Recog. 8.   † Orat. cont. Idolos.   ‡ In Psal. cxxxvi. 6.
‖ In Psal. xxiv.   § Comment. in Isa. l. 13.

of precepts; and therefore the stars must needs have rational souls. Of this opinion was Philo the Jew*: nay, many of the rabbies conclude, that they do every hour sing praises unto God with an audible real voice †; because of that in Job xxxviii. 7. which speaks of the morning stars singing together. And Psal. xix. 3, 4. where it is said of the heavens, that there is no speech nor language where their voice is not heard, and their words are gone to the ends of the world. And whereas we translate that place in the tenth of Joshua, concerning the standing still of the heavens; the original word, דום does properly signify silence, and according to their opinion, Joshua did only bid them hold their peace. From such grounds it is likely did Origen‡ fetch his opinion, that the stars should be saved. I might set down many other the like instances, were it not for being already weary of raking into the errors of antiquity, or uncovering the nakedness of our forefathers. That excuse of Acosta ‖ may justly serve to mitigate the mistakes of these ancient divines: *facile condonandum est patribus, si cum cognoscendo colendoque creatori toti vacarent, de creatura minus apte aliqua ex parte opinati sunt.* Those good men were so wholly busied about the knowledge and worship of the creator, that they had not leisure enough for an exact search into the essence of the creatures. However, these examples that have been already cited, may sufficiently manifest how frequently others have been deceived, in concluding the points of philosophy from the expressions of scripture. And therefore it is not certain, but that in the present case also, it may be insufficient for such a manner of arguing.

* De plant. Noe.   † Tostatus in Josh. c. 10. quest. 13, 14.
‡ Tom. 1. in Johan.   ‖ De nat. novi orbis, l. 1, c. 2.

PROP. V.

That the scripture, in its proper construction, does not any where affirm the immobility of the earth.

THE same answer which was insisted on before, concerning the conformity of scripture expressions to men's capacity and common opinion, may well enough satisfy all those other arguments, which seem thence to affirm the earth's settledness and immobility; since this is as well agreeable to outward appearance and vulgar apprehension as the other. But now for more full satisfaction, I shall set down the particular places that are urged for it; which being thoroughly examined, we may plainly discern that none of them, in their proper meaning, will serve to infer any such conclusion.

One of these sayings is that of the preacher, Eccles. i. 4. One generation cometh, and another passeth, but the earth endureth for ever; where the original word is, עמד, and the vulgar, *stat*; from whence our adversaries * conclude that it is immoveable.

I answer: the meaning of the word, as it is here applied, is permanent; or as we translate it, endureth. For it is not the purpose of this place to deny all kind of motion to the whole earth, but that of generation and corruption, to which other things in it are liable. And though Pineda and others keep a great deal of impertinent stir about this scripture, yet they grant this to be the natural meaning of it: which you may more clearly discern, if you consider the chief scope of this book; wherein the preacher's intent is, to shew the extraordinary vanity of all earthly contentments, ver. 2. the utter unprofitableness of all a man's labour, ver. 3. and this he illustrates by the shortness and un-

* Vallesius Sacra Phil. c. 62.   Fuller, Miscell. l. 1. c. 15.   Pineda Comment. in locum.

certainty of his life, in which respect he is below many of his fellow creatures, as may be manifested from these four comparisons.

1. From the earth, which though it seem to be but as the sediment of the world, as the rubbish of the creation; yet is this better than man in respect of his lastingness; for one generation passeth away, and another cometh; but the earth that abideth for ever, ver. 4.

2. From the sun; who though he seem frequently to go down, yet he constantly seems to rise again, and shines with the same glory*, ver. 5. but man dieth, and wasteth away, yea, man giveth up the ghost, and where is he? he lieth down, and riseth not till the heavens be no more.

3. From the wind, the common emblem of uncertainty; yet it is more constant than man, for that knows its circuits, and whirleth about continually, ver. 6. whereas our life passeth away as doth the wind, but returneth not again †.

4. From the sea; though it be as uncertain as the moon, by whom it is governed, yet it is more durable than man and his happiness. For though the rivers run into it, and from it, yet it is still of the same quantity that it was at the beginning, ver. 7. but man grows worse as he grows older, and still nearer to a decay, So that in this respect he is much inferior to many other of his fellow creatures.

From whence it is manifest, that this constancy, or standing of the earth, is not opposed to its local motion, but to the changing or passing away of divers men in their several generations. And therefore thence to conclude the earth's immobility were as weak and ridiculous as if one should argue thus: one miller goes, and another comes, but the mill remains still; ergo, the mill hath no motion ‡.

Or thus: one pilate goes, and another comes, but the ship remains still; *ergo*, the ship does not stir.

R. Moses ‖ tells us, how that many of the Jews did from this place conclude, that Solomon thought the earth to be

* Job xiv. 10, 12.   † Psal. lxxviii. 39.
‡ Mr. Carpenter's Geog. l. 1. c. 4.   ‖ Perplex. l. 2. c. 29.

eternal, because he saith it abideth לעולם for ever; and questionless, if we examine it impartially, we shall find that the phrase seems more to favour this absurdity, than that which our adversaries would collect from hence, that it is without motion.

But Mr. Fuller urging this text against Copernicus, tells us, if any should interpret these phrases concerning the earth's standing still, ver. 4. and the sun's motion, ver. 5. in reference only to appearance, and common opinion; he must necessarily also understand those two other verses which mention the motion of the wind and rivers in the same sense. As if he should say; because some things appear otherwise than they are, therefore every thing is otherwise than it appears: or, because scripture speaks of some natural things, as they are esteemed according to man's false conceit, therefore it is necessary that every natural thing mentioned in scripture must be interpreted in the like sense: or, because in one place we read of the ends of a staff, 1 Kings viii. 8. and in many other places of the ends of the earth, and the ends of heaven; therefore the earth and heavens have as properly ends as a staff. It is the very same consequence of that in the objection. Because in this place of Ecclesiastes we read with the rest of the earth, and the motion of the sun; therefore these phrases must needs be understood in the same proper construction as those afterwards, where motion was attributed to the wind and rivers. Which inference you see is so weak, that the objector need not triumph so much in its strength as he doth.

Another proof like unto this is taken from St. Peter, Epist. 2. cap. iii. ver. 5. where he speaks of the earth standing out of the water, and in the water, γη συνεστωσα, and therefore the earth is immoveable.

I answer: it is evident that the word here is equivalent with *fuit*; and the scope of the apostle is to shew, that God made all the earth, both that which was above the water, and that which was under it. So that from this expression, to collect the rest and immobility of the earth, would be such an argument as this other. Such a man made that part of a mill-wheel, or a ship, which stands below the water, and that part which stands above the water; therefore those things are immoveable.

To such vain and idle consequences does the heat of opposition drive our adversaries.

A third argument stronger than either of the former, they conceive may be collected from those scriptures*, where it is said, the world is established, that it cannot be moved.

To which I answer: these places speak of the world in general, and not particularly of our earth; and therefore may as well prove the immobility of the heavens, they being the greatest part of the world; in comparison to which, our earth is but as an insensible point.

If you reply, that the word in these places is to be understood by a synechdoche, as being meant only of this habitable world, the earth:

I answer: first, this is only said, not proved: secondly, David but a little before seems to make a difference between the world and the earth, Psal. xc. 2. where he says, before thou hadst formed the earth and the world. But thirdly, in another place there is the same original word applied expressly to the heavens; and which is yet more, the same place does likewise mention this supposed settledness of the earth, Prov. iii. 19. The Lord by wisdom hath founded the earth; and by understanding hath he established the heavens. So that these places can no more prove an immobility in the earth than in the heavens.

If you yet reply, that by the heavens there is meant the seat of the blessed, which does not move with the rest:

I answer: though by such an evasion a man might possibly avoid the force of this place; yet, first, it is but a groundless shift, because then that verse will not contain a full enumeration of the parts in the world, as may seem more agreeable to the intention of it; but only shew, that God created this earth where we live, and the heaven of

* 1 Chron. xvi. 30. Psal. xciii. 1. item xcvi. 10.

heavens. So that the heaven of the stars and planets shall be shifted out from the number of the other creatures. Secondly, there is another place which cannot be so avoided, Psal. lxxxix. 37. where the Psalmist uses this expression, יכן it shall be established as the moon. So Psal. viii. 4. the moon and the stars, אשר כוננתה which thou hast established. Thus likewise, Prov. viii. 27. when he established the heavens: and in the next verse, our English translation reads it, when he established the clouds. And yet our adversaries will affirm the moon, and stars, and clouds to be subject unto natural motions: why then should the very same expressions be counted as sufficient arguments to take it away from the earth?

If it be replied, that by establishing the heavens, is meant only the holding of them up, that they do not fall down to us (as Lorinus* explains that in the eighth psalm, and quotes Euthymius for the same interpretation;) *fundand' i verbum significat decidere non posse, aut dimoveri a loco ubi collocata sunt.* I answer, why may not we as well interpret the words thus of the earth; so that by establishing of it, is meant only the keeping of it up in the vast places of the open air, without falling to any other place.

From hence it is plain, that these scriptures are to be understood of such an immobility in the earth, as may likewise agree with the heavens: the same original word being so promiscuously applied to both.

Ay, but (you will say) there are some other places which do more peculiarly apply this settledness and establishment to the earth. So Psal. cxix. 90. Thy faithfulness is unto all generations: Thou hast established the earth, and it abideth. Thus likewise, Psal. civ. 5. Who laid the foundations of the earth, that it should not be moved for ever. The latter of which, being well weighed in its original (saith Mr. Fuller†) does in three emphatical words strongly conclude the earth's immobility.

As first, when he says יסד *fundavit*, he hath founded it;

---

* Lorinus Comment. in Psal. viii.　　　† Miscel. l. 1, cap. 15.

wherein it is implied, that it does not change his place. To which may be added all those texts, which so frequently speak of the foundations of the earth; as also that expression of the Psalmist, where he mentions the pillars of the earth, Psal. lxxv. 3.

The second word is מכונה translated basis; and by the Septuagint, επι την ασφαλειαν αυτης; that is, he hath founded it upon its own firmness; and therefore it is altogether without motion.

The third expression is בל־תמוט from the root מוט which signifies, *declinare*; implying, that it could not wag with the least kind of declination.

To these I answer severally:

First, for the word, יסד fundavit, it cannot be understood properly, as if the natural frame of the earth, like other artificial buildings, did need any bottom to uphold it; for he hangeth the earth upon nothing, Job xxvi. 7. But it is a metaphor, and signifies God's placing or situating this globe of land and water. As David tells us of the pillars of the earth; so Job mentions pillars of the heavens, Job xxvi. 11. and yet that will not prove them to be immoveable.

True indeed, we read often concerning the foundations of the earth: but so we do likewise of the ends, sides, and corners of the earth; and yet these scriptures will not prove it to be of a long or square form. Besides, we read also of the foundations of heaven, מוסדות, 2 Sam. xxii. 8. And yet we must not hence infer, that they are without all motion: as also of the planting of the heavens, Isa. li. 6. which may as well prove them to be immoveable, as that which follows in the same verse concerning the foundations of the earth.

Which phrase (if I have observed right) in several places of scripture, is to be understood according to these three interpretations.

1. It is taken sometimes for the lower parts of the earth, as appears by that place, 2 Sam. xxii. 16. The channels of the sea appeared, the foundations of the world were discovered*.

* So Psal. xviii. 15.

2. Sometimes for the beginning and first creation of it. Isa. xl. 2. Hath it not been told you from the beginning, have ye not understood from the foundations of the earth? and in many other places, before the foundation of the world was laid *; that is, before the first creation.

3. Sometimes it signifies the magistrates and chief governors of the earth. So, many interpret that place in Micah, where it is said, vi. 2. Hear O ye mountains the Lord's controversy, and ye strong foundations of the earth. So Psal. lxxxii. 5. The foundations of the earth are out of course; and in Sam. ii. 8. they are called pillars. For the pillars of the earth are the Lord's, and he hath set the world upon them. Hence it is, that the Hebrews derive their word for master, or lord, from a root which signifies a basis or bottom. אדון, ab אדן. And the Greek word for king, does in its primitives import as much as the foundation of the people, βασιλευς, quasi βασις τ8 λα8 †. But now, none of all the several interpretations of this phrase, will in the least manner conduce to the confirmation of the present argument.

As for the second word, מכוניה basis ejus: I answer, the proper signification of it, is locus dispositus, sedes, or statio, an appointed seat or station; and according to this sense, is it most frequently used in scripture. And therefore, the heavens are sometimes called מכין the seat of God's habitation. And for this reason likewise, do Aquila and Symmachus translate it by the word εδρα, a seat or appointed situation, which may as well be attributed to the heavens.

The third expression is בל תמוט, that it should not be moved, from the primitive, מוט, which does not signify barely to move, but declinare, or vacillare, to decline or slip aside from its usual course. Thus is it used by David, Psal. xvii. 5. where he prays, hold up my goings in thy paths, בל נמטו פעמי that my footsteps slide not: he does not mean that his feet should not move. So Psal. cxxi. 3. He will not suffer thy foot to be moved. Thus likewise, Psal.

---

* John xvii. 24. Ephes. i. 4.　　　　† Etymol. mag.

xvi. 8. *Because the Lord is at my right hand, I shall not be moved.* Which last place is translated in the New Testament* by the Greek word σαλευω, which signifies *fluctuare,* or *vacillare,* to be shaken by such an uncertain motion as the waves of the sea. Now as David's feet may have their usual motion, and yet in this sense be said not to move, that is, not to decline or slip aside; so neither can the same phrase applied to the earth, prove it to be immoveable.

Nor do I see any reason, why that of Didacus Astunica † may not be truly affirmed, that we may prove the natural motion of the earth, from that place in Job ix. 6. *Qui commovet terram e loco suo,* as well as its rest and immobility from these.

From all which, it is very evident, that each of these expressions, concerning the founding or establishing both of heaven or earth, were not intended to shew the unmoveableness of either; but rather, to manifest the power and wisdom of providence, who had so settled these parts of the world in their proper situations, that no natural cause could displace them, or make them decline from their appointed course. As for such who do utterly dislike all new interpretation of scripture, even in such matters as do merely concern opinion, and are not fundamental, I would only propose unto them a speech of St. Hierom, concerning some that were of the same mind in his time. *Cum novas semper expetant voluptates, et gulæ eorum vicina maria non sufficiant, cur in solo studio scripturarum, veteri sapore contenti sunt.*

Thus have I in some measure cleared the chief arguments from scripture, against this opinion. For which notwithstanding, I have not thence cited any; because I conceive the holy writ, being chiefly intended to inform us of such things as concern our faith and obedience, we cannot thence take any proper proof for the confirmation of natural secrets.

* Act. ii. 25.   † Comment. in Job,

PROP. VI.

That there is not any argument from the words of scrip-
ture, principles of nature, or observations in astronomy,
which can sufficiently evidence the earth to be in the cen-
tre of the universe.

OUR adversaries do much insult in the strength of those
arguments which they conceive do unanswerably conclude the earth to be in the centre of the world. Whereas,
if they were but impartially considered, they would be
found altogether insufficient for any such conclusion, as
shall be clearly manifested in this following chapter.

The arguments which they urge in the proof of this,
are of three sorts; either such as are taken,

1. From expressions of scripture.
2. From principles of natural philosophy.
3. From common appearances in astronomy.

Those of the first kind are chiefly two: the first is
grounded on that common scripture-phrase, which speaks
of the sun, as being above us. So Solomon often mentioning human affairs, calls them, the works which are
done under the sun *. From whence it appears, that the
earth is below it, and therefore nearer to the centre of the
universe, than the sun.

I answer: Though the sun in comparison to the absolute frame of the world, be in the midst; yet this does not
hinder, but that in respect to our earth, he may be truly
said to be above it; because we usually measure the
height or lowness of every thing, by its being further off,
or nearer unto this centre of our earth. From which,
since the sun is so remote, it may properly be affirmed that
we are under it, though notwithstanding that be in the
centre of the world.

* Eccles i. 14, &c.

A second argument of the same kind, is urged by Fromondus.

It is requisite, that hell (which is in the centre of the earth *) should be most remotely situated from the seat of the blessed.   But now this heaven, which is the seat of the blessed, is concentrical to the starry sphere : and therefore it will follow, that our earth must be in the midst of this sphere ; and so consequently in the centre of the world.

I answer: this argument is grounded upon these uncertainties ;

1. That hell must needs be situated in the centre of our earth.

2. That the heaven of the blessed must needs be concentrical to that of the stars.

3. That places must be as far distant in situation as in use.

Which because they are taken for granted, without any proof, and are in themselves but weak and doubtful, therefore the conclusion (which always follows the worser part) cannot be strong, and so will not need any other answer.

The second sort of arguments taken from natural philosophy, are principally these three.

1. First, from the vileness of our earth, because it consists of a more sordid and base matter than any other part of the world ; and therefore must be situated in the centre, which is the worst place, and at the greatest distance from those purer incorruptible bodies, the heavens.

I answer: this argument does suppose such propositions for grounds, which are not yet proved, and therefore not to be granted.   As,

1. That bodies must be as far distant in places, as in nobility.

2. That the earth is of a more ignoble substance than any of the other planets, consisting of a more base and vile matter.

* Antar. c. 12. item Vesta. tract. 5. c. 2.

3. That the centre is the worst place.

All which are (if not evidently false) yet very uncertain.

2. From the nature of the centre, which is the place of rest, and such as in all circular motions is itself immoveable, and therefore will be the fittest situation for the earth; which by reason of its heaviness, is naturally unfit for motion.

I answer: this argument likewise is grounded upon these two false foundations; as,

1. That the whole frame of nature does move round, excepting only the earth.

2. That the whole earth, considered as whole, and in its proper place, is heavy, or more unfit for a natural motion, than any of the other planets.

Which are so far from being such general grounds from which controversies should be discussed, that they are the very thing in question betwixt us and our adversaries.

3. From the nature of all heavy bodies, which is to fall towards the lowest place. From whence they conclude, that our earth must be in the centre.

I answer: this may prove it to be a centre of gravity, but not of distance, or that it is in the midst of the world. Yea, (but say our adversaries) Aristotle for this urges a demonstration, which must needs be infallible. Thus the motion of light bodies does apparently tend upward towards the circumference of the world: but now the motion of heavy bodies is directly contrary to the ascent of the other; wherefore it will necessarily follow, that these do all of them tend unto the centre of the world.

I answer: though Aristotle were a master in the art of syllogisms, and he from whom we received the rules of disputation; yet in this particular, it is very plain that he was deceived with a fallacy, whilst his argument does suppose that which it does pretend to prove.

That light bodies do ascend unto some circumference which is higher and above the earth, is plain and undeniable. But that this circumference is the same with that of the world, or concentrical unto it, cannot be reasonably affirmed, unless he suppose the earth to be in the centre of the universe, which is the thing to be proved.

I would fain know from what grounds our adversaries can prove, that the descent of heavy bodies is to the centre; or the ascent of light bodies, to the circumference of the world. The utmost experience we can have in this kind, does but extend to those things that are upon our earth, or in the air above it. And alas! what is this unto the vast frame of the whole universe, but punctulum, such an insensible point, which does not bear so great a proportion to the whole, as a small sand does unto the earth. Wherefore it were a senseless thing, from our experience of so little a part, to pronounce any thing infallibly concerning the situation of the whole. The arguments from astronomy, are chiefly these four; each of which are boasted of to be unanswerable.

1. The horizon does every where divide all the great circles of a sphere into two equal parts; so there is always half the equinoctial above it, and half below. Thus likewise, there will constantly be six signs of the zodiac above the horizon, and other six below it. And besides, the circles of the heaven and earth, are each way proportionable to one another; as fifteen German miles on the earth, are every where agreeable to one degree in the heavens; and one hour in the earth, is correspondent to fifteen degrees in the equator. From whence it may be inferred, that the earth must necessarily be situated in the midst of these circles; and so consequently, in the centre of the world.

I answer: this argument does rightly prove the earth to be in the midst of these circles; but we cannot hence conclude, that it is in the centre of the world: from which, though it were never so much distant, yet would it still remain in the midst of those circles, because it is the eye that imagines them to be described about it. Wherefore it were a weak and preposterous collection, to argue thus, that the earth is in the centre of the world, because in the midst of those circles; or because the parts and degrees of the earth are answerable in proportion to the parts and de-

grees in heaven.   Whereas, it follows rather on the contrary, that these circles are equally distant and proportional in
their parts, in respect of the earth, because it is our eye
that describes them about the centre of it.

So that though a far greater part of the world did appear
at one time than at another, yet in respect of those circles
which our eye describes about the earth, all that we could
see at once, would seem to be but a perfect hemisphere;
as may be manifested by this following figure

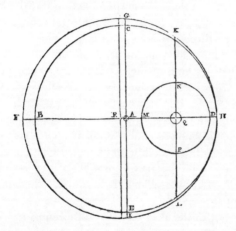

Where if we suppose A to be our earth, B C D E one of
the great circles which we fancy about it, F G H I the orb
of fixed stars, R the centre of them: now though the ark
G F I be bigger than the other G H I, yet notwithstanding,
to the eye on the earth A, one will appear a semicircle as
well as the other; because the imagination does transfer all
those stars into the lesser circle B C D E, which it does
fancy to be described above that centre.   Nay, though
there were a habitable earth at a far greater distance from
the centre of the world, even in the place of Jupiter, as suppose at Q; yet then also would there be the same appearance.   For though the ark K F L in the starry heaven,
were twice as big as the other K H L, yet notwithstanding
at the earth Q they would both appear but as equal hemi-

spheres, being transferred into that other circle M N O P, which is part of the sphere that the eye describes to itself about that earth.

From whence we may plainly discern, that though the earth be never so far distant from the centre of the world, yet the parts and degrees of that imaginary sphere about it, will always be proportional to the parts and degrees of the earth.

2. Another demonstration like unto this former, frequently urged to the same purpose, is this. If the earth be out of the centre of the world, then must it be situated in one of these three positions : either in the equator, but out of the axis; or 2dly, in the axis, but out of the equator; or 3dly, besides both of them. But it is not placed according to any of these situations, therefore must it needs be in the centre *.

1. It is not in the equator, and beside the axis: for then, 1st, there will be no equinox at all in some places, when the days and nights shall be of an equal length; 2dly, the afternoons and forenoons will not be of the same length; because, then our meridian line must divide the hemisphere into unequal parts.

2. It is not in the axis, but out of the equator; for then, first, the equinox would not happen when the sun was in the middle line betwixt the two solstices, but in some other parallel, which might be nearer to one of them, according as the earth did approach to one tropic more than another. Secondly, there would not be such a proportion between the increase and decrease of days and nights, as now there is.

3. It is not besides both of them: for then, all these inconveniencies, and sundry others must with the same necessity of consequence be inferred. From whence it will follow, that the earth must be situated there where the axis and equator meet, which is in the centre of the world.

To this we grant, that the earth must needs be placed

* Vid. Carp. Geog. l. 1. c. 5.

both in the axis and equator; and so consequently, in the centre of that sphere which we imagine about it. But yet this will not prove, that it is in the midst of the universe: for let our adversaries suppose it to be as far distant from that, as they conceive the sun to be; yet may it still be situated in the very concourse of these two lines; because the axis of the world is nothing else, but that imaginary line which passes through the poles of our earth, to the poles of the world. And so likewise the equator is nothing else but a great circle in the midst of the earth, betwixt both the poles, which by imagination is continued even to the fixed stars. Thus also, we may affirm the earth to be in the plane of the zodiac, if by its annual motion it did describe that imaginary circle: and in the plane of the equator, if by its diurnal motion about its own axis, it did make several parallels, the midst of which should be the equator. From whence it appears, that these two former arguments proceed from one and the same mistake; whilst our adversaries suppose the circumference and centre of the sphere, to be the same with that of the world.

Another demonstration of the same kind, is taken from the eclipses of the sun and moon; which would not always happen when these two luminaries are diametrically opposed, but sometimes when they are less distant than a semicircle, if it were so that the earth were not in the centre.

I answer: this argument, if well considered, will be found most directly to infer this conclusion; that in all eclipses, the earth is in such a strait line (betwixt the two luminaries) whose extremities do point unto opposite parts of the zodiac. Now, though our adversaries should suppose (as Copernicus does) the earth to be situated in that which they would have to be the sun's orb, yet would there not be any eclipse, but when the sun and moon were diametrically opposite, and our earth betwixt them; as may clearly be manifested by this figure, where you see the two luminaries in opposite signs: and according as any part of our earth is situated by its diurnal revolution, so will every eclipse be either visible, or not visible unto it.

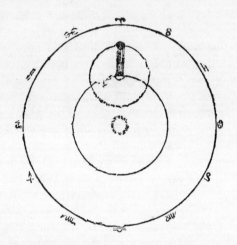

The last and chief argument, is taken from the appearance of the stars; which in every horizon, at each hour of the night, and at all times of the year, seem of an equal bigness*. Now this could not be, if our earth were sometimes nearer unto them by 2000000 German miles, which is granted to be the diameter of that orb wherein the earth is supposed to move.

I answer: this consequence will not hold, if we affirm the earth's orb not to be big enough for the making of any sensible difference in the appearance of the fixed stars.

Yea, but (you will say) it is beyond conceit, and without all reason, to think the fixed stars of so vast a distance from us, that our approaching nearer unto them by 2000000 German miles, cannot make any difference in the seeming quantity of their bodies †.

I reply: there is no certain way to find out the exact distance of the starry firmament; but we are fain to con-

---

* Arist. de cœlo, lib. 2. c. 14.   † Copern. l. 1. cap. 5, 6.

clude of it by conjectures, according as several reasons and observations seem most likely unto the fancies of divers men. Now that this opinion of Copernicus does not make it too big, may be discerned from these following considerations.

The words great and little, are relative terms, and do import a comparison to something else: so that where the firmament, (as it is according to Copernicus) is said to be too big, it is likely that this word is to be understood in reference to some other thing of the same kind, the least of which is the moon's orb. But now if its being so much bigger than this, may be a sufficient reason why it should be thought too great, then it seems that every thing which exceeds another of the same kind in such a proportion, may be concluded to be of too big a quantity; and so consequently, we may affirm that there is no such thing in the world. And hence it will follow, that whales and elephants are mere chimæras, and poetical fictions, because they do so much exceed so many other living creatures. If all this eighth sphere, (saith Galilæus) as great as it is, were a light body, and placed so far from us that it appeared but as one of the lesser stars, we should then esteem it but little; and therefore we have no reason now to thrust it out from being amongst the works of nature, by reason of its too great immensity. It is a frequent speech of our adversaries, Tycho, Fromondus, and others, in excuse of that incredible swiftness which they imagine in their *primum mobile*, that it was requisite the motion of the heavens should have a kind of infinity in it, the better to manifest the infiniteness of the creator. And why may not we as well affirm this concerning the bigness of the heavens? *Difficilius est accidens præter modulum subjecti intendere, quam subjectum sine accidente augere* (saith Keplar.) His meaning is, that it is less absurd to imagine the eighth sphere of so vast a bigness, as long as it is without motion, or at least has but a very slow one; than to attribute unto it such an incredible celerity, as is altogether disproportionable to its bigness.

2. It is the acknowledgment of Clavius*, and might easily be demonstrated, that if the centre were fastened upon the pole of the world, the orb wherein he supposes the sun to move would not be able to reach so far in the eighth sphere (being considered according to Ptolemy's hypothesis) as to touch the pole star; which notwithstanding (saith he) is so near the pole itself, that we can scarce discern it to move: nay, that circle which the pole-star makes about the pole, is above four times bigger than the orb of the sun. So that according to the opinion of our adversaries, though our earth were at that distance from the centre, as they suppose the sun to be, yet would not this eccentricity make it nearer to any one part of the firmament, than the pole-star is to the pole; which according to his confession, is scarce sensible. And therefore according to their opinion, it would cause very little difference in the appearance of those stars, the biggest of which does not seem to be of above five seconds in its diameter.

3. It is considerable, that the spheres of Saturn, Jupiter, Mars, are, according to the general opinion, of very great extension; and yet each of them is appointed only to carry about its particular planet, which are but very little in comparison of the fixed stars. Now if for the situation of these fixed stars, there should be allotted a proportionable part of the world, it is certain that their orb must be far bigger than it is commonly supposed, and very near to this opinion of Copernicus.

4. We usually judge the bigness of the higher orbs by their different motions: as because Saturn finishes his course in thirty years, and Jupiter in twelve, therefore we attribute unto those orbs such a different proportion in their bigness. Now if by this rule we would find out the quantity of the eighth sphere, we shall discern it to be far nearer unto that bigness which Copernicus supposeth it to have, than that which Ptolemy, Tycho, and others ordinarily ascribe unto

---

* Comment. in Sphær. cap. 1.

it: for the starry heaven (say they) does not finish his course under 26000 years; whereas Saturn, which is next unto it, does compass his orb in thirty years. From whence it will probably follow, that there is a very great distance betwixt these in place, because they have such different terms of their revolutions.

But against this answer unto the last argument, our adversaries thus reply :

1. If the fixed stars are so far distant from us, that our approaching nearer unto them by 1000000 German miles, does not make any sensible difference in their appearance ; then Galilæus's perspective could not make them seem of a bigger form than they do to the bare eye, which yet is contrary to common experience *.

2. From hence it may be inferred, that the least fixed star is bigger than all this orb wherein we suppose the earth to move; because there is none of them but are of a sensible bigness in respect of the firmament, whereas this it seems is not †.

3. Since God did at first create the stars for the use of all nations that are under the whole heavens, Deut. iv. 19. it might have argued some improvidence in him, if he had made them of such vast magnitudes; whereas they might as well bestow their light and influences, and so consequently be as serviceable to that end for which they were appointed, if they had been made with less bodies, and placed nearer unto us. And it is a common maxim, that nature in all her operations, does avoid superfluities, and use the most compendious way ‡.

I answer:

1. To the first, whether the perspective do make the fixed stars appear bigger than they do to the bare eye, cannot certainly be concluded, unless we had such an exact glass, by which we might try the experiment. But if in this kind we will trust the authority of others, Keplar ‖ tells

---

* Fromond. Vesta, tract. 5. cap. 1.   † Ibid,   ‡ Ibid.
‖ Astron. Copern. lib. 4, par. 1.

us from the experience of skilful men, that the better
the perspective is, by so much the less will the fixed stars
appear through it, being but as meer points, from which the
beams of light do disperse themselves like hairs. And it is
commonly affirmed by others, that the dog-star, which
seems to be the biggest star amongst those of the first magnitude, does yet appear through this glass but as a little
point no bigger than the fiftieth part of Jupiter. Hence it
is, that though the common opinion hold the stars of the
first magnitude to be two minutes in their diameter, and
Tycho three ; yet Galilæus *, who hath been most versed
in the experiments of his own perspective concludes them
to be but five seconds.

2. To the second : first we affirm, the fixed stars to be of
a vast magnitude. But however, this argument does not
induce any necessity that we should conceive them so big
as the earth's orb. For it might easily be proved, that
though a star of the sixth magnitude were but equal in diameter unto the sun (which is far enough from the greatness of the earth's orb ;) yet the starry heaven would be at
such a distance from us, that the earth's annual motion
could not cause any difference in its appearance.

Suppose the diameter of the sun to be about half a
degree †, as our adversaries grant ; whereas a star of the
sixth magnitude is 50 thirds, which is comprehended in
that of the sun 2160 times. Now if the sun were removed
so far from us, that its diameter would seem but as one of
that number whereof it now contains 2160 ; then must his
distance from us be 2160 times greater than now it is :
which is all one, as if we should say, that a star of the
sixth magnitude is severed from us by so many semidiameters of the earth's orb. But now according to common
consent, the distance of the earth from the sun does contain 128 semidiameters of the earth, and (as was said before) this supposed distance of the fixed stars does comprehend 2160 semidiameters of the earth's orb. From whence
it is manifest, that the semidiameter of the earth, in com-

* System. Mundi. Coll. 3.   † Vid. Gal. ibid.

parison to its distance from the sun, will be almost doubly bigger than the semidiameter of the earth's orb, in comparison to this distance of the stars. But now, the semidiameter of the earth does make very little difference in the appearance of the sun, because we see common observations upon the surface of it, are as exactly true to the sense as if they were made from the centre of it. Wherefore, that difference which would be made in these fixed stars, by the annual course of the earth, must needs be much more unobservable, or rather altogether insensible.

2. The consequence of this argument is grounded upon this false supposition, that every body must necessarily be of an equal extension to that distance from whence there does not appear any sensible difference in its quantity. So that when I see a bird flying such a height in the air, that my being nearer unto it, or farther from it, by ten or twenty foot, does not make it seem unto my eyes either bigger or less; then I may conclude, that the bird must needs be either ten or twenty foot thick: Or when I see the body of a tree that may be half a mile from me, and perceive that my approaching nearer to it by 30 or 40 paces, does not sensibly make any different appearance, I may then infer, that the tree is forty paces thick; with many the like absurd consequences, that would follow from that foundation upon which this argument is bottomed.

To the third I answer: it is too much presumption, to conclude that to be superfluous, the usefulness of which we do not understand. There be many secret ends in these great works of Providence, which human wisdom cannot reach unto; and as Solomon speaks of those things that are under the sun, so may we also of those things that are above it; that no man can find out the works of God; for though a man labour to seek it out, yea further, though a wise man think to know it, yet shall he not be able to find it *. He that hath most insight into the works of nature, is not able to give a satisfying reason, why the

* Eccles. viii. 17.

planets or stars should be placed just at this particular
distance from the earth, and no nearer or farther. And
besides, this argument might as well be urged against the
hypothesis of Ptolemy or Tycho, since the stars, for ought
we know, might have been as serviceable to us, if they had
been placed far nearer, than either of those authors suppose
them. Again, were there any force in such a consequence,
it would as well conclude a great improvidence of nature,
in making such a multitude of those lesser stars, which have
lately been discovered by the perspective. For to what
purpose should so many lights be created for the use of
man, since his eyes were not able to discern them? So
that our disability to comprehend all those ends which
might be aimed at in the works of nature, can be no sufficient argument to prove their superfluity. Though scripture do tell us that these things were made for our use, yet
it does not tell us, that this is their only end. It is not
impossible, but that there may be elsewhere some other
inhabitants, by whom these lesser stars may be more
plainly discerned. And (as was said before) why may not
we affirm that of the bigness, which our adversaries do
concerning the motion of the heavens? That God, to
shew his own immensity, did put a kind of infinity in the
creature.

There is yet another argument to this purpose, urged
by Al. Ross *. which was not referred to any of the former
kind, because I could scarcely believe I did rightly understand it : since he puts it in the front of his other arguments, as being of strength and subtilty enough to be a
leader unto all the rest ; and yet in the most likely sense of
it, it is so extremely simple to be pressed in a controversy,
that every fresh-man would laugh at it. The words of it
are these : *Quod minimum est in circulo debet esse centrum
illius; at terra longe minor est sole, & æquinoctialis terrestris est omnium in cælo circulus minimus ; ergo, &c.*

By the same reason, it would rather follow, that the

* Lib. 1. sect. 2. c. 1.

moon or Mercury were in the centre, since both these are less than the earth. And then, whereas he says that the æquinoctial of the earth is the least circle in the heavens, it is neither true nor pertinent, and would make one suspect, that he who should urge such an argument, did scarce understand any thing in astronomy.

There are many other objections like unto this, not worth the citing: the chief of all have been already answered; by which you may discern, that there is not any such great necessity as our adversaries pretend, why the earth should be situated in the midst of the universe.

PROP. VII.

It is probable that the Sun is in the centre of the world.

THE chief reasons for the confirmation of this truth, are implied in the conveniences of this hypothesis above any other; whereby we may resolve the motions and appearances of the heavens into more easy and natural causes.

Hence will the frame of nature be freed from that deformity which it has according to the system of Tycho; who though he make the sun to be in the midst of the planets, yet without any good reason denies it to be in the midst of the fixed stars; as if the planets, which are such eminent parts of the world, should be appointed to move about a distinct centre of their own, which was beside that of the universe.

Hence likewise are we freed from many of those inconveniences in the hypothesis of Ptolemy, who supposed in the heavens, epicycles and eccentrics, and other orbs, which he calls the deferents of the apoge and perige. As if nature in framing this great engine of the world, had been put unto such hard shifts, that she was fain to make use of wheels and screws, and other the like artificial instruments of motion.

There be sundry other particulars, whereby this opinion concerning the sun's being in the centre, may be strongly evidenced ; which because they relate unto several motions also, cannot therefore properly be insisted on in this place. You may easily enough discern them, by considering the whole frame of the heavens, as they are according to the system of Copernicus , wherein all those probable resolutions that are given for divers appearances amongst the planets, do mainly depend upon this supposition, that the sun is in the centre. Which arguments (were there no other) might be abundantly enough for the confirmation of it. But for the greater plenty, there are likewise these probabilities considerable.

1. It may seem agreeable to reason, that the light which is diffused in several stars, through the circumference of the world, should be more eminently contained, and (as it were) contracted in the centre of it, which can only be by placing the sun there.

2. It is an argument of Clavius *, and frequently urged by our adversaries, That the most natural situation of the sun's body was in the midst, betwixt the other planets ; and that for this reason, because from thence he might more conveniently distribute amongst them both his light and heat. The force of which may more properly be applied to prove him in the centre.

3. It is probable that the planetary orbs (which are special parts of the universe) do move about the centre of the world, rather than about any other centre which is remote from it. But now it is evident that the planets Saturn, Jupiter, Mars, Venus, Mercury, do by their motion encompass the body of the sun. It is likely therefore that this is situated in the midst of the world.

As for the three upper planets, it is found by observation, that they are always nearest to the earth when in opposition to the sun, and farthest from us when in conjunction with it ; which difference is so eminent, that Mars in his perige

* In prim. c. Spher.

does appear sixty times bigger than when he is in the apoge, and at the greatest distance.

Now, that the revolution of Venus and Mercury also is about the sun, may from hence be evidenced: First, because they are never at any great distance from him. Secondly, because they are seen sometimes above, and sometimes below him. Thirdly, because Venus, according to her different situation, does change her appearance as the moon.

4. There is yet another argument, which Aristotle * himself does repeat from Pythagoras. The most excellent body should have the best place; but the sun is the most excellent body, and the centre is the best place; therefore it is likely the sun is in the centre. In the frame of nature (which is supposed to be of an orbicular form) there are but two places of any eminency, the circumference and the centre. The circumference being of so wide a capacity, cannot so fitly be the peculiar seat of a body, that is so little in respect of it: and besides, that which is the most excellent part of the world, should be equally preserved in itself, and shared in its virtues by all the other parts, which can only be done by its being placed in the midst of them. This is intimated unto us in that frequent speech of Plato, that the soul of the world does reside in the innermost place of it; and that in Macrobius †, who often compares the sun in the world to the heart in a living creature.

Unto this Aristotle answers by a distinction: there is *medium magnitudinis,* so the centre is the middle of a sphere, and there is *medium naturæ,* or *informationis,* which is not always the same with the other; for in this sense the heart is the middle of a man; because from thence (saith he) as from the centre, the vital spirits are conveyed to all the members: and yet we know that it is not the centre of magnitude, or at an equal distance from all the other parts.

And besides, the middle is the worst place, because most circumscribed, since that is more excellent which does

* De Cœlo, l. 2. c. 13.   † Saturnal. l. 1. c. 17, &c.

limit any thing, than that which is bounded by it.   For this reason is it, that matter is amongst those things which are terminated, and form, that which does circumscribe.

But against this answer of Aristotle, it is again replied :

1. Though it be true, that in living creatures the best and chiefest part is not placed always just in the midst, yet this may be, because they are not of an orbicular form, as the world is *.

2. Though that which bounds another thing be more excellent than that which is terminated by it, yet this does not prove the centre to be the worst place, because that is one of the terms or limits of a round body, as well as the circumference.

There are likewise other arguments to this purpose, much insisted on by eminent astronomers †, taken from that harmonical proportion which there may be betwixt the several distance and bigness of the orbs, if we suppose the sun to be in the centre.

For according to this (say they) we may conceive an excellent harmony both in the number and the distance of the planets : (and if God made all other things *numero &* *mensurá*, much more then those greater works, the heavens) ; for then the five mathematical bodies, so much spoken of by Euclid ‡, will bear in them a proportion answerable to the several distances of the planets from one another.

Thus a cube will measure the distance betwixt Saturn and Jupiter ; a pyramis or tetraëdron, the distance betwixt Jupiter and Mars ; a dodecaëdron, the distance betwixt Mars and the earth ; an icosaëdron, the distance betwixt the earth and Venus ; and an octaëdron the distance betwixt Venus and Mercury ; that is, if we conceive a circumference described immediately without the cube, and another within it, the distance between these two will shew what proportional distance there is betwixt the orb of Saturn and that of

---

* Keplar, Astr. Copern. l. 4. part 2.

† Mæslin. præ. ad Narrat. Rhetici, Keplar, Mysterium Cosmographicum.

‡ Lib. 13. prop. 14, 15, &c.

Jupiter. Thus also if you conceive a circumference described on the outside of a pyramis or tetraedron, and another within it, this will shew such a proportional distance as there is betwixt the orb of Mars from that of Jupiter. And so of the rest.

Now if any ask why there are but six planetary orbs? Keplar answers: *Quia non oportet plures quàm quinque proportiones esse, totidem nempè quot regularia sunt in mathesi corpora. Sex autèm termini consummant hunc proportionum numerum.* Because there are but five proportions, so many as there are regular bodies in mathematics, each of whose sides and angles are equal to one another. But now there are six terms required to consummate this number of proportions; and so consequently, there can be but six primary planets.

Thus likewise by placing the sun in the centre, we may conceive such a proportion betwixt the bodies of the planets, as will be answerable unto their several spheres: then Mercury, which has the least orb, will have the least body; Venus bigger than that, but less than any of the other; our earth bigger than Venus, but less than the rest; Mars bigger than the earth, but less than Jupiter; Jupiter bigger than Mars, and less than Saturn; Saturn being the highest, should also be the biggest. All which harmony would be disturbed by putting in the sun amongst them; and therefore it may be more convenient for him to sit still in the centre.

There are sundry other arguments in this kind to be found out, by a consideration of this whole hypothesis: He that does rightly understand it, may therein easily discern many strong probabilities, why the sun should be in the midst of the world, rather than in any other position.

PROP. VIII.

That there is not any sufficient reason to prove the earth incapable of those motions which Copernicus ascribes unto it.

THE two chief motions in the world, which are more especially remarkable above the rest, are the diurnal, and annual.

The diurnal, which makes the difference betwixt night and day, is caused by the revolution of our earth upon its own axis, in the space of four and twenty hours.

The annual, which makes the difference betwixt winter and summer, is likewise caused by the earth, when being carried through the ecliptic in its own orb, it finishes its course in a year.

The first is usually stiled, *motus revolutionis:* the second, *motus circumlationis:* there is likewise a third, which Copernicus calls, *motus inclinationis:* but this being thoroughly considered, cannot properly be stiled a motion, but rather an immutability, it being that whereby the axis of the earth does always keep parallel to itself, from which situation it is not his annual course that does make it in the least manner to decline.

As for the difficulties which concern the second of these, they have been already handled in the sixth proposition, where the earth's eccentricity was maintained.

So that the chief business of this chapter, is to defend the earth's diurnal motion, against the objections of our adversaries. Sundry of which objections, to speak (as the truth is) do bear in them a great shew of probability, and such too (as it seems) was very efficacious; since Aristotle and Ptolemy, &c. Men of excellent parts and deep judgments did ground upon them, as being of infallible and necessary consequence.

I shall reckon them up severally, and set down such answers unto each, as may yield some satisfaction to every indifferent seeker of truth.

1. First then, it is objected from our senses ; if the earth did move, we should perceive it. The western mountains would then appear to ascend towards the stars, rather than the stars to descend below them.

I answer : the sight judges of motion according as any thing does desert the plain whereon itself is seated ; which plain everywhere keeping the same situation and distance, in respect of the eye, does therefore seem immoveable unto it, and the motion will appear in those stars and parts of the heaven, through which the vertical line does pass.

The reason of such deceit may be this : motion being not a proper object of the sight, nor belonging to any other peculiar sense, must therefore be judged of by the *sensus communis*, which is liable to mistake in this respect ; because it apprehends the eye itself to rest immoveable, whilst it does not feel any effects of this motion in the body : as it is when a man is carried in a ship ; so that sense is but an ill judge of natural secrets. It is a good rule of Plato, Εις τον νεν αφοραν δει Φιλοσοφον και μη εις την οψιν : a philosopher must not be carried away by the bare appearance of things to sight, but must examine them by reason. If this were a good consequence, the earth does not move, because it does not appear so to us, we might then as well argue, that it does move when we go upon the water, according to the verse :

Provehimur portu, terræque, urbesque recedunt.

Or if such arguments would hold, it were an easy matter to prove the sun and moon not so big as a hat, or the fixed stars as a candle.

Yea, but if the motion of the heavens be only apparent, and not real, then the motion of the clouds will be so too, since the eye may be as well deceived in the one as the other *.

I answer : it is all one, as if he should infer that the sense was mistaken in every thing, because it was so in one

* Al. Ross. l. 1. sect. 1. c. 1.

thing: and this would be an excellent argument to prove that opinion of Anaxagoras, that the snow was black.

The reason why that motion which is caused by the earth does appear as if it were in the heavens, is, because the *sensus communis* in judging of it, does conceive the eye to be itself immoveable (as was said before) there being no sense that does discern the effects of any motion in the body; and therefore it does conclude every thing to move, which it does perceive to change its distance from it: so that the clouds do not seem to move sometimes, when as notwithstanding they are everywhere carried about with our earth, by such a swift revolution; yet this can be no hindrance at all, why we may not judge aright of their other particular motions, for which there is not the same reason. Though to a man in a ship, the trees and banks may seem to move, yet it would be but a weak argument, to conclude from hence, that therefore such a one could not tell whether his friend does really stir, whom he sees to walk up and down in the ship: or that he might as well be deceived in judging the oars to move when they do not

It is again replied by the same objector *, that it is not credible the eye should be mistaken in judging of the stars and heavens; because those being light bodies, are the primary and proper objects of that sense.

I answer: the deceit here is not concerning the light or colour of those bodies, but concerning their motion; which is neither the primary nor proper object of the eye, but reckoned amongst the *objecta communia*.

2. Another common argument against this motion, is taken from the danger that would thence arise, unto all high buildings, which by this would quickly be ruinated, and scattered abroad.

I answer: this motion is supposed to be natural; and those things which are according to nature, have contrary effects to other matters, which are by force and violence †. Now it belongs unto things of this latter kind to be incon-

---

* Al. Ross. l. 1. sect. 1. c. 1.   † Coper. l. 1. c. 8.

sistent and hurtful; whereas those of the first kind must be regular, and tending to conservation. The motion of the earth is always equal and like itself; not by starts and fits. If a glass of beer may stand firmly enough in a ship, when it moves swiftly upon a smooth stream, much less then will the motion of the earth, which is more natural, and so consequently more equal, cause any danger unto those buildings that are erected upon it. And therefore to suspect any such event, would be like the fear of Lactantius, who would not acknowledge the being of any antipodes, lest then he might be forced to grant that they should fall down unto the heavens *. We have equal reason to be afraid of high buildings, if the whole world above us were whirled about with such a mad celerity as our adversaries suppose; for then there would be but small hopes that this little point of earth should escape from the rest.

But supposing (saith Rosse †) that this motion were natural to the earth, yet it is not natural to towns and buildings, for these are artificial.

To which I answer: ha, ha, he.

3. Another argument to this purpose is taken from the rest and quietness of the air about us; which could not be, if there were any such swift motion of the earth. If a man riding upon a fleet horse, do perceive the air to beat against his face, as if there were a wind, what a vehement tempest should we continually feel from the east, if the earth were turned about with such a swift revolution as is supposed.

Unto this it is usually answered, that the air also is carried along with the same motion of the earth: for if the concavity of the moon's orb, which is of so smooth and glabrous a superficies, may (according to our adversaries) drive along with it the greatest part of this elementary world, all the regions of fire, and all the vast upper regions of air, and (as some will have it) the two lower regions, together with the sea likewise; for from hence (saith Alex. Rosse, l. 1. sect. 1. c. 3.) is it, that betwixt the tropics there is a constant

* Gilbert de Magn. l. 6. c. 5.   † Lib. 1. sect. 1. c. 3.

eastern wind, and a continual flowing of the sea westward :
I say, if the motion of the heavens, which are smooth bodies, may be able to carry with it so great a part of the elementary world: or if the rugged parts of the moon's body
be able to carry with it so great a part of the air, as Fromondus (Ant. c. 16.) affirms; much more then may our
earth, which is a rugged mountainous body, be able to turn
about so little a part of the world, as that vaporous air next
unto it.

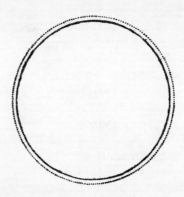

Suppose the inward circle to represent the earth ; and
the outward the thicker air, which encompasses it.   Now
it is easily conceivable, that the revolution of so great a
body as this globe of earth, may turn about by its mere
motion (if there were nothing else) so little a part of the
adjoining air, as is here represented : and yet,

1. The disproportion betwixt the thickness of the earth,
and this orb of air, is far greater than could be expressed in
the figure, being but as twenty miles; which is at most the
thickness of this air, unto 3456 miles, which is the semidiameter of our earth, and so is but as an insensible number
in respect of this other.

2. Besides the mere motion of the earth, which in probability (being such a rugged body) might be enough to carry
so little a part of the air along with it; there is also (as we
suppose) a magnetical vigour which proceeds from it,

whereby it is more able to make all things that are near
unto it, to observe the same revolution.

But if it be so (saith Alex. Ross *.) that not only the
man, but the medium also, and the object be moved: this
must needs be such a great hindrance to the sight, that the
eye cannot judge exactly of any thing. For, suppose the
man alone to be in a motion, he could not see so well as
when he is still; but now if not only he, but his spectacles
and book were all moved, he would not be able to discern
any thing distinctly.

I answer: the consequence were pertinent, if all these
were several motions; but if the subject, and medium, and
object, were all carried with one and the same equal motion, (as it is here supposed) this could be no impediment
to the act of seeing, but it would be all one with the rest;
because by this means, they are not severed from one another, and therefore the species are not disturbed. It is an
excellent saying of Galilæus †, and may serve for the resolution of many such doubts as these: *motus eatenus tanquam motus operatur, quatenus relationem habet ad eas res
quæ ipso distituuntur, in iis vero rebus, quæ totæ æqualiter
de eo participant, nihil operatur, et ita se habet ac si nullus
esset.* If a man be within some room of a ship, he may
read altogether as easily when the ship moves, as when it
stands still.

4. Another argument against this circular motion of the
earth, is grounded upon that common principle amongst
the Aristotelians: *unius corporis simplicis unus tantum est
motus.* One kind of body has but one kind of motion.
But now the earth and water has a motion of descent; the
air a motion of ascent; and therefore none of them can
have any circular motion natural unto them.

I answer: first, these right motions of elementary bodies
belong only to the parts of them, and that too when they
are out of their proper places; so that the whole to which
they belong, may notwithstanding this, have another mo-

* Lib. 1 sect. 1. cap. 5.   † Syst. Mundi, Colloq. 2.

tion of its own.   But secondly, this saying which Aristotle calls a principle, will not consist with other evident experiments of nature.   Thus, though a loadstone, in respect of its matter and condensity, naturally tends downward; yet this does not hinder, but that in respect of some other qualities, as its desire of union and coition to another loadstone, it may also naturally move upwards.   From whence it will follow, that the same elementary body may have divers natural motions.

5. The gravity and magnitude of this earthy globe do make it altogether unfit for so swift a motion.

I answer: first, heaviness can only be applied unto those bodies which are out of their proper places, or unto such parts as are severed from the whole to which they belong. And therefore the globe of earth, (considered as whole, and in its right place) cannot truly be called heavy.   I deny not, but that there is in it, and so likewise in the other planets, an ineptitude to motion, by reason of the matter and condensity of their bodies: and so likewise there is as truly (though not according to the same degrees) in the least particle of a material condensed substance: so that this cannot reasonably be pretended as a just impediment, why the earth should be incapable of such a motion.   Secondly, and though this globe be of so vast a magnitude, yet as nature bestows upon other creatures (for instance, an eagle and a fly) spirits, and motive powers, proportionable to their several bodies; so likewise may she endow the earth with a motive faculty answerable to its greatness.   Or if this may make the earth incapable of so swift a motion as is supposed, much more then will the heavens be disabled for that greater swiftness which is imagined in them.   I might add, the globe of the sun and Jupiter are observed to move about their own centres; and therefore the earth, which is far less than either of them, is not, by reason of its too great magnitude, made unfit for such a revolution.   Thirdly: as for the swiftness of the earth's course, it does not exceed (all circumstances well considered) the celerity of some other motions, with which we are acquainted; as that of the clouds, when driven by a tempestuous wind; that of a bullet shot from a cannon, which in the space of a minute does fly four miles*: or as another hath observed, in the second scruple of an hour it may pass the fifteenth part of a German mile. Than which, there is not any point in the earth's equinoctial that moves faster: and though a bullet be much slower in moving a greater distance, yet for so little a space, while the force of the powder is most fresh and powerful, it does equal the swiftness of the earth. And yet,

1. A bullet or cloud is carried in its whole body, being fain to break its way through the air round about it: but now the earth, (in respect of this first motion) does remain still in the same situation, and move only about its own centre.

2. The motion of a bullet is violent, and against its nature, which does strongly incline it to move downwards: whereas the earth, being considered as whole, and in its proper place, is not heavy, nor does it contain any repugnancy to a circular motion.

6. The chief argument on which our adversaries do most insist, is this. If there were such a motion of the earth as is supposed, then those bodies which are severed from it in the air, would be forsaken by it †. The clouds would seem to rise and set as the stars: the birds would be carried away from their nests: no heavy body could fall perpendicular: an arrow or bullet being shot from east to west by the same violence, will not be carried an equal distance from us, but we should by the revolution of our earth, overtake that which was shot to the east, before it could fall. If a man leaping up, should abide in the air but one second scruple of an hour, or the sixtieth part of a minute, the earth in that space would withdraw itself from him almost a quarter of a mile. All these, and many other such strange inferences, which are directly contrary to sense and experience, would follow from this motion of the earth.

* Meslin præfat. ad Narrat. Rhet. Fromond. Vesta. tract. 1. cap. 3.
† Arist. de Cælo, lib. 2. cap. 13.

There are three several ways most frequently used for the resolving of these kind of doubts.

1. From those magnetical qualities, which all elementary bodies do partake of.

2. From the like motion of other things, within the room of a sailing ship.

3. From the like participation of motion in the open parts of a ship.

1. For those magnetical properties, with which all these bodies are endowed. For the better understanding of this, you must know, that besides those common elementary qualities of heat, coldness, dryness, moisture, &c. which arise from the predominancy of several elements, there are likewise other qualities (not so well known to the ancients) which we call magnetical, of which every particle in the terrestrial globe does necessarily participate: and whether it be joined to this globe by continuity or contiguity, or whether it be severed from it, as the clouds in the second region, a bird, or bullet in the air; yet does it still retain its magnetical qualities, together with all those operations that proceed from them.

Now from these properties, do we suppose the circular motion of the earth to arise.

If you ask what probabilities there are, to prove that the earth is endowed with any such affections; I answer: it is likely, that the lower parts of this globe do not consist of such a soft fructifying earth, as there is in the surface, (because there can be no such use for it, as here, and nature does nothing in vain,) but rather of some hard rocky substance; since we may well conceive, that these lower parts are pressed close together by the weight of all those heavy bodies above them. Now it is probable, that this rocky substance is a loadstone, rather than a jaspis, adamant, marble, or any other; because experience teacheth us, that the earth and loadstone do agree together in so many properties. Suppose a man were to judge the matter of divers bodies, each of which should be wrapt up in some covering from his eye, so that he might only examine them by

some other outward signs: if in this examination he should
find any particular body which had all the properties that
are peculiar to a loadstone, he should in reason conclude it
to be of that nature, rather than any other.   Now there is
altogether as much reason why we should infer, that the
inward parts of the earth do consist of a magnetical substance.   The agreement of these two you may see largely
set forth in the treatise of D. Gilbert.   I will instance only
in one example; which of itself may sufficiently evidence,
that the globe of earth does partake of the like affections
with the loadstone.   In the mariners needle you may observe the magnetical motions of direction, variation, declination, the two last of which are found to be different, according to the variety of places.   Now this difference cannot proceed from the needle itself, because that is the same
every where.   Nor can we well conceive how it should be
caused by the heavens; for then the variation would not be
always alike in the same place, but diverse, according to
those several parts of the heaven, which at several times
should happen to be over it: and therefore it must necessarily proceed from the earth, which being itself endowed
with magnetical affections, does diversly dispose the motions
of the needle, according to the difference of that disponent
virtue which is in its several parts.

Now to apply this unto the particular instances of the objection; we say, though some parts of this great magnet,
the earth, may according to their matter be severed from
the whole; yet are they always joined to it by a communion
of the same magnetical qualities; and do no less observe
these kind of motions, when they are separated from the
whole, than if they were united to it.   Nor need this seem
incredible, that a heavy bullet, in such a swift violent course,
should be able to observe this magnetical revolution of the
whole earth; when as we see that those great bodies of
Saturn, Jupiter, &c. hanging in the vast spaces of the æthereal air, do so constantly and regularly move on, in their
appointed courses.   Though we could not shew any simi-

litude of this motion in these inferior bodies, with which we are acquainted; yet we must know, there may be many things which agree to the whole frame, that are not discernible in the divers parts of it. It is natural unto the sea to ebb and flow; but yet there is not this motion in every drop or bucket of water. So if we consider every part of our bodies severally, the humours, bones, flesh, &c. they are all of them apt to tend downwards, as being of a condensed matter; but yet consider them according to the whole frame, and then the blood or humours may naturally ascend upwards to the head, as well as descend to any of the lower parts. Thus the whole earth may move round, though the several parts of it have not any such particular revolution of their own. Thus likewise, though each condensed body being considered by itself, may seem to have only a motion of descent; yet in reference to that whole frame of which it is a part, it may also partake of another motion that may be natural unto it.

But some may here object; though the earth were endowed with such magnetical affections, yet what probability is there that it should have such a revolution? I answer; it is observed of those other magnetical bodies of Saturn, Jupiter, and the sun, that they are carried about their own centres; and therefore it is not improbable, but that it may be so with the earth also; which if any deny, he must shew a reason why in this respect they should be unlike.

Yea, but though the earth did move round, what ground is there to affirm that those bodies which are severed from it, as a bullet, or the clouds, should follow it in the same course?

I answer; those spots which are discovered about the sun, and are thought to be clouds or evaporations from his body, are observed to be carried about according to his revolution. Thus the moon is turned round by our earth; the four lesser planets by the body of Jupiter. Nay, thus all the planets in their several orbs, are moved about by the revolution of the sun, upon its own axis, (saith Keplar;) and therefore much more may an arrow or bullet be carried round by the magnetical motion of our earth.

The second way, whereby some answer unto the instances of this argument, is, by shewing the like motions of other things within some room of a sailing ship. Thus experience teaches (say they) that a candle, as also the fumes that come from it, will always keep the same situation in the swiftest motion of a ship, as if it did rest immoveably, and the flame will not more especially bend one way, or have any troubled fluctuation; but burn as strait and quietly, as if it did stand still. Again, it has been found (say those that have been versed in these kind of experiments,) that the same force will cast a body but at an equal distance, whether or no the body do move with, or against the motion of the ship. As also that any weight being let fall, will descend in as true a perpendicular, as if the ship did stand still. If a man leaping up, do tarry in the air one second minute of an hour; yet the ship will not in its greatest swiftness (as it should according to the calculation of our adversaries) be carried from him at least fifteen foot. If we suppose a man to jump in such a ship, he will not be able to pass farther, when he jumps against the motion of it, than when he jumps with it. All which particulars may argue, that these things are carried along together, by the common motion of the ship. Now if bodies may be thus jointly moved by such a preternatural motion, much more then will they accompany the earth in its diurnal revolution, which we suppose to be natural unto them, and as a law imposed by God in their first creation.

If the flame of a candle, or the smoke that comes from it, (things that are so easily moveable) are notwithstanding carried so equally, and without any disturbance, by the motion of a ship; then also the clouds in the air, and all other light bodies, may well enough be turned about by the revolution of our earth.

If an equal force will cast an heavy body but at an equal distance, whether or no it move with, or against the motion of the ship; then may we easily conceive, that an arrow or bullet being shot with the same violence, will pass but the same space on the earth, whether or no it be shot towards the east or west.

If a heavy body, while the ship does move, will fall down in a strait line, then it is not the revolution of our earth that can hinder a perpendicular descent.

If a man leaping up in a ship, may abide in the air one second scruple of an hour, and yet this ship in its greatest swiftness not withdraw itself fifteen foot; then will not the earth in that space go from him almost a quarter of a mile.

But against this it is objected, that the earth has the similitude of an open ship, and not of any room that is close*. And though it be true, that when the roof and the walls do all move together, the air which is included betwixt them, must be carried along by the same motion; yet it is not so with the earth, because that hath not any such walls or roof, wherein it may contain and carry along with it the medium. And therefore experience will rather argue against this supposed revolution. Thus it is observed, that a stone being let fall from the mast of a ship that moves swiftly, will not descend to the same point, as if the ship did stand still. From whence it will follow, that if our earth had such a circular motion, then any heavy body being let fall from some high tower, or other steep place, would not descend unto that point of earth which was directly under it at the beginning.

To this we answer; that the air which moves along with our earth, is as well limited in certain bounds, as that which is included in a room. If you ask where these bounds are terminated; I answer, neither by the utmost parts of the world, nor yet by the concavity of the moon's orb (as Fromondus would have us affirm;) but by the sphere of vaporous air that encompasses our earth; or which is all one, by the orb of magnetical vigour, which proceeds from it. And besides, it is considerable that all earthly bodies are

* Fromondus. Vest. Tract. 2. cap. 2.

not only contained within these limits, as things are in a close room, but also as parts in that whole to which they belong.

2. Though the carrying along of the medium may solve the motion of light bodies in a ship, as the flame of a candle, smoke, or the like; yet this cannot concur to that which hath been said of heavy bodies, as a man leaping up, a bullet descending, &c. since it is not the motion of the mere air that is able to make these partake of the same motion with the ship.   Unto that argument which he urges from the experiment of a stone falling in an open ship, we answer:

1. Though the instance of a ship may serve as a proof for this opinion, it being an argument *a minori ad majus*, from an accidental motion to a natural; yet it will not serve against it.   For though it were not thus in accidental motions; yet this would not hinder but that it might be so in those that are supposed to be proper and natural.

2. As for that experiment itself, it is but a groundless imagination, and was never yet confirmed by any particular experience; because it is certain the event would be clean otherwise, as shall be proved in the third way of answering.

3. The third and last way of clearing the doubts in the sixth argument, is by shewing the like participation of motion, in those things that are in the open parts of a ship. To which purpose Galilæus* urges this experiment: If any one should let fall a stone from an high mast, he would find *lapidem in eundem semper navis locum decidere, seu consistat illa, seu quantacunque velocitate moveatur:* that the stone would always descend unto the very same place, whether or no the ship did move or stand still.   The reason of which is, because the motion of the ship is likewise impressed in the stone: which impression is not equally prevalent in a light body, as a feather, or wool, because the air which has power over them, is not carried along by

* Syst. Mund. Colloq. 2.

the same motion of the ship. Thus likewise will it be in this other experiment: if a man upon a running horse should in his swiftest course let fall a bullet or stone, these heavy bodies, besides their own descent, would also participate that transverse motion of the horse. For as those things that are thrown from us, do continue their motion when they are out of the hand in the open air; so likewise must it be when the force is conferred by that motion which the arm has from the horse. While a man is riding, his arm is also carried by the same swiftness of the horse; therefore, if he should only open his hand and let fall any thing, it would not descend in a strait line, but must necessarily be driven forward, by reason of that force impressed in it by the swiftness of the horse, which is also communicated to the arm; it being all one in effect, whether or no the arm be moved by a particular motion of its own, as it is in casting of things from us; or by the common motion of the body, as it is in dropping of any thing from us, either when we are on the top of some sailing ship, as in the former; or on some running horse, as in this latter instance.

What hath been said concerning the motion of descent, is likewise appliable, both to that which is upward, and that which is transversal. So that when it is objected, if the earth did move, then a bullet that were shot up perpendicularly would be forsaken by it, and not descend to the place from whence it arose: we answer, that the cannon which is upon the earth, together with the bullet in it, do partake of the same circular motion with the earth; and this perhaps our adversaries will grant, whilst we suppose the bullet to remain still in the cannon; all the difficulty will be to shew how it must necessarily observe the same motion, when it is shot out into the open air*. For the better explication of this, you may note this following figure.

* Gall. Syst. Colloq. 2.

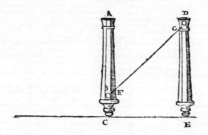

Where we suppose A C to be a cannon perpendicularly, erected with a bullet in it at B, which if it were immove-able, we grant that the bullet being discharged, must ascend in a just perpendicular. But now conceive this cannon to move along with the earth, then in that space of time while the bullet by the force of the powder is ascending to the top of the bore, the cannon will be transferred to the situation D E; so that the bullet must be moved according to the line F G, which is not directly upright, but somewhat declining. Now the motion of the bullet in the air, must necessarily be conformed unto that direction that is impressed in it by the cannon from whence it is shot, and so consequently it must be continued according to the line F G, and therefore will always keep perpendicularly over the point from which it did ascend.

If you reply, that the motion of the bullet in the cannon must needs be so swift, that the earth cannot carry the cannon from C to E, in the same space of time wherein the bullet does move from B to A. I answer; it is not material whether the earth be of a greater or lesser swiftness than the bullet, because the declination must always be proportionable to the motion of the earth; and if we suppose this to be slower than the bullet, then the declination of the line F G, will be so much the less.

This truth may yet farther be illustrated by the practice of those fowlers, who used to kill birds as they are flying :

concerning which art, it is commonly thought that these men direct their aims to some certain space in the air, just before the birds, where they conceive the bullet will meet with them in their flight; whereas the truth is, they proceed in this case, the very same way, as if the birds did stand still, by a direct aiming at their bodies, and following of their flight by the motion of the piece, till at length, having got a perfect aim, they discharge, and do hit altogether as surely, as if the birds were sitting upon a tree. From whence we may observe, that the motion of the piece, as in our aiming it is made to follow the birds in their flight (though it be but slow,) yet is communicated to the bullet in the air.

But here it may seem very difficult to give any reason according to those grounds concerning the flight of birds; which being animated, have a liberty to fly here or there, to tarry for a good space of time in the open air, and so it is not easy to conceive what means there is, by which they should participate of the earth's diurnal revolution.

To this Galilæus answers, that the motion of the air, as it does turn about the clouds, so doth it also carry with it the birds, together with such other like things that are in it. For if some violent wind be able to drive with such swiftness a full laden ship, to throw down towers, to turn up trees, and the like; much more then may the diurnal motion of the air, (which does so far exceed in swiftness the most tempestuous wind) be able to carry with it the bodies of birds.

But if all things be turned about by this revolution, then it should seem there is no such thing as a right motion, whether of ascent, or descent in a strait line.

I answer; the moving of heavy or light bodies, may be considered in a double relation.

1. According to the space wherein they move, and we grant their motions not to be simple, but mixed of a direct and circular.

2. According to the body or medium wherein they move, and then they may properly be said to have right

motions, because they pass through the medium in a strait
line; and therefore it is, that unto us they seem directly to
ascend or descend.   Aristotle himself would not deny, but
that fire may ascend in a strait line unto its sphere; and yet
participate also of that circular motion which he supposes
to be communicated from the heaven, unto the upper part
of the air, and its own region.   So likewise must it be for
the descent of any thing.   Suppose a ship in its swiftest
motion, and a man in it, having some vessel filled with
water, should let fall into it a little ball of wax, or some
other matter which may be slow in its sinking, so that in
one minute it should scarce descend the space of a cubit,
though the ship (it may be) in the same time may pass at
least a hundred cubits; yet would this still seem unto the
eye to descend in a strait line; and the other motion which
is communicated unto it by the ship, would not at all be
discernible in it.   And though in this case, the motion
were in itself composed of a circular and direct; yet in respect of us it would appear, and so might be stiled, exactly
strait.

   Now if it be thus in those which are generally granted to
be preternatural motions; we need not doubt then the
possibility of the like effect in that motion which we conceive to be proper and natural, both to the earth, and the
things that belong unto it.

   There is yet another objection to this purpose urged by
Malapertius *, a late jesuit; who, though he do with much
eagerness press this argument concerning a bullet or stone,
against the opinion of Copernicus; yet he grants that it
might easily be resolved, if the defenders of it would affirm
that the air did move round with the earth.   But this, says
he, they dare not avouch; for then the comets would always seem to stand still, being carried about with the revolution of this air; and then they could not rise or set, as
experience shews they do.

   To this it may be answered, that most comets are above

that sphere of air which is turned round with our earth, as
is manifest by their height. The motion that appears in
them, is caused by the revolution of our earth, whereby we
are turned from them.

As for those which are within the orb of our air, these
do seem to stand still. Such a one was that mentioned by
Josephus*, which did constantly hang over Jerusalem; and
that likewise which appeared about the time of Agrippa's
death, and for many days together did hang over the city
of Rome. Wherefore Seneca† does well distinguish out
of Epigenes, betwixt two sorts of comets; the one being
low, and such as seem immoveable, the other higher, and
such as did constantly observe their risings and settings, as
the stars.

I have done with all the arguments of any note or difficulty, that are urged against this diurnal motion of the
earth. Many other cavils there are, not worth the naming,
which discover themselves to be rather the objections of a
captious, than a doubtful mind. Amongst which, I might
justly pass over those that are set down by Alex. Rosse‡.
But because this author does proceed in his whole discourse
with so much scorn and triumph, it will not be amiss therefore to examine what infallible evidence there is in those
arguments upon which he grounds his boastings.

We have in one chapter no less than these nine.

1. If the earth did move, then would it be hotter than
the water, because motion does produce heat: and for this
reason likewise, the water would be so hot and rarified,
that it could not be congealed; since that also does partake
of the same motion with the earth.

2. The air which is next the earth, would be purer, as
being rarified with motion.

3. If the earth did move the air, it would cause some
sound; but this is no more audible, than Pythagoras's harmony of the heavens.

De bello Judaico, l. 7. cap. 12.   Dion. l. 54.
† Nat. Qu. lib. 7. cap. 6.   ‡ Lib. 1. sect. 2. cap. 6.

4. It would have been in vain for nature to have endowed the heavens with all conditions requisite for motion, if they had been to stand still. As first, they have a round figure. Secondly, they have neither gravity nor levity. Thirdly, they are incorruptible. Fourthly, they have no contrary.

5. All similary parts are of the same nature with the whole: but each part of the earth does rest in its place; therefore also doth the whole.

6. The sun in the world is as the heart in a man's body; but the motion of the heart ceasing, none of the members do stir: therefore also if the sun should stand still, the other parts of the world would be without motion.

7. The sun and heavens do work upon these inferior bodies by their light and motion. So the moon does operate upon the sea.

8. The earth is the foundation of buildings, and therefore must be firm and stable.

9. It is the constant opinion of divines, that the heavens shall rest after the day of judgment; which they prove from Isa. vi. 20. Thy sun shall no more go down, neither shall thy moon withdraw itself. So likewise, Rev. x. 6. The angel swears that there shall be time no longer; and therefore the heavens must rest, since by their motion it is that time is measured. And St. Paul says, Rom. viii. 20. That all the creatures are subject to vanity. Now this can be no other in the heavens, than the vanity of motion, which the wise man speaks of, Eccles. i. 4. The sun riseth, and the sun goeth down, &c.

To these it may be answered:

In the first you may note a manifest contradiction, when he will have the earth to be hotter than the water, by reason of this motion; when as notwithstanding, he acknowledges the water to move along with it: and therefore too in the next line, he infers that the water, because of that heat and rarefaction which it receives from this motion with the earth, must be incapable of so much cold, as to be congealed into ice.

But unto that which may be conceived to be his meaning in this and the next argument; I answer: if he had fully understood this opinion which he opposes, he would easily have apprehended that it could not be prejudiced by either of these consequences. For we suppose that not only this globe of earth and water, but also all the vaporous air which environs it, are carried along by the same motion. And therefore, though what he says concerning the heat; which would be produced by such a motion, were true, yet it would not be pertinent, since our earth and water, and the air next unto them, are not by this means severed from one another, and so do not come within the compass of this argument.

If any reply, that this will notwithstanding hold true concerning the upper part of the air, where there is such a separation of one body from another; and so consequently, an answerable heat.   I answer,

1. It is not generally granted, that motion in all kind of bodies does produce heat; some restrain it only to solid bodies, affirming, that in those which are fluid, it is rather the cause of coldness. This is the reason, say they, why running waters are ever to our sense the coolest; and why, amongst those winds which proceed from the same coasts of heaven, about the same time of the year, the strongest always is the coldest? If you object, that running waters are not so soon frozen as others, they answer; this is not because they are thereby heated, but because unto congelation it is requisite that a body should settle and rest, as well as be cold.

2. If we should grant a moderate heat in those parts of the air, we have not any experiment to the contrary, nor would it prejudice the present opinion, or common principles.

As the sound of this motion is not more heard than the harmony of the heavens; so neither is there any reason why this motion should cause a sound, more than the supposed motion of the heavens, which is likewise thought to be continued unto the air hard by us.

This will prove the earth to move as well as the heavens: for that has, first, a round figure, as is generally granted. Secondly, being considered as whole, and in its proper place, it is not heavy, as was proved before. And as for the two other conditions, neither are they true of the heavens, nor if they were, would they at all conduce to their motion.

1. This argument would prove that the sea did not ebb and flow, because there is not the same kind of motion in every drop of water; or that the whole earth is not spherical, because every little piece of it is not of the same form.

This is rather an illustration than a proof; or if it do prove any thing, it may serve as well for that purpose unto which it is afterward applied, where the motion of every planet is supposed to depend upon the revolution of the sun.

That the sun and planets do work upon the earth by their own real daily motion, is the thing in question; and therefore must not be taken for a common ground.

We grant that the earth is firm and stable from all such motions whereby it is joggled or uncertainly shaken.

1. For the authority of those divines, which he urges for the interpretation of these scriptures; this will be but a weak argument against that opinion which is already granted to be a paradox.

2. The scriptures themselves, in their right meaning, will not at all conduce to the present purpose.

As for that in Isaiah, if we consult the coherence, we shall find that the scope of the prophet is to set forth the glory of the church triumphant. Wherein he says there shall not be any need of the sun or moon, but God's presence shall supply them both: for the Lord shall be unto thee an everlasting light, and thy God thy glory, ver. 19. and as for this sun and moon, it shall not go down, or withdraw itself, but he shall be an everlasting light without intermission.   So that it is evident he speaks of that light which shall hereafter be instead of the sun and moon *.

As for that in the Revelations, we yield that time shall cease; but to say that this depends upon the cessation of the heavens, is to beg the question, and to suppose that which is to be proved; viz. that time is measured by the motion of the heavens, and not of the earth. Perrerius † (from whom this last argument was borrowed without acknowledgment) might have told him in the very same place, that time does not absolutely and universally depend upon the motion of the heavens, *sed in motu et successione, cujuslibet durationis,* but in any such succession, by which duration may be measured.

As for that in the Romans, we say, that there are other vanities to which the heavenly bodies are subject: as first, unto many changes and alterations; witness those comets which at several times have been discerned amongst them; and then likewise to that general corruption, in which all the creatures shall be involved at the last day. When they shall pass away with a great noise, and the elements shall melt with fervent heat ‡.

Thus you see, there is not any such invincible strength in these arguments, as might cause the author of them to triumph before-hand with any great noise of victory.

Another objection like unto these is taken from the etymology of several words. Thus the heavens are called *Æthera, ab αει Ͽειν,* because they are always in motion, and the earth *Vesta, qui vi stat,* because of its immobility.

To which I answer: it were no difficult matter to find such proofs for this opinion, as well as against it.

Thus we may say that the Hebrew word ארץ is derived from רוץ *quia currit;* and *terra, non quod terratur, sed quod perenni cursu omnia terat,* saith Calcagnius. However, though we suppose the etymology to be never so true and

---

* Vid. Revel. xxi. 23. item xxii. 5.
† Gen. c. 1. l. 2. quæst. 6.   ‡ 2 Pet. iii. 10, 12.

genuine, yet it can at the best but shew what the more common opinion was of those times when such names were first imposed.

But suppose all this were so, that the earth had such a diurnal revolution; yet how is it conceivable that it should at the same time have two distinct motions?

I answer: this may easily be apprehended, if you consider how both these motions do tend the same way from west to east. Thus a bowl being turned out of the hand, has two motions in the air; one, whereby it is carried round; the other, whereby it is cast forward.

From what hath been delivered in this chapter, the indifferent reader may gather some satisfaction for those arguments which are usually urged against this diurnal motion of the earth.

PROP. IX.

That it is more probable the earth does move, than the sun or heavens.

AMONGST those many arguments that may be urged for the confirmation of this truth, I shall set down only these five.

1. If we suppose the earth to be the cause of this motion, then will those vast and glorious bodies of the heavens be freed from that inconceivable, unnatural swiftness, which must otherwise be attributed unto them.

For if the diurnal revolution be in the heavens, then it will follow according to the common hypothesis*, that each star in the equator must in every hour move at the least 4529538 German miles. So that according to the observation of Cardan†, who tells us that the pulse of a

* Vid. Mesl. Epit. Astr. l. 1. in fine.
† De Prop. l. 5. prop. 58.

well-tempered man does beat 4000 times in an hour, one of these stars in that space, whilst the pulse beats once, must pass 1132 German miles (saith Alphraganus :) or according to Tycho, 732 German miles. But these numbers seem to be somewhat of the least, and therefore many others do much enlarge them, affirming that every star in the equator, in one beating of the pulse, must move 2528 of these miles.

It is the assertion of Clavius *, that though the distance of the orbs, and so consequently their swiftness, seem to be altogether incredible ; yet it is rather far greater in itself than astronomers usually suppose it ; and yet saith he, according to the common grounds, every star in the equator must move $42398437\frac{1}{2}$ miles in an hour. And though a man should constantly travel forty miles a day. yet he would not be able to go so far as a star does in one hour, under 2904 years : or if we will suppose an arrow to be of the same swiftness, then must it compass this great globe of earth and water 1884 times in an hour. And a bird that could but fly as fast, might go round the world seven times in that space, whilst one could say, *Ave Maria, gratia plena, Dominus tecum.*

Which though it be a pretty round pace, yet you must conceive that all this is spoken only of the eighth sphere ; and so being compared to the swiftness of the *primum mobile,* is but a slow and heavy motion.

For (saith the same author) the thickness of each orb is equal to the distance of its concave superficies from the centre of the earth. Thus the orb of the moon does contain as much space in its thickness, as there is betwixt the nearest parts of that and the centre. Thus also the eighth sphere is as thick as that whole space betwixt the centre of the earth and its own concave superficies. So likewise must it be in those three other orbs, which he supposes to be above the starry heaven. Now if we proportion their swiftness according to this difference in their

---

* Comment, in prim. cap. Sphæra,

bigness, you may then conceive (if you can) what a kind of celerity that must be, by which the *primum mobile* will be whirled about.

Tycho makes the distance of the stars to be much less, and their motion slower; and yet he is fain to confess, that it is *omni cogitatione celerior.*

Clavius likewise speaking concerning the swiftness of the starry orb, does acknowledge, *Quod velocitas ejus captum humani ingenii excedit.* What then could he think of the *primum mobile?*

Dr. Gilbert * being it seems astonished at the conside-ration of this strange swiftness, says of it, that it is *motus supra omnes cogitationes, somnia, fabulas & licentias poeticas insuperabilis, ineffabilis, incomprehensibilis.* A man may more easily conceive the possibility of any fable or fiction, how beasts and trees might talk together, than how any material body should be moved with such a swiftness.

Not but that it is possible for God to turn them about with a far greater velocity. Nay it is possible for art to contrive a motion, which shall be equally slow in that pro-portion as this is swift. But however, the question here is not what can be done, but what is most likely to be done according to the usual course of nature. It is the part of a philosopher, in the revolution of natural events, not to fly unto the absolute power of God, and tell us what he can do, but what according to the usual way of providence is most likely to be done, to find out such causes of things, as may seem most easy and probable to our reason.

If you ask what repugnancy there is in the heavens, unto so great a swiftness: we answer, their being such vast ma-terial condensed substances, with which this inconceivable motion cannot agree.

Since motion and magnitude are two such geometrical things, as bear a mutual proportion to one another; there-fore it may seem convenient, that slowness should be more agreeable to a great body, and swiftness to a lesser: and so it should be more consonant to the principles of nature, that

* De magnete, l. 6. c. 3.

the earth, which is of a lesser quantity, should be appointed to such a motion as is somewhat proportionable to its bigness, than that the heavens that are of such a vast magnitude, should be whirled about with such an incredible swiftness, which does as far exceed the proportion of their bigness, as their bigness does exceed this earth, that is but a point or centre to them.   It is not likely that nature in these constant and great works, should so much deviate from that usual harmony and proportion which she observes in lesser matters.   If this globe of earth only were appointed to move every day round the orb of the fixed stars, though it be but a little body, and so more capable of a swift motion ; yet that swiftness would be so extremely disproportionable unto it, that we could not with reason conceive it possible, according to the usual course of nature.   But now that the heavens themselves, of such strange bigness, with so many stars, which do so far exceed the magnitude of our earth, should be able to turn about with the same celerity, oh ! it is altogether beyond the fancy of a poet or a madman.

For answer unto this argument, our adversaries tell us: that there is not in the heavens any repugnancy to so swift a motion ; and that whether we consider the nature of those bodies ; or, secondly, the swiftness of this motion.

I. For the nature of those bodies, either   { Qualities.
their   { Quantity.

1. There is not in them the qualities of lightness or heaviness, or any the least contrariety that may make them reluctant to one another.

2. Their magnitude will help them in their swiftness * : for the greater any body is, the quicker will it be in its motion, and that not only when it is moved by an inward principle, as a millstone will descend faster than a little pebble ; but also when its motion does proceed from some external agent ; as the wind will drive a great cloud, or a heavy ship, when it is not able to stir a little stone.

* Ross, l. 1. sect. 1. c. 1.

II. As for the swiftness of this motion, the possibility of it may be illustrated by other particulars in nature : as,

1. The sound of a cannon, in a little time is carried for twenty miles distance *.

2. Though a star be situated so remotely from us, yet the eye discerns it in a moment, which is not without some motion, either of the species of the star, or the rays of the eye.   Thus also the light does in an instant pass from one side of the heaven to another †.

I. If the force of powder be able to carry a bullet with so great a swiftness, we need not doubt then, but that the heavens are capable of such a celerity as is usually attributed unto them.

Unto these it may be answered :

1. Where they say that the heavenly bodies are without all gravity, we grant it, in the same sense as our earth also, being considered as whole, and in its proper place, may be denied to be heavy : Since this quality in the exactest sense, can only be ascribed unto such parts as are severed from the whole to which they belong.   But however, since the heavens or stars are of a material substance, it is impossible but there should be in them some ineptitude to motion; because matter is of itself a dull and sluggish thing, and by so much the more, as it is kept close and condensed together.   And though the followers of Ptolemy do with much confidence deny the heavens to be capable of any reluctancy to motion, yet it were easy to prove the contrary out of their own principles.   It is not conceivable how the upper sphere should move the nether, unless their superficies were full of rugged parts (which they deny) : or else one of the orbs must lean upon the other with its weight, and so make it partake of its own motion.   And besides, they tell us, that the farther any sphere is distant from the *primum mobile*, the less it is hindered by that in its proper course, and the sooner does it finish its own revolution.

---

* Ross. l. 2. sect. 1. c. 5.   † Idem, l. 1. sect. 1. c. 2.

From whence it will easily follow, that these bodies have resistency from one another.

I have often wondered why amongst the enchanted buildings of the poets, they have not feigned any castle to be made of the same materials with the solid orbs, since in such a fabric there would have been these eminent conveniences.

1. It must needs be very pleasant, by reason of its perspicuity, because it is more diaphanous than the air itself, and so the walls of it could not hinder the prospect any way.

2. Being so solid and impenetrable, it must needs be excellent against all violence of weathers, as also against the assaults of the enemy, who should not be able to break it with the most furious batteries of the ram, or pierce it with any cannon shot.

3. Being void of all heaviness, a man may carry it up and down with him, as a snail does his house ; and so whether he follow the enemy, or fly from him, he has still this advantage, that he may take his castle and defence along with him.

But then again, there are on the other side as many inconveniencies. For,

1. Its perspicuity would make it so open, that a man should not be able to retire himself into any private part of it. And then,

2. Being so extremely solid, as well as invisible, a man should be still in danger of knocking his head against every wall and pillar ; unless it were also intangible, as some of the peripatetics affirm.

3. Its being without all gravity, would bring this inconvenience, that every little puff of wind would blow it up and down ; since some of the same sect are not ashamed to say, that the heavens are so utterly devoid of heaviness, that if but a little fly should jostle against the vast frame of the celestial spheres, he would move them out of their places.

A strong fancy, that could be at leisure, might make excellent sport with this astronomical fiction.

So that this first evasion of our adversaries will not shelter them from the force of that argument, which is taken from the incredible swiftness of the heavens.

2. Whereas they tell us in the second place, that a bigger body, as a millstone, will naturally descend swifter than a less, as a pebble. I answer: this is not because such a great body is in itself more easily moveable, but because the bigger any thing is which is out of its own place, the stronger will be its natural desire of returning thither, and so consequently, the quicker its motion. But now those bodies that move circularly, are always in their proper situations, and so the same reason is not appliable unto them. And then, whereas it is said, that magnitude does always add to the swiftness of a violent motion (as wind will move a great ship sooner than a little stone: we answer: this is not because a ship is more easily moveable in itself than a little stone: for I suppose the objector will not think he can throw the one as far as the other; but because these little bodies are not so liable to that kind of violence from whence their motion does proceed.

As for those instances, which are cited to illustrate the possibility of this swiftness in the heavens, we answer: the passage of a sound is but very slow in comparison to the motion of the heavens. And then besides, the swiftness of the species of sound or sight which are accidents, are not fit to infer the like celerity in a material substance: and so likewise for the light which Aristotle himself *, and with him the generality of philosophers, do for this very reason prove not to be a body, because it moves with such swiftness, of which (it seems) they thought a body to be incapable. Nay, the objector † himself in another place, speaking of light in reference to a substance, does say: *Lumen est accidens, sic species rei visæ, & alia est ratio substantiarum, alia accidentium.*

To that of a bullet, we answer: he might as well have illustrated the swiftness of a bullet, which will pass four or five miles in two minutes, by the motion of a hand in a

---

* De Anima, l. 2. c. 7.   † Ross. l. 2. sect. 1. c. 4.

watch, which passes two or three inches in twelve hours;
there being a greater disproportion betwixt the motion of
the heavens and the swiftness of a bullet, than there is betwixt the swiftness of a bullet and the motion of a hand in
a watch.

Another argument to this purpose may be taken from
the chief end of the diurnal and annual motions, which is
to distinguish betwixt night and day, winter and summer;
and so consequently, to serve for the commodities and seasons of the habitable world.   Wherefore it may seem more
agreeable to the wisdom of providence, for to make the
earth as well the efficient, as the final cause of this motion;
especially since nature in her other operations does never
use any tedious difficult means to perform that which may
as well be accomplished by shorter and easier ways.   But
now, the appearances would be the same, in respect of us,
if only this little point of earth were made the subject of
these motions, as if the vast frame of the world, with all
those stars of such number and bigness were moved about it.
It is a common maxim, Μηδεν ειχη την Φυσιν εργαζεσθαι *.
Nature does nothing in vain, but in all her courses does take
the most compendious way.   It is not therefore (I say)
likely, that the whole fabric of the heavens, which do so
much exceed our earth in magnitude and perfection, should
be put to undergo so great and constant a work in the service of our earth, which might more easily save all that labour by the circumvolution of its own body; especially,
since the heavens do not by this motion attain any farther
perfection for themselves, but are made thus serviceable to
this little ball of earth.   So that in this case it may seem to
argue as much improvidence in nature to employ them in
this motion, as it would in a mother †, who in warming her
child, would rather turn the fire about that, than that about
the fire : or in a cook ‡, who would not roast his meat by
turning it about to the fire; but rather, by turning the fire
about it : or in a man ||, who ascending some high tower, to

* Galen.   † Lansberg.   ‡ Keplar. || Galil.

save the labour of stirring his head, should rather desire that all the regions might successively be turned before his eye, that so he might easily take a view of them.

We allow every watchmaker so much wisdom as not to put any motion in his instrument, which is superfluous, or may be supplied an easier way: and shall we not think that nature has as much providence as every ordinary mechanic? or can we imagine that she should appoint those numerous and vast bodies, the stars, to compass us with such a swift and restless motion, so full of confusion and uncertainties, when as all this might as well be done by the revolution of this little ball of earth?

Amongst the several parts of the world, there are six planets which are generally granted to move. As for the sun and the earth, and the fixed stars, it is yet in question, which of them are naturally endowed with the same condition. Now common reason will dictate unto us, that motion is most agreeable to that which in kind and properties is most near to those bodies that undoubtedly are moved. But now there is one eminent qualification, wherein the earth does agree with the planets; whereas the sun, together with the fixed stars, do in the same respect differ from them: and that is light, which all the planets, and so too the earth, are fain to borrow elsewhere, whilst the sun and the stars have it of their own. From whence it may be probably concluded, that the earth is rather the subject of this motion than the other. To this it may be added, that the sun and stars seem to be of a more excellent nature than the other parts of the world; and therefore should in reason be endowed with the best qualifications. But now motion is not so noble a condition as rest. That is but a kind of wearisome and servile thing; whereas, this is usually ascribed to God himself: of whom it is said:

Immotus stabilisque manens dans cuncta moveri *.

Aristotle † tells us, it is very agreeable to reason that the time appointed for the revolution of each orb should

* Boet. de Consol, Phil. l. 3.   † De Cœlo, l. 2. c. 10.

be proportionable to its bigness. But now this can only be by making the earth a planet, and the subject of the annual and diurnal motions. Wherefore it is probable, that this does rather move than the heavens.

According to the common hypothesis, the *primum mobile* will move round in a day. Saturn in thirty years. Jupiter in twelve. Mars in two. The Sun, Venus, and Mercury, which have several orbs, yet will agree in their revolutions, being each of them about a year in finishing their courses : whereas by making the earth a planet, there will be a just proportion betwixt the bigness of the orbs and the time of their motions : for then, next to the sun or centre, there will be the sphere of Mercury ; which as it is but narrower in its diameter, so likewise is it quick in its motion, running its course in 88 days. Venus, that is next unto it, in 224 days. The earth in 365 days, or a year. Mars in 687 days, Jupiter in 4332 days, Saturn in 10759 days. Thus likewise is it with those Medicean stars that encompass Jupiter. That which is lowest amongst them, finishes his course in two and twenty hours ; the next in three days and a half ; the third in seven days ; and the farthest in seventeen days. Now as it is (according to Aristotle's confession) more likely that nature should observe such a due proportion betwixt the heavenly orbs ; so is it more probable, that the earth should move, rather than the heavens.

This may likewise be confirmed from the appearance of comets : concerning which there are three things commonly granted, or if they were not, might be easily proved : namely,

1. That there are divers comets in the air, betwixt the moon and our earth.

2. That many of these comets do seem to rise and set as the stars.

3. That this appearing motion is not properly their own, but communicated unto them from somewhat else.

But now, this motion of theirs cannot be caused by the

heavens; and therefore it must necessarily proceed from the revolution of our earth.

That the moon's orb cannot carry along with it the greater part of the air, wherein these comets are placed, might easily be proved from the common grounds. For the concave superficies of that sphere is usually supposed to be exactly terse and smooth; so that the meer touch of it cannot turn about the whole element of fire, with a motion that is not natural unto it. Nor could this elementary fire, which they imagine to be of a more rarified and subtle nature, communicate the same motion to the thicker air, and that to the waters (as some affirm:) for by what means could that smooth orb take hold of the adjoining air? To this Sarsius answers, that there are great gibbosities and mountainous inequalities in the concavity of the lowest sphere, and by these is it enabled to carry along with it the fire and air. But Fromondus * tells him, *Fictitia ista & ad fugam reperta sunt.* And yet his own conjecture is scarce so good, when he affirms, that this motion of the æthereal air, as also of that elementary air hard by us, is caused by that ruggedness which there is in the bodies of the planets; of which opinion we may with as good reason say as he says to Sarsius, *fictitia ista & ad fugam reperta :* these things are mere fictions invented for shifts, and without any probable ground.

But now this appearance of the comets may easily be resolved, if we suppose the earth to move. For then, though they did still remain in their wonted places; yet this, by its diurnal revolution successively withdrawing itself from them, they will appear to rise and set. And therefore, according to this common natural experiment, it is more probable that the earth should move, than the heavens.

Another argument urged by some to prove that this globe of earth is easily moveable, is taken from the opinion of those who affirm that the access of any weight unto a

* Antar. cap. 16.

new place *, as suppose an army, does make the earth poise itself afresh, and change the centre of gravity that it had before : but this is not generally granted ; and therefore not to be insisted on as a common ground.

To this purpose likewise is that inference of Lansbergius, who from Archimedes his saying, that he could move the earth, if he knew where to stand and fasten his instrument ; concludes, that the earth is easily moveable ; whereas it was the intent of Archimedes in that speech, to shew the infinite power of engines : there being no weight so great, but that an instrument might be invented to move it.

Before we finish this chapter, it is requisite that we inquire what kind of faculty that is from which these motions that Copernicus ascribes unto the earth, do proceed : whether or no it be some animal power, that does assist (as Aristotle) or inform (as Keplar thinks,) or else some other natural motive quality which is intrinsical unto it.

We may observe, that when the proper genuine cause of any motion is not obvious, men are very prone to attribute unto that which they discern to be the most frequent original of it in other things, life. Thus the stoics affirm the soul of the water to be the cause of the ebbing and flowing of the sea. Thus others think the wind to proceed from the life of the air, whereby it is able to move itself several ways, as other living creatures †. And upon the same grounds do the Platonics, Stoics, and some of the Peripatetics, affirm the heavens to be animated. From hence likewise it is, that so many do maintain Aristotle his opinion concerning intelligences ; which some of his followers, the schoolmen, do confirm out of scripture, from that place in Matthew xxiv. 29. where it is said, the powers of the heavens shall be shaken. In which words, by powers (say they) are meant the angels, by whose power it is, that the heavens are moved. And so likewise in that, Job ix. 13. where the vulgar has it, *sub quo curvantur, qui portant orbem* ; that is,

---

* Vid. Vasq. l. 1. diff. 2. cap. 8. 16.
† Sen. Nat. Quest. l. 5 cap. 5, 6.

the intelligences. Which text might serve altogether as well, to prove the fable of Atlas and Hercules. Thus Cajetan concludes from that place in the Psalm cxxxvi. 5. where it is said, " God by wisdom made the heavens ; or according to the vulgar, *Qui fecit cælos intellectu,* that the heavens are moved by an intelligent soul.

If we consider the original of this opinion, we shall find it to proceed from that mistake of Aristotle, who thought the heavens to be eternal ; and therefore to require such a moving cause, as being of an immaterial substance, might be exempted from all that weariness and inconstancy which other things are liable unto.

But now this ground of his is evidently false, since it is certain that the heavens had a beginning, and shall have an end. However, the employing of angels in these motions of the world, is both superfluous, and very improbable.

1. Because a natural power, intrinsical to those bodies, will serve the turn as well. And as for other operations, which are to be constant and regular, nature does commonly make use of some inward principle.

2. The intelligences being immaterial, cannot immediately work upon a body ; nor does any one tell us what instruments they should make use of in this business. They have not any hands to take hold of the heavens, or turn them about. And that opinion of Aquinas, Durand, Soncinus, with other schoolmen, seems to be without all reason ; who make the faculty whereby the angels move the orbs, to be the very same with their understandings and will : so that if an angel do but merely suspend the act of willing their motion, they must necessarily stand still : and on the contrary, his only willing them to move, shall be enough to carry them about in their several courses: since it were then a needless thing for providence to have appointed angels unto this business, which might have been done as well by the only will of God. And besides, how are the orbs capable of perceiving this will in the intelligences ? Or if they were, yet what motive faculty have they of themselves, which can enable them to obey it ?

Now as it would be with the heavens, so likewise is it with the earth, which may be turned about in its diurnal revolution, without the help of intelligences, by some motive power of its own, that may be intrinsical unto it.

If it be yet inquired, what cause there is of its annual motion : I answer ; it is easily conceivable, how the same principle may serve for both these, since they tend the same way from west to east.

However, that opinion of Keplar is not very improbable, that all the primary planets are moved round by the sun, which once in twenty-five or twenty-six days, does observe a revolution about its own axis, and so carry along the planets that encompass it ; which planets are therefore slower or swifter. according to their distances from him. If you ask by what means the sun can produce such a motion ? he answers ; by sending forth a kind of magnetic virtue in strait lines, from each part of its body ; of which there is always a constant succession : so that as soon as one beam of this vigour has passed a planet, there is another presently takes hold of it, like the teeth of a wheel.

But how can any virtue hold out to such a distance ?

He answers : first, as light and heat, together with those other secret influences which work upon minerals in the bowels of the earth ; so likewise may the sun send forth a magnetic, motive virtue, whose power may be continued to the farthest planets. Secondly, if the moon, according to common philosophy, may move the sea, why then may not the sun move this globe of earth ?

In such queries as these, we can conclude only from conjectures : that speech of the wise man, Eccles. iii. 11. being more especially verified of astronomical questions concerning the frame of the whole universe, that no man can find out the works of God from the beginning to the end. Though we may discern divers things in the world, which may argue the infinite wisdom and power of the author, yet there will be always some particulars left for our dispute and inquiry, and we shall never be able with all our industry, to attain a perfect comprehension of the creatures, or to find them wholly out, from the beginning to the end.

The providence of God having thus contrived it *, that so man might look for another life after this, when all his longing and thirst shall be fully satisfied. For since no natural appetite is in vain, it must necessarily follow, that there is a possibility of attaining so much knowledge as shall be commensurate unto these desires; which because it is not to be had in this world, it will behove us then to expect and provide for another.

PROP. X.

That this hypothesis is exactly agreeable to common appearances.

IT hath been already proved, that the earth is capable of such a situation and motion as this opinion supposes it to have. It remains, that in the last place we shew how agreeable this would be unto those ordinary seasons of days, months, years, and all other appearances in the heavens.

1. As for the difference betwixt days and nights; it is evident, that this may be as well caused by the revolution of the earth, as the motion of the sun; since the heavenly bodies must needs seem after the same manner to rise and set, whether or no they themselves by their own motion, do pass by our horizon and vertical point; or whether our horizon and vertical point, by the revolution of our earth, do pass by them. According to that of Aristotle †, ȣδεν διαφερει κινειν την οψιν η το ορωμενον, there will not appear any difference, whether or no the eye be moved from the object, or the object from the eye. And therefore I cannot chuse but wonder that a man of any reason or sense, should

* Valles. sacr. Philos. c. 64.   † De Cœlo, lib. 2. cap. 8.

make choice of no better an argument to conclude his book withal, than that which we read at the latter end of Al. Rosse, where he infers, that the earth does not move, because then the shadow in a sun-dial would not be altered.

2. As for the difference of months, we say, that the diverse illumination of the moon, the different bigness of her body, her remaining for a longer or shorter time in the earth's shadow, when she is eclipsed, &c. may well enough be solved by supposing her to move above our earth, in an eccentrical epicycle.   Thus,

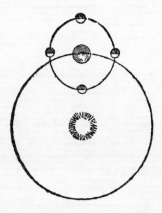

In which kind of hypothesis, there will be a double difference of motion ; the one caused by the different situations of the moon's body, in its own eccentric ; the other by the different situations of the moon's orb, in the earth's eccentric : which is so exactly answerable to the motions and appearances of this planet, that from hence Lansbergius draws an argument for this system of the heavens, which in the strength of his confidence he calls, *demonstrationem επι στημονικην, cui nulla ratione potest contradici.*

4. As for the difference betwixt winter and summer ; betwixt the number and length of days, which appertain to each of those seasons ; the seeming motion of the sun from one sign to another in the zodiac : all this may easily be

solved, by supposing the earth to move in an eccentrical
orb about the sun. Thus,

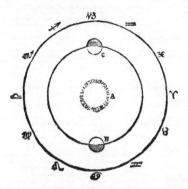

Suppose the earth to be at C, then the sun at A will seem
to be in the sign ♋, and at the greatest distance from us,
because the earth is then in the farthest part of its eccentric.   When after by its annual motion it hath passed successively by the signs ♒ ♓ ♈ ♉ ♊, at length it comes to
the other solstice at B, where the sun will appear in ♑, and
seem biggest, as being in its perige, because our earth is
then in the nearest part of its eccentric.

As for all other appearances of the sun which concern
the annual motion, you may see by the following figure,
that they are exactly agreeable to this hypothesis.

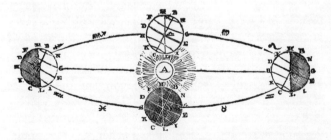

Where you have the earth described about the sun at A,
in the four chief points of the zodiac; namely, the two

equinoctials at ♈ and ♎, and the solstices at ♑ and ♋. Through all which points the earth does pass in his annual motion from west to east.

The axis upon which our earth does move, is represented by the line B C, which axis does always decline from that of the ecliptic, about 23 degrees, 30 minutes. The points B C are imagined to be the poles, B the north-pole, and C the south.

Now if we suppose this earth to turn about its own axis by a diurnal motion, then every point of it will describe a parallel circle, which will be either bigger or lesser, according to its distance from the poles. The chief of them are the equinoctial D, E. The two tropics, F, G; and H, I, the two polar circles. M, N, the arctic, and K, L, the antarctic; of which the equinoctial only is a great circle, and therefore will always be equally divided by the line of illumination M, L, whereas the other parallels are thereby distributed into unequal parts. Amongst which parts, the diurnal arches of those that are towards B, the north pole, are bigger than the nocturnal, when our earth is in ♑ and the sun appears in ♋: insomuch, that the whole arctic circle is enlightened, and there is day for half a year together under that pole.

Now when the earth proceeds to the other solstice at ♋, and the sun appears in ♑, then that hemisphere must be involved in darkness, which did before partake of light. And those parallels towards the north and south poles will still be divided by the same inequality. But those bigger parts which were before enlightened, will not be darkened, *et vice versa*. As when the earth was in N, the arctic circle M, N, was wholly enlightened, and the antarctic, K, L, altogether in the dark. So now, when it is in A, the antarctic K, L, will be wholly in the light, and the other M, N, altogether obscured. Whereas the sun before was vertical to the inhabitants at the tropic F, G; so now is he in the same situation to those that live under the other tropics, H, I. And whereas before the pole did incline 23 degrees 30 minutes towards the sun, so now does it decline as much from him.   The whole difference will amount to 47 degrees, which is the distance of one tropic from the other.

But now in the two other figures, when the earth is in either of the equinoctials ♈ ♎, the circle of illumination will pass through both the poles, and therefore must divide all the parallels into equal parts.   From whence it will follow, that the day and night must then be equal in all places of the world.

As the earth is here represented in ♎, it turns only the enlightened part towards us: as it is in ♈ we see its nocturnal hemisphere.

So that according to this hypothesis, we may easily and exactly reconcile every appearance concerning the difference betwixt days and nights, winter and summer, together with all those other varieties which depend upon them.

If you would know how the planets (according to the system of the heavens) will appear direct, stationary, retrograde; and yet still move regularly about their own centres, you may plainly discern it by this following diagram.

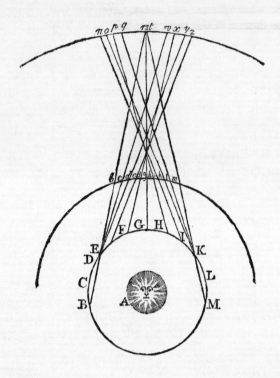

Where suppose the sun to be at A, the circle (B, G, M)
to be the orb of the earth's motion, and that above it noted
with the same letters, to be the sphere of Jupiter; and the
uppermost of all, to be a part of the zodiac in the starry
heaven.

Now if you conceive the letters A B C D E F G H I K L
M, and *b c d e f g h i k l m*, to divide the earth's orb and
that of Jupiter, into several parts, proportionable to the
slowness or swiftness of their different motions (Jupiter
finishes his course in twelve years, and the earth in one)
then supposing the earth to be at the point (B) and Jupiter
likewise in his orb to be situated at (*b*,) he will appear unto
us to be in the zodiac at the point (*r*.) But afterwards
both of them moving forwards to the letter (C *c*) Jupiter
will seem to be in the zodiac at (*v*,) as having passed di-

rectly forward according to the order of the signs.   And so
likewise each of them being transferred to the places (D *d*)
(E *e*) Jupiter will still appear direct, and to have moved in
the zodiac unto the points (*y z.*)   But now when the earth
comes to be more immediately interposed betwixt this planet and the sun; as when both of them are at the letter
(F *f*) then will Jupiter be discerned in the zodiac at (*x.*)   So
that all the while the earth was passing the arch (E F) Jupiter did still remain betwixt the points (*z*) and (*x,*) and
therefore must seem unto us as if he were stationary ; but
afterwards both of them being carried to (G *g,*) then Jupiter
will appear at (*s,*) as if by a hasty motion he had returned
from his former course the space (*x s.*)   Both of them passing to (H *h,*) this planet will still seem to be swiftly retrograde, and appear in the point at (*p,*) but when they come
to the points (I *i,*) Jupiter will then seem to be slower in
this motion, and to have only passed the space (*p n.*)   Both
of them being transferred to (K *k,*) Jupiter will then appear
in the zodiac at (*o*) as being again direct, going forward according to the order of the signs, and while the earth did
pass the arch (I K) Jupiter then remained between the
points (*n o,*) and so consequently did again seem to be stationary.   Both of them coming to (L *l,*) and thence to
(M *m,*) Jupiter will still appear direct, and to have gone
forward in the zodiac from (*q*) to (*t.*)   So that all the space
wherein Jupiter is retrograde, is represented by the arch
(*n z.*)   In which space he himself moves in his own orb,
the arch (*e i,*) and so the earth in its orb, a proportional
space (E I).

As it hath been said of this planet, so likewise is it appliable to the other, Saturn, Mars, Venus, Mercury; all
which are thus made to appear direct, stationary, and retrograde, by the motion of our earth, without the help of
those epicycles and excentrics, and such unnecessary
wheel-work, wherewith Ptolemy hath filled the heavens.
Insomuch, that here Fromondus * is fain to confess, *nullo*

* Antarist. c. 18.   Vest. tract. 4. c. 3.

argumento in speciem probabiliori, motum terræ annum a Copernicanis astrui, quam illo stationis, directionis, regressionis planetarum. There is not any more probable argument to prove the annual motion of the earth, than its agreeableness to the station, direction, and regression of the planets.

Lastly, that Copernicus's system of the heavens is **very** answerable to the exactest observations, may be manifest from this following description of it.

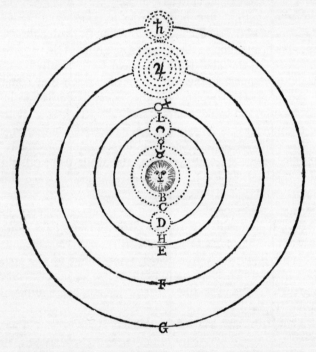

Suppose the sun to be situated at A: now because Mercury is found by experience to be always very near the sun, so that he does for the most part lie hid under his rays; as also because this planet hath a more lively vigorous light than any of the other; therefore we may infer, that his orb is placed next unto the sun, as that at B.

As for Venus, it is observed, that she does always keep

THAT THE EARTH MAY BE A PLANET. 253

at a set distance from the sun, never going from him above 40 degrees, or thereabouts; that her body appears through the perspective to be forty times bigger at one time than at another; that when she seems biggest and nearest unto us, we then discern her as being perfectly round. Therefore doth this planet also move in a circle that encompasses the sun. Which circle does not contain the earth within it; because then Venus would sometimes be in opposition to the sun; whereas it is generally granted, that she never yet came so far as to be in a sextile.

Nor is this circle below the sun (as Ptolemy supposeth) because then this planet, in both its conjunctions, would appear horned, which she does not *.

Nor is it above the sun, because then she would always appear in the full, and never horned.

From whence it will follow, that this orb must necessarily be betwixt the earth and the sun, as that at C.

As for Mars, it is observed, that he does appear sixty times bigger when he is near us, than at his greatest distance; that he is sometimes in opposition to the sun. From whence we may conclude that his orb does contain our earth within it. It is observed also, that he does constantly appear in the full, and never horned: from whence likewise it is manifest, that the sun is comprehended within its orb, as it is in that which is represented by the circle E.

And because the like appearances are observed in Jupiter and Saturn (though in less degrees) therefore we may with good reason conceive them to be in the heavens, after some such manner as they are here set down in the figure, by the circles F G.

As for the moon, because she is sometimes in opposition to the sun, therefore must her orb comprehend in it the earth; because she appears dark in her conjunction, and sometimes eclipses the sun; therefore that must necessarily be without her orb, as it is in that epicycle at H. In the centre of which, the earth must necessarily be situated,

* Matutina Vespertina.

according to all those appearances mentioned before. So that the orb of its annual motion will be represented by the circle D.

All which appearances cannot so well be reconciled by Ptolemy, Tycho, Origanus, or by any other hypothesis, as by this of Copernicus. But the application of these to the several planets, together with sundry other particulars, concerning the theorical part of astronomy, you may see more fully set down by those who have purposely handled this subject, Copernicus, Rhetichus, Galilæus; but more especially Keplar: unto whom I do acknowledge myself indebted for sundry particulars in this discourse.

I have done with that which was the chief purpose of the present treatise; namely, the removal of those common prejudices that men usually entertain against this opinion. It remains, that by way of conclusion, I endeavour to stir up others unto these kind of studies, which by most men are so much neglected.

It is the most rational way, in the prosecution of several objects, to proportion our love and endeavour after every thing, according to the excellency and desirableness of it. But now amongst all earthly contentments, there is nothing either better in itself, or more convenient for us, than this kind of learning; and that, whether you consider it according to its general nature, as a science; or according to its more special nature, as such a science.

1. Consider it as a science. Certain it is, that amongst the variety of objects, those are more eligible which conduce unto the welfare of that which is our best part, our souls. It is not so much the pleasing of our senses, or the increasing of our fortunes, that does deserve our industry, as the information of our judgments, the improvement of our knowledge. Whatever the world may think, yet it is not a vast estate, a noble birth, an eminent place, that can add any thing to our true real worth; but it must be the degrees of that which makes us men, that must make us better men, the endowments of our soul, the enlargement of our reason. Were it not for the contemplation of philosophy,

the heathen Seneca* would not so much as thank the gods for his being: *nisi ad hæc admitterer non fuit opere pretium nasci. Detrahe hoc inestimabile bonum non est vita tanti, ut sudem, ut æstuem.* Take but away this benefit, and he would not think life worth the sweating for. So much happiness could he discern in the studies of nature. And therefore as a science in general, it may very well deserve our love and industry.

2. Consider it as such a particular science, astronomy: the word signifies the law of the stars; and the Hebrews (who do not ordinarily admit of composition) call it in two words, חקות שמים, *cælorum statuta*, or the ordinances of heaven †; because they are governed in their courses by a certain rule, as the Psalmist speaks in the cxlviiith Psal. ver. 6. God has given them a law which shall not be broken.

Now this of all other natural sciences may best of all challenge our industry; and that, whether you consider it,

1. Absolutely, as it is in itself: or,

2. As it stands in reference to us.

1. As it is in itself. The excellency of any science may be judged of (saith the philosopher) first, by the excellency of the object. Secondly, by the certainty of its demonstrations.

1. For the object. It is no less than the whole world (since our earth also is one of the planets) more especially those vast and glorious bodies of the heavens. So that in this respect it far exceeds all those barren, empty speculations about *materia prima,* and *universale,* and such like cobwebs of learning; in the study of which so many do misplace their younger years. And for the same reason likewise is it to be preferred before all those other sciences, whose subjects are not either of so wide an extent, or so excellent a nature.

2. For the demonstrations of astronomy, they are as infallible as truth itself; and for this reason also does it excel all other knowledge, which does more depend upon con-

* Præf. ad l. 1. Nat. Quest.　　† Job xxxviii. 33. Jer. xxxiii. 25.

jectures and uncertainty. They are only those who want skill in the principles of this science, that mistrust the conclusions of it. Since therefore in these respects, it is one of the most excellent sciences in nature, it may best deserve the industry of man, who is one of the best works of nature. Other creatures were made with their heads and eyes turned downwards: would you know why man was not created so too? why it was, that he might be an astronomer.

> *Os homini sublime dedit, celumque tueri*
> *Jussit, et erectos ad sydera tollere vultus.*
>
> God gave to man an upright face, that he
> Might view the stars, and learn astronomy.

2. Consider it in reference to us; and so it is,

1. Most useful.

2. Most pleasant.

1. Most useful, and that in sundry respects. It proves a God and a providence, and incites our hearts to a greater admiration and fear of his omnipotency. We may understand by the heavens, how much mightier he is that made them; for by the greatness and beauty of the creatures, proportionably the maker of them is seen, saith the book of Wisdom, xiii. 4, 5. It was hence that Aristotle did fetch his chief argument to prove a *primus motor*. It was the consideration of these things that first led men to the knowledge and worship of God (saith Tully *) *hæc nos primum ad deorum cultum, tum ad modestiam, magnitudinemque animi erudivit.* And therefore when God by the prophet would convince the people of his deity, he bids them lift up their eyes on high, and behold who hath created those things; that bringeth out their host by number, that calleth them all by their names, &c. Isa. xl. 26. which occasioned that saying of Lactantius †; *Tanta rerum magnitudo, tanta dispositio, tanta in servandis ordinibus, temporibusque constantia; non potuit aut olim sine provido artifice oriri,*

---

* Tuscul. 1. item Plut. de Placit. Phil. l. 1. c. 6.
† Instit. l. 2. c. 5.

aut constare tot sæculis sine incola potente, aut perpetuum gubernari sine perito et sciente rectore, quod ratio ipsa declarat. Such a great order and constancy amongst those vast bodies, could not at first be made but by a wise providence, nor since preserved without a powerful inhatant, nor so perpetually governed without a skilful guide.

True indeed, an ordinary view and common apprehension of these celestial bodies, must needs manifest the excellency and omnipotency of their maker; but yet a more accurate and diligent enquiry into their natures, will raise our understandings unto a nearer knowledge, and a greater admiration of the deity: as it is in those inferior things, where the meer outside of a man, the comeliness and majesty of his countenance, may be some argument from whence to infer the excellency of his creator. But yet the subtle anatomist, who searches more deeply into this wonderful structure, may see a clear evidence for this in the consideration of the inward fabric, the muscles, nerves, membranes, together with all those secret contrivances in the frame of this little world. Thus also is it in the great universe, where the common apprehension of things is not at all considerable, in comparison to those other discoveries, which may be found out by a more exact enquiry.

As this knowledge may conduce to the proving of a God, and making men religious; so likewise may it serve to confirm unto us the truth of the holy scriptures: since the sacred story, in the order of its narrations, does so exactly agree with the conversions of heaven, and logistical astronomy.

It may also stir us up to behave ourselves answerably unto the noble and divine nature of our souls. When I consider the heaven, the works of thy fingers, the moon and the stars which thou hast ordained, what is man, that thou art so mindful of him * ? as to create such vast glorious bodies for his service.

Again, when I consider with myself the strange immen-

* Psal. viii. 3. 6.

sity and bigness of this great universe, in comparison to which, this earth of ours is but as an undiscernible point : when I consider that I carry a soul about me, of far greater worth than all this, and desires that are of a wider extent, and more unbounded capacity than this whole frame of nature; then, methinks, it must needs argue a degenerateness and poverty of spirit, to busy my faculties about so ignoble, narrow a subject as any of these earthly things. What a folly is it in men to have such high conceits of themselves, for some small possessions which they have in the world above others; to keep so great a bustle about so poor a matter? *Hoc est punctum quod inter tot gentes ferro et igni dividitur**. It is but a little point which with so much ado is distributed unto so many nations by fire and sword. What great matter is it to be monarch of a small part of a point? Might not the ants as well divide a little mole-hill into divers provinces, and keep as great a stir in disposing of their government? *punctum est illud in quo navigatis, in quo bellatis, in quo regna desponitis*. All this place wherein we war, and travel, and dispose of kingdoms, is but a point far less than any of those small stars, that at this distance are scarce discernible. Which when the soul does seriously meditate upon, it will begin to despise the narrowness of its present habitation, and think of providing for itself a mansion in those wider spaces above; such as may be more agreeable to the nobleness and divinity of its nature.

Why should any one dream of propagating his name, or spreading his report through the world? When although he had more glory than ambition can hope for, yet as long as all this habitable earth is but an inconsiderable point, what great matter can there be in that fame which is included within such strait contracted limits?

> *Quicunque solam mente præcipiti petit*
> *Summumque credit gloriam,*

---

* Sen. Nat. Quæst. l. 1. Nonne ô terrena animalia consideratis, quibus præsidere videamini? Nam si inter mares videres unum aliquam, jus sibi ac potestatem præ cæteris vindicentem, quanto movereris cachinno, &c. Boetius de Consol. l. 2.

Late patentes ætheris cernat plagas,
   Arctumque terrarum situm.
Brevem replere non valentis ambitum,
   Pudebit aucti nominis *.

" He that to honour only seeks to mount,
" And that his chiefest end doth count;
" Let him behold the largeness of the skies,
" And on the strait earth cast his eyes;
" He will despise the glory of his name,
" Which cannot fill so small a frame."

Why should any one be taken up in the admiration of these lower outsides, these earthly glories? *Respicite cœli spatium, firmitudinem, celeritatem, et aliquando definite vilia mirari†.* He that rightly understands the nature of the heavens, will scarce esteem any other thing worth his notice, much less his wonder.

Now when we lay all this together, that he who hath most in the world, hath almost nothing of it: that the earth itself, in comparison to the universe is but an inconsiderable point; and yet that this whole universe does not bear so great a proportion to the soul of man, as the earth does unto that. I say, when a man in some retired thoughts shall lay all this together, it must needs stir up his spirits to a contempt of these earthly things, and make him place his love and endeavour upon those comforts that may be more answerable to the excellency of his nature.

Without this science, what traffic could we have with foreign nations? What would become of that mutual commerce, whereby the world is now made but as one commonwealth.

Vosque mediis in aquis stellæ, pelagoque timendo.
Decretum monstrastis iter, totique dedistis,
Legibus inventis hominum, commercia mundo.

'Tis you bright stars, that in the fearful sea,
Do guide the pilot through his purposed way.
'Tis your direction that doth commerce give,
With all those men that through the world do live.

* Boetius de Consol. l. 2.   † Idem, lib. 3.

2. As this science is thus profitable in these and many other respects; so likewise is it equally pleasant. The eye (saith the philosopher) is the sense of pleasure, and there are no delights so pure and immaterial as those which enter through that organ. Now to the understanding, which is the eye of the soul, there cannot be any fairer prospect, than to view the whole frame of nature, the fabric of this great universe, to discern that order and comeliness which there is in the magnitude, situation, motion of the several parts that belong unto it; to see the true cause of that constant variety and alteration which there is in the different seasons of the year*. All which must needs enter into a man's thoughts with a great deal of sweetness and complacency. And therefore it was that Julius Cæsar in the broils and tumult of the camp, make choice of this delight:

——————— *Media inter prælia semper,*
Stellarum, cælique plagis, superisque vacavit. †

He always leisure found amidst his wars,
To mark the coast of heaven, and learn the stars.

And for this reason likewise did Seneca, amidst the continual noise and bustle of the court, betake himself to this recreation.

O quam juvabat, quo nihil majus, parens
Natura genuit, operis immensi artifex,
Cælum intueri solis, et currus sacros
Mundique motus, solis alternas vices,
Orbemque Phæbes, astra quem cingunt vaga
Lateque fulgens ætheris magni decus.

O what a pleasure was it to survey
Nature's chief work, the heavens; where we may
View the alternate courses of the sun,
The sacred chariots, how the world doth run:
The moon's bright orb, when she's attended by
Those scattered stars, whose light adorns the sky.

And certainly those eminent men who have this way bestowed a great part of their employment, such as were

* Wis. vii. 18, 19.   † Lucan, l. 10.

Ptolomy, Julius Cæsar, Alphonsus king of Spain, the noble
Tycho, &c. have not only by this means pitched upon that
which for the present was a more solid kind of pleasure and
contentment; but also a surer way to propagate their me-
mories unto future ages. Those great costly pyramids
which were built to perpetuate the memory of their foun-
ders, shall sooner perish and moulder away into their primitive dust, than the names of such worthies shall be forgotten. The monuments of learning are more durable
than the monuments of wealth or power.

All which encouragements may be abundantly enough
to stir any considering man, to bestow some part of his
time in the study and inquisition of these truths.

> *Fœlices animæ, quibus hæc cognoscere primum,*
> *Inque domos superas scandere cura fuit.*

END OF VOL. I.

THE

MATHEMATICAL AND PHILOSOPHICAL

WORKS

OF THE

RIGHT REV. JOHN WILKINS,

LATE LORD BISHOP OF CHESTER.

TO WHICH IS PREFIXED

THE AUTHOR's LIFE,

AND

AN ACCOUNT OF HIS WORKS.

IN TWO VOLUMES.

VOL. II.

CONTAINING,

I. Mercury; or, the Secret and Swift Messenger. Shewing how a Man may with Privacy and Speed communicate his Thoughts to a Friend at any Distance.

II. Mathematical Magic: or the Wonders that may be performed by Mechanical Geometry.
III. An Abstract of his Essay towards a Real Character, and a Philosophical Language.

LONDON:

PRINTED BY C. WHITTINGHAM,
Dean Street, Fetter Lane,

FOR VERNOR AND HOOD, POULTRY; CUTHELL, AND MARTIN, MIDDLE-ROW, HOLBORN; AND J. WALKER, PATERNOSTER-ROW.

1802.

CONTENTS.

VOL. II.

MERCURY,
THE SECRET AND SWIFT MESSENGER.

CHAP. I.

ARCHIMEDES; OR, MECHANICAL POWERS.

BOOK I.

DÆDALUS; OR, MECHANICAL MOTIONS.

BOOK II.

MERCURY:

OR, THE

SECRET AND SWIFT MESSENGER.

SHEWING

HOW A MAN MAY WITH PRIVACY AND SPEED COMMUNICATE
HIS THOUGHTS TO A FRIEND AT A DISTANCE.

TO

THE RIGHT HONOURABLE

GEORGE LORD BERKLEY,

BARON OF BERKLEY, MOBRAY, SEGRAVE, AND BRUCE,

AND KNIGHT OF THE NOBLE ORDER OF THE BATH.

My Lord,

I Do here once more present your Lordship with the fruit of my leisure studies, as a testimony of my readiness to serve you in those sacred matters, to which I devote my more serious hours. I should not have presumed to this dedication, had I not been encouraged by that generousness and sweetness of disposition, which does so eminently adorn your Lordship's place and abilities.

If your Lordship please to excuse this boldness, and to vouchsafe this pamphlet a shelter under your favourable patronage, you shall thereby encourage me in those higher studies, which may be more agreeable to that relation wherein I stand, as being

Your Lordship's servant and chaplain,

J. W.

TO

THE READER.

THAT which first occasioned this discourse, was
the reading of a little pamphlet, stiled *Nuntius
Inanimatus*, commonly ascribed to a late reverend
bishop; wherein he affirms, that there are certain
ways to discourse with a friend, though he were in
a close dungeon, in a besieged city, or a hundred
miles off.

Which promises, at the first perusal, did rather
raise my wonder than belief, having before that
time observed nothing that might give any satisfaction in these particulars. And I should have esteemed them altogether fabulous, had it not been
for the credit of their reputed author.

After this, I did collect all such notes to this
purpose, as I met with in the course of my other
studies.

From whence when I have received full satisfaction, I did for mine own farther delight compose
them into this method.

I have already attained mine own ends, both in the delight of composing this, and the occasion of publishing it: and therefore need not either fear the censure of others, or beg their favour. I could never yet discern, that any reader hath shewed the more charity for the author's bespeaking it.

Farewell.

J. W.

TO MERCURY THE ELDER:

ON THE

MOST LEARNED MERCURY THE YOUNGER.

———————

REST Maia's son, sometimes interpreter
   Of gods, and to us men their messenger:
Take not such pains as thou hast done of old,
To teach men hieroglyphics, and to unfold
Egyptian hidden characters, and how
Men writ in dark obscurity: for now
Trithemius and Selenus both are grown
Such cryptographers, as they scarce will own
Thee for their master; and decipherers know
Such secret ways to write, thou ne'er didst show.
These are but artists which thou didst inspire;
But now thou of a Mercury art sire
Of thine own name, a post with whom the wind,
Should it contend, would be left far behind.
Whose message, as thy metal, strikes the gold
Quite through a wedge of silver uncontrol'd ;
And in a moment's space doth pass as far
As from the arctic to th' antarctic star
So proving what is said of influence,
May now be said of his intelligence,
They neither of them having such a quality
As a relation to locality :
No places distance hindering their commerce,
Who freely traffic through the universe ;
And in a minute can a voyage make
Over the ocean's universal lake.
This son of thine, could any words or praise,
His learning, worth, or reputation raise,
We should be suitors to him to bestow
Encomiums on himself, which we do owe
Unto his worth, and use that eloquence,
Which as his own, must claim pre-eminence :
For thee, 'tis glory enough thou hast a son
Of art, that hath thyself in art outdone.

Sir FRANCIS KINASTON, Knt.

xiv

TO THE UNKNOWN AUTHOR.

OF old, who to the common good apply'd
  Or mind or means, for it were deified:
But chiefly such who new inventions found;
Bacchus for wine, Ceres that till'd the ground.
I know no reason time should breed such odds,
(W' have warrant for't) men now may be stil'd gods.
By hiding who thou art, seek not to miss
The glory due to such a work as this;
But set thy name, that thou may'st have the praise,
Lest to the unknown God we altars raise.

ANTHONY AUCHER, Esq.

TO MY FRIEND THE AUTHOR.

TO praise thy work, were to anticipate
  Thy reader's judgment, and to injure fate;
Injustice to thyself; for real worth
Needs not arts flattery to set it forth.
Some chuse selected wits to write as friends,
Whose verses, when the work fails, make amends,
So as the buyer has his pennyworth,
Though what the author write prove spumy froth.
Thou, of a humour cross to that, hast chose
A friend or two, whose verse hops like rough prose;
From whose inexpert vein thou canst not look
For lines that may enhance the price o'th' book.
Let it commend itself, all we intend
Is but to shew the world thou art our friend.

RICHARD HATTON, Esq.

TO THE READER.

READER, this author has not long ago
  Found out another world to this below:
Though that alone might merit great renown,
Yet in this book he goes beyond the moon:
Beyond the moon indeed, for here you see
That he from thence hath fetched down Mercury;
One that doth tell us things both strange and new,
And yet believe 't they're not more strange than true.
I'm loth to tell thee what rare things they be,
Read thou the book, and then thou lt tell them me.

TOB. WORLRICH, J. C. Doct.

TO HIS HONOURED FRIEND J. W.

ON HIS LEARNED TRACT ,

THE SECRET AND SWIFT MESSENGER.

INIMITABLE Sir, we here discern
  Maxims the Stagirite himself might learn.
Were Plato now alive he'd yield to you,
Confessing something might be known anew.
Fresh heresies (new-nothings) still appear
As almanacks, the births of every year.
This Dutchman writes a comment; that translates;
A third transcribes; your pen alone creates
New necessary sciences: this art
Lay undiscovered as the world's fifth part.
But secrecy's now publish'd; you reveal
By demonstration how we may conceal.
  Our legates are but men, and often may
Great state affairs unwillingly betray;
Caught by some sifting spies, or tell-tale wine,
Which dig up secrets in the deepest mine.
Sometimes, like fire pent in, they outward break,
And 'cause they should be silent, therefore speak.
  Nor are kings' writings safe: to guard their fame,
Like Scævola they wish their hand i'th' flame.
Ink turns to blood; they oft participate
By wax and quill sad Icarus's fate.
Hence noblemen's bad writing proves a plot;
Their letters are but lines, their names a knot.
  But now they shall no more seal their own fall;
No letters prove killing, or capital.
Things pass unknown, and each ambassador's
Strict as the breast of sacred confessors:
Such as the inquisition cannot see;
Such as are forc'd neither by rack, nor fee.
Swift secrecy descends to human powers;
That which was Pluto's helmet, now is ours.
We shall not henceforth be in pay for air,
Transported words being dear as precious ware;
Our thoughts will now arrive before they're stale;
They shall no more wait on the carrier's ale
And hostess, two land-remoraes, which bind
All to a tortoise pace, though words be wind.

This book's a better ark; we brook no stay,
Maugre the deepest flood, or foulest way,
Commerce of goods and souls we owe to two,
(Whose fames shall now be twins) Noah and You.
Each bird is turn'd a parrot, and we see
Esop's beasts made more eloquent by thee,
Wooers again may wing their fetter'd love
By Noah's trusty messenger the dove.
Torches which us'd only to help our sight,
(Like heavenly fires) do give our reason light.
Death's harbingers, arrows, and bullets prove
Like Cupid's darts, ambassadors of love.
Then your diviner hieroglyphics tell,
How we may landskips read, and pictures spell.
You teach how clouds inform, how smokes advise;
Thus saints with incense talk to deities.
Thus by dumb creatures we instructed are,
As the wise men were tutor'd by a star.
　　Since we, true serpents like, do little wrong
With any other member but the tongue;
You tell us how we may by gestures talk;
How feet are made to speak, as well as walk;
How eyes discourse, how mystic nods contrive;
Making our knowledge too, intuitive.
A bell no noise but rhetoric affords;
Our music notes are speeches, sounds are words.
Without a trope there's language in a flow'r,
Conceits are smelt without a metaphor.
Dark subtilties we now shall soon define,
Each organ's turn'd the sense of discipline.
'Tis to your care we owe that we may send
Business unknown to any but our friend.
That which is English friendship to my brother,
May be thought Greek or nonsense to another.
We now may Homer's Iliads confine,
Not in a nut-shell, but a point, or line.
Which art though't seem to exceed faith, yet who
Tries it will find both truth and reason too.
'Tis not like jugglers tricks, absurd, when shown;
But more and more admir'd, the more 'tis known.
Writing's an act of emanation,
And thoughts speed quick and far as day doth run.

RICHARD WEST, C. C. OX.

MERCURY,

THE SECRET AND SWIFT MESSENGER.

CHAP. I.

The dependance of this knowledge in nature. The authors that have treated of it. Its relation to the art of grammar.

EVERY rational creature, being of an imperfect and dependent happiness, is therefore naturally endowed with an ability to communicate its own thoughts and intentions ; that so by mutual services, it might the better promote itself in the prosecution of its own well-being.

And because there is so vast a difference betwixt a spirit and a body, therefore hath the wisdom of Providence contrived a distinct way and means, whereby they are each of them enabled to discourse, according to the variety of their several natures.

The angels or spiritual substances, *per insinuationem specierum*, (as the schoolmen speak *) by insinuating of the species, or an unveiling of their own natures in the knowledge of such particulars as they would discover to another. And since they are of an homogeneous and immaterial essence, therefore do they hear, and know, and speak, not with several parts, but with their whole sub-

---

* Aquinas part 1. Quæst. 107. Zanch. de operibus Dei, part 1. l. 3. c. 19.

stance. And though the apostle mentions the tongue ot angels*, yet that is only *per concessionem, et ex hypothesi.*

But now, men that have organical bodies, cannot communicate their thoughts so easy and immediate a way. And therefore have need of some corporeal instruments, both for the receiving and conveying of knowledge. Unto both which functions, nature hath designed several parts. Amongst the rest, the ear is chiefly the sense of discipline or learning, and the tongue the instrument of teaching. The communion betwixt both these, is by speech or language, which was but one at first, but hath since been confounded into several kinds. And experience now shews, that a man is equally disposed for the learning of all, according as education shall direct him †. Which would not be, if (as some fondly conceive) any one of them were natural unto us. For *intus existens prohibet alienum.*

Or suppose that a man could be brought up to the speaking of another tongue ‡, yet this would not hinder, but that he should still retain his knowledge of that which was natural. For if those which are gotten by art do not hinder one another, much less would they be any impediment to that which is from nature. And according to this it will follow, that most men should be of a double language, which is evidently false. Whence likewise you may guess at the absurdity of their enquiries, who have sought to find out the primitive tongue, by bringing up infants in such silent solitary places, where they might not hear the speech of others.

Languages are so far natural unto us, as other arts and sciences. A man is born without any of them, but yet capable of all.

Now, because words are only for those that are present both in time and place ; therefore to these there hath been added, the invention of letters and writing, which are such a

* 1 Cor. xiii. 1.   † Vallesius Sacr. Phil. cap. 3.
‡ Cæl. Rhod. Ant. lect. l. 2. 9. c. 14.

representation of our words (though more permanent) as our words are of our thoughts. By these we may discourse with them that are remote from us, not only by the distance of many miles, but also of many ages. *Hujus usu scimus maxime constare humanitatem vitæ, memoriam, ac hominum immortalitatem*, saith Pliny*. *Quid hoc magnificentius? Quid æque mirandum? in quod ne mortis quidem avida rapacitas jus ullum habeat*, saith Rhodiginus. This being the chiefest means both for the promoting of human society, and the perpetuating our names unto following times.

How strange a thing this art of writing did seem at its first invention, we may guess by the late discovered Americans, who were amazed to see men converse with books, and could scarce make themselves believe that a paper should speak; especially, when after all their attention and listening to any writing (as their custom was) they could never perceive any words or sound to proceed from it.

There is a pretty relation to this purpose, concerning an Indian slave; who being sent by his master with a basket of figs and a letter, did by the way eat up a great part of his carriage, conveying the remainder unto the person to whom he was directed; who when he had read the letter, and not finding the quantity of figs answerable to what was spoken of, he accuses the slave of eating them, telling him what the letter said against him †. But the Indian (notwithstanding this proof) did confidently abjure the fact, cursing the paper, as being a false and lying witness. After this, being sent again with the like carriage, and a letter expressing the just number of figs that were to be delivered, he did again, according to his former practice, devour a great part of them by the way; but before he meddled with any, (to prevent all following accusations) he first took the letter, and hid that under a great stone,

---

* Nat. Hist. l. 14. c. 11. Antiq. lect. l. 4. c. 3.
† Hermannus Hugo de Orig. Scribendi Præf.

assuring himself, that if it did not see him eat the figs, it could never tell of him; but being now more strongly accused than before, he confesses the fault, admiring the divinity of the paper, and for the future does promise his best fidelity in every employment.

Such strange conceits did those wilder nations entertain, concerning this excellent invention. And doubtless it must needs argue a vast ability both of wit and memory in that man who did first confine all those different sounds of voice, (which seem to be almost of infinite variety) within the bounds of those few letters in the alphabet.

The first inventor of this was thought to be the Egyptian Mercury*, who is therefore stiled the messenger of the Gods. To which purpose the poets have furnished him with wings for swiftness and dispatch in his errands. And because the planet of that name was thought to observe a more various and obscure revolution than any of the rest, therefore likewise did they attribute unto him such secret and subtle motions, as might make him a trusty and private messenger, and so the fitter for that preferment to which for this invention they had advanced him.

There is yet another way of discoursing, by signs and gestures; and though it be not so common in practice as either of the other, yet in nature perhaps it is before them both, since infants are able this way to express themselves, before they have the benefit of speech.

But now, because none of these ways in ordinary use, are either so secret or swift as some exigencies would require; therefore many of the ancients have busied themselves in a further enquiry, how both these deficiencies may be remedied; as conceiving that such a discovery would be of excellent use, especially for some occasions that are incident to statesmen and soldiers.

That the ignorance of secret and swift conveyances, hath often proved fatal, not only to the ruin of particular

* Cic. l. 3. de Nat. Deor. Polyd. Vir. de Inventor. l. 1. c. 6. Vossius de Grammatica, l. 1. c. 9. Natal. Comes Mytho. l. 5. c. 5.

persons, but also of whole armies and kingdoms, may easily appear to any one that is but little versed in story. And therefore the redressing of these may be a subject worth our enquiry.

Amongst the ancients that have most laboured in these particulars, Æneas[1], Cleomenes, and Democritus, (as they are cited by Polybius[2]) were for their inventions of this kind, more remarkably eminent. And that author[3] himself hath given us such an exact relation of the knowledge of antiquity in these things, that it is a wonder these following ages should either take no more notice, or make no more use of it. Besides these, there is also Julius Africanus, and Philo Mechanicus, two ancient Grecians, who have likewise treated of this subject.

The military significations in use amongst the Romans, are handled by Vegetius[4] and Frontinus[5].

Their notes of secrecy, and abbreviation in writing, are largely set down by Valerius Probus[6], and Pet. Diaconus. There is likewise a volume of these set forth by Janus Gruterus, which for their first invention are commonly ascribed unto Cicero and Seneca[7].

In latter times these particulars have been more fully handled by the Abbot Trithemius[8], Theodorus Bibliander[9], Baptista Porta[10], Cardan. Subtil. l. 17. de var. C. 12. 6. Isaac Casaubon[11], Johannes Walchius[12], Gustaphus Selenus[13], Gerardus Vossius[14], Hermannus Hugo[15], and divers others in particular languages.

Amongst the rest, our English Aristotle, the learned Verulam, in that work truly stiled the advancement of learning, hath briefly contracted the whole substance of what may be said in this subject. Where he refers it to the art of Grammar, noting it as a deficient part. And in refe-

---

[1] Poliorcetica. [2] Hist. l. 10. [3] Polybius, ib. juxta finem. [4] De re militia. l. 3. c. 5. [5] De Strat. [6] L. de notis antiquus. [7] The father [8] L. de Polygraph. item de Stenograph. [9] Tract de ratione commun. linguarum. [10] Lib. de Zyphris. [11] Notis in Æneæ Polyorcetica. [12] Fab. 9. [13] De Cryptog. [14] De Gram. L. 1. c. 40. [15] L. de Or. Scrib. de Augm. Scientiar. l. 6. c. 1.

rence to this is it handled by most of those authors who
have treated of it.

That art, in its true latitude comprehending a treaty,
concerning all the ways of discourse, whether by speech,
or by writing, or by gesture, together with the several circumstances pertaining to them. And so this subject belongs to the mint of knowledge ; expressions being current
for conceits, as money is for valuations.

Now as it will concern a man that deals in traffic, to understand the several kinds of money, and that it may be
framed of other materials besides silver and gold : so likewise does it behove them who profess the knowledge of
nature or reason, rightly to apprehend the several ways
whereby they may be expressed.

So that besides the usefulness of this subject for some
special occasions, it doth also belong unto one of the liberal arts.

From which considerations we may infer, that these
particulars are not so trivial, as perhaps otherways they
would seem ; and that there is sufficient motive to excite
any industrious spirit unto a further search after them.

In this following discourse I shall enquire,

1. Concerning the secrecy of means, whereby to communicate our thoughts.

2. Concerning their swiftness, or quick passing at any
great distance.

3. How they may be both joined together in the conveyance of any message.

In the prosecution of which, I shall also mention (besides the true discoveries) most of those other ways,
whether magical, or fabulous, that are received upon common tradition.

CHAP. II.

The conditions requisite to secrecy : the use of it in the matter of speech, either

By { FABLES OF THE HEATHEN.
{ PARABLES OF SCRIPTURE.

TO the exactness of secrecy in any way of discourse, there are these two qualifications requisite.

1. That it be difficult to be unfolded, if it should be doubted of, or examined.

2. That it be (if possible) altogether devoid of suspicion; for so far as it is liable to this, it may be said to come short in the very nature of secrecy; since what is once suspected, is exposed to the danger of examination, and in a ready way to be discovered, but if not, yet a man is more likely to be disappointed in his intentions, when his proceedings are mistrusted.

Both these conditions together are to be found but in few of the following instances; only they are here specified, to shew what a man should aim at, in the inventions of this nature.

The art of secret information in the general, as it includes all significatory signs, may be stiled *cryptomeneses*, or private intimations.

The particular ways of discoursing, were before intimated to be threefold.

1. By speaking.
2. By writing.
3. By signs or gestures.

According to which variety, there are also different ways of secrecy.

1. *Cryptologia.*
2. *Cryptographia.*
3. *Semæologia.*

Cryptologia, or the secrecy of speaking, may consist either,

        1. In the matter.

        2. In the words.

1. In the matter : when the thing we would utter is so concealed under the expression of some other matter, that it is not of obvious conceit. To which purpose are the metaphors, allegories, and divers other tropes of oratory; which, so far as they concern the ornament of speech, do properly belong to rhetoric; but as they may be applied for the secrecy of speech, so are they reducible unto this part of grammar.

To this likewise appertains all that ænigmatical learning, unto which not only the learned heathen, but their gods also were so much devoted, as appears by the strange and frequent ambiguities of the oracles and sybils. And those were counted the most profound philosophers amongst them, who were best able for the invention of such affected obscurities.

Of this kind also were all those mysterious fables, under which the ancients did veil the secrets of their religion and philosophy, counting it a prophane thing to prostitute the hidden matters of either, unto vulgar apprehension. *Quia sciunt inimicam esse naturæ, apertam nudamque expositionem sui; quæ, sicut vulgaribus hominum sensibus, intellectum sui, vario rerum tegmine operimentoque subtraxit, ita a prudentibus arcana sua voluit per fabulosa tractari,* saith Macrobius*. The gods and nature would not themselves have hidden so many things from us, if they had intended them for common understandings, or that others should treat of them after an easy and perspicuous way : hence was it that the learned men of former times were so generally inclined to involve all their learning, in obscure and mysterious expressions. Thus did the Egyptian priests, the Pythagoreans, Platonicks, and almost all other sects and professions.

* In Somn. Scip. lib. 1. cap. 2.

And to this general custom of those ages (we may guess) the Holy Ghost does allude, in the frequent parables both of the Old and New Testament. *Parabola est sermo similitudinarius, qui aliud dicit, aliut significat*, saith Aquinas *. It is such a speech of similitude, as says one thing and means anothei. The disciples do directly oppose it to plain speaking†, Behold now speakest thou plainly and no parables.

And elsewhere it is intimated, that our Saviour did use that manner of teaching for the secrecy of it: that those proud and perverse auditors, who would not apply themselves to the obedience of his doctrine, might not so much as understand it ‡. To whom it is not given to know the mysteries of the kingdom of God, to them all things are done in parables, that seeing they may see and not perceive, and hearing they may hear and not understand.

The art of these was so to imply a secret argument §, that the adversary might unawares be brought over to an acknowledgment and confession of the thing we would have. Thus did Nathan unexpectedly discover to David, the cruelty and injustice of his proceedings in the case of Uriah ||. Thus did another prophet make Ahab condemn himself, for suffering the king of Syria to escape ¶. And by this means did our Saviour in the parable of the vineyard, and the unjust husbandman **, force the unbelieving Jews to a secret acknowledgment of those judgments they had themselves deserved.

Of this nature was that argument of an ancient orator, who when the enemies had proposed peace upon this condition, that the city should banish their teachers and philosophers, he steps up and tells the people a tale, of certain wars betwixt the wolves and the sheep, and that the wolves promised to make a league, if the sheep would put away

* Commen. in Isai. xiv.   † John xvi. 29.
‡ Mat. xiii. 10, 11.   Mark. iv. 11, 12.   § Glos. Phil. l. 2. par. 1.
par. 1. Tract. 2. Sect. 5. || 2 Sam. xii.   ¶ 1 Kings xx. 39.
** Mat. xxi. 31.

their mastiff-dogs.   By this means better instructing them of the danger and madness there would be, in yielding to such a condition.

The jewish doctors do generally in their Talmud, and all their other writings, accustom themselves to a parabolical way of teaching; and it is observed, that many of those horrid fables that are fathered upon them, do arise from a misapprehension of them in this particulars: whilst others interpret that according to the letter *, which they intended only for the moral.   As that which one rabby relates, concerning a lion in the forest of Elay, that at the distance of four hundred leagues, did with his roaring shake down the walls of Rome, and make the women abortive. Wherein he did not affirm the existence of any such monster, but only intimate the terribleness and power of the divine majesty.   But this by the way.

By this art many men are able in their ordinary discourses, so secretly to convey their counsels, or reproofs, that none shall understand them, but those whom they concern.   And this way of teaching hath a great advantage above any other, by reason it hath much more power in exciting the fancy and affections.   Plain arguments and moral precepts barely proposed, are more flat in their operation, not so lively and persuasive, as when they steal into a man's assent, under the covert of a parable.

To be expert in this particular, is not in every man's power; like poetry, it requires such a natural faculty as cannot be taught.   But so far as it falls under the rules and directions of art, it belongs to the precepts of oratory.

In the general it is to be observed, That in these cases a man must be very careful to make choice of such a subject, as may bear in it some proper analogy and resemblance to the chief business.   And he must before-hand in his thoughts, so aptly contrive the several parts of the similitude, that they may fitly answer unto those particular passages which are of greatest consequence.

* Scickard Examen. Commen. Rabbin. dis. 7.

CHAP. III.

Concerning that secrecy of speech, which consists in the words, either

By inventing new ones, ⎧ CANTING.
   as in. . . . . . . ⎩ CONJURING.

Or by a changing ⎧ INVERSION.
  of the known ⎫ TRANSMUTATION.
  language, whe- ⎬ DIMINUTION.
  ther. . . . . ⎭ AUGMENTATION.

THE secret ways of speaking, which consist in the matter of discourse, have been already handled. Those
that are in the words are twofold. Either,

1. By inventing new words of our own, which shall signify upon compact.

2. Or by such an alteration of any known language,
that in pronunciation it shall seem as obscure, as if it were
altogether barbarous.

To the first kind we may refer the canting of beggars;
who though they retain the common particles, yet have
imposed new names upon all such matters as may happen
to be of greatest consequence and secrecy.

And of this nature the charms of witches, and language
of magicians seem to be. Though of these it may well be
doubted, whether they have any signification at all. And
if they have, whether any understand them, but the devil
himself. It is probable he did invent such horrid and barbarous sounds, that by them he might more easily delude
the weak imaginations of his credulous disciples. Martinus
de Arles*, an archdeacon in Navar, speaking of a conju-
ring-book, that was found in a parish under his visitation,

* Tract. de superstitionibus.

       †

repeats out of it these forms of discoursing with the devil. *Conjuro te per œlim, per œlion, per seboan, per adonay, per allelujah, per tanti, per archabuløn,* &c.   And a little after, *Sitis allegati & constricti per ista sancta nomina Dei, hir, œlli, habet, sat, mi, filisgœ, adrotiagundi, tat, chamiteram,* &c.   And in another place, *Coriscion, Matatron, Caladafon, Ozcozo, Yosiel,* &c.

In which forms the common particles and words of usual sense, are plainly set down in ordinary Latin; but many of the other, which seem to have the greatest efficacy, are of such secret sense, as I think no linguist can discover.

The inventions of this kind do not fall under any particular rule or maxim, but may be equally infinite to the variety of articulate sounds.

The second way of secrecy in speech *, is by an alteration of any known language, which is far more easy, and may prove of as much use for the privacy of it, as the other.   This may be performed four ways.

1. By inversion, when either the letters or syllables are spelled backwards.

Mitto tibi METULAS *cancros imitare legendo,* where the word SALUTEM is expressed by an inversion of the letters. Or as in this other example, *Stisho estad, veca biti,* which by an inversion of the syllables, is *Hostis adest, cave tibi.*

2. By transmutation, or a mutual changing of one letter for another in pronunciation; answerable to that form of writing, mentioned in the seventh chapter.   And though this may seem of great difficulty, yet use and experience will make it easy.

3. By contracting some words, and leaving part of them out; pronouncing them after some such way as they were wont to be both written and printed in ancient copies. Thus *ā ā* stands for *anima,* *Arl's* for *Aristoteles.*   But this can be but of small use in the English tongue, because that does consist most of monosyllables.

* Porta de furi. lit. l. 1. cap 5.   Selenus de Cryptographia l 2. c. 1.

4. By augmenting words with the addition of other letters. Of which kind is that secret way of discoursing in ordinary use, by doubling the vowels that make the syllables and interposing G. or any other consonant, K. P. T. R. &c. or other syllables, as Porta lib. 1. cap. 5. de furtiv. liter. notis. Thus if I would say, Our plot is discovered, it must be pronounced thus, *Ougour plogot igis digiscogovegereged.* Which does not seem so obscure in writing, as it will in speech and pronunciation. And it is so easy to be learnt, that I have known little children, almost as soon as they could speak, discourse to one another as fast this way, as they could in their plainest English.

But all these latter kinds of secrecy in speech, have this grand inconvenience in them, that they are not without suspicion *.

There are some other ways of speaking by inarticulate sounds, which I shall mention afterwards.

CHAP. IV.

Concerning the secret conveyances of any written message in use amongst the ancients.

Either by { LAND.
WATER.
THE OPEN AIR.

THE secrecy of any written message { Conveyance. may consist either in the { Writing.

1. In the conveyance, when the letter is so closely concealed in the carriage of it, as to delude the search and suspicion of the adversary. Of which kind ancient historians do furnish us with divers relations, reducible in the general unto these three heads. Those that are

* Chap. 17, 18.

1. By Land.
2. By Water.
3. Through the open Air.

1. The secret conveyances by land, may be of numberless variety; but those ancient inventions of this nature, which to my remembrance are most obvious and remarkable, are these.

That of Harpagus the Mede (mentioned by Herodotus and Justin *) who when he would exhort Cyrus to a conspiracy against the king his uncle, (and not daring to commit any such message to the ordinary way of conveyance, especially since the king's jealousy had stopped up all passages with spies and watchmen) he puts his letters into the belly of a hare, which, together with certain hunters nets, he delivered unto a trusty servant, who under this disguise of a huntsman, got an unsuspected passage to Cyrus. And Astyages himself was by this conspiracy bereaved of that kingdom which was then the greatest monarchy in the world.

To this purpose likewise is that of Demaratus †, king of Sparta, who being banished from his own country, and received in the Persian court, when he there understood of Xerxes his design and preparation for a war with Greece, he used these means for the discovery of it unto his countrymen. Having written an epistle in a tablet of wood ‡, he covered over the letters with wax, and then committed it unto a trusty servant, to be delivered unto the magistrates of Lacedæmon; who when they had received it, were for a long time in a perplexed consultation what it should mean; they did see nothing written, and yet could not conceive but that it should import some weighty secret; till at length the king's sister did accidentally discover the writing under the wax: by which means the Grecians

* Herod. l. 1. cap. 123. Justin. l. 1.
† Justin. l. 2. See the like related of Hamucar. Ib. l. 21.
‡ Such as formerly they were wont to write upon, whence the phrase *Rasa tabula,* and *litera a litura.*

were so well provided for the following war, as to give a defeat to the greatest and most numerous army that is mentioned in history.

The fathers of the council of Ephesus *, when Nestorius was condemned, being strictly debarred from all ordinary ways of conveyances, were fain to send unto Constantinople by one in the disguise of a beggar.

Some messengers have been sent away in coffins as being dead: some others in the disguise of brute creatures, as those whom Josephus mentions in the siege of Jotapata †, who crept out of the city by night like dogs.

Others have conveyed letters to their imprisoned friends, by putting them into the food they were to receive, which is related of Polycrita. Laurentius Medicus ‡ involving his epistles in a piece of bread, did send them by a certain nobleman in the form of a beggar. There is another relation of one, who rolled up his letters in a wax-candle, bidding the messenger tell the party that was to receive it, that the candle would give him light for his business. There is yet a stranger conveyance spoken of in Æneas ‖, by writing on leaves, and afterwards with these leaves covering over some sore or putrid ulcer, where the enemy would never suspect any secret message.

Others have carried epistles inscribed upon their own flesh, which is reckoned amongst those secret conveyances mentioned by Ovid.

> *Caveat hoc custos, pro charta, conscia tergum*
> *Præbeat, inquæ suo corpore verba ferat* §.

But amongst all the ancient practices in this kind, there is none for the strangeness, to be compared unto that of Hystiæus, mentioned by Herodotus, and out of him in Aulus Gellius ¶; who whilst he resided with Darius in Per-

---

* Isaac Casa. Notis in Æneæ Polior. c. 31.
† De Bello Judaic. l. 3. c. 8.
‡ Herm. Hugo de Orig. Scrib. c. 15.   Solemn. de Crytographia, l. 8. c. 7.   ‖ Poliorcet. c. 31.   § De Arte Amand.
¶ Herod. l. 5. c. 35. Noctes Atti. l. 17. c. 10.

sia, being desirous to send unto Aristagoras in Greece, about revolting from the Persian government (concerning which they had before conferred together) but not knowing well how at that distance to convey so dangerous a business with sufficient secrecy, he at length contrived it after this manner: he chose one of his houshold-servants that was troubled with sore eyes, pretending that for his recovery his hair must be shaved, and his head scarified; in the performance of which Hystiæus took occasion to imprint his secret intentions on his servant's head; and keeping him close at home till his hair was grown, he then told him, that for his perfect recovery, he must travel into Greece unto Aristagoras, who by shaving his hair the second time, would certainly restore him. By which relation you may see what strange shifts the ancients were put unto, for want of skill in this subject that is here discoursed of.

It is reported of some fugitive Jews * at the siege of Jerusalem, who more securely to carry away their gold, did first melt it into bullets, and then swallow it down, venting it afterwards amongst their other excrements †. Now if a man had but his faculty, who could write Homer's Iliads in so small a volume as might be contained in a nut-shell; it were an easy matter for him, by this trick of the Jews, securely to convey a whole pacquet of letters.

When all the land-passages have been stopped up, then have the ancients used other secret conveyances by water; writing their intentions on thin plates of lead, and fastening them to the arms or thighs of some expert swimmer. Frontinus § relates, that when Lucullus would inform a besieged city of his coming to succour them, he put his letters into two bladders, betwixt which a common soldier in the disguise of a sea-monster, was appointed to swim into the city. There have been likewise more exquisite inventions to pass under the water, either by a man's self, or in a boat, wherein he might also carry provision, only

* Joseph. de Bello Juda. l. 6. c. 15.   † Solin. Polyhist. c. 5.
§ De Stratag. l. 3. c. 13.

having a long trunk or pipe, with a tunnel at the top of it, to let down fresh air. But for the prevention of all such conveyances, the ancients were wont in their strictest sieges, to cross the rivers with strong nets *, to fasten stakes in several parts of the channel with sharp irons, as the blades of swords, sticking upon them.

3. Hence was it that there have been other means attempted through the open air, either by using birds, as pigeons and swallows, instead of messengers, of which I shall treat more particularly in the sixteenth chapter. Or else by fastening a writing to an arrow, or the weight that is cast from a sling.

Somewhat of this nature, was that intimation agreed upon betwixt David and Jonathan †, though that invention does somewhat savour of the ancient simplicity and rudeness. It was a more exact invention mentioned by Herodotus ‡ concerning Artabazus and Timoxenus, who when they could not come together, were wont to inform one another of any thing that concerned their affairs, by fastening a letter unto an arrow, and directing it unto some appointed place, where it might be received.

Thus also Cleonymus ‖ king of Lacedæmon, in the siege of the city Trezene, enjoined the soldiers to shoot several arrows into the town, with notes fastened unto them having this inscription, Ηκω τον πολιν ελευθερωσαν. I come that I may restore this place to its liberty. Upon which the credulous and discontented inhabitants were very willing to let him enter.

When Cicero was so straightly besieged by the Gauls, that the soldiers were almost ready to yield; Cæsar being desirous to encourage him with the news of some other forces that were to come unto his aid, did shoot an arrow into the city, with these words fastened unto it, *Cæsar Ciceroni fiduciam optat, expecta auxilia.* By which means

---

* Plin. l. 10. c. 37. † 1 Sam. xx.
‡ Urania, sive l. 8. c. 128. ‖ Polyænus, l. 2. See Plutarch in Cimon.

the soldiers were persuaded to hold out so long, till these new succours did arrive and break up the siege.

The same thing might also be done more securely, by rolling up a note within the head of an arrow, and then shooting of it to a confederate's tent, or to any other appointed place.

To this purpose is that which Lypsius * relates out of Appian, concerning an ancient custom for the besieged to write their minds briefly in a little piece of lead, which they could with a sling cast a great distance, and exactly hit any such particular place as should be agreed upon, where the confederate might receive it, and by the same means return an answer.

Of this nature likewise are those kind of bullets, lately invented in these German wars, in which they can shoot, not only letters, corn, and the like, but (which is the strangest) powder also into a besieged city.

But amongst all other possible conveyances through the air, imagination itself cannot conceive any one more useful, than the invention of a flying chariot, which I have mentioned elsewhere †.   Since by this means a man may have as free a passage as a bird, which is not hindered, either by the highest walls, or the deepest rivers and trenches, or the most watchful centinels.   But of this perhaps I may have occasion to treat more largely in some other discourse.

* Poliorcet. l. 4. c.   Dialog. 2. mentioned also by Heliodor. Hist.
Æthio. l. 9.   † World in the Moon, chap. 14.

CHAP. V.

*Of that secrecy which consists in the materials of writing,
whether the paper or ink.*

THE several inventions of the ancients, for the private conveyance of any written message, were the subject of the last chapter.

The secrecy of writing may consist,

Either in { THE MATERIALS,
or,
THE FORM.

1. The materials of writing, are, the paper and ink * (or that which is instead of them), both which may be so privately ordered, that the inscribed sense shall not be discoverable, without certain helps and directions.

1. The chief contrivance of secrecy by the paper in use among the ancients, was, the Lacedemonian scytale; the manner of which was thus: there were provided two round staves, of an equal length and size, the magistrates always retaining one of them at home, and the other being carried abroad by the general, at his going forth to war. When there was any secret business to be writ by it, their manner was, to wrap a narrow thong of parchment about one of these staves, by a serpentine revolution, so that the edges of it might meet close together; upon both which edges they inscribed their epistle; whereas, the parchment being taken off, there appeared nothing but pieces of letters on the sides of it, which could not be joined together into the right sense, without the true scytale. Thus is it briefly and fully described by Ausonius †.

Vel Lacedemoniam scytalen imitare libelli,
Segmina pergamei, tereti, circumdata ligno,
Perpetuo inscribens versu, deinde solutus,
Non respondentes sparso dabit ordine formas.

---

* Selenus de Cryptogra. l. 8. c. 1. 4.　　† Ausonius ad Paulinum.

You may read in Plutarch, how by this means Pharna-
baz did deceive Lysander *.

It is true, indeed, that this way was not of such inextri-
cable secrecy, but that a little examination might have
easily discovered it (as Scaliger † truly observes); however, in those ages, which were less versed in these kinds
of experiments, it seemed much more secret than now it
does unto us; and in these times, there are such other
means of private discoursing, which even Scaliger's eyes
(as good as they were) could not discover ‡. And therefore it was too inconsiderate and magisterial a sentence of
him, from thence to conclude all this kind of learning to
be vain and useless, serving only for imposture, and to perplex the enquirer.

It is certain, that some occasions may require the exactest privacy; and it is as certain, that there may be some
ways of secrecy, which it were madness for a man to think
he could unfold. *Furori simile esse videtur, sibi aliquem
persuadere, tam circumspectum hominem esse posse, ut se à
furtivo quodam scripto, abditaque machinatione tueri possit;
nam astans quilibet, vel procul distans loquitur, & factum
nunciat, ut non solum à nemine percipiatur, sed ne sic quidem significare quippiam posse existimet,* saith Vegetius §.
And Baptista Porta ‖, who had a strange and incredible ability in discovering of secret writings, yet doth ingeniously
confess, *Multa esse posse furtiva scripta, quæ se interpre-
taturum quenquam polliceri, furorem ac delirium plane
existimarem.*

So that though the ancient inventions of this kind were
too easily discoverable, yet Scaliger had no reason to conclude this to be a needless art, or that therefore he could
unfold any other way that might be invented. But this by
the by.

2. The other material of writing, is, the ink, or that li-

---

* In Vita Lysandri.   † Exerc. 327.
‡ Vossius de Arte Gram. l. 1. c. 40.   § Veget. de re milit. l. 3.
‖ Proœm. l. 3. de furtivis notis.

quor which is used instead of it; by which means also there are sundry ways of secrecy, commonly mentioned in natural magic *.

Thus, if a man write with salt armoniac dissolved in water, the letters will not appear legible, till the paper be held by the fire: this others affirm to be true also in the juice of onions, lemons, with divers the like acid and corroding moistures.

And on the contrary, those letters that are written with dissolved alum, will not be discernible, till the paper be dipped in water.

There are some other juices, that do not appear, till the paper be held betwixt a candle and the eye.

That which is written with the water of putrified willow, or the distilled juice of glow-worms, will not be visible but in the dark; as Porta affirms from his own experience †.

There is also a secret way of writing with two several inks, both of them alike in colour, but the one being of that nature, that it will easily be rubbed or washed off, and the other not.

A man may likewise write secretly with a raw egg, the letters of which being thoroughly dried, let the whole paper be blacked over with ink, that it may appear without any inscription; and when this ink is also well dried, if you do afterwards gently scrape it over with a knife, it will fall off from those places, where before the words were written.

Those letters that were described with milk, or urine, or fat, or any other glutinous moisture, will not be legible, unless dust be first scattered upon them; which, by adhering to those places, will discover the writing. This way is mentioned by Ovid ‡:

Tuta quoque est, fallitque oculos è lacte recenti
Litera, carbonis pulvere tange, leges.

* Porca Magiæ, l. 16. Wecker. de Secret. l. 14. Joach. Fortius Experient. Cardan. Subt. l. 17. Item de varietate, l. 12. c. 61.
† Bibliander de Ratione com. linguarum. De furtiv. lit. l. 1. c. 15.
‡ De Arte Amandi.

And it is thought that Attalus made use of this device, the better to excite the courage of his soldiers. Being before the battle to sacrifice to the gods for success, as he pulled out the entrails of the beast, he described upon them these words, *Regis victoria*, which he had before written backward in his hand with some gummy juice. The entrails being turned up and down by the priest, to find out their signification, the letters did by that means gather so much dust as to appear legible. By which omen the soldiers were so strangely heightened in their hopes and valour, that they won the day.

Unto these experiments of secrecy in the materials of writing, some add those other ways of expressing any private intimation, by drawing a string through the holes of a little tablet or board*; these holes should be of the same number with the letters, unto which by compact they should be severally applied. The order of the threads passing through them, may serve to express any words, and so consequently any sense we would discover.

To this purpose likewise is that other way of secret information, by divers knots tied upon a string, according to certain distances, by which a man may as distinctly, and yet as secretly, express his meaning, as by any other way of discourse. For who would mistrust any private news or treachery to lie hid in a thread, wherein there was nothing to be discerned, but sundry confused knots, or other the like marks?

The manner of performing it is thus: let there be a square piece of plate, or tablet of wood like a trencher, with the twenty-four letters described on the top of it, at equal distances, and after any order that may be agreed upon before-hand; on both the opposite sides let there be divers little teeth, on which the string may be hitched or fastened for its several returns, as in the following figure.

---

* Gust. Selenus de Cryptographia, l. 8. c. 3.

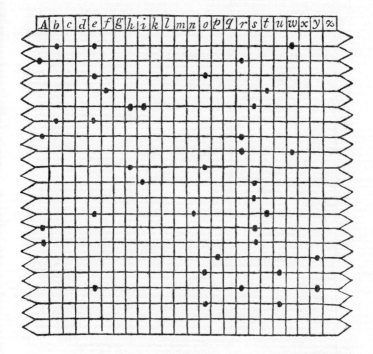

Where the string is supposed to be fastened by a loop on the first tooth, towards the letter A, and afterwards to be drawn successively over all the rest. The marks upon it do express the secret meaning: *Beware of this bearer, who is sent as a spy over you.* When it is taken off, and sent to a confederate, he may easily understand its intention, by applying it to his own tablet, which must be answerable unto this. The instrument may be made much longer than is here expressed: but if the matter to be revealed should happen to be more than the tablet would bear, then may it be supplied either by another string, or else by beginning again with that part of the same string wherein the last letter was terminated.

There may be divers other inventions of this kind, but I have not observed any more remarkable than those which are already mentioned.

CHAP. VI.

Secret writing with the common letters, by changing of their places.

THAT secrecy which does consist in the form of writing, is when the words or letters are so framed by compact, that they are not of ordinary signification *. The inventions of this kind may, both for their pleasure and benefit, justly challenge a place amongst our other studies †.

St. Austin speaking of such human inventions as are to be embraced or avoided, and rejecting all magical institutions and commerce with the devil, he adjoins, *Ea vero quæ homines cum hominibus habent, assumenda, & maxime literarum figuræ, &c. Ex eo genere sunt etiam notæ, quas qui didicerunt, proprie notarii appellantur. Utilia sunt ista, nec discuntur illicite, nec superstitiose implicant, nec luxu enervant, si'tantum occupent, ut majoribus rebus, quibus inservire debent, non sint impedimento ‡.*

This way of secret writing may be contrived, either,

1. By the common letters.

2. Or by some invented notes and characters instead of them.

Both these being distinguishable into those kinds that contain either,

1. Equal.

2. Or more.

3. Or fewer signs than are naturally required to the true framing of the word.

The particulars of these may be altered to such great variety as cannot be reckoned, and therefore I shall specify

---

* Selenus de Cryptographia, l. 2. c. 5.

† Ars notarum occultandi inter artes subtilitate præstantes annumeranda est. Cardan. Subtil. l. 17.   ‡ De Doctrin. Christiana, l. 2. c. 26.

those only which seem most remarkable, either for their antiquity or usefulness.

The way of secret writing by equal letters, is, either by changing of

1. Their places, or
2. Their powers.

1. By altering of the places;

Either of the $\begin{cases} \text{LINES.} \\ \text{LETTERS.} \\ \text{BOTH.} \end{cases}$

1. A man may obscure the sense, by perplexing the order of the lines. If they be written, not only from the left hand to the right, but also from the right hand to the left, as in the eastern languages; or from the top to the bottom, and so upward again, as is commonly related to be usual amongst the inhabitants of Taprobana in the South Sea, with those in China and Japan *: according to this following example.

```
e  r  f  d  l  e  e  l  l  t
i  e  t  o  o  s  w  i  i  h
l  s  u  u  h  h  s  n  t  e
p  h  o  t  o  a  v  c  s  p
p  a  h  t  t  l  t  r  h  e
u  n  t  h  e  l  s  e  t  s
s  d  i  e  l  n  g  a  o  t
y  s  w  s  b  o  n  s  d  i
d  p  e  i  a  t  o  e  c  l
e  e  g  e  e  b  m  a  n  e
```

In the reading of which, if you begin at the first letter towards the right hand, and so downwards, and then upwards again, you may find these words expressed:

The pestilence doth still increase amongst us; we shall not be able to hold out the siege without fresh and speedy supply.

* Diodor. Sic. Biblioth. l. 2.   Herman. Hugo de Orig. Scrib. c. 8.

2. A man may obscure the sense of his writing, by trans-posing each letter, according to some unusual order. As, suppose the first letter should be at the latter end of the line, the second at the beginning, or the like.

3. The meaning of any written message may be con-cealed, by altering the order both of the letters and the lines together. As if a man should write each letter in two several lines. thus:

T e o l i r a e l m s f m s e s p l v o w e u t e l
h s u d e s r a l o t a i h d, u p y s r e m s y i d

The souldiers are almost famished; supply us, or we must yield.

This way may be yet further obscured, by placing them in four lines *, and after any discontinuate order. As, suppose that the first letter be in the beginning of the first line, the second in the beginning of the fourth line, the third in the end of the first, the fourth in the end of the fourth, the fifth in the beginning of the second line, the sixth in the beginning of the third, the seventh in the end of the second, the eighth in the end of the third; and so of the rest: as in this example.

W m r p i t a h h s c t e i n p k e
h a t h f o n o i h k f t o e n i l
a n o e r r o c g t t t h m n v r l
e a u o m h t e i n l e n e t t es

Which in its resolution is this:
We shall make an irruption upon the enemy from the north, at ten of the clock this night.

This way will yet seem more obscure, if each line be severed into such words as may seem barbarous †.

All these kinds may be varied unto divers other more in-

* Or as many more as the length of the epistle shall require.
† Walchius, Fab. 9.

tricate transpositions, according as a man's fancy or occasion shall lead him.

CHAP. VII.

Concerning secret Writing with equal letters, by changing their powers. The use of this amongst the Jews and Romans. The key-character.

AS a written message may be concealed by changing the places of the letters, so likewise by changing of their powers, putting one of them for another, as suppose L for A, and A for L, or the like : answerable to that kind of cabalism in the Jewish learning, which the rabbies call צירופ, or *combinatio* ; when the letters of the alphabet are severally transposed, and taken one for another, after any known order *. Of which there be as many kinds, as there may be several combinations of the letters but amongst the rest, they observe two of more frequent use. The first is stiled from the four first correspondent letters אלבם *albam;* in which they are thus opposite to one another.

א ב ג ד ה ו ז ח ט י כ

ל מ נ ס ע פ צ ק ר שת

The other is from the same reason called אתבש *athbash,* wherein the letters are thus mutually opposed :

א ב ג ד ה ו ז ח ט י כ

ת ש ר ק צ כ ע ס נ מ ל

Both these kinds of secret writing, the Jewish doctors think to be frequently used by the sacred penmen of holy writ; amongst whom, the prophet Isaiah and Jeremiah are observed to be of more especial note for their skill in cabalisms.

---

* Schickard in Becbinath.　Haperus. Disp. l. 4.　Glassius Philolog. l. 2. par. tract. 2.

By the first of these combinations, called *Albam*, that place of Isaiah vii. 6. is usually interpreted ; where there is a person mentioned, under the unknown name of טבאל *Tabeal*, whom the prophet affirms to aspire unto the crown of Judah ; meaning, by a secret transmutation of the letters, רמלה Remaliah the king of Israel, whom he was loth more expressly to nominate : and therefore he veils it by this kind of secrecy, instead of ר writing the letter above it ט ; for מ, the correspondent letter ב ; and so ל for א, and א for ל. Which being joined together, do make טבאל, instead of רמלא.

By the second of these combinations, called *Athbash*, is that place, Jerem. li. 1. translated ; where by the original לב קמי *Cor insurgentium contra me*, is meant כשדים the Chaldæans : and therefore both the Targum, and the Septuagint do unanimously translate it so * ; as if in their version of it, they had chiefly respect unto this kind of cabalism. So likewise in 41 verse of the same chapter, by the feigned name of ששך, is meant בבל.

This way of secret writing hath been also in use amongst the ancient Romans : thus Suetonius † relates of Julius Cæsar, when he would convey any private business, he did usually write it, *per quartam elementorum literam;* that is D for A, E for B, and so of the rest, after this order.

```
d e f g h i k l m n o p q r s t u w x y z a b c
a b c d e f g h i k l m n o p q r s t u w x y z
```

Hasten unto me.
Ldwxhq yqxr ph.

And the same author reports of Octavius Augustus, that in the writing of his secrets, he did *secundum elementum proprii loco substituere*, set down the second letter for the first, as B for A, C for B, and for A a double x x.

---

* Item c. 25. v. 26. fide Hieron. com. in eundem locum.
† Sueton. in vita ejus.   A. Gellius Noct. Attic. l. 17. c. 9.

But now, because such an epistle might be easily unfolded, being altogether written by the same way ; therefore this kind of secrecy hath, by later invention, been further obscured, by writing each several word, or line, or
letter, by a diverse alphabet.

For the performance of this, two friends must before-
hand, by compact, agree upon some certain form of words,
that may be instead of a key, serving both to close, and
to unlock the writing; which words would be less discoverable, if they be barbarous, and of no signification.

But for the easier apprehending of this, I shall explain
it in an example.

Suppose the key agreed upon, were only this one word
prudentia.

Having first framed several alphabets, according to each
of its letters, thus:

A	b c	d e f	g h i	k l m	n o p	q r s	t u w	x y z
P	q r	f t v	w x y	z a b	c d e	f g h	i k l	m n o
R	s t	u w x	y z a	b c d	e f g	h i k	l m n	o p q
U	w x	y z a	b c d	e f g	h i k	l m n	o p q	r s t
D	e f	g h i	k l m	n o p	q r s	t u w	x y z	a b c
E	f g	h i k	l m n	o p q	r s t	u w x	y z a	b c d
N	o p	q r s	t u w	x y z	a b c	d e f	g h i	k l m
T	u w	x y z	a b c	d e f	g h i	k l m	n o p	q r s
I	k l	m n o	p q r	s t u	w x y	z a b	c d e	f g h
A	b c	d e f	g h i	k l m	n o p	q r s	t u w	x y z

I may write each line, or word, or letter, according as
the order of these alphabets shall direct.   As in these,

1. In the lines.

Ixt hdkasytgh bkiycn
xfi nrel fx matlmrck;
npkkfs pn, im oczs qdff
uhyrox xr xlh hqmpmh.

2. In the words.

Ixt kfmcuawik gpodhs
iru aery bs oiwnotem;
bdyytg vs, dg lzwp qdff
uhyrox ys gur ygcfcy.

3. In the letters.

Izz wshemitin in pzgcwy
vfm zean xf kaxxznebr
skgkoc hm, xr izzb awet
rtm iox gh cht whmqwy.

Which examples being unfolded, do each of them express this inward meaning:

The souldiers mutiny
For want of victuals;
Supply us, or they will
Revolt to the enemy.

These ways may be yet further obscured, if the first alphabet, (according to which the rest are described) be contrived after any mixed order. As, suppose instead of the ordinary A b c, &c. there be written these letters, after this manner.

R z k m p s e b l a u f t c y g w h x o q i n d.

And then will they be liable to all those other differences of secrecy, that are usually invented by the wheel character, which you may see largely described by Porta.

There may be divers other ways to this purpose, but by these you may sufficiently discern the nature of the rest.

CHAP V.

Of secret writing by more letters than are requisite to the intended meaning.

THE different kinds of secrecy by equal letters have been already handled. The next particular to be discussed, is concerning the ways of hiding any private sense under more letters than are required to the words of it.

Of which kind there may be divers particulars, some of them in use amongst the ancients.

1. A writing may be so contrived, that only one letter in a verse shall be significant. As it was in those remarkable acrosticks made by a Sybil concerning our Saviour*; where the lettters at the beginning of each verse, being put together, made up these words, Ιησας Χριστος Θεα υιος σωτηρ. Jesus Christ the son of God, a Saviour.

The translation of these you may see in St. Augustin de Civit. Dei, lib. 18. cap. 23 †. And the original are mentioned by Ludovicus Vives, in his notes upon that place.

According unto this doth Plautus contrive the names of his comedies in the first letters of their arguments But this way is so ordinary in practice, that it needs not any further explication.

2. The inward sense hath likewise been conveyed by some single letters of several words in the same verse. As in that common distich.

> *Mitto tibi caput Veneris, ventremque Dianæ*
> *Latronisque caput, posteriora canE.*

3. Sometimes one letter in each word was only significant. By which way óf secret expression, the Holy Ghost (say the rabbies) hath purposely involved many sacred mysteries in scripture. When these significant letters were at

---

* Sybilla Erythræa.   † Beda, l. de Sybillis.

the beginning of each word, the cabalists in their learning, called such an implicit writing ראשי תיבות *capita dictionum.* When they were at the latter end, then was it stiled סופי תיבות *fines dictionum.* Both being reckoned as species of that cabalism which they called נוטריקון *notaricon,* imposed by some later rabbies from the Latin word *notarius.*

Of the first sort, is that collection from those eminent words, Gen. xlix. 10. יבא שילה ורו. Shilo shall come, and in him, &c. where the capital letters make up the word ישו Jesu.

So Psal. lxxii. 17. ינין שמו יתברכרבו His name shall continue, and in him shall be blessed, &c. which place does expressly treat concerning the Messias his name, and therefore seems unto the Jews, to be of strong consequence for the proof of christianity. For so much is that nation befooled in their absurd dotage upon these trivial literal collections, that a reason of this nature is of greater force unto them, than the most evident solid demonstration that may be urged. Ludovicus Carret*, a famous Jew, physician to the French king, being himself converted, and writing an epistle to this purpose, unto those of his own nation, he does chiefly insist upon the arguments of this kind, as being in his opinion of greatest efficacy to prove the truth of christian religion.

Of the other sort is that passage, Gen. i. 1. היס את ברא אל where the final letters make up the word אמח or truth. Which kind of cabalism is six times repeated in the history of the creation. As if Moses by such an artificial contrivance of the letters at the beginning of his writings, did purposely commend unto our belief his following books. Unto this David is thought to allude, Psal. cxix. 160. The beginning of thy word is אמח truth. Of this natu e likewise is that observation from Exod. iii. 13. לי מה שמו מה. When they shall say unto me, what

---

* Lib. Visorum Divinorum.

is his name, &c. Where the final letters answer יהוה
Jehovah.

It were an easy matter for a man that had leisure and
patience for such enquiries, to find out sundry arguments
of this kind for any purpose.

4. There is another way of hiding any secret sense under an ordinary epistle, by having a plate* with certain
holes in it, through which (being laid upon the paper) a
man may write those letters or words, that serve to express the inward sense; the other spaces being afterwards
filled up with such other words, as in their conjunction to
these former, shall contain some common unsuspected
business.

5. There is also another intricate way to this purpose,
much insisted on by Trithemius, Porta, and Sylenus.
When each usual word or form of an epistle, is varied to
as many differences as there are letters, unto which they
must all of them be severally assigned. But these two latter inventions (though they be of great secrecy, yet) because they require so much labour and trouble in the
writer, I shall therefore pass them over without any further enlargement.

---

* Cardan de subtil. l. 17. Porta de furt. l. 2. c. 18.

CHAP. IX.

Of concealing any written sense under barbarous words,
and such as shall not seem to be of any signification.
How all the letters may be expressed by any five, three,
or two of them. Of writing with a double alphabet.
How from these two last ways together, there may be
contrived the best kind of secret writing.

ALL the ways of secrecy by more letters, already specified, do make the writing appear under some other
sense, than what is intended, and so consequently are
more free from suspicion : there are likewise some other
inventions to express any inward sense by barbarous words,
wherein only the first, and middle, and last letters shall be
significant.   As in this example.

Fildy, fagodur wyndeeldrare discogure rantibrad.

Which in its resolution is no more than this :

Fly for we are discovered.

To this purpose likewise is that other way of expressing
the whole alphabet by any five, or three, or two of the
letters repeated.   And though such a writing, to ordinary
appearance, will seem of no signification at all, and so may
seem of less use ; yet because a right apprehension of these
ways may conduce to the explication of some other particulars that follow, it will not be amiss therefore to set them
down more distinctly.

All the letters may be expressed by any five of them
doubled.   Suppose A B C D E.

A B C D E F G H I K L M N
aa ab ac ad ae ba bb bc bd be ca cb cc

O P Q R S T V W X Y Z. &
cd ce da db dc dd de ea eb ec ed ee

According to which, these words, *I am betrayed*, may
be thus described.

Bd aacb abaedddbaaecaead.

Three letters being transposed through three places, do give sufficient difference, whereby to express the whole alphabet.

A B C D E F G H I
aaa aab aac baa bba bbb bbc caa cca

K L M N O P Q R S
ccb ccc aba abb abc aca acb acc bca

T V W X Y Z &.
bcb bcc bab cba cbb cbc bac

Hasten unto me.

Caa aaa bca bcb bba abb bcc abb bcb abc aba bba.

Two letters of the alphabet being transposed through five places, will yield thirty-two differences, and so will more than serve for the four and twenty letters; unto which they may be thus applied.

A.   B.   C.   D.   E.   F.   G.
aaaaa. aaaab. aaaba. aaabb. aabaa. aabab. aabba.

H.   I.   K.   L.   M.   N.   O.
aabbb. abaaa. abaab. ababa. abaab. abbaa. abbab.

P.   2.   R.   S.   T.   V.   W.
abbba. abbbb. baaaa. baaab. baaba. baabb. babaa.

X.   Y.   Z.
babab. babba. babbb.

aababababababba.   aaaaababaaaaaaababba.

f   l   y   a   w   a   y.

There is yet another way of secrecy by more letters than are naturally required to the inward sense; if we write with a double alphabet, wherein each letter shall in the fashion of it, bear some such small distinction from the other of the same kind, as is usual in common mixed writing. For example.

The first Alphabet.

Aa.Bb.Cc.Dd.Ee.Ff.gg. H h
Ji.Kk.LLMm.Nn.Oo.Pp. Qq.
Rr.Ss.Tt.Vuv.Ww.Xx. Yy.Zz.

the second Alphabet.

Aa.Bb.Cc.Dd.Ee.ff.Gg.Hh
Ji.Kk.LL.Mm.Xn.Oo.Pp.Qq.
Rr.Ss.Ts.Vuv.Ww.Xx.Yy.Zz.

1. Write an epistle of an ordinary matter, or (if it be needful) contrary to what you intend. Let the body of it consist chiefly of the first alphabet, only inserting (as you have occasion) such letters of the second, as may express that inward meaning which you would reveal to a confederate.

For example, from those that are besieged.

Weeprosper stillin our af=
faires.and shall(without

hauing anyfurtherhelpe)
endure the siege.

In which clause, the letters of the second alphabet are only significant, expressing this inward sense.

Weeperiſh with hunger

helpe us

But because the differences betwixt these two alphabets may seem more easily discoverable, since they are both generally of the same kind, the letters of the second being all of them more round and full than the other ; therefore for their better secrecy in this particular, it were safer to mix them both by compact, that they might not in themselves be distinguishable.

Now if this kind of writing be mixed with the latter way of secrecy, by two letters transposed through five places, we may then write *omnia per omnia*, (which as a learned man speaks*) is the highest degree of this cyphering.

For supposing each letter of the first alphabet to be instead of the letter A, and those of the other for B, we may easily inscribe any secret sense in any ordinary letter, only by a quintuple proportion of the writing infolding to the writing infolded.   As for example.

* Bacon. Augment. Scient. l. 6. c. 8.

All things do happen ac
cording to our desires,the
particulars you shall vnder
stand when wee meete at
the appointed time and place
of which you must not faile
by any means The successe of
our affairs dos much depend
vpon the meeting that wee
have agreed vpon.

The involved meaning of which clause is this :

Fly, for we are discovered, I am forced to write this.

If you suppose each letter of the first alphabet to be instead of A, and those of the second for B, then will the former clause be equivalent to this following description.

Aabab	ababa	babba	aabab	abbab	baaaa	babaa
F	l	y	f	o	r	w
aabaa	aabaa	aaaaa	baaaa	aabaa	aaabb	abaaa
e	e	a	r	e	d	i
baaab	aaaba	abbab	baabb	aabaa	baaaa	aabaa
s	c	o	v	e	r	e
aaabb	abaaa	aaaaa	ababb	aabab	abbab	baaaa
d,	I	a	m	f	o	r
aaaba	aabaa	aaabb	baaba	abbab	babaa	baaaa
c	e	d	t	o	w	r
abaaa	baaba	aabaa	baaba	aabbb	abaaa	baaab.
i	t	e	t	h	i	s.

This way of secrecy may be serviceable for such occasions as these. Suppose a man were taken captive, he may by this means discover to his friends the secrets of the enemy's camp, under the outward form of a letter persuading them to yield. Or, suppose such a man were forced by his own hand-writing to betray his cause and party, though the words of it in common appearance may express what the enemy does desire; yet the involved meaning (which shall be legible only to his confederates), may contain any thing else which he has a mind to discover to them: as in the former example.

But now if there be a threefold alphabet (as is easy to contrive), then the inward writing will bear unto the outward but a triple proportion, which will be much more convenient for enlarging of the private intimations.

And this way of writing is justly to be preferred before any of the other, as containing in it more eminently, all those conditions that are desirable in such kind of inventions. As,

1. It is not very laborious either to write or read.
2. It is very difficult to be decyphered by the enemy.
3. It is void of suspicion.

But by the way, it is to be generally observed, that the mixture of divers kinds of secret writing together (as sup-

pose this with the key-character) will make the inward
sense to be much more intricate and perplexed.

CHAP. X.

*Of writing any secret sense by fewer letters than are re-
quired to the words of it. The use of this amongst the
Jews and Romans.*

AS the sense may be obscured by writing it with more
letters than are required to the words of it, so likewise by fewer. Abbreviations have been anciently used
in all the learned languages, especially in common forms,
and phrases of frequent use. Sometimes by contracting
words, when some parts of them did stand for the whole*.
So in the Hebrew, וכו׳ for וכולו *et totum illud*, which is all
one with our *et cetera*, &c. כל׳ for כלומר *secundum dicere*,
equivalent to our *viz.* or *v. g. verbi gratia*. So likewise in
the Greek, Χϱς for Χϱιστος, and ανϴ⦿ for ανϴρωπος. And in
the Latin, D̄n̄s for *Dominus*; *āā* for *anima*, and the like.
But these were rather for the speed of writing, than the
secrecy.

Sometimes words were expressed only by their first letters. Thus did the Jews write all their memorials, and
common forms, which are largely handled by Buxtorf.
Hence was it, that their captain Judas had his name of
Maccaby; for being to fight against Antiochus, he gave that
saying for his watch-word, Exod. xv. מי למכה באלהים יהוה.
Who is like unto thee (O Lord) amongst the gods? in-
scribing in his ensigns the capital letters of it, מכבי Mac-
cabi. Whereupon after the victory, the soldiers stiled
their captain by that name.

It is observed by the Rabbies, that many grand mysteries
are this way implied in the words of Scripture. Thus, where

* Buxtorf. de Abbreviat. in initio.

it is said, Psalm iii. רבים Many rise up against me, it is interpreted from the several letters, Resh the Romans, Beth
the Babylonians, Jod the Ionians or Grecians, Mem the
Medes. Answerable unto which, that place in Gen. xlix.
10. (speaking of Shilo, unto whom יקהת the gathering of
the people shall be) is by another Rabby applied to the
Jews, Christians, Heathens, and Turks.

Upon these grounds likewise, is that argument to prove
the trinity, from the first verse of Genesis. ברא אלהים The
word אלהים Elohim, being of the plural number, is thought
to be that divine name which denoteth the persons of
the deity; which persons are more particularly intimated in the letters of the verb ברא, that answers unto it:
ב Beth being put for בן the Son, ר Resh for רוח the Holy
Ghost, א Aleph for אב the Father. And if you will believe the Jews, the holy spirit hath purposely involved in
the words of scripture, every secret that belongs to any art
or science, under such cabalisms as these. And if a man
were but expert in unfolding of them, it were easy for him
to get as much knowledge as Adam had in his innocency,
or human nature is capable of.

These kind of mysterious interpretations from particular
letters, do seem to be somewhat favoured, by God's addition of the letter ה unto the name of Abraham and Sarah *,
upon the renewing of his covenant with them; which in
all likelihood was not without some secret mystery. That
being the chief letter of the tetragrammaton, might perhaps
intimate that amongst their other posterity, with the promise of which he had then blessed them, they should also
be the parents of the Messias, who was Jehovah.

This likewise others have confirmed from the example
of Christ †, who calls himself Alpha and Omega. Rev. i. 8.

But though such conjectures may be allowable in some
particulars, yet to make all scriptures capable of the like
secrets, does give such a latitude to men's roving and corrupt fancies, as must needs occasion many wild and strange

---

* Gen. xvii. 5. 15.   † Vide Tertul. l. de præscr. c. 50.

absurdities. And therefore Irenæus* does fitly observe, that from such idle collections as these, many heresies of the Valentinians and Gnostics had their first beginnings.

As this way of short writing by the first letters, was of ancient use among the Jews, so likewise amongst the Romans, which appears from many of their contractions yet remaining, as *S. P. D. Salutem plurimum dicit. S. Pq. R. Senatus populusque Romanus. C. R. Civis Romanus. U. C. Urbs condita.* And the like.

These single letters were called *syglæ, per syncopen,* from the obsolete word *sigillæ,* whence *sigillatim.* They were usually inscribed in their coins, statues, arms, monuments, and public records. You may see them largely treated of by Valerius Probus †, where he affirms the study of them to be very necessary for one that would understand the Roman affairs. *His enim exprimebant nomina curiarum, tribuum, comitiorum, sacerdotiorum, potestatum, magistratuum, præfecturarum, sacrorum ludorum, rerum urbanarum, rerum militarium, collegiorum, decuriarum, fastorum, numerorum, mensurarum, juris civilis,* & *similium.*

They were first used by their notaries, at senates and other public assemblies, and from thence retained in their statutes and civil laws: whence Manilius makes it the note of a good lawyer.

> —— *Qui legum tabulas* & *condita jura*
> *Noverit, atque notis levibus pendentia verba.*

Thus (saith Isidor‡) (A) inversed Ʌ did formerly stand for *pupilla,* and M inversed ꟽ for *mulier.* By these letters *D. E. R. I. C. P.* is signified, *De ea re ita censuerunt patres.*

When the judges were to inscribe their several opinions on a little stone or tessera, to be cast into the urn; by the note Λ, they did absolve, by K § condemn; by *N. L. Non*

---

* Iren. l. 1. c. 13.

† Lib. de liter. antiquis. As it is set forth by Jacobus Mazochius.

‡ Isidor. Bibliand. de ratione com. ling. Pet. Crinit. Honest. Disc. l. 6. c. 8.

§ From the Greek κατ*α*δικ*α*ζειν.

liquet, they did intimate that they could not tell what to make of the business, and did therefore suspend their judgments.

But because of those many ambiguities which this contracted way of writing was liable unto, and the great inconveniences that might happen thereupon in the misinterpretation of laws; therefore the emperor Justinian did afterward severely forbid any further use of them, as it were, calling in all those law-books that were so written *. *Neque enim licentiam aperimus ex tali codice in judicium aliquid recitari.*

The chief purpose of these ancient abbreviations amongst the Romans, was properly for their speed. But it is easy to apprehend how by compact they may be contrived also for secrecy.

CHAP. XI.

Of writing by invented characters.

The distinction of these into such as signify, either, { LETTERS. WORDS. NOTIONS. }

The general rules of unfolding and obscuring any letter-characters. How to express any sense, either by points, or lines, or figures.

BESIDES the ways of secret writing by the common letters, there may likewise be divers others by invented notes.

The difference of characters, whereby several languages are expressed, is part of the second general curse in the confusion of tongues; for as before there was but one way of speaking, so also but one way of writing. And as now, not only nations, but particular men, may discover their

* Lib. 1. Cod. Tit. 17. leg. 1, 2.

thoughts by any different articulate sounds, so likewise by any written signs.

These invented characters in the general, are distinguishable into such as signify, either

1. *Letters.*
2. *Words.*
3. *Things, and notions.*

First, concerning those that signify letters : to which kind some learned men * refer the Hebrew character that is now in use ; affirming, that Ezra first invented it, thereby the better to conceal the secrets of their law, and that they might not have so much as their manner of writing common with the Samaritans and other schismatics.

It were but needless to set down any particulars of this kind, since it is so easy for any ordinary man to invent or vary them at pleasure.

The rules that are usually prescribed for the unfolding of such characters, are briefly these.

1. Endeavour to distinguish betwixt the vowels and consonants. The vowels may be known by their frequency, there being no word without some of them. If there be any single character in English, it must be one of these three vowels, *a, i, o.*

2. Search after the several powers of the letters : for the understanding of this, you must mark which of them are most common, and which more seldom used. (This the printers in any language can easily inform you of, who do accordingly provide their sets of letters.) Which of them may be doubled, and which not, as *H, 2, X, Y.* And then, for the number of vowels or consonants in the beginning, middle, or end of words, a man must provide several tables, whence he may readily guess at any word, from the number and nature of the letters that make it : as, what words consist only of vowels ; what have one vowel, and one consonant ; whether the vowel be first, as in these

---

* Hieronym. præf ad lib. Regum.   Joseph Scal. notis ad Euseb.

words, *am, an, as, if, in, is, it, of, on, or, us*; or last, as in these words, *Be, he, me, by, dy, ly, my, ty, do, to, so,* &c. And so for all other words, according to their several quantities and natures.

These tables must be various, according to the difference of languages. There are divers the like rules to be observed, which are too tedious to recite; you may see them largely handled by Baptista Porta, and Gustavus Selenus.

The common rules of unfolding being once known, a man may the better tell how to delude them; either by leaving out those letters that are of less use, as *H, K, 2, X, Y*; and putting other characters instead of them, that shall signify the vowels: so that the number of this invented alphabet will be perfect, and the vowels, by reason of their double character, less distinguishable. Or a man may likewise delude the rules of discovery, by writing continuately, without any distinction betwixt the words, or with a false distinction, or by inserting nulls and non-significants, &c.

These characters are besides liable to all those other ways whereby the common letters may be obscured, whether by changing their places, or their powers.

The particulars of this kind, may be of such great variety, as cannot be distinctly recited : but it is the grand inconvenience of all these ways of secrecy by invented characters, that they are not without suspicion.

For the remedying of which, there have been some other inventions of writing by points, or lines, or figures ; wherein a man would never mistrust any private message, there being nothing to be discerned in these kinds of intimation, but only either some confused and casual, or else some mathematical descriptions ; as you may see in these following examples.

By Points alone.

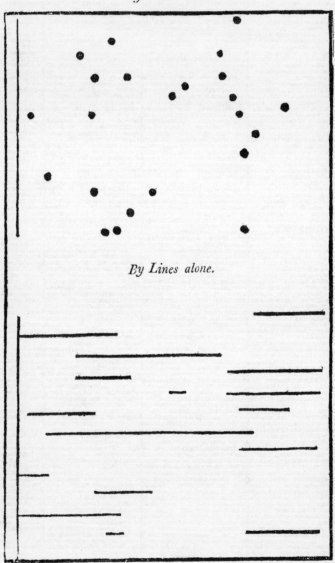

By Lines alone.

By Mathematical Figures.

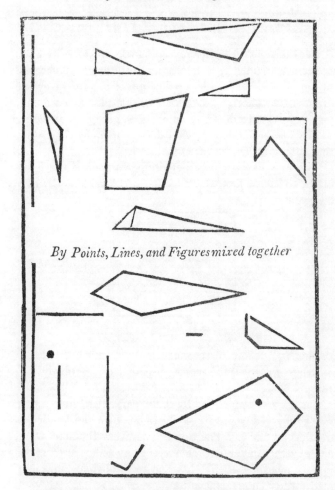

By Points, Lines, and Figures mixed together

Each of which figures do express these words :

There is no safety but by flight.

The direction both for the making and unfolding of these descriptions, is this : let the alphabet be described at equal distances, upon some thin and narrow plate, pasteboard, or the like, thus :

A b c d e f g h i k l m n o p q r s t u w x y z

Let the sides of the paper which you are to write upon, be secretly divided into equal parts, according to the breadth of the plate ; and then by application of this to the epistle, it is easy to conceive how such a writing may be both composed and resolved. The points, the ends of the lines, and the angles of the figures, do each of them, by their different situations, express a several letter.

This may likewise be otherwise performed, if the alphabet be contrived in a triangular form, the middle part of it being cut out.

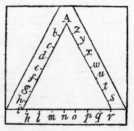

The larger these directories are, by so much the less liable unto error will the writing be, that is described from them.

It is easy to apprehend by these particulars, how a man may contrive any private saying in the form of a landscape, or other picture*. There may be divers the like ways, whereby this invention of secrecy may be further obscured; but they are in themselves so obvious, that they need not any larger explication.

* Joh. Walchius, Fab. 9.

CHAP. XII.

Of characters that express words. The first invention of these. Of those that signify things and notions, as hieroglyphics, emblems.

THE next particular to be discoursed of, is, concerning characters that express words. The writing by these is properly stiled Stenography, or short-hand; *Scripturæ compendium, cum verba non perscribimus, sed signamus,* saith Lypsius*. The art of them is, to contrive such figures for several syllables, as may easily be joined together in one form, according as different words shall require. Thus it is ordinary to represent any proper name by some such unusual character, as may contain in it all the letters of that name for which it is intended. Of this nature was that angular figure so much used by the Grecians of old, which might be resolved into the letters *υγιεα* †.

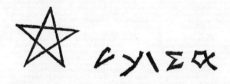

This mark was esteemed so sacred amongst the ancients, that Antiochus Soter, a perpetual conqueror, did always instamp it upon his coin, and inscribe it on his ensigns; unto which he did pretend to be admonished in a dream, by an apparition of Alexander the Great. And there are many superstitious women in these times, who believe this to be so lucky a character, that they always work it upon the swaddling clothes of their young children, thinking thereby to make them more healthful and prosperous in

---

* Cent. 1. ad Belg. Epist. 27.   † Schikard Happer. Disp. 5.

their lives.   Unto this kind also, some refer the characters that are used in magic, which are maintained to have, not only a secret signification, but likewise a natural efficacy.

This short-hand writing is now so ordinary in practice (it being usual for any common mechanic both to write and invent it) that I shall not need to set down any particular example of it.   In ancient times it was not so frequently used ; but then there was a twofold kind of it.

PRIVATE.

PUBLIC.

These private characters were practised by the Roman magistrates, and others of eminent favour amongst them ; who being often importuned to write in the commendation of those persons they knew not, were fain to agree upon some secret notes, whereby their serious epistles might be distinguished from those of form *.   Whence the proverb arose, *De meliori nota commendare.*

The other characters of public and common use, are many of them explained by Valerius Probus, in his book *de Literis Antiquis*; and there is a whole volume, or dictionary of them, set forth by Janus Gruterus.   From the practice of these came the word *notarius*, as St. Austin † observes.

The first invention of them is commonly ascribed to Tyro, who was a servant unto Cicero.   So Eusebius ‡, and Polydore Virgil §.   But Trithemius affirms, that Cicero himself writ a treatise on this subject, which was afterwards augmented by St. Cyprian : and that he had found in an old library, the copy of a psalter written in these characters, inscribed by some ignorant man with this title, *Psalterium in Lingua Armenica.*

That Cicero ‖ was not unacquainted with these notes,

---

* And therefore Pancirollus reckons it amongst these later inventions, l. de Repert. tit. 14.   Casaubon. notis in Æne. Poliorcet. c. 31.   De notis Tyronis & Senec.

† De Doct. Christ. l. 2. c. 26.   ‡ In Chron.

§ De invent. rerum, l. 2. c. 8   De Polygr.

‖ Lib. 13. ad Attic. Ep. 32.

may be evident from that passage to Atticus: *Quod ad te de legatis scripsi, parum intellexit, credo, quia διᾳ σημειων scripseram.*

Pet. Diaconus * attributes the first invention of these to the old poet Ennius ; whose beginnings in this kind, did afterwards receive successive addition from the works of Tyro, Philargirus, Aquila, and Seneca the father; by whom they were increased to the number of 5000.

But Hermannus Hugo †, a late jesuit, will have this short-hand writing to be of far more ancient use ; affirming, that David alludes to the practice of it, in that phrase, Psalm xlv. 1. The pen of a ready writer. And that the writing upon the wall, in Dan. v. 25. which so puzzled the Chaldean wizards, was described in such kind of characters. But whether this were so, or not, is not much material : it is sufficiently pertinent to the present enquiry, that the use of these word-characters may well enough conduce to the secrecy of any written message.

The third and last sort of signs, that have been anciently used for the expression of things and notions, are either hieroglyphics, or emblems.

1. Concerning hieroglyphics. The word signifies sacred sculptures, which were engraven upon pillars, obelisks, pyramids, and other monuments, before the invention of letters. Thus the Egyptians ‡ were wont to express their minds, by the pictures of such creatures as did bear in them some natural resemblance to the thing intended §. By the shape of a bee, they represented a king; intimating, that he should be endowed with industry, honey, and a sting. By a serpent, with his tail in his mouth, the year, which returns into itself: and (which was a kind of prophetical hieroglyphic) by the sign of a cross, they did anciently denote *spem venturæ salutis,* or *vitam eternam,* as

---

* Prolog. not. Conrad. Imp. Isidor. Orig. l. 1. c. 21.
† De Orig. scribendi, c. 18. juxta finem   ‡ Tacit. Annal. l. 11.
§ Pol. Virgil. de Invent. l. 3. c. 11.

Pet. Crinitus relates out of Ruffinus[*].   Philo [†] reckons up the knowledge of these amongst those other abstruse Egyptian arts, wherein Moses is said to be so expert.   And Clemens relates of Pythagoras, how he was content to be circumcised, that so he might be admitted to the understanding of those many and great mysteries which were this way delivered by the ancient priests, who did conceal all their learning under such kind of magical expressions, as the poet [‡] stiles them.

> *Nondum flumineas Memphis contexere byblos*
> *Noverat, & saxis tantum voluⱦresque færæque,*
> *Sculptaque servabant magicas animalia linguas.*

Plutarch [§] speaks of a temple in Egypt dedicated to Minerva, in the front of which there was placed the image of an infant, an old man, a hawk, by which they did represent God; a fish, the expression of hatred; and a sea-horse, the common hieroglyphic of impudence: the construction of all being this; O ye that are born to die, know that God hateth impudence.

Of this nature were those presents sent unto Darius [||], when he was almost wearied in his war against the Scythians; which were, a bird, a mouse, a frog, and certain arrows; intimating, that unless the Persians could fly as birds, or hide themselves under water as frogs, or inhabit the caverns of the earth as mice, they should not escape the Scythian arrows. Of this kind likewise were some military signs amongst the Romans.   When any thing was to be carried with silence and secrecy, they lifted up the representation of a minotaur [¶]; thereby teaching the captains, that their counsels and contrivances must be as inextricable as a labyrinth, which is feigned to be the habitation of that monster.

---

* De honesta disciplina, l. 7. c. 2.
† Lib. de vita Mosis. Lib. 1. Stromat.   ‡ Lucan. l. 3.
§ Lib. de Isid. & Osiride.
|| Herodot. Melpom. l. 4. c. 130.   Cl. Alex. Strom. 5.
¶ Pierius Hieroglyph. l. 3. c. 38.

2. Like unto these hieroglyphics, are the expressions by emblems *. They were usually inserted as ornaments upon vessels of gold, and other matters of state or pleasure. Of this nature are the stamps of many ancient medals, the impresses of arms, the frontispieces of books, &c.

The kinds of them are chiefly twofold.

1. Natural. Which are grounded upon some resemblance in the property and essence of the things themselves. So a dolphin, which is a swift creature, being described upon an anchor, which serves for the stay and rest of a ship, signifies *festina lente*, deliberation in counsel, and dispatch in execution: a young stork carrying the old one, filial gratitude.

2. Historical. Those that refer to some common relation. So the picture of Prometheus gnawed by a vulture, signifies the desert of over-much curiosity. Phaeton, the folly of rashness. Narcissus, the punishment of self-love.

It was formerly esteemed a great sign of wit and invention, handsomely to convey any noted saying under such kind of expressions.

CHAP. XIII.

Concerning an universal character, that may be legible to all nations and languages. The benefit and possibility of this.

AFTER the fall of Adam, there were two general curses inflicted on mankind: the one upon their labours, the other upon their language.

Against the first of these we do naturally endeavour to provide, by all those common arts and professions about

* Emblems, from the Greek word εμβαλλεσθαι, interserere, injicere·

which the world is busied; seeking thereby to abate the sweat of their brows in the earning of their bread.

Against the other, the best help that we can yet boast of, is the Latin tongue, and the other learned languages, which by reason of their generality, do somewhat restore us from the first confusion. But now if there were such an universal character to express things and notions, as might be legible to all people and countries, so that men of several nations might with the same ease both write and read it, this invention would be a far greater advantage in this particular, and mightily conduce to the spreading and promoting of all arts and sciences: because that great part of our time which is now required to the learning of words, might then be employed in the study of things. Nay, the confusion at Babel might this way have been remedied, if every one could have expressed his own meaning by the same kind of character. But then perhaps the art of letters was not invented.

That such a manner of writing is already used in some parts of the world, the kingdoms of the high Levant, may evidently appear from divers credible relations. Trigaultius affirms, that though those of China and Japan* do as much differ in their language as the Hebrew and the Dutch; yet either of them can, by this help of a common character, as well understand the books and letters of the others, as if they were only their own.

And for some particulars, this general kind of writing is already attained amongst us also.

1. Many nations do agree in the characters of the common numbers, describing them either the Roman way by letters, as I. II. V. X. C. D. M. or else the Barbarian way by figures, as 1. 2. 3. 10. &c. So likewise for that which we call philosophical number, which is any such measure whereby we judge the differences betwixt several substances, whether in weight, or length, or capacity; each of

* Histor. Sinens. l. 1. c. 5. Bacon Augment. Scient. l. 6. c. 13. Voss. Gr. l. 1. c. 41. Herm. Hugo de Orig. scrib. c. 4.

these are expressed in several languages by the same character. Thus פ signifies a scruple, ן a drachm, and so of the rest.

2. The astronomers of several countries do express both the heavenly signs, and planets, and aspects by the same kind of notes, as ♈, ♉, ♊, ♋, &c. ♄, ♃, ♂, ♀, &c. ☌, ✶, △, □, ☍. Which characters (as it is thought) were first invented by the ancient astrologers for the secrecy of them, the better to conceal their sacred and mysterious profession from vulgar capacity.

3. The chymical treatises that are written in different languages, do all of them agree in the same form of writing their minerals. Those that are attributed to any of the planets, are decyphered by the character of the planet to which they belong. The rest by other particular signs, as △ for salt ammoniac, ♄ for arsenic, &c.

4. Musical notes in most countries are the same: nor is there any reason why there may not be such a general kind of writing invented for the expression of every thing else as well as these particulars.

In the contrivance of this there must be as many several characters as there are primitive words. To which purpose the Hebrew is the best pattern, because that language consists of fewest radicals.

Each of these primitives must have some particular marks to distinguish the cases, conjugations, or other necessary variations of those derivatives that depend upon it.

In the reading of such a writing, though men of several countries should each of them differ in their voices, and pronouncing several words, yet the sense would be still the same. As it is in the picture of a man, a horse, or tree ; which to all nations do express the same conceit, though each of these creatures be stiled by several names, according to the difference of languages.

Suppose that astronomical sign ♉ were to be pronounced, a Jew would call it שור; a Grecian ταυρον; an Italian, toro; a Frenchman, *taureau*; a German, *stier*; an Englishman, *a bull*.

So likewise for that character, which in Tiro's notes signifies the world, a Jew would read it תבל; a Grecian Κοσμ☉; an Italian, *il monde*; a Frenchman, *le monde*; a German, *belt*. Though several nations may differ in the expression of things, yet they all agree in the same conceit of them.

The learning of this character will not be more difficult than the learning of any one language, because there needs not be more signs for the expression of things, than there is now for the expression of words. Amongst those in China and Japan, there is said to be about seven or eight thousand.

The perfecting of such an invention were the only way to unite the seventy-two languages of the first confusion; and therefore may very well deserve their endeavours who have both abilities and leisure for such kind of enquiries.

CHAP. XIV.

Concerning the third way of secret discoursing by signs and gestures, which may signify, either

$$\text{Ex} \begin{cases} \text{CONGRUO.} \\ \text{PLACITO.} \end{cases}$$

THE third way of discoursing was by signs and gestures, which (as they are serviceable to this purpose) may be distinguished into such as are significant, either

1. EX CONGRUO.
2. OT EX PLACITO.

1. *Ex congruo*, when there is some natural resemblance and affinity betwixt the action done, and the thing to be

exprest. Of which kind are all those outward gestures, whereby not only dumb creatures, but men also do express their inward passions, whether of joy, anger, fear, &c. For,

Sæpe tacens vocem verbaque vultus habet.

And the wise man notes it of the scorner, That he winketh with his eyes, he speaketh with his feet, he teacheth with his fingers *.

Of this kind likewise are many religious actions, and circumstances of divine worship, not only amongst the ancient heathen, but some that were particularly enjoined the priests and levites of the old law; and some too that are now in use in these times of the gospel. For by such bodily gestures and signs, we may as well speak unto God as unto men.

To this kind also are reducible those actions of form, that are required as necessary circumstances in many civil affairs and public solemnities, which are usually such, as in themselves are apt to signify the thing for which they are meant.

But now sometimes the intended meaning of these gestures is concealed under a secret similitude. As it was in that act of Thrasybulus, who being consulted with, how to maintain a tyranny that was newly usurped: he bid the messenger attend him in the field; where with his wand he whipt off those higher ears of corn that did over-top the rest; intimating, that it consisted in cutting off the peers and nobility, who were likely to be most impatient of subjection. This I may call a parabolical way of speaking by gestures.

2. *Ex placito*, when these signs have their signification from use and mutual compact; which kind of speaking, as it refers to lascivious intimations, is largely handled by *Ovid, de Arte amandi.*

* Prov. vi. 13.

Verba superciliis sine voce loquentia dicam,
Verba leges digitis, &c.

By the help of this it is common for men of several nations, who understand not one another's languages, to entertain a mutual commerce and traffic.   And it is a strange thing to behold, what dialogues of gestures there will pass betwixt such as are born both deaf and dumb ; who are able by this means alone, to answer and reply unto one another as directly if they had the benefit of speech.   It is a great part of the state and majesty belonging to the Turkish emperor, that he is attended by mutes, with whom he may discourse concerning any private business, which he would not have others to understand.

It were a miserable thing for a rational soul to be imprisoned in such a body as had no way at all to express its cogitations ; which would be so in all that are born deaf, if that which nature denied them, were not in this respect supplied by a second nature, custom and use.

But (by the way) it is very observable which Valesius*
relates of Pet. Pontius a friend of his, who by an unheard-of art taught the deaf to speak.   *Docens primum scribere, res ipsas digito indicando, quæ characteribus illis significarentur ; deinde ad motus linguæ, qui characteribus responderent provocando.*   First learning them to write the name of any thing he should point to ; and afterwards provoking them to such motions of the tongue as might answer the several words.   It is probable that this invention well followed, might be of singular use for those that stand in need of such helps.   Though certainly that was far beyond it. (if true) which is related of an ancient doctor, Gabriel Neale, that he could understand any word by the mere motion of the lips, without any utterance.

The particular ways of discoursing by gestures, are not to be numbered, as being almost of infinite variety, according as the several fancies of men shall impose significations

* Sacra Philos. c. 3.

upon all such signs or actions as are capable of sufficient difference.

But some there are of more especial note for their use and antiquity. Such is that upon the joints and fingers of the hand, commonly stiled *arthrologia*, or *dactylologia*; largely treated of by the venerable Bede[*], Pierius[†], and others. In whom you may see, how the ancients were wont to express any number by the several postures of the hands and fingers: the numbers under a hundred, were denoted by the left hand, and those above, by the right hand. Hence Juvenal[‡], commending Rylias for his old age, says, that he reckoned his years upon his right hand.

> *Fœlix nimirum qui tot per sæcula vitam*
> *Distulit, atque suos jam dextra computat annos.*

There are divers passages in the ancient authors, both sacred and profane, which do evidently allude to this kind of reckoning.

Hence it is easy to conceive, how the letters as well as the numbers, may be thus applied to the several parts of the hand, so that a man might with divers touches, make up any sense that he hath occasion to discover unto a confederate.

This may be performed, either as the numbers are set down in the authors before-cited; or else by any other way of compact that may be agreed upon.

As for example: let the tops of the fingers signify the five vowels; the middle parts, the five first consonants; the bottoms of them, the five next consonants; the spaces betwixt the fingers the four next. One finger laid on the side of the hand may signify T, two fingers V the consonant, three W, the little finger crossed X, the wrist Y, the middle of the hand Z.

But because such various gesticulations as are required to this, will not be without suspicion, therefore it were a bet-

---

[*] Lib. de loquelâ per gestum digitorum sive de indigitatione.

[†] Hieroglyphic. l. 37. c. 1. &c. Cælius antiq. lect. l. 23. c. 12.

[‡] Satyr. 10.

ter way, to impose significations upon such actions as are
of more common unsuspected use ; as scratching of the
head, rubbing the several parts of the face, winking of
the eyes, twisting of the beard, &c.   Any of which, or all
of them together, may be as well contrived to serve for
this purpose, and with much more secrecy.

In which art, if our gaming cheats, and popish miracle-
impostors, were but well versed, it might much advantage
them, in their cozening trade of life.

CHAP. XV.

*Concerning the swiftness of informations, either by quali-
ties, as the impression of imagination, and the sensitive
species; or by spiritual substances, as angles.*

HAVING already treated concerning the several ways
of secrecy in discoursing, I shall in the next place
enquire, how a man may with the greatest swiftness and
speed, discover his intentions to one that is far distant
from him.

There is nothing (we say) so swift as thought, and yet
the impression of these in another, might be as quick almost as the first act, if there were but such a great power
in imagination, as some later philosophers * have attributed to it.

Next to the acts of thought, the species of sight do
seem to be of the quickest motion.   We see the light of
the east will in a moment fill the hemisphere, and the eye

* Marsil. Ficin. Theolog. Platon. l. 3, c. 1.   Pomponatius de Incantat.
Paracelsus.

THE SECRET AND SWIFT MESSENGER.

does presently discern an object that is very remote. How we may by this means communicate our thoughts at great distances, I shall discourse afterwards.

The substances that are most considerable for the swiftness of their motion, are

Either { SPIRITUAL.
{ CORPOREAL.

Amongst all created substances, there are not any of so swift a motion as angels or spirits. Because there is not either within their natures, any such indisposition and reluctancy, or without them in the medium, any such impediment as may in the least manner retard their courses. And therefore have the ancient philosophers employed these as the causes of that mad celerity of the celestial orbs; though according to their suppositions, I think it would be a hard match, if there were a race to be run betwixt the *primum mobile* and an angel. It being granted that neither of them could move in an instant, it would be but an even lay which should prove the swifter.

From the fitness of spirits in this regard to convey any message, are they in the learned languages called messengers*.

Now if a man had but such familiarity with one of these, as Socrates is said to have with his tutelary genius †; if we could send but one of them upon any errand, there would be no quicker way than this for the dispatch of business at all distances.

That they have been often thus employed, is affirmed by divers relations. Vatinius being at Rome, was informed by an apparition of that victory which Paulus their general had obtained over king Perses in Macedon, the very same day wherein the battle was fought; which was a long time before any other messenger could arrive with the news ‡.

* מלאך, αγγελος, Angelus.
† Plutarch. Maximus Tyrius. Dissertat. 26. 27,
‡ Lactant. Inst. l. 2. ep. 8. Val. Max. l. 1. c. 8. Florus, lib. 2 c. 12.

And it is storied of many others, that whilst they have resided in remote countries, they have known the death of their friends, even in the very hour of their departure; either by bleeding, or by dreams, or some such way of intimation. Which, though it be commonly attributed to the operation of sympathy; yet it is more probably to be ascribed unto the spirit or genius. There being a more especial acquaintance and commerce betwixt the tutelary angels of particular friends, they are sometimes by them informed (though at great distances) of such remarkable accidents as befall one another.

But this way there is little hopes to advantage our enquiry, because it is not so easy to employ a good angel, nor safe dealing with a bad one.

The abbot Trithemius, in his books concerning the several ways of secret and speedy discoursing, does pretend to handle the forms of conjuration, calling each kind of character by the name of spirits, thereby to deter the vulgar from searching into his works. But under this pretence, he is thought also to deliver some diabolical magic. Especially in one place, where he speaks of the three saturnine angels, and certain images, by which, in the space of twenty-four hours, a man may be informed of news from any part of the world *. And this was the main reason, why by Junius his advice, Frederic the second, prince palatine, did cause the original manuscript of that work to be burned. Which action is so much (though it should seem unjustly) blamed by Selenus †.

---

* Vossius Gram. l. 1. c. 41.   Polygraph. l. 3. c. 16.
† Cryptogr. l. 3. c. 15.

CHAP. XVI

Concerning the swiftness of conveyance by bodies, whether inanimate, as arrows, bullets; or animate, as men, beasts, birds.

THE bodies that are most eminent for their swiftness, may be distinguished into such as are

Either { INANIMATE.
{ ANIMATE.

These inanimate bodies, as arrows, bullets, &c. have only a violent motion; which cannot therefore be continued to so great a distance, as some occasions would require: but for so much space as they do move, they are far swifter than the natural motion of any animated body. How these have been contrived to the speedy conveyance of secret messages, hath been formerly discoursed, in the fourth chapter, which I now forbear to repeat.

Those living bodies that are most observable for their speed and celerity in messages, are either men, beasts, birds: though I doubt not, but that fishes also may be serviceable for this purpose, especially the dolphin, which is reported to be of the greatest swiftness, and most easily circurated, or made tame.

Amongst the ancient footmen, there are some upon record for their incredible swiftness. Lædas is reported to be so quick in his running, *Ut arenis pendentibus & cavo pulvere, nulla indicia relinqueret vestigiorum* * ; that he left no impression of his footsteps on the hollow sands. And it is related of a boy amongst the Romans, being but eight years old, that did run five and forty miles in an afternoon. Anistius and Philonides, two footmen unto Alexander the Great, are said to have run 1200 stadia in

---

* Solinus Polyhist. c. 6.

a day. Which relations will seem less incredible, if we
consider the ancient exercises and games of this kind, together with the public fame and rewards for those that
were most eminent.

Amongst the variety of beasts, there are some of more
especial note for their strength and swiftness. Scaliger *
mentions a story, (though he distrusts the truth of it) of a
certain beast called ellend, two of which being joined in a
little cart, are said to pass three hundred leagues a day
upon the ice.

In former ages, and in other countries, the dromedary,
and camel, and mule, were of more common use; but in
these times and places, the horse (for the most part) serves
instead of them all; by the help of which, we have our
swiftest means of ordinary conveyance. The custom of
riding post, by renewing both horse and man at set stages,
is of ancient invention. Herodotus † relates it to be used
by Xerxes in the Grecian war; and that it was by the
Persians called Αγγαρηιον. The particulars that concern
these kind of conveyances amongst the ancients, are
largely handled by *Hermannus Hugo, Lib. 3. de Origine
scribendi, c.* 14.

Pliny ‡ tells us of certain mares in Lusitania, which do
conceive merely by the west wind; that alone (without
the copulation of any male) serving to actuate their heat,
and to generate their young. Which are likewise mentioned by Virgil § :

> *Exceptantque auras leves, & sæpe sine ullis
> Conjugiis, vento gravidæ, &c.*

Methinks these children of the wind should, for their
fleetness, make excellent post-horses, and much conduce
to the speedy conveyance of any message.

The Paracelsians talk of natural means to extract the
metal and spirit out of one horse, and infuse it into

* Exer. 205.   † Lib. 8. 98.
‡ Nat. Hist. l. 8. c. 42.   § Georg. 3.

another; of enabling them to carry a man safely and swiftly through enemies, precipices, or other dangerous places. And such horses (say they) were used by the wise men of the East at our Saviour's nativity; for they had not otherwise been able to have kept pace with a star, or to have passed so great a journey as it was to Jerusalem, which is thought to be five or six hundred miles at the least, from the places of their habitation. If this conceit were feasible, it would much promote the speed of conveyances; but I think it may justly be referred amongst the other dreams of the melancholic chymics.

Amongst all animate bodies, there is not any that have naturally so swift a motion as birds; which if a man could well employ in the dispatch of any errand, there would be but little fear that such messenger should be either intercepted, or corrupted.

That this hath been attempted, and effected by many of the ancients, is affirmed by divers relations. Pliny * tells us of Volaterranus, that he discovered a conquest he had gotten unto the city of Rome, by sending out swallows, which should fly thither, being anointed over with the colour of victory. And of another, who sending one of these birds into a besieged city (whence she was before taken from her young ones), and tying a string unto her with certain knots upon t, did thereby shew, after what number of days their aids would come; at which time they should make an irruption upon the enemy.

And elsewhere, in the same book †, he relates, how Hircius the consul, and Brutus who was besieged in Mutina, did this way maintain mutual intelligence, by tying their letters unto such pigeons, as were taught beforehand to fly from the tents to the city, and from thence to the tents again.

How Thaurosthenes did by this means send the news of

* Nat. Hist. l. 10. c. 24.   † Cap. 37.

his victory at Olympia, to his father at Ægina, is related by
Ælian *.

Anacreon has an ode upon such a pigeon, which he himself had often used as a messenger, wherein the bird is
feigned to say,

> Εγο δ' Ανακοιοντι
> Διακονω τοσαυτα
> Και νυν ὁρᾳς εκεινε
> Επιστολας κομεζω.

Unto this invention also, Juvenal † is thought to allude;
where he says,

> —— Tanquam è diversis partibus orbis,
> Anxia præcipiti venisset epistola penna.

Lypsius relates out of Varro ‡, that it was usual for the
Roman magistrates when they went unto the theatre, or
other such public meetings, whence they could not return
at pleasure, to carry such a pigeon with them; that if any
unexpected business should happen, they might thereby
give warning to their friends or families at home.

By which relations you may see how commonly this invention was practised amongst the ancients. Nor hath it
been less used in these later times, especially in those countries where by reason of continual wars and dissensions,
there have been more particular and urgent necessity for
such kind of conveyances. *Nunc vulgatissima res est, co-*
lumbas habere, ad ejusmodi jussa paratas, saith Casaubon.
Harum opere, nostrates hoc bello civili, frequenter adjuti
sunt, saith Godesc. Stewechius §.

There are divers other stories to this purpose, but by
these you may sufficiently discern the common practices of

---

* Hist. Animalium, l. 6. c. 7.   † Sat. 4. juxta fin.
‡ Saturn. Serm. l. 2. c. 6.
§ Not. in Æneæ Poliorcet. c. 31. Comment. in Veget. l. 3. c. 5.
See Nunt. Inanimat. concerning Amiraldus. Porta de furt. lit. l. 2.
c. 21. concerning marches. Herm. Hugo de Orig. scribendi, c. 15.
Thuanus Hist. l. 17.

this kind. As it is usual to bring up birds of prey, as hawks, cormorants, &c. to an obedience of their keepers; so likewise have some attempted it in these other birds, teaching them the art of carrying messages. There is a smaller sort of pigeon, of a light body, and swift flight, which is usually made choice of for such particulars; and therefore the kind of them is commonly called by the name of Carriers.

CHAP. XVII.

Of secret and swift informations by the species of sound.

HAVING in the former chapters treated severally concerning the divers ways of secrecy and swiftness in discourse; it remains that I now enquire (according to the method proposed), how both these may be joined together in the conveyance of any message. The resolution of which, so far as it concerns the particulars already specified, were but needless to repeat.

That which does more immediately belong to the present quære, and was the main occasion of this discourse, does refer to other ways of intimation, besides these in ordinary use, of speaking, or writing, or gestures. For in the general we must note, that whatever is capable of a competent difference, perceptible to any sense, may be a sufficient means whereby to express the cogitations. It is more convenient, indeed, that these differences should be of as great variety as the letters of the alphabet; but it is sufficient if they be but twofold, because two alone may, with somewhat more labour and time, be well enough contrived to express all the rest. Thus any two letters or numbers, suppose A. B. being transposed through five places, will yield thirty-two differences, and so consequently will superabundantly serve for the four and twenty letters, as was before more largely explained in the ninth chapter.

Now the sensitive species, whereby such informations must be conveyed, are, either the species of sound, or the species of sight : the ear and the eye being the only senses that are of quick perception, when their objects are remote.

Vegetius * distinguisheth all significatory signs into these three sorts.

1. *Vocalia.* By articulate sounds.
2. *Semivocalia.* By inarticulate sounds.
3. *Muta.* By the species of sight.

The two last of these are chiefly pertinent to the present enquiry. Concerning which, in the general it may be concluded, that any sound, whether of trumpets, bells, cannons, drums, &c. or any object of sight, whether flame, smoke, &c. which is capable of a double difference, may be a sufficient means whereby to communicate the thoughts.

The particular application of these, to some experiments, I shall treat more distinctly in the remainder of this discourse.

First, Concerning the secrecy and swiftness of any message by the species of sound. Though these audible species be much slower than those of sight, yet are they far swifter than the natural motion of any corporeal messenger. The chief use of these is for such as are within some competent nearness, as perhaps a mile off. But they may also by frequent multiplication be continued to a far greater distance.

There is a relation in Joach Camerarius †, of some that have heard their friends speaking to them distinctly, when they have been many miles asunder. *Habui notos homines, neque leves, & non indoctos, qui affirmabant, se audiisse secum colloquentes diserte, eos quos tunc multorum millium pas-*

* De re milit. l. 3. c. 5.
† Procem. in lib. Plutar. de defectu oraculorum.

suum abesse certe scirent. But this he justly refers to diabolical magic, and the illusion of spirits.

There are other natural experiments in this kind, of
more especial note for their antiquity. Such was that of
king Xerxes, related by Cleomenes, as he is cited by Sardus *. *Cleomenes in libro de circulis cœlestibus scribit
Xerxem toto itinere à Perside in Grœciam stationes statu-
isse, & in iis homines ita prope, ut vocem alterius alter ex-
audiret; quo modo quadraginta horarum spatio, ex Grœciâ
in Persidem res nunciari poterat.* But this invention, besides the great trouble and uncertainty of it, is also too
gross for imitation, savouring somewhat of the rudeness of
those former and more barbarous ages.

Much beyond it was that experiment of the Romans, in
the contrivance of the Picts wall, related by our learned
Cambden †; this wall was built by Severus in the north
part of England, above a hundred miles long. The towers
of it were about a mile distant from one another. Betwixt
each of these towers there passed certain hollow pipes or
trunks in the curtains of the wall, through which the defendants could presently inform one another of any thing
that was necessary, as concerning that place wherein the
enemy was most likely to assault them, &c.

Since the wall is ruined, and this means of swift adver-
tisement taken away, there are many inhabitants thereabouts, which hold their land by a tenure in cornage (as
the lawyers speak) being bound by blowing of a horn to discover the irruption of the enemy.

There is another experiment to this purpose mentioned
by Walchius ‡, who thinks it possible so to contrive a
trunk or hollow pipe, that it shall preserve the voice entirely for certain hours or days, so that a man may send his
words to a friend instead of his writing. There being al-

---

* De rerum Inventor. lib. 2.

† Britan. de Vallo, sive the Picts Wall, p. 654. Boter. Geog. l. 2. &
l. 4. where he mentions also another wall of 8000 furlongs in China.

‡ Fabul. 9

ways a certain space of intermission, for the passage of the
voice, betwixt its going into these cavities, and its coming
out; he conceives that if both ends were seasonably stopped, whilst the sound was in the midst, it would continue
there till it had some vent. *Huic tubo verba nostra insu-
surremus, & cum probe munitur tabellario committamus,*
&c.   When the friend to whom it is sent, shall receive and
open it, the words shall come out distinctly, and in the
same order wherein they were spoken.   From such a contrivance as this (saith the same author), did Albertus Magnus make his image, and friar Bacon his brazen head, to
utter certain words.   Which conceit (if it have any truth)
may serve somewhat to extenuate the gross absurdity of
that Popish relic, concerning Joseph's [hah] or the noise
that he made (as other carpenters use) in fetching of a
blow; which is said to be preserved yet in a glass amongst
other ancient relics.

But against these fancies it is considerable, that the species of sound are multiplied in the air, by a kind of continuation and efflux from their first original, as the species of
light are from any luminous body; either of which being
once separated from their causes, do presently vanish and
die.   Now as it would be a mad thing for a man to endeavour to catch the sun-beams, or inclose the light; upon
the same grounds likewise must it needs be absurd, for
any one to attempt the shutting in of articulate sounds:
since both of them have equally the same intrinsical and
inseparable dependance upon their efficient causes.

True, indeed, the species of sound may seem to have
some kind of self-continuance in the air, as in echoes;
but so likewise is it in proportion with those of sight, as in
the quick turning round of a fire-stick, which will make the
appearance of a fiery circle: and though the first kind of
these be more lasting than the other, by reason their natural motion is not so quick, yet neither of them are of such
duration as may be sufficient for the present enquiry.

None of all these inventions already specified, do sufficiently perform the business that is here enquired after;

nor are they either so generally or safely applicable for all places and exigencies.

The discovery that is here promised, may be further serviceable for such cases as these.

Suppose a friend were perfidiously clapped up in some close dungeon, and that we did not know exactly where, but could only guess at the place, within the latitude of half a mile or somewhat more; a man might very distinctly by these other inventions, discourse unto him. Or suppose a city were straitly besieged, and there were either within it or without it, such a confederate, with whom we should necessarily confer about some design ; we may by these means safely discover to him our intentions. By which you may guess that the messenger which is here employed, is of so strange a nature, as not to be barred out with walls, or deterred by enemies.

To the performance of this, it is requisite that there be two bells of different notes, or some such other audible and loud sounds, which we may command at pleasure, as muskets, cannons, horns, drums, &c. By the various sounding of these (according to the former table) a man may easily express any letter, and so consequently any sense.

These tables * I shall again repeat in this place : that of two letters may be contrived thus :

A.	B.	C.	D.	E.	F.	G.
aaaaa.	aaaab.	aaaba.	aaabb.	aabaa.	aabab.	aabba.

H.	I.	K.	L.	M.	N.	O.
aabbb.	abaaa.	abaab.	ababa.	ababb.	abbaa.	abbab.

P.	Q.	R.	S.	T.	V.	W.
abbba.	abbbb.	baaaa.	baaab.	baaba.	baabb.	babaa.

X.	Y.	Z.
babab.	babba.	babbb.

Suppose the word victuals were this way to be expressed , let the bigger sound be represented by A, and the lesser by

* Cap. 9.

B, according to which, the word may be thus made up by five of these sounds for each letter.

V.   I.   C.   T.   U.   A.   L.
baabb. abaaa. aaaba. baaba. baabb. aaaaa. ababa.

S.
baaab.

That is, the lesser note sounded once, and then the bigger twice, and then again the lesser twice, as (baabb) will signify the letter (V.) So the bigger once, and then the lesser once, and after that the bigger thrice together, as (abaaa) will represent the letter (I.) and so of the rest.

If the sounds be capable of a triple difference, then each letter may be expressed by a threefold sound, as may appear by this other alphabet.

A.   B.   C.   D.   E.   F.   G.   H.   I.   K.   L.
aaa. aab. aac. baa. bab. bba. bbb. bbc. caa. cba. cbb.

M.   N.   O.   P.   Q.   R.   S.   T.   V.   W.   X.
cbc. cca. ccb. ccc. aba. abb. abc. aca. acb. acc. bca.

Y.   Z.
bcb. bcc.

V.   I.   C.   T.   U.   A.   L.   S.
acb. caa. aac. aca. acb. aaa. cbb. abc.

If these sounds do contain a quintuple difference, then may every letter be signified by two sounds only, (which will much conduce to the speed and dispatch of such a message.) As you may see in this other table.

A. B. C. D. E. F. G. H, I. K. L. M. N. O. P.
aa. ab. ac. ad. ae. ba. bb. bc. bd. be. ca. cb, cc. cd. ce.

Q. R. S. T. V. W. X. Y. Z.
da. db. dc. dd. de. ea. eb. ec. ed.

V.   I.   C.   T.   U.   A   L.   S.
de. bd. ac. dd. de. aa. ca. dc.

It is related by Porta *, that when the citizens in the siege of Navarre were reduced to such great extremities

* De furt. lit. l. 1. c. 6.

that they were ready to yield, they did discover to their friends the greatness and kind of their wants, by discharging divers cannons and ordnances in the night-time, according to a certain order before agreed upon ; and by this means did obtain such fitting supplies as preserved the city.

CHAP. XVIII.

Concerning a language that may consist only of tunes and musical notes, without any articulate sound.

IF the musical instrument that is used to this purpose, be able to express the ordinary notes, not only according to their different tones, but their times also, then may each letter of the alphabet be rendered by a single sound.

Whence it will follow, that a man may frame a language, consisting only of tunes and such inarticulate sounds, as no letters can express. Which kind of speech is fancied to be usual amongst the lunary inhabitants, who (as Domingo Gonsales * hath discovered) have contrived the letters of the alphabet upon the notes after some such order as this.

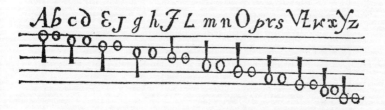

Where the five vowels are represented by the minnums on each of the five lines, being most of them placed according to their right order and consequence, only the

* Or the Man in the Moon, written by the same author of Nuntius Inanimat.

letters K. and Q. are left out, because they may be otherwise expressed.

According to this alphabet of notes, these words, *Gloria
Deo soli*, must be thus contrived *.

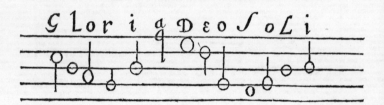

By this you may easily discern how two musicians may
discourse with one another, by playing upon their instruments of music, as well as by talking with their instruments
of speech. (And which is a singular curiosity) how the
words of a song may be contrived in the tune of it.

I suppose that these letters and notes might be disposed
to answer one another, with better advantage than here
they are expressed. And this perhaps, would be easy
enough for those that are thoroughly versed in the grounds
of music, unto whose further enquiry I do here only propose this invention.

But now if these inarticulate sounds be, contrived for the
expression, not of words and letters, but of things and notions (as was before explained, concerning the universal
character), then might there be such a general language,
as should be equally speakable by all people and nations;
and so we might be restored from the second general curse,
which is yet manifested, not only in the confusion of writing, but also of speech.

The utterance of these musical tunes may serve for the
universal language, and the writing of them for the universal character. As all nations do agree in the same conceit
of things, so likewise in the same conceit of harmonies.

This curiosity (for aught I know) has not yet been men-

* See Dom. Gonsal. 94.

tioned by any author, but it may be (if well considered) of such excellent use, as to deserve a more full and particular enlargement in a treatise by itself.

CHAP XIX.

Of those common relations that concern secret and swift informations by the species of sight; which are either fabulous, or magical.

THE usual relations that concern secret and swift conveyances by the species of sight, may be distinguished into such as are, either

1. FABULOUS.
2. MAGICAL.
3. NATURAL AND TRUE.

First, of those that are fabulous. In which kind, that of the loadstone is most remarkable, as it is maintained by Famianus Strada *, in his imitation of Lucretius's stile, and divers others. The manner that is usually prescribed for the performance of it, is thus : let there be two needles provided, of an equal length and bigness, being both of them touched with the same loadstone : let the letters of the alphabet be placed in the circles on which they are moved, as the points of the compass under the needle of the mariner's chart. Let the friend that is to travel take one of them with him, first agreeing upon the days and hours wherein they should confer together : at which times, if one of them move the needle of his instrument to any letter of the alphabet, the other needle, by a sympathy, will move unto the same letter in the other instrument, though they be never so far distant : and thus by several motions of the needle to the letters, they may easily make up any words or sense which they have a mind to express.

* Lib. 2. Prol. 6.

O utinam hæc ratio scribendi prodeat usu;
Cautior & citior properaret epistola, nullas
Latronum verita insidias, fluviosque morantes,
Ipse suis princeps manibus sibi conficeret rem, &c.

Saith Strada.   But this invention is altogether imaginary,
having no foundation in any real experiment.   You may
see it frequently confuted in those that treat concerning
magnetical virtues.   *Non solum exhibilandi sunt, sed etiam*
male mulctandi philosophicâ ferulâ, fabularum isti procus-
sores, qui suis portentis deterrent homines à præclarissimo
causarum studio; saith Cabæus to this purpose *.

The first occasion of these relations, was, the proof of
that strange immaterial power of the loadstone, whereby it
did work through thick and solid bodies, as a table, or
wall, or the like ; as also of that directive virtue, whereby
it always tends to the poles ; from whence others have
conjectured, that it might be serviceable also for such a business, at so great a distance.

But against this, it is considerable,

1. That every natural agent is supposed to have some
certain sphere, which determines its activity.

2. That magnetical operations do not arise (as some
fondly conceive) from a sympathetical conformation of natures, which is the same at all distances; but from such a
diffusion of these magnetical qualities through the medium,
that they may be continued from the agent to the patient.
And so these natural powers will not be of so great an extent, as they are supposed in this experiment.

The utmost distance, at which we may discourse with
another by these magnetical virtues, is, two or three feet,
or thereabouts ; and this we may do, though it be through
a wall of that thickness.   *Fieri enim posse me docuit expe-*
rientia, ut ope magnetis, & instrumenti ad id aptati, amicus
cum amico, in cubiculo proximo, trans crassum murum
(puta bipetalem) colloquatur, animi sui sententiam imper-
tiat, & ad quæsita respondeat; saith a late author †.   But

---

* Philosoph. Magnet. l. 4. c. 10.

† S. Ward Magnetis Reduct. c. 40. See Cabæus Phil. Magn. l. 4. c. 11.

in this experiment, it is not only the secondary virtue of the needles that can be thus effectual (as is supposed in the former invention), but there must be the help also of the loadstone itself.

As for the reason why these magnetical powers are able to work through solid bodies; it is considerable, that any quality may be diffused through such a substance, as hath no natural repugnancy unto it. We see, the light does pass as well through hot bodies as cold, through solid as fluid, &c. only opacity keeps it out, because that quality alone is contrary to its nature. So likewise is it with magnetical virtues, which do equally spread themselves through all kind of bodies, whether rare or dense, diaphanous or opacous; there being no quality contrary to this, because it is that general endowment of the whole globe, that universal quality to which all other particulars are naturally subservient.

The second sort of relations to this purpose, are such as refer to diabolical magic; of which kind is that invention thought to be, which is commonly ascribed to Pythagoras; of whom it is reported, that he could write any thing in the body of the moon, so as it might be legible to another at a great distance. Agrippa * affirms this to be naturally possible, and the way of performing it not unknown to himself, with some others in his time. And Fredericus Risner † seems to believe it; for speaking of the strange experiments to be wrought by some glasses, he adds, *Denique certo artificio, depictas imagines, aut scriptas literas, nocte serena, plenæ lunæ sic opponi possunt, ut radiis lunam irradiantibus, ideoque reflexis, videas & legas, quæ Constantinopoli Lutetiam tibi nuncientur.*

There is an experiment in optics, to represent any writing by the sun-beams, upon a wall, or a front of a house: for which purpose, the letters must be first described with wax, or some other opacous colour, upon the surface of the

* Occult. Philosoph. l. 1. c. 6.
† Optic. l. 3. prop. 6. Speculorum persuasio hoc pervasit, &c.

glass, in an inverted form; which glass afterwards reflecting the light upon any wall in the shade, will discover these letters in the right form and order. Unto some such invention I did first (before I had well considered these particulars) attribute the performance of those strange promises in *Nuncius inanimatus**; but upon better thoughts it will be found, that the species of reflection in this experiment are so weak, that unless the glass and the letters be very big, and the wall somewhat near, there will be no distinct appearance of the writing. And therefore this way there can be no thoughts of contriving any reflected species, that shall be visible at so great a distance as the moon. Nor is there any other natural means conceivable, by which so strange an effect may be performed; which is the reason that it is so frequently attributed to diabolical magic, by almost all the writers that have occasion to treat of it.

But Agrippa in another place† speaking concerning this invention, affirms that it was performed thus: Pythagoras did first describe with blood any letters which he thought fit, in some great glass, and then opposing the glass against the full moon, the letters would appear through it, as if they were writ in the circumference of her body. *Quæ collibuisset sanguine perscripsit in speculo, quo, ad pleni luminis lunæ orbem obverso, stanti à tergo, res exaratas in disco lunæ commonstravit.* In which passage he seems to intimate, that this writing in the moon could not be visible at any great distance, (as it is related in common tradition) but that it did appear to such only, betwixt whose eyes and the moon this glass might be interposed. And according to this, the wonder of the relation ceases, nor may it truly be referred to diabolical magic.

More properly reducible to this kind, are those inchanted glasses mentioned in divers authors‡: in which some magicians are said to contain such familiar spirits, as do inform them of any business they shall enquire after.

---

* World in the Moon, c. 7.   † Agrippa de Vanit. Scient. c. 48.
‡ Joach. Camerar.   Procœm. in lib. Plut. de defect. Orac.

†

I have heard a great pretender to the knowledge of all secret arts, confidently affirm, that he himself was able at that time, or any other, to shew me in a glass what was done in any part of the world ; what ships were sailing in the Mediterranean; who were walking in any street of any city in Spain, or the like. And this he did aver with all the laboured expressions of a strong confidence. The man, for his condition, was an Italian doctor of physic ; for his parts, he was known to be of extraordinary skill in the abstruser arts, but not altogether free from the suspicion of this unlawful magic.

CHAP. XX.

Of informations by significatory fires and smoke. Their antiquity. The true manner of using them to this purpose. That these were meant in Nuntius inanimatus.

THE experiments of this kind that are true, and upon natural grounds, have been made either by fire in the night, or smoke and such other signs visible at a distance in the day-time.

These informations by significatory fires, have been of ancient use. The first invention of them is commonly ascribed to Sinon in the Trojan wars. *Specularem significationem Trojano Bello Sinon invenit,* (saith Pliny*) This was the sign upon which he agreed to unlock the wooden horse.

———— *Flammas cum regia puppis*
Extulerat † ————

* Nat. Hist. l. 7. c. 56.　　　　　† Virgil.

But Diodorus Siculus* affirms them to be practised by Medea in her conspiracy with Jason. And they are frequently mentioned in other ancient historians. Herodotus† speaks of them in the Grecian war against Xerxes: and Thucydides‡ testifies of them in the onsets that were made by the Peloponnesians against Salamis, and in the siege of Corcyra. Appian speaking of Scipio at Numantia, how he divided his camp into divers companies, says, that he assigned each of them to several tribunes, with this charge, *Si impeterentur ab hoste, de die, panno rubro in hasta sublato significarent*§; *de nocte, igne.* If the enemy did charge any of them, they should signify it to the others, in the day-time by holding up a red cloth, in the night by fires. Vegetius‖ affirms it to be usual, when the army was divided, to inform one another, in the day by smoke, in the night by fires. These significatory fires were by the Grecians called Φρυκτοι (saith Suidas) and sometimes Πυρσεια. The use of them was chiefly for the answer of some particular quære¶, that was before agreed upon; as concerning the coming of aids or enemies; if the enemies were coming, they were wont to shake these torches, if the aids, they held them still (saith the scholiast upon Thucydides**).

But they have by more exact inventions been enlarged to a greater latitude of signification: so that now, any thing which we have occasion to discover, may be expressed by them ††.

The ways by which they may be contrived to this purpose, are divers; I shall specify only the chief of them.

That which in ancient times was used by the Grecians, and is particularly treated of in Polybius‡‡, adviseth thus.

Let the letters be divided into five tablets or columns.

---

* Biblioth. l. 4.   † Polymn. l. 7. c. 182.   ‡ Hist. l. 2. Item, l. 3. So Curtius of Alex. M. l. 5.   § To this purpose the flags of truce or defiance.   ‖ De re milit. l. 3. c. 5.   Lips. de milit. Rom. lib. 5. Dialog. 9.   ¶ Æneas Poliorc. c. 31.   ** Schol. in l. 2. Thucyd. †† Wecker de Secretis, l. 14. c. 1.   Port. de Furt. lit. l. 1. c. 10. Cardan, de Variet. Rerum, l. 12. c. 61.   ‡‡ Hist. l. 10. juxta fin.

	I	II	III	IV	V
1	a	f	l	q	w
2	b	g	m	r	x
3	c	h	n	$ſ$	y
4	d	i	o	t	z
5	e	k	p	u	

Let there be provided ten torches, five being placed on the right hand, and five on the left: let so many torches be lifted up on the right hand, as may shew the number of the table; and so many on the left, as may shew the number of that letter in it which you would express: as in this following example, wherein the several numbers, both at the right and left hand, do signify the word HASTEN.

The right hand.   *The left hand.*

II	H	3
I	A	1
IV	S	3
IV	T	4
I	E	5
III	N	3

That is, two lights being lifted up on the right hand, shew the second column; and at the same time three torches appearing on the left hand, denote the third letter in that column, which is H. Thus a single torch being discovered on both sides, doth signify the first letter of the first column, which is A; and so of the rest.

There is another way mentioned by Joachimus Fortius*, unto the performance of which there are only three lights required : one torch being shewed alone, shall signify the eight first letters, $A. B. C. D. E. F. G. H.$ Two together, the eight next, $I. K. L. M. N. O. P. Q.$ And all three the rest, $R. S. T. V. W. X. Y. Z.$

One light being discovered once, signifies A; if twice, B: two lights being shewed once, do denote the letter I; if twice, K, &c.

According to this way, if I would express the word FAMIN, the torches must be contrived; one light must be lifted up six times for the letter F; one light once for A; two lights four times for M; two lights once for I; two lights five times for N.

But here it will be requisite that there be some intermission betwixt the expression of several letters, because otherwise there must needs be a great confusion amongst those that belong to the same number of torches. In which respect, this way is much more tedious and inconvenient than the former invention out of Polybius.

It is easy to conceive, how by the alphabet consisting of two letters transposed through five places, such a manner of discoursing may be otherwise contrived, only by two torches. But then there must be five shews, to express every letter.

There is another way of speaking, by the differences of motion in two lights; which for its quickness and speed, is much to be preferred before any of the rest; the manner of it is thus: provide two torches on long poles : let them be placed so far from one another, that they may

* Lib. de Experiment.

seem unto your confederate to be about four cubits distance. By the divers elevations or depressions of these, inclining of them to the right hand, or to the left, severally or both together, it is easy to express all the alphabet.

One light alone being discovered, must stand for *A*; lifted up, for *E*; depressed, for *I*; inclined to the right hand, for *O*; unto the left hand, for *V*.

Two lights elevated, for *B*; depressed, for *C*; inclined to the right hand, for *D*; to the left hand, for *F*.

Two lights being still discovered, and the torch at the right hand being lifted up, shall signify *G*; being depressed, *H*; inclined to the right hand, *K*; to the left hand, *L*.

The torch at the left hand, being elevated, shall stand for *M*; depressed, for *N*; inclined to the right hand, for *P*; to the left hand for *Q*.

The torch at the right hand being moved towards the left hand, and that at the left hand being at the same time moved towards the right hand, shall signify *R*: the right hand torch being inclined to the left hand, and the other at the same time being elevated, signifies *S*; being depressed, *T*: the left hand torch being inclined to the right hand, and the other at the same time being elevated, signifies *W*; being depressed, *X*.

The right hand torch being inclined to the right hand, and the other at the same time being elevated, may stand for *Y*; being depressed, for *Z*.

When any thing is thus to be expressed, the two torches being discovered, must remain without any motion, so long, till the confederate shall by other lights shew some sign, that he is ready to take notice. After every one of these particular motions, the torches must be carefully hidden and obscured, that so the several letters expressed by them, may be the better distinguished.

The day-time informations by smoke, cannot so conveniently be ordered according to this latter contrivance, and therefore must be managed by some of those other ways that were specified before: to which purpose there must be some tunnels provided, for the orderly inclosing and conveying up the smoke. The other particulars concerning this, are in themselves easy enough to be apprehended.

How these significatory signs will be visible at a great distance. How by multiplication of them in several places, they may be contrived for many scores of miles, will easily be discerned from the situation and use of beacons *, by which the intimations of public danger and preparations, have been oftentimes suddenly spread over this whole island.

This may further be advantaged by the use of Galilæus his perspective.

It is storied of the inhabitants in China, that when any merchants do happen upon the shores of that kingdom, they are presently examined, whence they come, what commodities they bring, and of what number they are † : which being known, the watch (set for that purpose) do presently inform the king of their answers, by smoke in the day, and fires in the night: who by the same means does as speedily return them his pleasure, whether they shall be admitted or kept out: and so that is easily dispatched in some few hours, which could not be performed the ordinary way, without the trouble of many days.

The practice of all these secret and swift messages, may perhaps seem very difficult at the first; but so does also the art of writing and reading to an unlettered man ‡ : custom and experience will make the one as facile and ready as the other.

That these ways of information already explained, whether by the species of sound or sight, are the same with those intimated in Nuntius Inanimatus, may be clearly evident to any one who does but thoroughly peruse that discourse, and compare it with divers other the like passages of the same author in his Domingo Gonsales.

1. For the species of sound, his words are these §, *Auribus nihil percipi nisi personum, neminem fugit. Erit*

---

* See Barcla. Argen. l. 1.   † Busbequius Epist. Tur. ep. 4.
‡ Polyb. l. 10.   § Nunc. Inanim. p. 16.

igitur necesse ut is, cui aliquid auditu mediante nunciatum fuerit, sonos audiat, eosque distinguibiles pro numero audiendorum; quæ cum sint infinita, infinita, etiam sit oportet, sonorum edendorum varietas. Satis tamen erit ut distinguantur vel genere, vel tempore, modo etiam & numero. Which passage together with that other invention in Domingo Gonsales, concerning the language of the lunary inhabitants, before explained in the eighteenth chapter; I say, both these, being compared with the discoveries and experiments of the same kind that are here discoursed of, may plainly manifest, that they are both performed by the same means.

2. For the species of sight, his words are these *, *Si oculis amici absentis aliquid cupis representare, idque citius quam corpus aliquod sublunare ad locum tam longo intervallo disjunctum possit perferri; oportet ut ideæ, sive formæ visibiles, augeantur, quantitate, multiplicentur numero, & pro rerum significandarum varietate varientur, vel qualitate, vel quantitate, vel situ, vel ordine.* Which passage being compared with that other way of compact, betwixt Gonsales and his man Diego, mentioned in the other discourse; it may evidently appear, that the ways of intimation which were there meant, are performed after the same manner, according to which they are here discoursed of.

He does indeed mention out of Busbequius, the practice of those informations amongst the inhabitants of China, and thinks that they were used too by the Romans; but withal he wonders how that now amongst us, they should be altogether forgotten; and the restoring of them to these places and times, seems to be his chief aim, in the promises of that discourse.

The particular example which he mentions, is this : suppose that one at London would send a message to Bristol, Wells, Exeter, or though it were any remoter place : *Neque enim longinquitatem viæ multum moror, si detur facultas*

---

* Nunc. Inanim. p. 16.

sternendi, & permeabilem efficiendi. That is, the greatness
of distance can be no impediment, if the space betwixt be
fitted with such high mountains, and beacon hills, as may
serve for these kind of discoveries. Suppose (I say) this
messenger should set forth from London, in the very point
of noon, he would notwithstanding arrive at Bristol before
twelve of the clock that day: that is, a message may by
these means be conveyed so great a distance, in fewer minutes than those which make' the difference betwixt the
two meridians of those places.

If according to this, we should interpret that passage out
of Trithemius*, concerning the three saturnine angels,
that in twenty-four hours can convey news from any part
of the world ; that author might then in one respect, be
freed from the aspersion of diabolical magic, which for
this very reason hath heretofore been imputed to him.
But this by the way.

It may be, the resolution of those great promises in Nuncius Inanimatus, to such easy causes as they are here
ascribed unto, will not be answerable to men's expecta-
tion; every one will be apt to mistrust some greater matter than is here exprest : but it is thus also in every other
the like particular; for ignorance is the mother of wonder,
and wonder does usually create unto itself many wild imaginations ; which is the reason why men's fancies are so
prone to attribute all unusual and unknown events, unto
stranger causes than either nature or art hath designed
for them.

CONCLUSION.

The poets † have feigned Mercury to be the chief pa-
tron of thieves and treachery,

Αρχος Φηλητιων.

* See before cap. 15.
† Horat. l. 1. Od. 10.   Ovid. Metam. l. 11.   Homer. in Hymnis.
Nat. Comes. Mytholog. l. 5. c. 5.

To which purpose they relate that he filched from Venus her girdle, as she embraced him in congratulation of a
victory; that he robbed Jupiter of his sceptre, and would
have stolen his thunderbolt too, but that he feared to burn
his fingers. And the astrologers observe, that those who
are born under this planet, are naturally addicted to theft
and cheating.

If it be feared that this discourse may unhappily advantage others in such unlawful courses; it is considerable,
that it does not only teach how to deceive, but consequently also how to discover delusions. And then besides,
the chief experiments are of such nature, that they cannot
be frequently practised, without just cause of suspicion,
when as it is in the magistrates power to prevent them.
However, it will not follow, that every thing must be sup-
prest which may be abused. There is nothing hath more
occasioned troubles and contention, than the art of writing, which is the reason why the inventor of it is fabled to
have sown serpents teeth *. And yet it was but a barbarous act of Thamus, the Egyptian king, therefore to forbid the learning of letters: we may as well cut out our
tongues, because that member is a world of wickedness †.
If all those useful inventions that are liable to abuse,
should therefore be concealed, there is not any art or
science which might be lawfully profest.

* Cali. Rho. antiq. lect. 1. 22. c. 15. † James iii.

MATHEMATICAL MAGIC:

OR,

THE WONDERS

THAT MAY BE PERFORMED BY

MECHANICAL GEOMETRY.

IN TWO BOOKS.

CONCERNING

MECHANICAL $\begin{cases} \text{POWERS.} \\ \text{MOTIONS.} \end{cases}$

Being one of the most easy, pleasant, useful (and yet most neglected Part) of the Mathematics.

Not before treated of in this Language.

HIS HIGHNESS THE

PRINCE ELECTOR PALATINE.

May it please your Highness,

I SHOULD not thus have presented my diversions where I owe my study and business, but that where all is due, a man may not justly with-hold any part.

This following discourse was composed some years since, at my spare hours in the university. The subject of it is mixed mathematics; which I did the rather at such times make choice of, as being for the pleasure of it more proper for recreation, and for the facility, more suitable to my abilities and leisure.

I should not, Sir, have been ambitious of any so great (I could not of any better) patronage, had not my relation both engaged and emboldened me to this dedication.

They that know your Highness, how great an encourager you are, and how able a judge in all kind of ingenious arts and literature, must needs acknowledge your pressures and low condition to be none of the least mischiefs (amongst those many other) under which the commonwealth of learning does now suffer.

DEDICATION.

It would in many respects much conduce to the general advancement of religion and learning, if the reformed churches, in whose cause and defence your family hath so deeply suffered, were but effectually mindful of their engagements to it. And particularly, if these present unhappy differences of this nation, did not occasion too much forgetfulness of their former zeal and professions for the vindicating of your family, and the restoring of your Highness: the hastening and accomplishment of which, together with the increase of all heavenly blessings upon your Highness, shall be the hearty daily prayer of,

Your Highness's

most humble and most devoted

servant and chaplain,

JOHN WILKINS.

THE READER.

IT is related of Heraclitus, that when his scholars had found him in a tradesman's shop, whither they were ashamed to enter; he told them, *Quod neque tali loco dii desunt immortales;* that the gods were as well conversant in such places, as in others: intimating, that a divine power and wisdom might be discerned, even in those common arts which are so much despised: and though the manual exercise and practice of them be esteemed ignoble, yet the study of their general causes and principles, cannot be prejudicial to any other (though the most sacred) profession.

It hath been my usual custom in the course of my other studies, to propose divers mathematical or philosophical enquiries, for the recreation of my leisure hours; and as I could gather satisfaction, to compose them into some form and method.

Some of these have been formerly published, and I have now ventured forth this discourse; wherein, besides the great delight and pleasure (which every rational reader must needs find in such notions as carry with them their own evidence and demonstration) there is also much real benefit to be learned; particularly for such gentlemen as employ their estates in those chargeable adventures of draining mines, coalpits, &c. who may from hence learn the chief grounds and nature of engines, and thereby more easily avoid the delusions of any cheating impostor: and also for such common artificers, as are well skilled in the practice of these arts, who may be much advantaged by the right understanding of their grounds and theory.

Ramus * hath observed, that the reason why Germany hath been so eminent for mechanical inventions, is, because there have been public lectures of this kind instituted amongst them; and those, not only in the learned languages, but also in the vulgar tongue, for the capacity of every unlettered ingenious artificer.

This whole discourse I call Mathematical Magic; because the art of such mechanical inventions as are here chiefly insisted upon, hath been formerly so stiled †, and in allusion to vulgar opinion, which doth commonly attribute all such strange operations unto the power of magic; for which reason the ancients did name this art, Θαυματοποιητικη, or *Mirandorum Effectrix.*

The first book is called Archimedes, because he was the chiefest in discovering of mechanical powers.

The second is stiled by the name of Dædalus, who is related to be one of the first and most famous amongst the ancients, for his skill in making automata, or self-moving engines: both these being two of the first authors, that did reduce mathematical principles unto mechanical experiments.

Other discourses of this kind, are for the most part large and voluminous, of great price, and hardly gotten; and besides, there are not any of them (that I know of) in our vulgar tongue, for which these mechanical arts of all other are most proper. These inconveniences are here in some measure remedied; together with the addition (if I mistake not) of divers things very considerable, and not insisted upon by others.

* Schol. Mathem. l. 2.   † Agrippa, de Vanit. Scient. c. 42.

ARCHIMEDES;

OR,

MECHANICAL POWERS.

BOOK I.

CHAP. I.

*The excellency of these arts. Why they were concealed by
the ancients. The authors that have treated of them.*

ALL those various studies about which the sons of
men do busy their endeavours, may be generally
comprised under these three kinds,

> DIVINE.
> NATURAL.
> ARTIFICIAL.

To the first of these, is reducible, not only the speculation of theological truths, but also the practice of those
virtues, which may advantage our minds in the enquiry
after their proper happiness. And these arts alone may
truly be stiled liberal, *Quæ liberum faciunt hominem, quibus curæ virtus est,* (saith the divine Stoic*) which set a
man at liberty from his lusts and passions.

---

* Sen. Ep. 88.

To the second may be referred all that knowledge which concerns the frame of this great universe, or the usual course of providence in the government of these created things.

To the last do belong all those inventions, whereby nature is any way quickened or advanced in her defects : these artificial experiments being (as it were) but so many essays, whereby men do naturally attempt to restore themselves from the first general curse inflicted upon their labours.

The following discourse does properly appertain to this latter kind.

Now art may be said, either to imitate nature, as in limning and pictures; or to help nature, as in medicine; or to overcome and advance nature, as in these mechanical disciplines, which in this respect are by so much to be preferred before the other, by how much their end and power is more excellent. Nor are they therefore to be esteemed less noble, because more practical; since our best and most divine knowledge is intended for action; and those may justly be counted barren studies, which do not conduce to practice as their proper end.

But so apt are we to contemn every thing which is common, that the ancient philosophers esteemed it a great part of wisdom to conceal their learning from vulgar apprehension or use, thereby the better to maintain it in its due honour and respect. And therefore did they generally veil all their arts and sciences under such mystical expressions as might excite the people's wonder and reverence; fearing lest a more easy and familiar discovery, might expose them to contempt. *Sic ipsa mysteria fabularum cuniculis operiuntur, summatibus tantum viris, sapientia interprete, veri arcani consciis; contenti sint reliqui, ad venerationem, figuris defendentibus à vilitate secretum,* saith a Platonic*.

---

* Macrobius Somn. Scip. l. 1. c. 2.

Hence was it, that the ancient mathematicians did place all their learning in abstracted speculations; refusing to debase the principles of that noble profession unto mechanical experiments.   Insomuch that those very authors amongst them, who were most eminent for their inventions of this kind, and were willing by their own practice to manifest unto the world those artificial wonders that might be wrought by these arts, as Dædalus, Archytas, Archimedes, &c. were notwithstanding so much infected with this blind superstition, as not to leave any thing in writing concerning the grounds and manner of these operations.

Quintilian * speaking to this purpose of Archimedes, saith thus. *Quamvis tantum tamque singularem geometriæ usum, Archimedes, singularibus exemplis, & admirandis operibus ostenderit, propter quæ non humanæ sed divinæ scientiæ laudem sit adeptus, hæsit tamen in illa Platonis persuasione, nec ullam mechanicam literam prodere voluit.*

By which means, posterity hath unhappily lost, not only the benefit of those particular discoveries, but also the proficiency of those arts in general.   For when once the learned men did forbid the reducing of them to particular use, and vulgar experiment; others did thereupon refuse these studies themselves, as being but empty and useless speculations †.   Whence it came to pass that the science of geometry was so universally neglected, receiving little or no addition for many hundred years together.

Amongst these ancients, the divine Plato is observed to be one of the greatest sticklers for this fond opinion; severely dehorting all his followers from prostituting mathematical principles, unto common apprehension or practice ‡.   Like the envious emperor Tiberius, who is reported to have killed an artificer for making glass malleable, fearing lest thereby the price of metals might be debased.   So he, in his superstition to philosophy, would

* Quint. l. 1. c. 10.   † Pet. Ram. Schol. Mathem. l. 1.
‡ Plin. Nat. l. 36. c. 26.

rather chuse to deprive the world of all those useful and
excellent inventions which might be thence contrived,
than to expose that profession unto the contempt of the
ignorant vulgar.

But his scholar Aristotle *, (as in many other particulars,
so likewise in this) did justly oppose him, and became himself one of the first authors that hath writ any methodical
discourse concerning these arts ; chusing rather a certain
and general benefit, before the hazard that might accrue
from the vain and groundless disrespect of some ignorant
persons. Being so far from esteeming geometry disho-
noured by the application of it to mechanical practices,
that he rather thought it to be thereby adorned, as with
curious variety, and to be exalted unto its natural end.
And whereas the mathematicians of those former ages, did
possess all their learning as covetous men do their wealth,
only in thought and notion; the judicious Aristotle, like
a wise steward, did lay it out to particular use and improvement ; rightly preferring the reality and substance of
public benefit, before the shadows of some retired speculation, or vulgar opinion.

Since him there have been divers other authors who
have been eminent for their writings of this nature. Such
were Hero Alexandrinus, Hero Mechanicus, Pappus Alexandrinus, Proclus Mathematicus, Vitruvius, Guidus Ubaldus, Henricus Monantholius, Galileus, Guevara, Mersennus, Bettinus, &c. Besides many others that have treated
largely of several engines, as Augustin Ramelli, Vittorio
Zoncha, Jacobus Bessonius, Vegetius, Lipsius.

Most of which authors I have perused, and shall willingly
acknowledge myself a debtor to them for many things in
this following dicourse.

* Arist. Quæst. Mechan.

CHAP. II.

Concerning the name of this art. That it may properly be stiled liberal. The subject and nature of it.

THE word mechanic is thought to be derived *απο τ8 μηκ8ς και ανειν, multum ascendere, pertingere:* intimating the efficacy and force of such inventions. Or else *παρα μη χαινειν,* (saith Eustathius) *quia hiscere non sinit,* because these arts are so full of pleasant variety, that they admit not either of sloth or weariness *.

According to ordinary signification, the word is used in opposition to the liberal arts: whereas in propriety of speech those employments alone may be styled illiberal, which require only some bodily exercise, as manufactures, trades, &c. And on the contrary, that discipline which discovers the general causes, effects, and proprieties of things, may truly be esteemed as a species of philosophy.

But here it should be noted, that this art is usually distinguished into a twofold kind †.

1. RATIONAL.
2. CHIRURGICAL.

The rational is that which treats of those principles and fundamental notions, which may concern these mechanical practices.

The chirurgical or manual doth refer to the making of these instruments, and the exercising of such particular experiments. As in the works of architecture, fortifications, and the like.

The first of these is the subject of this discourse, and may properly be styled liberal, as justly deserving the pro-

---

* Lypsius Poliorcet. l. 2. Dial. 3. That's a senseless absurd etymology, imposed by some, *Quia intellectus in eis mæchatur,* as if these arts did prostitute and adulterate the understanding.

† Pappus Procem. in Collect. Mathem. l. 8.

secution of an ingenious mind. For if we consider it according to its birth and original, we shall find it to spring from honourable parentage, being produced by geometry on the one side, and natural philosophy on the other. If according to its use and benefit, we may then discern that to this should be referred all those arts and professions, so necessary for human society, whereby nature is not only directed in her usual course, but sometimes also commanded against her own law. The particulars that concern architecture, navigation, husbandry, military affairs, &c. are most of them reducible to this art, both for their invention and use.

Those other disciplines of logic, rhetoric, &c. do not more protect and adorn the mind, than these mechanical powers do the body.

And therefore are they well worthy to be entertained with greater industry and respect, than they commonly meet with in these times ; wherein there be very many that pretend to be masters in all the liberal arts, who scarce understand any thing in these particulars.

The subject of this art is concerning the heaviness of several bodies, or the proportion that is required betwixt any weight, in relation to the power which may be able to move it. And so it refers likewise to violent and artificial motion, as philosophy doth to that which is natural.

The proper end for which this art is intended, is to teach how by understanding the true difference betwixt the weight and the power, a man may add such a fitting supplement to the strength of the power, that it shall be able to move any conceiveable weight, though it should never so much exceed that force which the power is naturally endowed with.

The art itself may be thus described to be a mathematical discipline, which by the help of geometrical principles doth teach to contrive several weights and powers unto any kind, either of motion, or rest, according as the artificer shall determine.

If it be doubted how this may be esteemed a species of mathematics, when as it treats of weights, and not of quantity * : for satisfaction to this, there are two particulars considerable.

1. Mathematics in its latitude is usually divided into pure and mixed: and though the pure do handle only abstract quantity in general, as geometry, arithmetic: yet that which is mixed, doth consider the quantity of some particular determinate subject. So astronomy handles the quantity of heavenly motions ; music of sounds, and mechanics of weights and powers.

2. Heaviness or weight is not here considered, as being such a natural quality, whereby condensed bodies do of themselves tend downwards; but rather, as being an affection, whereby they may be measured. And in this sense, Aristotle himself refers it amongst the other species of quantity †, as having the same proper essence, which is to be compounded of integral parts. So a pound doth consist of ounces, drams, scruples. Whence it is evident, that there is not any such repugnancy in the subject of this art, as may hinder it from being a true species of mathematics.

* Dav. Rivaltus præf. in I. Archim. de centro gravitatis.
† Metaph. l. 10. c. 2.

CHAP. III.

Of the first mechanical faculty, the Balance.

THE mechanical faculties by which the experiments of this nature must be contrived, are usually reckoned to be these six.

1. *Libra.*	1. *The Balance.*
2. *Vectis.*	2. *The Leaver.*
3. *Axis in Peritrochio.*	3. *The Wheel.*
4. *Trochlea.*	4. *The Pulley.*
5. *Cuneus.*	5. *The Wedge.*
6. *Cochlea.*	6. *The Screw.*

Unto some of which, the force of all mechanical inventions must necessarily be reduced. I shall speak of them severally, and in this order.

First, concerning the balance: this and the leaver are usually confounded together, as being but one faculty; because the general grounds and proportions of either's force is so exactly the same. But for better distinction, and more clear discovery of their natures, I shall treat of them severally.

The first invention of the balance is commonly attributed to Astrea, who is therefore deified for the goddess of Justice; and that instrument itself advanced amongst the celestial signs.

The particulars concerning it are so commonly known, and of such easy experiment, that they will not need any large explication. The chief end and purpose of it, is for the distinction of several ponderosities: for the understanding of which, we must note, that if the length of the sides in the balance, and the weights at the ends of them, be both mutually equal, then the beam will be in a horizontal situation. But on the contrary, if either the weights alone be equal, and not their distances, or the distances alone, and not the weights, then the beam will accordingly decline.

As in this following diagram.

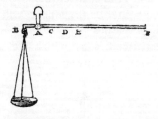

Suppose an equal weight at C, unto that at B; (which points are both equally distant from the centre A) it is evident that then the beam B F will hang horizontally. But if the weight supposed at C, be unequal to that at B, or if there be an equal weight at D E, or any of the other unequal distances; the beam must then necessarily decline.

With this kind of balance, it is usual, by the help only of one weight, to measure sundry different gravities, whether more or less, than that by which they are measured*. As by the example here described, a man may with one pound alone, weigh any other body within ten pounds; because the heaviness of any weight doth increase proportionably to its distance from the centre. Thus one pound at D, will equiponderate unto two pounds at B; because the distance A D is double unto A B. And for the same reason, one pound at *E*, will equiponderate to three pound at B; and one pound at F, unto ten at B; because there is still the same disproportion betwixt their several distances.

This kind of balance is usually stiled *Romana statera*. It seems to be of ancient use, and is mentioned by Aristotle † under the name of Φαλαγξ.

Hence it is easy to apprehend how that false balance may be composed, so often condemned by the wise men,

*Cardan. Subtil. l. 1.   † Mechan. c. 21.

as being an abomination to the Lord*.   If the sides of the
beam be not equally divided, as suppose one have 10 parts
and the other 11 ; then any two weights that differ according to this proportion, (the heavier being placed on the
shorter side, and the lighter on the longer) will equiponderate ; and yet both the scales being empty, will hang in
æquilibrio, as if they were exactly just and true† : as in
this description.

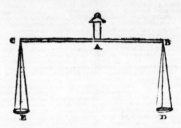

Suppose A C to have 11 such parts, whereof A B has
but 10, and yet both of them to be in themselves of equal
weight ; it is certain, that whether the scales be empty, or
whether in the scale D we put 11 pound, and at E 10
pound ; yet both of them shall equiponderate, because
there is just such a disproportion in the length of the sides
A C, being unto A B, as 11 to 10.

The frequency of such cozenages in these days, may be
evident from common experience ; and that they were
used also in former ages, may appear from Aristotle's testimony concerning the merchants in his time‡.   For the
remedying of such abuses, the ancients did appoint divers
officers, stiled ζυγοστάται ‖, who were to overlook the common measures.

So great care was there amongst the Jews, for the preservation of commutative justice from all abuse and falsi-
fication in this kind, that the public standards and originals,

---

* Prov. xi. 1. xvi. 11. item xx. 10. 23.

† Pappus Collect. Math. l. 8.   ‡ Quæstion. Mechan. c. 2. Budæus
‖ Hence the proverb, Zygostatica fides.

by which all other measures were to be tried and allowed, were with much religion preserved in the sanctuary; the care of them being committed to the priests and levites, whose office it was to look unto all manner of measures and size. Hence is that frequent expression, according to the shekel of the sanctuary; and that law, all thy estimations shall be according to the shekel of the sanctuary * : which doth not refer to any weight, or coin, distinct from, and more than the vulgar, (as some fondly conceive), but doth only oblige men in their dealing and traffic, to make use of such just measures, as were agreeable unto the public standards that were kept in the sanctuary.

The manner how such deceitful balances may be discovered is, by changing the weights into each other scale, and then the inequality will be manifest.

From the former grounds rightly apprehended, it is easy to conceive how a man may find out the just proportion of a weight, which in any point given, shall equiponderate to several weights given, hanging in several places of the beam.

Some of these balances are made so exact, (those especially which the refiners use) as to be sensibly turned with the eightieth part of a grain : which (though it may seem very strange) is nothing to what Capellus † relates of one at Sedan, that would turn with the four hundredth part of a grain.

There are several contrivances to make use of these, in measuring the weight of blows, the force of powder, the strength of strings, or other oblong substances; condensed air : the distinct proportion of several metals mixed together; the different gravity of divers bodies in the water, from what they have in the open air; with divers the like ingenious inquiries.

* 1 Chron. xxiii. 29. Exod. xxx. 13. Lev. xxvii. 25.
† De ponderibus & nummis, l, 1.

CHAP. IV.

Concerning the second mechanic faculty, the Leaver.

THE second mechanical faculty is the leaver: the first invention of it is usually ascribed to Neptune, and represented by his trident, which in the Greek are both called by one name*, and are not very unlike in form, being both of them somewhat broader at one end, than in the other parts.

There is one main principle concerning it, which is (as it were) the very sum and epitome of this whole art. The meaning of it is thus expressed by Aristotle: Ὁ το κινεμενον βαρος προς το κινεν, το μηκος προς το μηκος αντιπεπονθεν. That is, as the weight is to an equivalent power, so is the distance betwixt the weight and the centre unto the distance betwixt the centre and the power, and so reciprocally.   Or thus, the power that doth equiponderate with any weight, must have the same proportion unto it, as there is betwixt their several distances from the centre or fulciment ; as in this following figure.

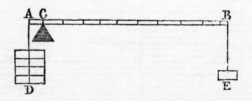

Where suppose the leaver to be represented by the length AB, the centre or prop † at the point C, the weight to be sustained D, the power that doth uphold it E.

---

* μοχλος.   Aristotle Quæst. Mechan. cap. 4.   Archimedes, de Æquiponderant. l. 1. prop. 7.   Vitruvius Architect. l. 10. c. 8.

† This Aristotle calls υπομοχλιον; Vitruvius, pressio; Whaldus, fulcimentum; Dan. Barbarus, scabellum.

Now the meaning of the foresaid principle doth import thus much ; that the power at E, must bear the same proportion to the weight D, as the distance C A doth to the other C B ; which, because it is octuple in the present example, therefore it will follow that one pound at B, or E, will equiponderate to eight pounds at A, or D ; as is expressed in the figure. The ground of which maxim is this, because the point C is supposed to be the centre of gravity, on either side of which, the parts are of equal weight.

And this kind of proportion is not only to be observed when the power doth press downwards, (as in the former example) but also in the other species of violent motion ; as lifting, drawing, and the like. Thus if the prop or fulciment were supposed to be at the extremity of the leaver,

as in this diagram at A, then the weight B would require such a difference in the strengths or powers that did sustain it, as there is betwixt the several distances A C, and B C. For as the distance A B is unto A C, so is the power at C to the weight at B ; that is the power at A must be double to that at C, because the distance B C is twice as much as B A *. From whence it is easy to conceive, how any burthen carried betwixt two persons, may be proportioned according to their different strengths. If the weight were imagined to hang at the number 2, then the power at C would sustain but two of those parts, whereof that at A did uphold 16. If it be supposed at the figure 3, then the strength at C, to that at A, would be but as three to fifteen. But if it were situated at the figure 9, then each of the extremities would participate of it alike ; because that being the middle, both the distances are equal. If at the number 12, then the strength at C is required to be double unto that at A. And in the like manner are we to conceive of the other intermediate divisions.

* The right understanding of this doth much conduce to the explication of the pulley.

Thus also must it be, if we suppose the power to be placed betwixt the fulciment and the weight, as in this example.

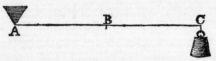

Where, as A C is to A B so is the power at B, to the weight at C.

Hence likewise may we conceive the reason why it is much harder to carry any long substance, either on the shoulders, or in the hand, if it be held by either of the extremes, than if it be sustained by the middle of it. The strength that must equiponderate at the nearer end, sometimes increasing the weight almost double to what it is in itself.

Imagine the point A to be the place where any long substance (as suppose a pike) is sustained; it is evident from the former principle, that the strength at B (which makes it lie level) must be equal to all the length A C, which is almost the whole pike.

And as it is in the depressing, or elevating, so likewise is it in the drawing of any weight, as a coach, plough, or the like.

Let the line D B represent the pole or carriage on which the burthen is sustained, and the line A C the cross-bar ; at each of its extremities, there is a several spring-tree G H, and I K, to which either horses or oxen may be fastened. Now because A and C are equally distant from the middle B, therefore in this case the strength must be equal on both sides ; but if we suppose one of these spring-trees to be fastened unto the points E or F, then the strength required to draw on that side, will be so much more, as the distance E B or F B is less than that of A B ; that is, either as three to four, as E B to B A, or as one to two, as F B to B A. So that the beast fastened at A, will not draw so much by a quarter as the other at E, but half as much as one at F.

Whence it is easy to conceive how a husbandman *(cum inæquales veniunt ad aratra juvenci)* may proportion the labour of drawing, according to the several strength of his oxen.

Unto this mechanical faculty should be reduced sundry other instruments in common use. Thus the oars, stern, masts, &c. according to their force whereby they give motion to the ship, are to be conceived under this head *.

Thus likewise for that engine, whereby brewers and dyers do commonly draw water, which Aristotle calls κηλονειον, and others tollenon. This being the same kind of instrument by which Archimedes drew up the ships of Marcellus †.

CHAP. V.

How the natural motion of living creatures is conformable to these artificial rules.

THE former principle being already explained, concerning artificial and dead motions, it will not be altogether impertinent, if in the next place we apply it unto those that

---

* Arist. Mechan. c. 5, 6, 7. Vide Guevar. Comment.

† Mechan. c. 29. Pet. Crinitus, de honesta disciplina, l. 19. c. 2. calls it corruptly Tellenon.

are natural in living bodies, and examine whether these also are not governed by the same kind of proportions.

In all perfect living creatures, there is a twofold kind of motive instruments :

1. Primary, the muscles.

2. Secondary, the members.

The muscles are naturally fitted to be instruments of motion, by the manner of their frame and composure; consisting of flesh as their chief material, and besides of nerves, ligatures, veins, arteries, and membranes.

The nerves serve for the conveyance of the motive faculty from the brain. The ligatures for the strengthening of them, that they may not flag and languish in their motions. The veins for their nourishment. The arteries for the supplying of them with spirit and natural vigour. The membranes for the comprehension or inclosure of all these together, and for the distinction of one muscle from another. There are besides divers fibræ, or hairy substances, which nature hath bestowed for the farther corroborating of their motions ; these being dispersed through every muscle, do so join together in the end of them, as to make entire nervous bodies, which are called tendons, almost like the gristles. Now this (saith *Galen* *) may fitly be compared to the broader part of the leaver, that is put under the weight; which, as it ought to be so much the stronger, by how much it is put to a greater force, so likewise by this, doth nature enable the muscles and nerves for those motions, which otherwise would be too difficult for them.

Whence it may evidently appear, that according to the opinion of that eminent physician, these natural motions are regulated by the like grounds with the artificial.

2. Thus also is it in those secondary instruments of motion, the members : amongst which, the hand is οργανον οργανων, the instrument of instruments, (as Galen † stiles it ;) and as the soul of man doth bear in it the image of the

---

* De Placit. Hippoc. & Platon. l. 1. cap. 10.

† De usu part. l. 1. c. 2.

divine wisdom and providence, so this part of the body seems in some sort to represent the omnipotency of God, whilst it is able to perform such various and wonderful effects by the help of this art.   But now for its own proper natural strength, in the lifting any great weight, this is always proportioned according to its extension from the body, being of least force when it is fully stretched out, or at arms-end, (as we say) because then the shoulder-joint is as the centre of its motion, from which the hand in that posture being very remote, the weight of any thing it holds must be accordingly augmented.   Whereas the arm being drawn in, the elbow-joint doth then become its centre, which will diminish the weight proportionably, as that part is nearer unto it than the other.

To this purpose also, there is another subtle problem proposed by Aristotle *, concerning the postures of sitting and rising up.   The quære is this : why a man cannot rise up from his seat, unless he first either bend his body forward, or thrust his feet backward ?

In the posture of sitting, our legs are supposed to make a right angle with our thighs, and they with our backs, as in this figure.

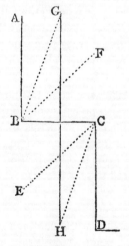

* Mechan. c. 31.

Where let A B represent the back, BC the thighs, C D the legs. Now it is evident, that a man cannot rise from this posture, unless either the back A B do first incline unto F, to make an acute angle with the thighs B C ; or else that the legs C D do incline towards E, which may also make an acute angle with the thighs B C ; or lastly, unless both of them do incline to the points G H, where they may be included in the same perpendicular.

For the resolution of which, the philosopher proposes these two particulars.

1. A right angle (saith he) is a kind of equality, and that being naturally the cause of rest, must needs be an impediment to the motion of rising.

2. Because when either of the parts are brought into an acute angle, the head being removed over the feet, or they under the head ; in such a posture the whole man is much nearer disposed to the form of standing, wherein all these parts are in one strait perpendicular line, than he is by the other of right angles, in which the back and legs are two parallels ; or that of turning these strait angles into obtuse, which would not make an erect posture, but declining.

But neither of these particulars (as I conceive) do fully satisfy the present quære ; neither do the commentators, Monantholius, or Guevara, better resolve it. Rather suppose BC to be a vectis or leaver, towards the middle of which is the place of the fulciment, A B as the weight, C D the power that is to raise it.

Now the body being situate in this rectangular form, the weight A B must needs be augmented proportionably to its distance from the fulciment, which is about half the thighs : whereas, if we suppose either the weight to be inclined unto F, or the power to E, or both of them to G H ; then there is nothing to be lifted up, but the bare weight itself ; which in this situation, is not at all increased with any addition by distance.

For in these conclusions concerning the leaver, we must always imagine that point which is touched by a perpendicular from the centre of gravity, to be one of the terms.

So that the diverse elevation or depression of the instrument, will infer a great alteration in the weight itself; as may more clearly be discerned by this following diagram.

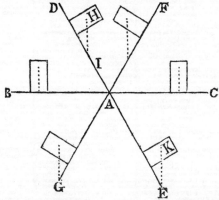

Where A is supposed to be the place of the prop, or fulciment; BC, a leaver which stands horizontally; the power and the weight belonging unto it being equal, both in themselves, and also in their distances from the prop.

But now suppose this instrument to be altered according to the situation D E; then the weight D will be diminished by so much, as the perpendicular from its centre of gravity H I, doth fall nearer to the prop or fulciment at A: and the power at E will be so much augmented, as the perpendicular from its centre K E does fall farther from the point at A. And so on the contrary, in that other situation of the leaver, F G: whence it is easy to conceive the true reason, why the inclining of the body, or the putting back of the leg, should so much conduce to the facility of rising.

From these grounds likewise may we understand, why the knees should be most weary in ascending, and the thighs in descending; which is, because the weight of the body doth bear most upon the knee-joints, in raising itself up; and most upon the muscles of the thighs, when it stays itself in coming down *

* Sir Francis Bacon's Natural History. Experiment 731.

There are divers other natural problems to this purpose, which I forbear to recite. We do not so much as go, or sit, or rise, without the use of this mechanical geometry.

CHAP. VI.

Concerning the Wheel.

THE third mechanical faculty is commonly stiled *axis in peritrochio* *. It consists of an axis, or cylinder, having a rundle about it, wherein there are fastened divers spokes, by which the whole may be turned round; according to this figure.

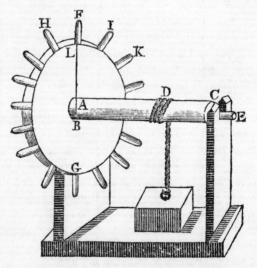

Where BC does represent the cylinder, which is supposed to move upon a smaller axis at E; (this being all one, in comparison to the several proportions, as if it were

* Called likewise ον@·. Arist. Mechan. c. 14.

a mere mathematical line;) L G is the rundle, or wheel; H F I K, several spokes or handles that are fastened in it; D, the place where the cord is fastened, for the drawing or lifting up of any weight.

The force of this instrument doth consist in that disproportion of distance which there is betwixt the semidiameter of the cylinder A B, and the semidiameter of the rundle with the spokes, F A. For let us conceive the line F B to be as a leaver, wherein A is the centre or fulciment, B the place of the weight, and F of the power. Now it is evident from the former principles, that by how much the distance F A is greater than A B, by so much less need the power be at F, in respect of the weight at B. Suppose A B to be as the tenth part of A F, then that power or strength, which is but as a hundred pound at F, will be equal to a thousand pound at B.

For the clearer explication of this faculty, it will not be amiss to consider the form of it, as it will appear, being more fully exposed to the view: as in this other diagram.

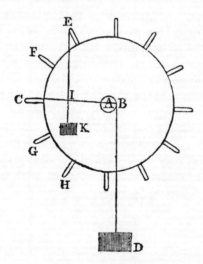

Suppose A B for the semidiameter of the axis or cylinder, and A C for the semidiameter of the rundle with the spokes; then the power at C, which will be able to support the weight D, must bear the same proportion unto it, as A B doth to A C : so that by how much shorter the distance A B is, in comparison to the distance A C, by so much less need the power be at C, which may be able to support the weight D hanging at B.

And so likewise is it for the other spokes or handles, E F G H ; at either of which, if we conceive any power, which shall move according to the same circumference wherein these handles are placed ; then the strength of this power will be all one, as if it were at C. But now, supposing a dead weight hanging at any of them, (as at E) then the disproportion will vary : the power being so much less than that at C, by how much the line A C is longer than A I ; the weight K being of the same force at E, as if it were hung at I, in which point the perpendicular of its gravity doth cut the diameter.

The chief advantage which this instrument doth bestow above that of the leaver, doth consist in this particular : in a leaver, the motion can be continued only for so short a space, as may be answerable to that little distance betwixt the fulciment and the weight ; which is always by so much lesser, as the disproportion betwixt the weight and the power is greater, and the motion itself more easy : but now in this invention, that inconvenience is remedied ; for by a frequent rotation of the axis, the weight may be moved for any height, or length, as occasion shall require.

Unto this faculty may we refer the force of all those engines, which consist of wheels with teeth in them.

Hence also may we discern the reason, why sundry instruments in common use, are framed after the like form with these following figures

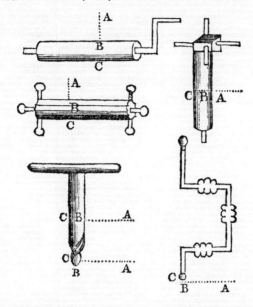

All which are but several kinds of this third mechanical faculty, in which the points A B C do represent the places of the power, the fulciment, and the weight; the power being in the same proportion unto the weight, as B C is unto B A.

CHAP. VII.

Concerning the Pulley.

THAT which is reckoned for the fourth faculty, is the pulley; which is of such ordinary use, that it needs not any particular description. The chief parts of it are divers little rundles, that are moveable about their proper axes *. These are usually divided, according to their several situations, into the upper and lower. If an engine

* Arist. Mechan. c. 19.

have two of these rundles above, and two below, it is usually called διπαστος, if three, τρισπαστος, if many, πολυσπαστος.

The lower pullies only do give force to the motion.   If we suppose a weight to hang upon any of the upper rundles, it will then require a power that in itself shall be fully equal for the sustaining of it.

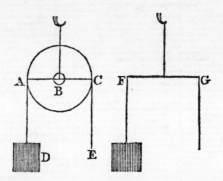

The diameter A C being as the beam of a balance, of which B is the prop or centre ; now the parts A and C being equally distant from this centre, therefore the power at E must be equal to the weight at D ; it being all one, as if the power and the weight were fastened by two several strings, at the ends of the balance F G.

Now all the upper pullies being of the same nature, it must necessarily follow, that none of them do in themselves conduce to the easing of the power, or lightening the weight, but only for the greater conveniency of the motion ; the cords by this means running more easily moved, than otherwise they would.

But now, suppose the weight to be sustained above the pulley, as it is in all those of the lower sort ; and then the power which supports it, need be but half as much as the weight itself.

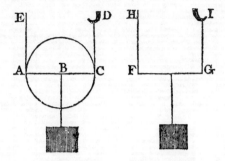

Let A C represent the diameter of a lower pulley, on whose centre at B the weight is fastened, one end of the cord being tied to a hook at D.   Now it is evident, that half the weight is sustained at D, so that there is but the other half left to be sustained by the power at E: it being all one, as if the weight were tied unto the middle of the balance F G, whose ends were upheld by two several strings, F H, and G I.

And this same subduple proportion will still remain, though we suppose an upper pulley joined to the power; as in these two other figures.

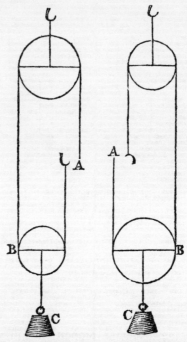

Where the power at A is equal to the weight at B: now the weight at B being but half the ponderosity C, therefore the power at A, notwithstanding the addition of the upper rundle, must be equivalent to half the weight; and as the upper pulley alone doth not abate any thing of the weight, so neither being joined with the lower ; and the same subduple difference betwixt the power and the weight, which is caused by the lower pulley alone, doth still remain unaltered, though there be an upper pulley added unto it.

Now, as one of these under-pullies doth abate half of that heaviness which the weight hath in itself, and cause the power to be in a subduple proportion unto it; so two of them do abate half of that which remains, and cause a subquadruple proportion betwixt the weight and the power; three of them a subsextuple, four a suboctuple: and so for five, six, or as many as shall be required; they will all of them diminish the weight, according to this proportion.

Suppose the weight in itself to be 1200 pound, the applying unto it one of these lower pulleys, will make it but as 600; two of them, as 300; three of them, as 150, &c.

But now, if we conceive the first part of the string to be fastened unto the lower pulley, as in this other figure at F;

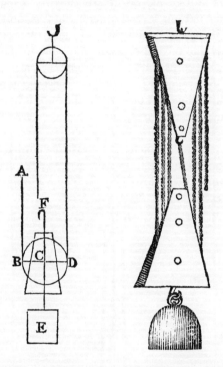

then the power at A, will be in a subtriple proportion to the weight E, because the heaviness would be then equally divided unto the three points of the lower diameter B, C, D, each of them supporting a like share of the burthen. If unto this lower pulley there were added another, then the power would be unto the weight in a subquintuple proportion. If a third, a subsextuple, and so of the rest. For we must note, that the cords in this instrument are as so many powers, and the rundles as so many leavers, or balances.

Hence it is easy to conceive, how the strength of the power may be proportioned according to any such degree, as shall be required; and how any weigh given may be moved by any power given.

It is not material to the force of this instrument, whether the rundles of it be big or little, if they be made equal to one another in their several orders: but it is most conveni- ent, that the upper should each of them increase as they are higher, and the other as they are lower; because by this means the cords will be kept from tangling.

These pulleys may be multiplied according to sundry different situations, not only when they are subordinate, as in the former examples, but also when they are placed col- laterally.

From the former grounds it it easy to contrive a ladder, by which a man may pull himself up unto any height. For the performance of this, there is required only an upper and a lower rundle.

To the uppermost of these at A, there should be fastened a sharp grapple or cramp of iron, which may be apt to take hold of any place where it lights.   This part being first cast up and fastened, and the staff D E, at the nether end, being put betwixt the legs, so that a man may sit upon the other B C, and take hold of the cord at F, it is evident that the weight of the person at E, will be but equal to half so much strength at F; so that a man may easily pull himself up to the place required, by leaning but little more than half of his own weight on the string F.   Or if the pulleys be multiplied, this experiment may then be wrought with less labour.

CHAP. VIII.

Of the Wedge.

THE fifth mechanical faculty is the wedge, which is a known instrument, commonly used in the cleaving of wood.   The efficacy and great strength of it may be resolved unto these two particulars:

1. The form of it.

2. The manner whereby the power is impressed upon it, which is by the force of blows.

1. The form of it represents (as it were) two leavers.

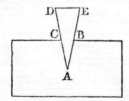

Each side A D, and A E, being one, the points B C, being instead of several props or fulciments; the weight to be moved at A, and the power that should move it, being applied to the top D E, by the force of some stroke or blow· as Aristotle * hath explained the several parts of this faculty.

* Mechan. c. 18.

But now, because this instrument may be so used that the point of it shall not touch the body to be moved, as in these other figures:

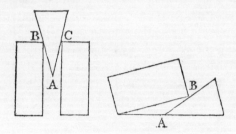

Therefore Ubaldus hath more exactly applied the several parts of it according to this form, that the point A, should be as the common fulciment, in which both the sides do meet, and (as it were) uphold one another; the points B, and C, representing that part of the leavers where the weight is placed.

It is a general rule, that the more acute the angles of these wedges are, by so much more easy will their motion be; tne force being more easily impressed, and the space wherein the body is moved, being so much the less.

The second particular whereby this faculty hath its force, is the manner whereby the power is imprest upon it, which is by a stroke or blow; the efficacy of which doth much exceed any other strength.   For though we suppose a wedge being laid on a piece of timber, to be pressed down with never so great a weight; nay, though we should apply unto it the power of those other mechanical engines, the pulley, screw, &c. yet the effect would be scarce considerable in comparison to that of a blow.   The true reason of which, is one of the greatest subtilties in nature, nor is it fully rendered by any of those who have undertaken the resolution of it.   Aristotle, Cardan, and Scaliger*, do generally ascribe it unto the swiftness of that motion: but there seems to be something more in the matter than so ;

---

* Mechan. c. 10.   Subtil. 1. 17.   Exercit. 331.

for otherwise it would follow that the quick stroke of a light hammer should be of greater efficacy than any softer and more gentle striking of a great sledge. Or according to this, how should it come to pass, that the force of an arrow or bullet discharged near at hand (when the impression of that violence whereby they are carried, is most fresh, and so in probability the motion at its swiftest) is yet notwithstanding much less than it would be at a greater distance. There is therefore further considerable, the quality of that instrument by which this motion is given, and also the conveniency of distance through which it passes.

Unto this faculty is usually reduced the force of files, saws, hatchets, &c. which are as it were but so many wedges fastened unto a vectis or leaver.

CHAP. IX.

Of the Screw.

THAT which is usually recited for the sixth and last mechanic faculty, is the screw, which is described to be a kind of wedge that is multiplied, or continued by a helical revolution about a cylinder, receiving its motion not from any stroke, but from a vectis at one end of it *. It is usually distinguished into two several kinds: the male which is meant in the former description, and the female which is of a concave superficies.

* Pappus Collect. Mathemat. 1. 8.

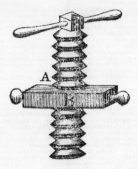

The former is noted in the figure with the letter A, the other with B.

Aristotle himself doth not so much as mention this instrument, which yet notwithstanding is of greater force and subtilty than any of the rest. It is chiefly applied to the squeezing or pressing of things downwards, as in the presses for printing; for wine, oil, and extracting the juice from other fruits. In the performance of which, the strength of one man, may be of greater force than the weight of a heavy mountain. It is likewise used for the elevating or lifting up of weights.

The advantage of this faculty above the rest, doth mainly consist in this: the other instruments do require so much strength for the supporting of the weight to be moved, as may be equal unto it, besides that other superadded power whereby it is out-weighed and moved; so that in the operations by these, a man does always spend himself in a continued labour.

Thus (for example) a weight that is lifted up by a wheel or pulley, will of itself descend, if there be not an equal power to sustain it. But now in the composure of a screw, this inconvenience is perfectly remedied; for so much force as is communicated unto this faculty from the power that is applied unto it, is still retained by the very frame and nature of the instrument itself, since the motion of it cannot possibly return, but from the very same place where it first began. Whence it comes to pass, that any weight lifted up with the assistance of this engine, may likewise be sustained by it without the help of any external power; and cannot again descend unto its former place, unless the handle of the screw (where the motion first began) be turned back: so that all the strength of the power may be employed in the motion of the weight, and none spent in the sustaining of it.

The chief inconvenience of this instrument is, that in a short space it will be screwed unto its full length, and then it cannot be of any further use for the continuance of the motion, unless it be returned back, and undone again as at the first. But this is usually remedied by another invention, commonly styled a perpetual screw, which hath the motion of a wheel, and the force of a screw, being both infinite.

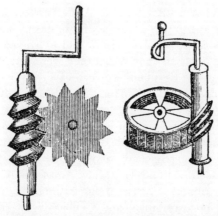

For the composure of which, instead of the female, or concave screw, there must be a little wheel with some notches in it, equivalent to teeth *, by which the other may take hold of it, and turn it round, as in these other figures.

This latter engine does so far exceed all other contrivances to this purpose, that it may justly seem a wonder why it is not of as common use in these times and places, as any of the rest.

* It is used in some watches.

CHAP. X.

*An enquiry into the magnificent works of the ancients,
which much exceeding our latter times, may seem to
infer a decay in these mechanical arts.*

THUS have I briefly treated concerning the general
principles of mechanics, together with the distinct
proportions betwixt the weight and the power in each several faculty of it : whence it is easy to conceive the truth
and ground of those famous ancient monuments, which
seem almost incredible to these following ages.   And because many of them recorded by antiquity, were of such
vast labour and magnificence, and so mightily disproportionable to human strength, it shall not therefore be impertinent unto the purpose I aim at, for to specify some of the
most remarkable amongst them, and to enquire into the
means and occasion upon which they were first attempted.

Amongst the Egyptians we read of divers pyramids of
so vast a magnitude, as time itself in the space of so many
hundred years hath not yet devoured.   Herodotus * mentions one of them, erected by Cleopes an Egyptian king,
wherein there was not any one stone less than 30 foot long,
all of them being fetched from Arabia.   And not much
after, the same author relates, how Amasis, another Egyptian, made himself a house of one entire stone, which was
21 cubits long, 14 broad, and 8 cubits high.   The same
Amasis is reported to have made the statue of a sphink,
or Egyptian cat, all of one single stone; whose length was
143 foot, its height 62 foot, the compass of this statue's head
containing 102 foot†.   In one of the Egyptian temples
consecrated to Jupiter, there is related to be an obelisk,
consisting of 4 smaragds or emeralds; the whole is 40 cubits high, 4 cubits broad at the bottom, and two at the
top ‡.   Sesostris the king of Egypt, in a temple at Mem-

---

* Lib. 2. c. 175.   † Plin. l. 36. c. 12.   ‡ Plin. l. 37. cap. 5.

phis, dedicated to Vulcan, is reported to have erected two
statues; one for himself, the other for his wife, both consisting of two several stones, each of which were 30 cubits
high*.

Amongst the Jews we read in sacred writ of Solomon's
temple, which for its state and magnificence, might have
been justly reckoned amongst the other wonders of the
world; wherein besides the great riches of the materials,
there were works too of as great labour.   Pillars of brass
18 cubits high, and 12 cubits round ; great and costly stones
for the foundation of it † : Josephus ‡ tells us that some of
them were 40 cubits, others 45 cubits long.   And in the
same chapter he mentions the three famous towers built
by Herod; wherein every stone being of white marble,
was 20 cubits long, 10 broad, and 5 high.   And which was
the greatest wonder, the old wall itself was situated on a
steep rising ground, and yet the hills upon it, on the tops
of which these towers were placed, were about 30 cubits
high, that it is scarce imaginable by what strength so many
stones of such great magnitude should be conveyed to so
high a place.

Amongst the Grecians we read of the Ephesian temple
dedicated to Diana; wherein there were 127 columns
made of so many several stones, each of them 60 foot
high, being all taken out of the quarries in Asia ||.   It is
storied also of the brazen colossus, or great statue in the
island of Rhodes, that it was 70 cubits high.   The thumbs
of it being so big that no man could grasp one of them
about with both his arms; when it stood upright, a ship
might have passed betwixt the legs of it, with all its sails
fully displayed; being thrown down by an earthquake, the
brass of it did load 900 camels §.   But above all ancient
designs to this purpose, that would have been most wonderful, which a Grecian architect ¶ did propound unto

---

* Diodor. Sicul. Biblioth. l. 1. sect. 2.

† 1 King. vii. 15. v. 17.   ‡ De Bello Jud. l. 6. cap. 6.

|| Plin. l. 36. cap. 14. Pancirol. Deperd. Tit. 32.

§ Plin. l. 34. cap. 3.   ¶ Vitruv. Archit. l. 2.

Alexander, to cut the mountain Athos into the form of a statue, which in his right hand should hold a town capable of ten thousand men, and in his left a vessel to receive all the water that flowed from the several springs in the mountain. But whether Alexander in his ambition did fear that such an idol should have more honour than he himself, or whether in his good husbandry, he thought that such a microcosm (if I may so style it) would have cost him almost as much as the conquering of this great world, or whatever else was the reason, he refused to attempt it.

Amongst the Romans we read of a brazen colossus, made at the command and charges of Nero *, which was 120 foot high ; Martial calls it sydereus, or starry.

Hic ubi sydereus propius videt astra colossus.

And it is storied of M. Curio † that he erected two theatres sufficiently capacious of people, contrived moveable upon certain hinges ; sometimes there were several plays and shows in each of them, neither being any disturbance to the other ; and sometimes they were both turned about, with the people in them, and the ends meeting together, did make a perfect amphitheatre ; so that the spectators which were in either of them, might jointly behold the same spectacles.

There were besides at Rome sundry obelisks ‡, made of so many entire stones, some of them 40, some 80, and others 90 cubits high.   The chief of them were brought out of Egypt, where they were dug out of divers quarries, and being wrought into form, were afterwards (not without incredible labour, and infinite charges) conveyed unto Rome. In the year 1586, there was erected an old obelisk which had been formerly dedicated unto the memory of Julius Cæsar. It was one solid stone, being an ophite or kind of spotted marble. The height of it was 107 foot, the breadth of it at the bottom was 12 foot, at the top 8. Its whole weight is reckoned to be 956148 pounds; besides the hea-

* Suet. Ner.   † Pancirol. Deperd. Tit. 28.   ‡ Idem Tit. 31.

viness of all those instruments that were used about it, which (as it is thought) could not amount to less than 1042824 pounds.   It was transplaced at the charges of pope Sixtus the fifth, from the left side of the Vatican unto a more eminent place about a hundred foot off, where now it stands.   The moving of this obelisk is celebrated by the writings of above 56 several authors, (saith Monantholius *,) all of them mentioning it, not without much wonder and praise.   Now if it seem so strange and glorious an attempt to move this obelisk for so little a space, what then may we think of the carriage of it out of Egypt, and divers other far greater works performed by antiquity? This may seem to infer that these mechanical arts are now lost, and decayed amongst the many other ruins of time: which yet notwith-standing cannot be granted, without much ingratitude to those learned men, whose labours in this kind we enjoy, and may justly boast of.   And therefore for our better un-derstanding of these particulars, it will not be amiss to en-quire both why, and how such works should be performed in those former and ruder ages, which are not, and (as it should seem) cannot be effected in these later and more learned times.   In the examination of which, we shall find that it is not the want of art that disables us for them, since these mechanical discoveries are altogether as perfect, and (I think) much more exact now, than they were heretofore; but it is, because we have not either the same motives to attempt such works, or the same means to effect them as the ancients had.

CHAP. XI.

That the ancients had divers motives and means for such vast magnificent works, which we have not.

THE motives by which they were excited to such mag-nificent attempts, we may conceive to be chiefly three:

* Comment. in Mechan. Arist. c. 19.

$$\left\{\begin{array}{l}\text{Religion.}\\\text{Policy.}\\\text{Ambition.}\end{array}\right.$$

1. Religion. Hence was it that most of these stately buildings were intended for some sacred use, being either temples or tombs *, all of them dedicated to some of their deities. It was an inbred principle in those ancient heathen, that they could not chuse but merit very much by being liberal in their outward services. And therefore we read of Crœsus †, that being overcome in a battle, and taken by Cyrus, he did revile the gods of ingratitude, because they had no better care of him, who had so frequently adored them with costly oblations. And as they did conceive themselves bound to part with their lives in defence of their religion, so likewise to employ their utmost power and estate about any such design which might promote or advance it. Whereas now, the generality of men, especially the wisest sort amongst them, are in this respect of another opinion, counting such great and immense labours, to be at the best but glorious vanities. The temple of Solomon indeed was to be a type, and therefore it was necessary that it should be so extraordinarily magnificent, otherwise perhaps a much cheaper structure might have been as commendable and serviceable.

2. Policy. That by this means they might find out employment for the people, who of themselves being not much civilized, might by idleness quickly grow to such a rudeness and barbarism, as not to be bounded within any laws of government. Again, by this means the riches of the kingdom did not lie idly in their kings treasuries, but was always in motion; which could not but be a great advantage and improvement to the commonwealth ‡. And perhaps some of them feared lest if they should leave too much money unto their successors, it might be an occasion to ensnare them in such idle and vain courses, as would ruin their kingdoms: whereas in these latter ages, none of

* As Pyramids, Obelisks.   † Herodot. l. 1.
‡ Plin. l. 6. c. 12.

all these politic incitements can be of any force, because now there is employment enough for all, and money little enough for every one.

3. Ambition to be known unto posterity; and hence likewise arose that incredible labour and care they bestowed, to leave such monuments behind them as might continue for ever *, and make them famous unto all after-ages. This was the reason of Absalom's pillar, spoken of in scripture, to keep his name in remembrance †. And doubtless this too was the end which many other of the ancients have aimed at, in those (as they thought) everlasting buildings.

But now these later ages are much more active and stirring; so that every ambitious man may find so much business for the present, that he shall scarce have any leisure to trouble himself about the future. And therefore in all these respects, there is a great disproportion betwixt the incitements of those former and these later times unto such magnificent attempts.

Again, as they differ much in their motives unto them, so likewise in the means of effecting them.

There was formerly more leisure and opportunity, both for the great men to undertake such works, and for the people to perfect them. Those past ages were more quiet and peaceable, the princes rather wanting employment, than being overpressed with it, and therefore were willing to make choice of such great designs, about which to busy themselves. Whereas now the world is grown more politic, and therefore more troublesome; every great man having other private and necessary business about which to employ both his time and means. And so likewise for the common people, who then living more wildly, without being confined to particular trades and professions, might be more easily collected about such famous employments; whereas now, if a prince have any occasion for an army, it is very hard for him to raise so great a multitude as were

* Psal. iv. 11.　　　† 2 Sam. i. 18.

usually employed about these magnificent buildings. We read of 360000 men that were busied for twenty years in making one of the Egyptian pyramids. And Herodotus * tells us of 1000000 men who were as long in building another of them. About the carriage of one stone for Amasis the distance of twenty days journey, there was for three years together employed 2000 chosen men, governors, besides many other under-labourers. It was the opinion of Josephus † and Nazianzen, that these pyramids were built by Joseph for granaries against the years of famine. Others think that the brick made by the children of Israel was employed about the framing of them, because we read that the tower of Babel did consist of brick or artificial stone, Gen. xi. 3. And if these were the labourers that were busied about them, it is no wonder though they were of so vast a magnitude; for we read that the children of Israel at their coming out of Egypt, were numbered to be six hundred thousand, and three thousand, and five hundred and fifty men, Numb. i. 46. So many handfuls of earth would almost make a mountain, and therefore we may easily believe that so great a multitude in so long a space as their bondage lasted, for above four hundred years, might well enough accomplish such vast designs.

In the building of Solomon's temple, there were threescore and ten thousand that bare burthens, and fourscore thousand hewers in the mountains, 1 Kings v. 15.

The Ephesian temple was built by all Asia joining together; the 127 pillars were made by so many kings, according to their several successions, the whole work being not finished under the space of two hundred and fifteen years. Whereas the transplacing of that obelisk at Rome by Sixtus the Vth, (spoken of before) was done in some few days by five or six hundred men; and as the work was much less than many other recorded by antiquity, so the means by which it was wrought, was yet far less in this respect than what is related of them.

* Lib. 2.   † Antiq. l. 2. c. 5.

2. The abundance of wealth, which was then ingrossed in the possession of some few particular persons, being now diffused amongst a far greater number. There is now a greater equality amongst mankind, and the flourishing of arts and sciences hath so stirred up the sparks of men's natural nobility, and made them of such active and industrious spirits, as to free themselves in a great measure from that slavery, which those former and wilder nations were subjected unto.

In building one of the pyramids, there was expended for the maintenance of the labourers with radish and onions, no less than eighteen hundred talents, which is reckoned to amount unto 1880000 crowns, or thereabouts. And considering the cheapness of these things in those times and places, so much money might go farther than a sum ten times greater could do in the maintenance of so many now.

In Solomon's temple we know how the extraordinary riches of that king, the general flourishing of the whole state, and the liberality of the people did jointly concur to the building of the temple. *Pecuniarum copia et populi largitas, majora dictu conabatur*, (saith Josephus*.) The Rhodian colossus is reported to have cost three hundred talents the making; and so were all those other famous monuments of proportionable expence.

Pancirollus† speaking of those theatres that were erected at the charges of some private Roman citizens, saith thus: *nostro hoc sæculo vel rex satis haberet quod ageret ædificio ejusmodi erigendo;* and a little after upon the like occasion, *res mehercule miraculosa, quæ nostris temporibus vix à potentissimo aliquo rege possit exhiberi.*

3. Add unto the two former considerations, that exact care and indefatigable industry which they bestowed in the raising of those structures; these being the chief and only designs on which many of them did employ all their best thoughts and utmost endeavours. Cleopes an Egyptian

* De Bell. Jud. l. 6. cap. 6.　　　† Deperd. Tit. 18.

king is reported to have been so desirous to finish one of the pyramids, that having spent all about it he was worth, or could possibly procure, he was forced at last to prostitute his own daughter for necessary maintenance. And we read of Ramises * another king of Egypt, how that he was so careful to erect an obelisk, about which he had employed 20000 men, that when he feared lest through the negligence of the artificers, or weakness of the engine, the stone might fall and break, he tied his own son to the top of it, that so the care of his safety might make the workmen more circumspect in their business. And what strange matters may be effected by the mere diligence and labour of great multitudes, we may easily discern from the wild Indians, who having not the art or advantage of engines, did yet by their unwearied industry remove stones of an incredible greatness. Acosta † relates that he himself measured one at Tiaguanaco, which was thirty-eight foot long, eighteen broad, and six thick; and he affirms, that in their stateliest edifices there were many other of much vaster magnitude.

From all which considerations, it may appear, that the strangeness of those ancient monuments above any that are now effected, does not necessarily infer any defect of art in these later ages. And I conceive, it were as easy to demonstrate the mechanical arts in these times to be so far beyond the knowledge of former ages, that had we but the same means as the ancients had, we might effect far greater matters than any they attempted, and that too in a shorter space, and with less labour.

* Plin. l. 36. c. 9.   † Histor. Ind. l. 6. c. 14.

CHAP. XII.

Concerning the force of the mechanic faculties; particularly the Balance and Leaver.   How they may be contrived to move the whole world, or any conceivable weight.

ALL these magnificent works of the ancients before specified, are scarce considerable in respect of art, if we compare them with the famous speeches and acts of Archimedes: of whom it is reported, that he was frequently wont to say, how that he could move *datum pondus, cum data potentiâ;* the greatest conceivable weight, with the least conceivable power: and that if he did but know where to stand and fasten his instrument, he could move the world, all this great globe of sea and land.   Which promises, though they were altogether above the vulgar apprehension or belief, yet because his acts were some-what answerable thereunto, therefore the king of Syracuse did enact a law, whereby every man was bound to believe whatever Archimedes would affirm.

It is easy to demonstrate the geometrical truth of those strange assertions, by examining them according to each of the forenamed mechanic faculties, every one of which is of infinite power.

To begin with the two first of them, the balance and the leaver, (which I here join together, because the proportions of both are wholly alike;) it is certain, though there should be the greatest imaginable weight, and the least imaginable power, (suppose the whole world, and the strength of one man, or infant;) yet if we conceive the same disproportion betwixt their several distances in the former faculties, from the fulciment, or centre of gravity, they would both equiponderate.   And if the distance of the power from the centre, in comparison to the distance of the weight, were but any thing more than the heaviness of the weight is in respect of the power, it may then be evident from the former principles, that the power would be of greater force than the weight, and consequently able to move it.

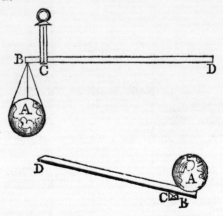

Thus, if we suppose this great globe at A to contain 2400000000000000000000000 pounds, allowing a hundred pounds for each cubical foot in it, (as Stevinius * hath calculated) yet a man or child at D, whose strength perhaps is but equivalent to one hundred, or ten pounds weight, may be able to outweigh and move it; if there be but a little greater disproportion betwixt the two distances C D and C B, than there is betwixt the heaviness of the weight, and the strength of the power; that is, if the distance C D, unto the other distance C B, be any thing more than 2400000000000000000000000 unto 100 or 10, every ordinary instrument doth include all these parts really, though not sensibly distinguished.

Under this latter faculty, I did before mention that engine, by which Archimedes drew up the Roman ships at the siege of Syracuse †. This is usually stiled Tollenon, being of the same form with that which is commonly used by brewers and dyers, for the drawing of water. It consists of two posts; the one fastened perpendicularly in the

---

* Static. l. 3. prop. 10.   † Lipsius Poliorcet. l. 1. Dialog. 6.

ground, the other being jointed on cross to the top of it. At the end he fastened a strong hook or grapple of iron, which being let over the wall to the river, he would thereby take hold of the ships, as they passed under; and after-wards, by applying some weight, or perhaps the force of screws to the other end, he would thereby lift them into the open air; where having swinged them up and down till he had shaken out the men and goods that were in them, he would then dash the vessels against the rocks, or drown them in their sudden fall: insomuch that Marcellus, the Roman general, was wont to say, τον μεν ναυσιν αυτ8 κυαδιζειν εκ θαλατΐης Αρχιμηδη *.   That Archimedes made use of his ships instead of buckets to draw water with.

This faculty will be of the same force, not only when it is continued in one, but also when it is multiplied in divers instruments; as may be conceived in this other form; which I do not mention, as if it could be serviceable for any other motion, (since the space by which the weight would be moved, will be so little as not to fall under sense) but only for the better explication of this mechanic principle, and for the right understanding of that force arising from multiplication in the other faculties, which do all depend upon this.   The wheel, and pulley, and screw, being but as so many leavers of a circular form and motion, whose strength may be therefore continued to a greater space.

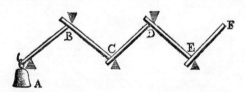

Imagine the weight A to be a hundred thousand pounds, and the distance of that point, wherein every leaver touches either the weight, or one another from the point where they touch the prop, to be but one such part, whereof the

* Plutarch in his life.

remainder contains ten; then according to the former grounds, 10000 at B will equiponderate to A, which is 100000; so that the second leaver hath but 10000 pounds to move. Now, because this observes the same proportions with the other, in the distances of its several points, therefore 1000 pounds at C will be of equal weight to the former: and the weight at C being but as a thousand pound, that which is but as a hundred at D, will be answerable unto it; and so still in the same proportion, that which is but 10 at E, will be equal to 100 at D; and that which is but one pound at F, will also be equal to ten at E. Whence it is manifest, that one pound at F is equal to 100000 at A; and the weight must always be diminished in the same proportion as ten to one, because in the multiplication of these leavers, the distance of the point where the instrument touches the weight, from that where it touches the prop, is but as one such part, whereof the remainder contains ten. But now if we imagine it to be as the thousandth part, then must the weight be diminished according to this proportion; and then in the same multiplication of leavers, 1 pound will be equal to 1000 000 000 000 000 pounds: so that though we suppose the weight to be never so heavy, yet let the disproportion of distances be greater, or the leavers more, and any little power may move it.

* See the figures, c. 6.

CHAP. XIII.

Of the Wheel: by multiplication of which, it is easy to move any imaginable weight.

THE wheel, or axis in peritrochio, was before demonstrated to be of equivalent force with the former faculties *. If we conceive the same difference betwixt the semidiameter of the wheels, or spokes A C, and the semidiameter of the axis A B, as there is betwixt the weight of the world, and the strength of a man; it may then be evident, that this strength of one man, by the help of such an instrument, will equiponderate to the weight of the whole world. And if the semidiameter óf the wheel A C, be but any thing more in respect of the semidiameter of the axis A B, than the weight of the world supposed at D, is in comparison to the strength of a man at C; it may then be manifest from the same grounds, that this strength will be of so much greater force than the weight, and consequently able to move it.

The force of this faculty may be more conveniently understood and used by the multiplication of several wheels *, together with nuts belonging unto each of them; as it may be easily experimented in the ordinary jacks that are used for the roasting of meat, which commonly consist but of three wheels; and yet if we suppose a man tied in the place of the weight, it were easy by a single hair fastened unto the fly or balance of the jack, to draw him up from the ground: as will be evident from this following figure.

* An engine of many wheels is commonly called glossocomus.

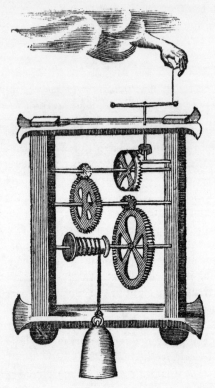

Where suppose the length of the fly or balance in comparison to the breadth of its axis, to be as 10 to one, and so for the three other wheels in respect of the nuts that belong unto them; (though this difference be oftentimes less, as we may well allow it to be); withal suppose the weight (or a man tied in the place of it) to be a hundred pounds: I say according to this supposition, it is evident that the power at the balance which shall be equal to the weight, need be but as 1 to 10000. For the first axis is conceived to be but as the tenth part of its wheel; and therefore though the weight in itself be as 10000, yet unto a power that hath this advantage, it is but as 1000, and therefore this thousand unto the like power at the second wheel, will be but as 100, and this 100 at the third but as 10; and lastly, this ten at the balance but as one. But the weight was before supposed to be 100, which to the first wheel will be but 10, to the second as one, to the third as a decimal, or one tenth to the sails as one hundredth part · so that if the hair be but strong enough to lift $\frac{1}{10000}$, that is, one ten thousandth part of a man, or (which is all one) one hundredth part of a pound, it may as well serve by the help of this instrument for the drawing of him up. And though there be not altogether so great a disproportion betwixt the several parts of a jack (as in many perhaps there is not;) and though a man may be heavier than is here supposed, yet it is withal considerable, that the strength of a hair is able to bear much more than the hundredth part of a pound.

Upon this ground Mersennus * tells us out of Solomon de Cavet, that if there were an engine of twelve wheels, each of them with teeth, as also the axes or nuts that belong unto them; if the diameter of these wheels were unto each axis as a hundred to one; and if we suppose these wheels to be so placed, that the teeth of the one might take hold of the axis that belongs unto the next, and that the axis of the handle may turn the first wheel, and the weight be tied unto the axis of the last; with such an engine as this, saith he, a child (if he could stand anywhere without this earth) might with much ease move it towards him.

For according to the former supposition, that this globe of sea and land did contain as many hundred pounds as it doth cubical feet, viz. 24000000000000000000000000, it may be evident that any strength, whose force is but equivalent to three pounds, will by such an engine be able to move it,

Of this kind was that engine so highly extolled by Stevinus †, which he calls pancration, or omnipotent, preferring it before the inventions of Archimedes. It consisted

---

* Comment in Gen. c. 1. v. 10. art. 6. De viribus motricibus, Theor. 16.
† De Static. praxi.

of wheels and nuts, as that before specified is supposed.
Hither also should be referred the force of racks, which
serve for bending of the strongest bows *, as also that little
pocket engine, wherewith a man may break or wrench open
any door, together with divers the like instruments in common use.

CHAP. XIV.

*Concerning the infinite strength of Wheels, Pullies, and
Screws. That it is possible by the multiplication of these,
to pull up any oak by the roots with a hair, lift it up with
a straw, or blow it up with one's breath, or to perform the
greatest labour with the least power.*

FROM what hath been before delivered concerning the
nature of the pulley, it is easy to understand how this
faculty also may be proportioned betwixt any weight, and
any power, as being likewise of infinite strength.

It is reported of Archimedes, that with an engine of pullies, to which he applied only his left hand, he lifted up
5000 bushels of corn at once †, and drew a ship with all its
lading upon dry land. This engine Zetzes calls trispatum,
or trispastum, which signifies only a threefold pulley : but
herein he doth evidently mistake, for it is not possible that
this alone should serve for the motion of so great a weight ;
because such an engine can but make a subsextuple, or at
most a subseptuple proportion betwixt the weight and
power ; which is much too little to reconcile the strength of
a man unto so much heaviness. Therefore Ubaldus ‡ doth
more properly style it, polyspaston ; or an instrument of
many pullies. How many, were easy to find out, if we

---

* Ramelli, fig. 160.   † 7000 saith Zetzes, Chiliad. 2. Hist. 35.
‡ Præf. ad. Mechan.

did exactly know the weight of those ancient measures;
supposing them to be the same with our bushel in England,
which contains 64 pints or pounds, the whole would amount
to 320000 pounds; half of which would be lightened by
the help of one pulley, three quarters by two pullies, and
so onward, according to this subduple, subquadruple, and
subsextuple proportion. So that if we conceive the strength
of the left hand to be equivalent unto twenty or forty
pounds, it is easy to find out how many pullies are required
to enable it for the motion of so great a weight.

Upon this ground Mersennus * tells us, that any little
child with an engine of an hundred double pullies, might
easily move this great globe of earth, though it were much
heavier than it is. And in reference to this kind of engine
(saith Monantholius †) are we to understand that assertion
of Archimedes, (as he more immediately intended it) concerning the possibility of moving the world.

The wedge was before demonstrated to be as a double
vectis or leaver, and therefore it would be needless to explain particularly how this likewise may be contrived of infinite force.

The screw is capable of multiplication, as well as any of
the other faculties, and may perhaps be more serviceable
for such great weights, than any of the rest. Archimedes
his engine of greatest strength, called caristion, is by some
thought to consist of these. *Axes habebat cum infinitis
cochleis* ‡. And that other engine of his called helix,
(mentioned by ‖ Athenæus) wherewith he lifted Hiero's
great ship into the sea, without any other help, is most
likely to be framed of perpetual screws, saith Rivaltus.

Whence it may evidently appear, that each of these
mechanic faculties are of infinite power, and may be contrived proportionable unto any conceivable weight. And
that no natural strength is anyway comparable unto these
artificial inventions.

* Comment in Gen. c. i. v. 10. art. 6.
† Præf ad. Mechan Aristotle.
‡ Stevin. de Static. prax. See Besson.
‖ Deipnosophist. l. 5. Oper. exter. Archimed.

It is reported of Sampson *, that he could carry the gates of a city upon his shoulders; and that the strongest bonds were unto him but as flax burnt with fire, and yet his hair being shaved off, all his strength departed from him. We read of Milo † that he could carry an ox upon his back, and yet when he tried to tear an oak asunder that was somewhat riven before, having drawn it to its utmost, it suddenly joined together again, catching his hands in the cleft, and so strongly manacled him, that he became a prey to the wild beasts.

But now by these mechanical contrivances, it were easy to have made one of Sampson's hairs that was shaved off, to have been of more strength than all of them when they were on. By the help of these arts it is possible (as I shall demonstrate) for any man to lift up the greatest oak by the roots with a straw, to pull it up with a hair, or to blow it up with his breath.

Suppose the roots of an oak to extend a thousand foot square, (which is almost a quarter of a mile) and forty foot deep, each cubical foot being an hundred pound weight; which though it be much beyond the extension of any tree, or the weight of earth; the compass of the roots in the ground (according to common opinion) not extending further than the branches of it in the air, and the depth of it not above ten foot, beyond which the greatest rain doth not penetrate (saith Seneca ‡.) *Ego vinearum diligens fossor affirmo nullam pluviam esse tam magnam, quæ terram ultra decem pedes in altitudinem madefaciat.* And because the root must receive its nourishment from the help of showers, therefore it is probable that it doth not go below them. So that (I say) though the proportions supposed do much exceed the real truth, yet it is considerable that some great overplus must be allowed for that labour which there will be in the forcible divulsion or separation of the parts of the earth which are continued.

* Judges xv.   † A. Gell. Noct. Att. l. 15. c. 16.
† Nat. Qu. l. 3. c. 7.

According to this supposition, the work of forcing up the
oak by the roots will be equivalent to the lifting up of
4000000000 pound weight, which by the advantage of such
an engine, as is here described, may be easily performed
with the least conceivable power.

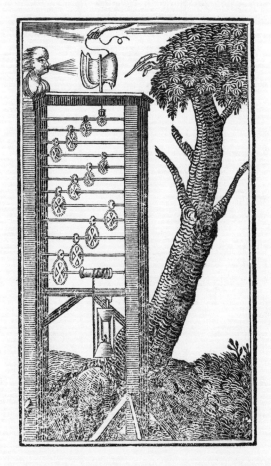

The whole force of this engine doth consist in two
double pullies, twelve wheels, and a sail. One of these
pullies at the bottom will diminish half of the weight, so
that it shall be but as 2000000000, and the other pulley will

abate $\frac{3}{4}$ three quarters of it ; so that it shall be but as 1000000000. And because the beginning of the string being fastened unto the lower pulley, makes the power to be in a subquintuple proportion unto the weight, therefore a power that shall be as 1000000000, that is, a sub-quadruple, will be so much stronger than the weight, and consequently able to move it *. Now suppose the breadth of all the axes and nuts to be unto the diameters of the wheel as ten to one ; and it will then be evident that to a power at the

> First wheel, the weight is but as 100000000 :
> To the second as 10000000 :
> To the third as 1000000 :
> To the fourth as 100000 :
> To the fifth as 10000 :
> To the sixth as 1000 :
> To the seventh as 100 :
> To the eighth as 10 :
> To the ninth as 1 :
> To the tenth as $\frac{1}{10}$, one decimal :
> To the eleventh as $\frac{1}{1000}$:
> To the twelfth as $\frac{1}{10000}$:
> And to the sails yet less :

So that if the strength of the straw, or hair, or breath, be but equal to the weight of one thousandth part of a pound, it may be of sufficient force to pull up the oak.

If in this engine we suppose the disproportion betwixt the wheels and nuts to be as a hundred to one, then it is very evident that the same strength of breath, or a hair, or a straw, would be able to move the whole world, as will be easily found by calculation Let this great globe of sea and land be imagined (as before) to weigh so many hundred pounds as it contains cubical feet ; namely, 24000000000000000000000000 pounds. This will be to the first pulley, 120000000000000000000000000. To the second less than 600000000000000000000000. But for

---

* See chap, viii.

more easy and convenient reckoning, let it be supposed to
be somewhat more, viz. 1000000000000000000000000. This
To the first wheel will be but as 100000000000000000000000.
To the second as . . . . 10000000000000000000000.
To the third as . . . . 1000000000000000000.
To the fourth as . . . . 10000000000000000.
To the fifth as . . . . . 100000000000000.
To the sixth as . . . . 1000000000000.
To the seventh as . . . . 10000000000.
To the eighth as . . . . 100000000.
To the ninth as . . . . 1000000.
To the tenth as . . . . 10000.
To the eleventh as . . . 100.
To the twelfth as . . . . 1.
To the sails as . . . . . . $\frac{1}{100}$.

So that a power which is much less than the hundredth
part of a pound will be able to move the world.

It were needless to set down any particular explication,
how such mechanical strength may be applied unto all
the kinds of local motion; since this is in itself so facil and
obvious, that every ordinary artificer doth sufficiently understand it.

The species of local violent motion are by Aristotle *
reckoned to be these four: pulsio, tractio, vectio, vertigo;
thrusting, drawing, carrying, turning; unto some of which
all these artificial operations must necessarily be reduced,
the strength of any power being equally appliable unto all
of them: so that there is no work impossible to these contrivances; but there may be as much acted by this art, as
can be fancied by imagination.

* Phys. l. 7. c. 3.

CHAP. XV.

Concerning the proportion of slowness and swiftness in mechanical motions.

HAVING already discoursed concerning the strength of these mechanical faculties; it remains, for the more perfect discovery of their natures, that we treat somewhat concerning those two differences of artificial motion : slowness, and swiftness : without the right understanding of which, a man shall be exposed to many absurd mistakes, in attempting of those things which are either in themselves impossible, or else not to be performed with such means as are applied unto them.   I may safely affirm, that many, if not most mistakes in these mechanical designs, do arise from a misapprehension of that difference which there will be betwixt the slowness or swiftness of the weight and power, in comparison to the proportion of their several strengths.

Hence it is, that so many engines invented for mines and waterworks, do so often fail in the performance of that for which they were intended ; because the artificers many times do forget to allow so much time for the working of their engine, as may be proportionable to the difference betwixt the weight and power that belong unto them : whereas, he that rightly understands the grounds of this art, may as easily find out the difference of space and time required to the motion of the weight and power, as he may their different strengths ; and not only tell how any power may move any weight, but also in what a space of time it may move it any space or distance.

If it were possible to contrive such an invention, whereby any conceivable weight may be moved by any conceivable power, both with the same quickness and speed, (as it is in those things which are immediately stirred by the hand, without the help of any other instrument ;) the works of

nature would be then too much subjected to the power of
art, and men might be thereby encouraged (with the
builders of Babel, or the rebel giants) to such bold designs
as would not become a created being. And therefore the
wisdom of providence hath so confined these human arts,
that what any invention hath in the strength of its motion,
is abated in the slowness of it ; and what it hath in the extraordinary quickness of its motion, must be allowed for in
the great strength that is required unto it.

For it is to be observed as a general rule, that the space
of time or place, in which the weight is moved, in comparison to that in which the power doth move, is in the same
proportion as they themselves are unto one another.

So that if there be any great difference betwixt the
strength of the weight and the power, the same kind of
differences will there be in the spaces of their motion.

To illustrate this by an example :

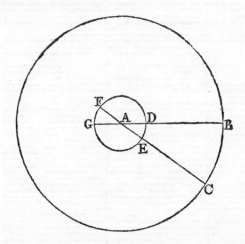

Let the line G A B represent a balance, or leaver; the
weight being supposed at the point G, the fulciment at A,
and the power sustaining the weight at B. Suppose the
point G, unto which the weight is fastened, to be elevated
unto F, and the opposite point B to be depressed unto C ;

it is evident that the arch, F G, or (which is all one) D E,
doth shew the space of the weight, and the arch B C the
motion of the power.   Now both these arches have the
same proportion unto one another, as there is betwixt the
weight and the power, or (which is all one) as there is betwixt their several distances from the fulciment.   Suppose
A G unto A B to be as one unto four; it may then be evident, that F G, or D E, will be in the same proportion unto
B C: for as any two semidiameters are unto one another,
so are the several circumferences described by them, as also
any proportional parts of the same circumferences.

And as the weight and power do thus differ in the spaces
of their motions, so likewise in the slowness of it; the one
moving the whole distance B C, in the same time wherein
the other passes only G F.   So that the motion of the
power from B to C, is four times swifter than that of the
weight from G to F.   And thus will it be, if we suppose the
disproportions to be far greater; whether or no we conceive
it, either by a continuation of the same instrument and faculty, as in the former example; or by a multiplication of
divers, as in pullies, wheels, &c.   By how much the power
is in itself less than the weight, by so much will the motion
of the weight be slower than that of the power.

To this purpose, I shall briefly touch at one of the dia-
grams expressed before in the twelfth chapter, concerning
the multiplication of leavers.

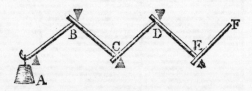

In which, as each instrument doth diminish the weight
according to a decuple proportion, so also do they diminish
the space and slowness of its motion.   For if we should
conceive the first leaver B to be depressed unto its lowest,
suppose ten foot, yet the weight A would not be raised

above one foot : but now the second leaver, at its utmost, could move but a tenth part of the first, and the third leaver but a tenth part of the second ; and so of the rest.   So that the last leaver F being depressed, will pass a space 100000 greater, and by a motion, 100000 swifter than the weight at A.

Thus are we to conceive of all the other faculties, wherein there is constantly the same disproportion betwixt the weight and power, in respect of the spaces and slowness of their motions, as there is betwixt their several gravities. If the power be unto the weight but as one unto a hundred, then the space through which the weight moves, will be a hundred times less, and consequently the motion of the weight a hundred times slower than that of the power.

So that it is but a vain and impossible fancy for any one to think that he can move a great weight with a little power, in a little space ; but in all these mechanical attempts, that advantage which is gotten in the strength of the motion, must be still allowed for the slowness of it.

Though these contrivances do so extremely increase the power, yet they do proportionably protract the time. That which by such helps one man may do in a hundred days, may be done by the immediate strength of a hundred men in one day.

CHAP. XVI.

That it is possible to contrive such an artificial motion, as shall be of a slowness proportionable to the swiftness of the heavens.

IT were a pretty subtilty to inquire after, whether or no it be not possible to contrive such an artificial motion, that should be in such a proportion slow, as the heavens are supposed to be swift.

For the exact resolution of which, it would be requisite that we should first pitch upon some medium, or indifferent motion, by the distance from which, we may judge of the proportions on either side, whether slowness, or swiftness. Now, because there is not any such natural medium, which may be absolutely stiled an indifferent motion, but that the swiftness and slowness of every thing is still proportioned either to the quantity of bodies in which they are, or some other particular end for which they are designed; therefore we must take liberty to suppose such a motion; and this we may conceive to be about 1000 paces, or a mile in an hour.

The starry heaven, or 8th sphere, is thought to move 42398437 miles in the same space: so that if it may be demonstrated that it is possible to contrive such a motion, which going on in a constant direct course, shall pass but the 42398437 part of a mile in an hour; it will then be evident, that an artificial motion may be slow, in the same proportion as the heavens are swift.

Now it was before manifested, that according to the difference betwixt the weight and power, so will the difference be betwixt the slownesss or swiftness of their motions; whence it will follow, that in such an engine, wherein the weight shall be 42398437 pounds, and the power that doth equiponderate it, but the 42398437 part of a pound (which is easy to contrive) in this engine the power being supposed to move with such a swiftness as may be answerable to a mile an hour, the weight will pass but the 42398437 part of a mile in the same space, and so consequently will be proportionably slow unto the swiftness of the heavens.

It is related by our countryman I. Dee *, that he and Cardan being both together in their travels, did see an instrument which was at first sold for twenty talents of gold, wherein there was one wheel, which constantly moving

---

* Preface to Euclid.

round amongst the rest, did not finish one revolution under the space of seven thousand years.

But if we farther consider such an instrument of wheels as was mentioned before in the fourteenth chapter, with which the whole world might be easily moved, we shall then find that the motion of the weight by that, must be much more slow, than the heavens are swift. For though we suppose (saith Stevinus *) the handle of such an engine with twelve wheels to be turned about 4000 times in an hour (which is as often as a man's pulse doth beat) yet in ten years space the weight by this would not be moved above $\frac{10512}{2400}$ 0000000000000000 parts of one foot, which is nothing near so much as a hair's breadth. And it could not pass an inch in 1000000 years, saith Mersennus †.

The truth of which we may more easily conceive, if we consider the frame and manner of this twelve wheeled engine. Suppose that in each axis or nut, there were ten teeth, and on each wheel a thousand : then the sails of this engine must be turned a hundred times, before the first wheel, (reckoning downward) could be moved round once, and ten thousand times before the second wheel can finish one revolution, and so through the twelve wheels, according to this multiplied proportion.

So that besides the wonder which there is in the force of these mechanical motions, the extreme slowness of them is no less admirable. If a man considers that a body should remain in such a constant direct motion, that there could not be one minute of time, wherein it did not rid some space and pass on further, and yet that this body in many years together should not move so far as a hair's breadth.

Which notwithstanding may evidently appear from the former instance. For since it is a natural principle, that there can be no penetration of bodies ; and since it is supposed, that each of the parts in this engine do touch one

* De stat. pract.   † Phænom. Mechan. Prop. 11.

another in their superficies ; therefore it must necessarily
follow, that the weight does begin and continue to move
with the power; and (however it is insensible) yet it is
certain there must be such a motion so extremely slow as
is here specified.   So full is this art of rare and incredible
subtilties.

I know it is the assertion of Cardan *, *Motus valde tardi,
necessario quietes habent intermedias.*   Extreme slow motions have necessarily some intermediate stops and rests.
But this is only said, not proved, and he speaks it from
sensible experiments, which in this case are fallible: our
senses being very incompetent judges of the several proportions, whether greatness or littleness, slowness or swiftness, which there may be amongst things in nature.   For
ought we know, there may be some organical bodies as
much less than ours, as the earth is bigger.   We see what
strange discoveries of extreme minute bodies, (as lice,
wheal-worms, mites, and the like) are made by the mi-
croscope, wherein their several parts (which are altogether
invisible to the bare eye) will distinctly appear: and perhaps there may be other insects that live upon them as they
do upon us.   It is certain that our senses are extremely dis-
proportioned for comprehending the whole compass and
latitude of things.   And because there may be such difference in the motion as well as in the magnitude of bodies; therefore, though such extreme slowness may seem
altogether impossible to sense and common apprehension,
yet this can be no sufficient argument against the reality
of it.

* De Varietate Rerum, l. 9. c. 47.

CHAP. XVII.

Of Swiftness : how it may be increased to any kind of proportion.   Concerning the great force of Archimedes his engines.   Of the Ballista.

B Y that which hath been already explained concerning the slowness of motion, we may the better understand the nature of swiftness, both of them (as is the nature of opposites) being produced by contrary causes.   As the greatness of the weight in respect of the power, and the great distance of the power from the fulciment in comparison to that of the weight, does cause a slow motion ; so the greatness of the power above the weight, and the greater distance of the weight from the centre, in comparison to that of the power, does cause a swift motion.

And as it is possible to contrive a motion unto any kind of slowness, by finding out an answerable disproportion betwixt the weight and power, so likewise unto any kind of swiftness : for so much as the weight does exceed the power, by so much will the motion of the weight be slower, and so much as the power does exceed the weight, by so much will the motion of the weight be swifter.

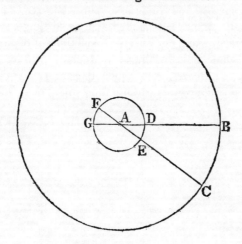

In the diagram set down before, if we suppose F to be
the place of the power, and C of the weight, the point A
being the fulciment or centre, then in the same space of
time wherein the power does move from F to G, the
weight will pass from C to B.   These distances having the
same disproportion unto one another, as there is betwixt
AF and A C, which is supposed to be quadruple.   So that
in this example, the weight will move four times swifter
than the power ; and according as the power does exceed
the weight in any greater disproportion, so will the swiftness of the weight be augmented.

Hence may we conceive the reason of that great force
which there is in slings, which have so much a greater
swiftness than a stone thrown from the hand, by how much
the end of the sling is farther off from the shoulder-joint,
which is the centre of motion.   The sacred history concerning David's victory over Goliath * may sufficiently
evidence the force of these.   Vegetius † relates that it was
usual this way to strike a man dead, and beat the soul out
of his body, without so much as breaking his armour, or
fetching blood.   *Membris integris læthale tamen vulnus
important, & sine invidia sanguinis, hostis lapidis ictu
intereat.*

In the use of these, many of the ancients have been
of very exquisite and admirable skill.   We read of seven
hundred Benjamites left-handed, that could sling a stone at
a hair's breadth, and not miss ‡.   And there is the like storied of a whole nation amongst the Indians, who from their
excellency in this art, were stiled Baleares ‖.   They were
so strict in teaching this art unto their young ones, *ut cibum
puer à matre non accipit, nisi quem ipsa monstrante per-
cussit* ; that the mother would not give any meat to her
child, till (being set at some distance) he could hit it with
slinging.

* 1 Sam. xvii. 49.   † Lipsius Polior. l. 4. Dialogue 21.
‡ Judges xx. 16.

‖ Απο τυ βαλλειν, Diodor. Sicul. Biblioth. l. 5.   L. Florus Hist. l. 3.
cap. 8.   Io. Boemus Aubanus de moribus gentium, l. 3. c. 26.

Foi the farther illustration of this subject, concerning the swiftness of motion, I shall briefly specify some particulars concerning the engines of war used by the ancients. Amongst these, the most famous and admirable were those invented by Archimedes ; by which he did perform such strange exploits, as (were they not related by so many and such judicious authors) would scarce seem credible even to these more learned ages.   The acts of that most famous engineer, are largely set down by Polybius*, Tzetzes †, Proclus ‡, Plutarch ||, Livy §, and divers others.   From the first of whom alone, we may have sufficient evidence for the truth of those relations : for besides that he is an author noted to be very grave and serious in his discourse, and does solemnly promise in one place ¶ that he will relate nothing, but what either he himself was an eye-witness of, or else what he had received from those that were so: I say, besides all this, it is considerable, that he himself was born not above thirty years after the siege of Syracuse. And afterwards having occasion to tarry some weeks in that city, when he travelled with Scipio, he might there perhaps see those engines himself, or at least take his information from such as were eye-witnesses of their force: so that there can be no colourable pretence for any to distrust the particulars related of them.

In brief, the sum of their reports is this.   When the Roman forces under the conduct of Marcellus, had laid siege unto that famous city, (of which, both by their former successes, and their present strength, they could not chuse but promise themselves a speedy victory;) yet the arts of this one mathematician, notwithstanding all their policies and resolutions, did still beat them back to their great disadvantage.   Whether they were near the wall, or farther from it, they were still exposed to the force of his engines, *και μακραν αφεστωτας και συνεγγυς οντας, 8 μονον απρακτες παρεσ-*

---

* Histor. l. 4.   † Histor. Chilios 2. Histor. 35.

‡ Lib. 2. c. 3. || Marcellus.   § Histor. l. 24.

¶ Histor. l. 4. juxta initium.

κευαζε προς τας ιδιας επιβολας, αλλα και διεφθειρε τας πλειστας αυτων. From the multitude of those stones and arrows which he shot agains᷉ them, was he stiled εκατογχειρ or Briareus *. Those defensive engines that were made by the Romans in the form of pent-houses †, for to cover the assailants from the weapons of the besieged, these would he presently batter in pieces with great stones and blocks. Those high towers erected in some of the ships, out of which the Romans might more conveniently fight with the defendants on the wall, these also were so broken by his engines, that no cannon, or other instrument of gunpowder, (saith a learned man‡) had they been then in use, could have done greater mischief. In brief, he did so molest them with his frequent and prodigious batteries, that the common soldiers were utterly discouraged from any hopes of success.

What was the particular frame and manner of these engines, cannot certainly be determined; but to contrive such as may perform the like strange effects, were not very difficult to any one who is thoroughly versed in the grounds of this art. Though perhaps those of Archimedes, in respect of divers circumstances, were much more exact and proper for the purposes to which they were intended, than the invention of others could be; he himself being so extraordinarily subtle and ingenious above the common sort of men.

It is probable that the general kind of these engines were the same with those that were used afterwards, amongst the Romans and other nations. These were commonly divided into two sorts; stiled ballistæ, catapultæ, both which names are sometimes used promiscuously ‖; but according to their propriety, ballista § does signify an engine

---

* Cæl. Rhod. Ant. lect. l. 2. c. 16.   † Pluteus Testudo.

‡ Sir Walt. Raleigh, Histor. l. 5. c. 3. § 16.

‖ Vid. Naudæum de Stud. Militar. l. 2.

§ Απο τυ εαλλειν, called also λιθοβολος, πετροβολος. Fundibalus, Petraria. lib. 3.

for the shooting of stones, and catapulta for darts or arrows.

The former of these was fitted either to carry divers lesser stones, or else one greatest one.   Some of these engines made for great stones, have been proportioned to so vast and immense a weight, as may seem almost incredible; which occasioned that in Lucan,

> *At saxum quoties ingenti verberis ictu*
> *Excutitur, qualis rupes quam vertice montis*
> *Abscidit impulsu ventorum adjuta vetustas,*
> *Frangit cuncta rumes; nec tantum corpora pressa*
> *Exanimat, totos cum sanguine dissipat artus.*

With these they could easily batter down the walls and towers of any fort.   So Ovid.

> *Quam grave ballistæ mœnia pulsat onus.*

And Statius

> *Quo turbine bellica quondam,*
> *Librati saliunt portarum in claustra molares.*

The stones that were cast from these, were of any form, *enormes et sepulchrales*, mill-stones or tomb-stones *. Sometimes for the farther annoyance and terror of any besieged place, they would by these throw into it dead bodies, either of men or horses, and sometimes only parts of them, as men's heads.

Athenæus† mentions one of these ballistæ that was proportioned unto a stone of three talents weight, each talent being 120 pounds (saith Vitruvius‡,) so that the whole will amount to 360 pounds.   But it is storied of Archimedes ‖, that he cast a stone into one of Marcellus his ships, which was found to weigh ten talents.   There is some difference amongst authors §, concerning what kind of talent this should be understood, but it is certain that in Plutarch's time, (from whom we have this relation) one talent did amount to 120 pounds (saith Suidas:) according

---

* Lipsius Poliorcet. l. 3. Dial. 3. † Deipnosoph. l. 5.
‡ Archit. l. 10. c. ult. λιθον δεκαταλαιτον. ‖ Plut. Marcell.
§ Dav. Rivaltus Comment. in Archim. Oper. Ext.

to which account, the stone itself was of no less than twelve
hundred pounds weight.   A weapon (one would think) big
enough for those rebel giants that fought against the gods.
Now the greatest cannon in use, does not carry above 64
pound weight, which is far short of the strength in these
mathematical contrivances *.   Amongst the Turks indeed,
there have been sometimes used such powder instruments,
as may equal the force of those invented by Archimedes.
Gab. Naudæus † tells us of one bullet shot from them at
the siege of Constantinople, which was of above 1200
pound weight; this he affirms from the relation of an archbishop, who was then present, and did see it; the piece
could not be drawn by less than a hundred and fifty yoke
of oxen, which might almost have served to draw away
the town itself.   But though there hath been perhaps some
one or two cannons of such a prodigious magnitude, yet it
is certain that the biggest in common use, does come far
short of that strength which was ordinarily in these mechanical engines.

There are divers figures of these ballistæ, set out by
Vegetius, Lipsius, and others ‡ ; but being without any explication, it is not very facil to discover in what their forces
did consist.

I have here expressed one of them most easy to be apprehended; from the understanding of which, you may the
better guess at the nature of the rest.

* Naudæus de Studio Milit. l. 2.   † De Stud. Mil. l. 2.
‡ See Rob. Valteurius de Re Milit. l. 10. c. 4.

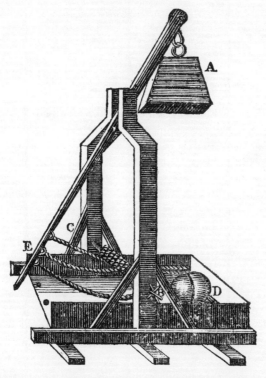

That great box or cavity at A, is supposed to be full of some heavy weight, and is forced up by the turning of the axis and spokes B C. The stone or bullet to be discharged, being in a kind of sling at D; which when the greater weight A descends, will be violently whirled upwards, till that end of the sling at E, coming to the top will fly off, and discharge the stone as the skilful artist should direct it.

CHAP. XVIII.

Concerning the Catapultæ, or engines for arrows.

THE other kind of engine was called catapulta *, απο της πελτης, which signifies a spear or dart, because it was used for the shooting off such weapons† : some of these were proportioned unto spears of twelve cubits long; they did carry with so great a force, *ut interdum nimio ardore scintillant*, (saith Ammianus ‡) that the weapons discharged from them were sometimes (if you can believe it) set on fire by the swiftness of their motion.

The first invention of these is commonly ascribed to Dionysius the younger ‖, who is said to have made them amongst his other preparations against Carthage. But we have good reason to think them of more ancient use, because we read in scripture, that Uzziah made in Jerusalem engines invented by cunning men to shoot arrows and great stones withal § : though it is likely these inventions were much bettered by the experience of after ages.

The usual form of these catapultæ, was much after the manner of great bows placed on carriages, and wound up by the strength of several persons. And from that great force which we find in lesser bows, we may easily guess at the greater power of these other engines ¶. It is related of the Turkish bow, that it can strike an arrow through a piece of steel or brass two inches thick, and being headed only with wood, it pierces timber of eight inches. Which though it may seem incredible, yet it is attested by the experience of divers unquestionable witnesses: Barclay in his *Icon Animorum*, a man of sufficient credit, affirms that he

---

* In Greek καταπελτης. † Athenæus. Deipnos. 1. 5.
‡ Lib. 23. Lipsius Poliorcet. 1. 3. Dial 2.
‖ Diod. Sicul. Biblioth. 1. 14 Sardus de Invent. Rerum, 1. 2.
§ 2 Chron. xxvi. 15. ¶ Sir Fran. Bacon, Nat. Hist. Exp. 704.

was an eye-witness, how one of these bows with a little
arrow did pierce through a piece of steel three fingers
thick.   And yet these bows being somewhat like the long
bows in use amongst us, were bent only by a man's immediate strength, without the help of any bender or rack that
are used to others.

Some Turkish bows are of that strength, as to pierce a
plank of six inches in thickness, (I speak what I have seen)
saith M. Jo. Greaves in his pyramodographia.   How much
greater force then may we conceive to be impressed by the
catapultæ ?

These were sometimes framed for the discharging of
two or three arrows together, so that each of them might
be directed unto a several aim.   But it were as easy to
contrive them after the like manner for the carriage of
twenty arrows, or more; as in this figure.

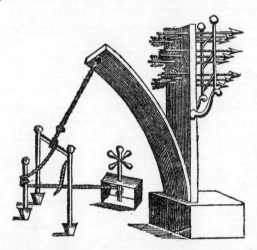

Both these kinds of engines, when they were used at the
siege of any city, were commonly carried in a great
wooden turret (first invented by Demetrius *.)   It was

* Who was therefore stiled Poliorcetes.   This kind of turret was first
used at the siege of Cyprus, and is thus described by Diodorus Sicul.
Biblioth. l. 20.

driven upon four wheels at the bottom, each of its sides being forty-five cubits, its height ninety. The whole was divided in nine several partitions, every one of which did contain divers engines for battery: from its use in the battering and taking of cities it is stiled by the name of helepolis.

He that would be informed in the nature of bows, let him consult *Mersennus de Ballistica et Acontismologia*, where there are divers subtile enquiries and demonstrations, concerning the strength required to the bending of them to any distance, the force they have in the discharge, according to several bents, the strength required to be in the string of them, the several proportions of swiftness and distance in an arrow shot vertically, or horizontally, or transversally.

Those strange effects of the Turkish bow (mentioned before) so much exceeding the force of others, which yet require far greater strength for the bending of them, may probably be ascribed either to the natural cause of attraction by similitude of substance (as the Lord Bacon conjectures :) for in these experiments the head of the arrow should be of the same substance (whether steel or wood) with that which it pierces : or else to that just proportion betwixt the weight of the arrow, and the strength of the bow, which must needs much conduce to the force of it, and may perhaps be more exactly discovered in these, than it is commonly in others.

CHAP. XIX.

A Comparison betwixt these ancient Engines, and the Gunpowder Instruments now in use.

IT shall not be altogether impertinent to enquire somewhat concerning the advantages and disadvantages betwixt those military offensive engines used amongst the ancients, and those of these later ages.

In which enquiry there are two particulars to be chiefly examined.

1. The force of these several contrivances, or the utmost that may be done by them.

2. Their price, or the greatness of the charges required unto them.

1. As for the force of these ancient inventions, it may sufficiently appear from those many credible relations mentioned before; to which may be added that in Josephus *, which he sets down from his own eye-sight, being himself a chief captain at the siege of Jotapata, where these events happened.   He tells us that besides the multitude of persons, who were slain by these Roman engines, being not able to avoid their force, by reason they were placed so far off, and out of sight; besides this, they did also carry such great stones, with so great a violence, that they did therewith batter down their walls and towers.   A great bellied woman walking about the city in the day-time, had her child struck out of her womb, and carried half a furlong from her.   A soldier standing by his captain Josephus, on the wall, had his head struck off by another stone sent from these Roman engines, and his brains carried three furlongs off.

To this purpose Cardan † relates out of Ammianus Marcellinus.   *Tanto impetu fertur lapis ut uno viso lapide, quamvis intacti barbari fuerint ab eo, destiterunt à pugnâ et abierunt.*   Many foreign people being so amazed at the strange force of these engines, that they durst not contest with those who were masters of such inventions.   It is frequently asserted, that bullets have been melted in the air, by that extremity of violent motion imprest from these slings.

> *Fundaque contorto transverberat aëra plumbo,*
> *Et mediis liquidæ glandes in nubibus errant.*

* De Bello Judaico, l. 3. c. 9.   † De Variet. l. 12. c. 58.

So Lucan, speaking of the same engines.

Inde faces et saxa volant, spatioque solutæ
Aeris et calidæ liquefactæ pondere glandes.

Which relations, though they may seem somewhat poetical and improbable, yet Aristotle himself (*de Cælo, lib.* 2. c. 7.) doth suppose them as unquestionable. From whence it may be inferred, that the force of these engines does rather exceed than come short of our gunpowder inventions.

Add to this that opinion of a learned man * (which I cited before) that Archimedes in the siege of Syracuse † did more mischief with his engines, than could have been wrought by any cannons, had they been then in use.

In this perhaps there may be some disadvantage, because these mathematical engines cannot be so easily and speedily wound up, and so certainly levelled as the other may.

2. As for the price or charges of both these, it may be considered under three particulars :

1. Their making.
2. Their carriage or conveyance.
3. Their charge and discharging.

In all which respects, the cannons now in use, are of much greater cost than these other inventions.

1. The making or price of these gun-powder instruments is extremely expensive, as may be easily judged by the weight of their materials. A whole cannon weighing commonly 8000 pounds, a half cannon 5000, a culverin 4500, a demiculverin 3000; which whether it be in iron or brass, must needs be very costly, only for the matter of them; besides the farther charges required for the form and making of them, which in the whole must needs amount to several hundred pounds. Whereas these mathematical inventions consisting chiefly of timber, and

---

* Sir Walt. Raleigh. Hist. l. 5. c. 3. sect. 16.
† See Lipsius de Militiâ Romanâ, l. 5.

cords, may be much more cheaply made; the several degrees of them which shall answer in proportion to the strength of those other, being at the least ten times cheaper; that is, ten engines that shall be of equal force either to a cannon or demicannon, culverin or demiculverin, may be framed at the same price that one of these will amount to : so that in this respect there is a great inequality.

2. As for their carriage or conveyance; a whole cannon does require at the least 90 men, or 16 horses, for the draught of it; a half cannon 56 men, or 9 horses; a culverin 50 men, or 8 horses; a demiculverin 36 men, or 7 horses; supposing the way to be hard and plain, in which notwithstanding the motion will be very slow. But if the passage prove rising and steep, or rotten and dirty, then they will require a much greater strength and charge for the conveyance of them. Whereas these other inventions are in themselves more light (if there be occasion for the draught of them) being easily taken asunder into several parts. And besides, their materials are to be found every where, so that they need not be carried up and down at all, but may be easily made in the place where they are to be used.

3. The materials required to the charging of these gunpowder instruments, are very costly. A whole cannon requiring for every charge 40 pounds of powder, and a bullet of 64 pounds; a half cannon 18 pounds of powder, and a bullet of 24 pounds; a culverin 16 pounds of powder, and a bullet of 19 pounds; a demiculverin 9 pounds of powder, and a bullet of 12 pounds: whereas those other engines may be charged only with stones, or (which may serve for terror) with dead bodies, or any such materials as every place will afford without any cost.

So then, put all these together: if it be so that those ancient inventions did not come short of these other in regard of force, and if they do so much excel them in divers other respects; it should seem then, that they are much more commodious than these latter inventions, and should be preferred before them. But this enquiry cannot be fully determined without particular experience of both.

CHAP. XX.

That it is possible to contrive such an artificial motion, as may be equally swift with the supposed motion of the heavens.

FOR the conclusion of this discourse, I shall briefly examine (as before concerning slowness) whether it be possible to contrive such an artificial motion, as may be equal unto the supposed swiftness of the heavens. This question hath been formerly proposed and answered by Cardan *, where he applies it unto the swiftness of the moon's orb; but that orb being the lowest of all, and consequently of a dull and sluggish motion, in comparison to the rest; therefore it will perhaps be more convenient to understand the question concerning the eighth sphere, or starry heaven.

For the true resolution of this, it should be first observed, that a material substance is altogether incapable of so great a celerity, as is usually ascribed to the celestial orbs, (as I have proved elsewhere †,) and therefore the quære is not to be understood of any real and experimental, but only notional, and geometrical contrivance.

Now that the swiftness of motion may be thus increased according to any conceivable proportion, will be manifest from what hath been formerly delivered concerning the grounds and nature of slowness and swiftness. For ac-

* De Variet. Rerum. l. 9. c. 47.   † Prop. 9.

cording as we shall suppose the power to exceed the
weight: so may the motion of the weight be swifter than
that of the power.

But to answer more particularly: let us imagine every
wheel in this following figure to have a hundred teeth in it,
and every nut ten:

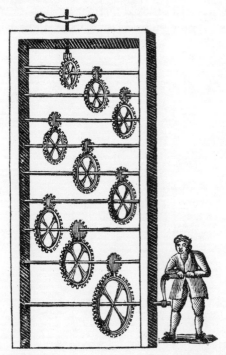

It may then be evident, that one revolution of the first
wheel, will turn the nut, and consequently the second wheel
on the same axis ten times, the third wheel a hundred
times, the fourth a thousand times, the fifth 10000, the
sixth a hundred thousand times, the seventh 1000000
times, the eighth 10000000 times, the ninth 100000000
times, the sails 1000000000 times: so that if we suppose
the compass of these sails to be five foot, or one pace:
and that the first wheel is turned about after the rate of one

thousand times in an hour : it will then be evident, that
the sails shall be turned 1000000000000 times, and consequently shall pass 100000000 miles in the same space.
Whereas a star in the equator (according to common hypothesis) does move but 42398437 miles in an hour : and
therefore it is evident that it is possible geometrically to
contrive such an artificial motion, as shall be of greater
swiftness then the supposed revolutions of the heavens.

DÆDALUS;

OR,

MECHANICAL MOTIONS.

BOOK II.

CHAP. I.

The divers kinds of Automata, or Self-movers. Of Mills, and the contrivance of several motions by rarified air. A brief digression concerning Wind-guns.

AMONGST the variety of artificial motions, those are of most use and pleasure, in which, by the application of some continued strength, there is bestowed a regular and lasting motion.

These we call the αυτοματα, or self-movers: which name, in its utmost latitude, is sometimes ascribed unto those motions, that are contrived from the strength of living creatures, as chariots, carts, &c. But in its strictness and propriety, it is only appliable unto such inventions, wherein the motion is caused either by something that belongs unto its own frame, or else by some external inanimate agent.

Whence these αυτοματα are easily distinguishable into two sorts:

1. Those that are moved by something which is extrinsical unto their own frame; as mills, by water or wind.

2. Those that receive their motion from something that does belong to the frame itself; as clocks, watches, by weights, springs, or the like.

Of both which sorts, there have been many excellent inventions: in the recital of them, I shall insist chiefly on such as are most eminent for their rarity and subtilty.

Amongst the αυτοματα that receive their motion from some external agent, those of more common use are mills.

And first, the water-mills; which are thought to be before the other, though neither the first author, nor so much as the time wherein they were invented is fully known. And therefore Polydore Virgil * refers them amongst other fatherless inventions. Pliny † indeed doth mention them, as being commonly used in his time; and yet others affirm, that Belisarius, in the reign of Justinian, did first invent them: whence Pancirollus ‡ concludes, that it is likely their use was for some space intermitted, and being afterwards renewed again, they were then thought to be first discovered.

However, it is certain that this invention hath much abridged and advantaged the labours of men, who were before condemned unto this slavery ‖, as now unto the galleys. And as the force of waters hath been useful for this, so likewise may it be contrived to divers other purposes. Herein doth the skill of an artificer chiefly consist, in the application of these common motions unto various and beneficial ends; making them serviceable, not only for the grinding of corn, but for the preparing of iron, or other ore; the making of paper, the elevating of water, or the like.

To this purpose also are the mills that are driven by wind, which are so much more convenient than the other, by how much their situations may be more easy and common. The motions of these may likewise be accommodated to as various uses as the other; there being scarce

---

* De Invent. Rerum, l. 3. c. 18.   † Nat. Hist. l. 18. c. 10.
‡ De Repert. Tit. 22.   ‖ Ad pistrinum.

any labour, to the performance of which, an ingenious artificer cannot apply them.   To the sawing of timber, the
ploughing of land, or any other the like service, which cannot be dispatched the ordinary way, without much toil and
tediousness.   And it is a wonderful thing to consider, how
much men's labours might be eased and contracted in sundry particulars, if such as were well skilled in the principles
and practices of these mechanical experiments, would but
thoroughly apply their studies unto the enlargement of such
inventions.

There are some other motions by wind or air, which
(though they are not so common as the other, yet) may
prove of excellent curiosity, and singular use.   Such was
that musical instrument invented by Cornelius Dreble ;
which being set in the sunshine, would of itself render a
soft and pleasant harmony ; but being removed into the
shade, would presently become silent.   The reason of it
was this : the warmth of the sun working upon some moisture within it, and rarifying the inward air unto so great an
extension that it must needs seek for vent or issue, did
thereby give several motions unto the instrument *.

Somewhat of this nature are the æolipiles, which are
concave vessels, consisting of some such material as may
endure the fire, having a small hole, at which they are filled
with water, and out of which (when the vessels are heated)
the air doth issue forth with a strong and lasting violence.
These are frequently used for the exciting and contracting
of heat in the melting of glasses, or metals : they may also
be contrived to be serviceable for sundry other pleasant
uses ; as for the moving of sails in a chimney-corner ; the
motion of which sails may be applied to the turning of a
spit, or the like.

* Marcell. Vrankhein. Epist. ad Joh. Ernestum.   Like that statue of
Memnon, in Egypt, which makes a strange noise whenever the sun begins to shine upon it.   Tacit. Annal. 2.   Strabo affirms, that he had both
seen and heard it.

But there is a better invention to this purpose, mentioned in Cardan *, whereby a spit may be turned (without the help of weights) by the motion of the air that ascends the chimney; and it may be useful for the roasting of many, or great joints: for as the fire must be increased according to the quantity of meat, so the force of the instrument will be augmented proportionably to the fire. In which contrivance, there are these conveniences above the jacks of ordinary use:

1. It makes little or no noise in the motion.

2. It needs no winding up, but will constantly move of itself, while there is any fire to rarify the air.

3. It is much cheaper than the other instruments that are commonly used to this purpose; there being required unto it only a pair of sails, which must be placed in that part of the chimney where it begins to be straitened; and one wheel, to the axis of which the spit-line must be fastened, according to this following diagram.

* De Variet. Rerum, l. 12. c. 58.

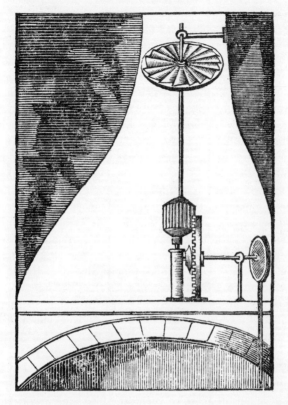

The motion of these sails may likewise be serviceable for sundry other purposes, besides the turning of a spit; for the chiming of bells, or other musical devices; and there cannot be any more pleasant contrivance for continual and cheap music.   It may be useful also for the reeling of yarn, the rocking of a cradle, with divers the like domestic occasions.   For (as was said before) any constant motion being given, it is easy for an ingenious artificer to apply it unto various services.

These sails will always move both day and night, if there is but any fire under them, and sometimes though there be none.   For, if the air without be much colder than that within the room, then must this which is more warm and

rarified, naturally ascend through the chimney, to give place
unto the more condensed and heavy, which does usually
blow in at every chink or cranny, as experience shews.

Unto this kind of motion may be reduced all those representations of living creatures, whether birds, or beasts,
invented by Ctesibius, which were for the most part performed by the motion of air, being forced up either by
rarefaction, with fire, or else by compression, through the
fall of some heavier body, as water, which by possessing the
place of the air, did thereby drive it to seek for some other
vent.

I cannot here omit (though it be not altogether so pertinent) to mention that late ingenious invention of the wind-
gun, which is charged by the forcible compression of air,
being injected through a syringe; the strife and distention
of the imprisoned air, serving by the help of little falls or
shuts within, to stop and keep close the vents by which it
was admitted. The force of it in the discharge is almost
equal to our powder-guns. I have found upon frequent
trials (saith Mersennus*) that a leaden bullet shot from one
of these guns against a stone wall, the space of 24 paces
from it, will be beaten into a thin plate. It would be a
considerable addition to this experiment, which the same
author mentions a little after, whereby he will make the
same charge of air to serve for the discharge of several arrows or bullets after one another, by giving the air only so
much room, as may immediately serve to impress a violence in sending away the arrow or bullet, and then screw-
ing it down again to its former confinement, to fit it for
another shooting. But against this there may be many
considerable doubts, which I cannot stand to discuss.

* Phænomena pneumatica, prop. 32.

CHAP. II.

Of a Sailing Chariot, that may without horses be driven on the land by the wind, as ships are on the sea.

THE force of wind in the motion of sails may be applied also to the driving of a chariot, by which a man may sail on the land, as well as by a ship on the water. The labour of horses or other beasts, which are usually applied to this purpose, being artificially supplied by the strength of winds.

That such chariots are commonly used in the champion plains of China, is frequently affirmed by divers credible authors. Boterus mentions that they have been tried also in Spain *, though with what success he doth not specify. But above all other experiments to this purpose, that sailing chariot at Sceveling in Holland, is more eminently remarkable. It was made by the direction of Stephinus, and is celebrated by many authors. Walceius † affirms it to be of so great a swiftness for its motion, and yet of so great a capacity for its burthen: *ut in medio freto secundis ventis commissas naves, velocitate multis parasangis post se relinquat, et paucarum horarum spatio, viginti aut triginta milliaria germanica continuo cursu emetiatur, concreditosque sibi plus minus vectores sex aut decem, in petitum locum transferat, facillimo illius ad clavum qui sedet nutu, quaqua versum minimo labore velis commissum, mirabile hoc continenti currus navigium dirigentis.* That it did far exceed the speed of any ship, though we should suppose it to be carried in the open sea with never so prosperous wind: and that in some few hours space it would convey six or ten persons, 20 or 30 German miles, and all this with very little labour of him that sitteth at the stern, who may easily guide the course of it as he pleaseth.

---

* De Incremento Urbium, l. 1. c. 10.
† Fabularum Decas, Fab. 9.

That eminent inquisitive man Peireskius, having travelled to Sceveling for the sight and experience of this chariot, would frequently after with much wonder mention the extreme swiftness of its motion. *Commemorare solebat stuporem quo correptus fuerat cum vento translatus citatissimo non persentiscere tamen, nempe tam citus erat quam ventus*.* Though the wind were in itself very swift and strong, yet to passengers in this chariot it would not be at all discernible, because they did go with an equal swiftness to the wind itself: men that ran before it seeming to go backwards, things which seem at a great distance being presently overtaken and left behind. In two hours space it would pass from Sceveling to Putten, which are distant from one another above 14 *horaria milliaria,* (saith the same author,) that is, more than two and forty miles.

Grotius is very copious and elegant in the celebrating of this invention, and the author of it, in divers epigrams.

> *Ventivolum Tiphys deduxit in æquora navim,*
> *Jupiter in stellas, æthereamque domum.*
> *In terrestre solum virtus Stevinia, nam nec*
> *Tiphy tuum fuerat, nec Jovis istud opus* †.

And in another place ‡:

> *Imposuit plaustro vectantem carbasa, malum*
> *An potius navi, subdidit ille rotas ?*
> ——— *Scandit aquas navis currus ruit aere prono,*
> *Et merito dicas hic volat, illa natat.*

These relations did at the first seem unto me, (and perhaps they will so to others) somewhat strange and incredible. But upon farther enquiry, I have heard them frequently attested from the particular eye-sight and experience of such eminent persons, whose names I dare not cite in a business of this nature, which in those parts is so very common, and little observed.

I have not met with any author who doth treat particu-

---

* Pet. Gassendus, Vita Peireskii, l. 2.
† Grotii Poemata, Ep. 19.   ‡ Ep. 5.

larly concerning the manner of framing this chariot, though
Grotius mentions an elegant description of it in copper by
one Geynius *: and Hondius in one of his large maps of
Asia, does give another conjectural description of the like
chariots used in China.

The form of it is related to be very simple and plain,
after this manner.

The body of it being somewhat like a boat, moving upon
four wheels of an equal bigness, with two sails like those in a
ship; there being some contrivance to turn and steer it, by
moving a rudder which is placed beyond the two hindmost
wheels; and for the stopping of it, this must be done,
either by letting down the sail, or turning it from the wind.

* Epig. 20. et 21.

Of this kind they have frequently in Holland other little vessels for one or two persons to go upon the ice, having sledges instead of wheels, being driven with a sail; the bodies of them like little boats, that if the ice should break, they might yet safely carry a man upon the water, where the sail would be still useful for the motion of it.

I have often thought that it would be worth the experiment to enquire, whether or no such a sailing chariot might not be more conveniently framed with moveable sails, whose force may be imprest from their motion, equivalent to those in a wind-mill. Their foremost wheels (as in other chariots) for the greater facility, being somewhat lower than the other, answerable to this figure.

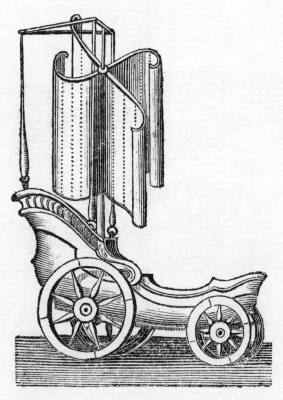

In which the sails are so contrived, that the wind from
any coast will have a force upon them to turn them about;
and the motion of these sails must needs turn the wheels,
and consequently carry on the chariot itself to any place
(though fully against the wind) whither it shall be
directed.

The chief doubt will be, whether in such a contrivance,
every little ruggedness or unevenness of the ground, will
not cause such a jolting of the chariot, as to hinder the
motion of its sails. But this perhaps (if it should prove so)
is capable of several remedies.

I have often wondered, why none of our gentry who
live near great plains, and smooth champions, have attempted any thing to this purpose. The experiments of
this kind being very pleasant, and not costly: what could
be more delightful, or better husbandry, than to make use
of the wind (which costs nothing, and eats nothing) instead
of horses? This being very easy to be effected by those,
the convenience of whose habitations doth accommodate
them for such experiments.

CHAP. III.

*Concerning the fixed automata, clocks, spheres, representing
the heavenly motions: the several excellencies that are
most commendable in such kind of contrivances.*

THE second kind of αυτοματα were described to be
such engines, as did receive a regular and lasting motion from something belonging to their own frame, whether
weights, or springs, &c.

They are usually distinguished into αυτοματα στατα, fixed
and stationary; υπαγοντα, moveable and transient.

1. The fixed are such as move only according to their
several parts, and not according to their whole frame; in

which, though each wheel hath a distinct rotation, yet the whole doth still remain unmoved. The chiefest kind of these are the clocks and watches in ordinary use, the framing of which is so commonly known by every mechanic, that I shall not trouble the reader with any explication of it. He that desires fuller satisfaction, may see them particularly described by Cardan *, D. Flood †, and others.

The first invention of these (saith Pancirollus ‡) was taken from that experiment in the multiplication of wheels, mentioned in Vitruvius ||, where he speaks of an instrument, whereby a man may know how many miles or paces he doth go in any space of time, whether or no he do pass by water in a boat, or ship, or by land in a chariot, or coach: they have been contrived also into little pocket-instruments, by which, after a man hath walked a whole day together, he may easily know how many steps he hath taken. I forbear to enter upon a larger explication of these kind of engines, because they are impertinent unto the chief business that I have proposed for this discourse. The reader may see them more particularly described in the above-cited place of Vitruvius, in Cardan §, Bessonius ¶, and others; I have here only mentioned them, as being the first occasion of the chiefest αυτοματα, that are now in use.

Of the same kind with our clocks and watches (though perhaps more elaborate, and subtle) was that sphere invented by Archimedes, which did represent the heavenly motions: the diurnal, and annual courses of the sun, the changes, and aspects of the moon, &c. ** This is frequently celebrated in the writings of the ancients, particularly in that known epigram of Claudian:

---

* De Variet. Rer. l. 9. c. 47.   † Tract. 2. part. 7. l. 1. cap. 4.
‡ Repert. Tit. 10. || Architect. l. 10. c. 14.   § Subtil. l. 18.
¶ Theatrum Instrumentorum.   Wecker de Secretis, l. 15. c. 32.
** Mentioned by Cicero, Tuscul. Quæst. l. 1. item De Nat. Deorum, l. 2.

Jupiter in parvo cum cerneret æthera vitro,
Risit, et ad superos talia dicta dedit ;
Huccine mortalis progressa potentia curæ ?
Jam meus in fragili luditur orbe labor.
Jura poli, rerumque fidem, legesque deorum,
Ecce Syracusius transtulit arte senex.
*Inclusus variis famulatur * spiritus astris,*
Et vivum certis motibus urget opus.
Percurrit proprium mentitus signifer annum ;
Et simulata novo Cynthia mense redit.
Jamque suum volvens audax industria mundum
Gaudet, et humaná sidera mente regit.
Quid falso insontem tonitru Salmonea miror ?
Æmula naturæ parva reperta manus.

Excellently translated by T. Randolph :

Jove saw the heavens fram'd in a little glass,
And laughing, to the gods these words did pass ;
Comes then the power of mortal cares so far?
In brittle orbs my labours acted are.
The statutes of the poles, the faith of things,
The laws of gods, this Syracusian brings
Hither by art : spirits inclos'd attend
Their several spheres, and with set motions bend
The living work : each year the feigned sun,
Each month returns the counterfeited moon.
And viewing now her world, bold industry
Grows proud, to know the heavens his subjects be.
Believe, Salmoneus hath false thunders thrown,
For a poor hand is nature's rival grown.

But, that this engine should be made of glass, is scarce credible. Lactantius † mentioning the relation of it, affirms it to consist of brass, which is more likely. It may be the outside or case was glass, and the frame itself of brass. Cœlius Rhodoginus ‡ speaking of the wonderous art in the contrivance of this sphere, breaks out into this quære. *Nonne igitur miraculorum omnium, maximum miraculum est homo ?* He might have said *mathematicus :*

---

* The secret force from which the motion was impressed.
† Instit. l. 2. c. 5.   ‡ Antiq. lect. l. 2. c. 16.

and another to this purpose *. *Sic manus ejus naturam, ut natura ipsa manum imitata putetur.* Pappus † tells us, that Archimedes writ a book *de sphæropæia,* concerning the manner of framing such engines; and after him, Possidonius composed another discourse on the same subject; though now either the ignorance, or the envy of time hath deprived us of both those works. And yet the art itself is not quite perished, for we read of divers the like contrivances in these latter times. Agrippa affirms ‡ that he himself had seen such a sphere; and Ramus tells us how he beheld two of them in Paris, the one brought thither amongst other spoils from Sicily, and the other out of Germany. And it is commonly reported, that there is yet such a sphere at Strasburg in Germany. Rivaltus ‖ relates how Marinus Burgesius a Norman made two of them in France for the king. And perhaps these latter (saith he) were more exact than the former, because the heavenly revolutions are now much better understood than before. And besides it is questionable, whether the use of steel-springs was known in those ancient times; the application of which unto these kind of spheres, must needs be much more convenient than weights.

It is related also of the consul Boethius §, that amongst other mathematical contrivances, (for which he was famous) he made a sphere to represent the sun's motion; which was so much admired, and talked of in those times, that Gundibaldus, king of Burgundy, did purposely send over ambassadors to Theodoricus the emperor, with intreaties that he would be a means to procure one of these spheres from Boethius; the emperor thinking hereby to make his kingdom more famous and terrible unto foreign nations, doth write an epistle to Boethius, persuading him

* Guid. Ubaldus Præf. ad Mechan.
† Collect. Mathem. Procem. ad l. 8.
‡ De Vanit. Scient. c. 22. Schol. Mathem. l. 1. So Cardan too, l. 17. Monanth. in Mecha. Arist. Com. c. 1. Dr. Hackwell, Apol. l. 3. c. 10, sect. 1.   ‖ De Vita Archimedis.
§ Cassiodor. Chron. Pet. Bertius Præf. ad Consolat. Philos.

to send this instrument. *Quoties non sunt credituri quod viderint? Quoties hanc veritatem lusoria somnia putabunt? Et quanto fuerint à stupore conversi, non audebunt se æquales nobis dicere, apud quos sciunt sapientes talia cogitasse.* So much were all these kind of inventions admired in those ruder and darker times: whereas the instruments that are now in use amongst us (though not so much extolled) yet do altogether equal (if not exceed) the other, both in usefulness and subtilty. The chiefest of these former engines receiving their motion from weights, and not from springs, (which as I said before) are of later and more excellent invention*.

The particular circumstances, for which the automata of this kind are most eminent, may be reduced to these four.

1. The lastingness of their motion, without needing of any new supply; for which purpose there have been some watches contrived to continue without winding up for a week together, or longer.

2. The easiness and simplicity of their composition; art itself being but the facilitating and contracting of ordinary operations; therefore the more easy and compendious such inventions are, the more artificial should they be esteemed. And the addition of any such unnecessary parts, as may be supplied some other way, is a sure sign of unskilfulness and ignorance. Those antiquated engines that did consist of such a needless multitude of wheels, and springs, and screws, (like the old hypothesis of the heavens) may be compared to the notions of a confused knowledge, which are always full of perplexity and complications, and seldom in order; whereas the inventions of art are more regular, simple, and perspicuous, like the apprehensions of a distinct and thoroughly-informed judgment. In this respect the manner of framing the ordinary automata hath been much bettered in these later times above the former, and shall hereafter perhaps be yet more advantaged. These kind of

---

* Polyd. Virgil de Invent. Rerum, l. 2. c. 5.   Cardan Subtil.

experiments (like all other human arts) receiving additions from every day's experiment.

To this purpose there is an invention consisting only of one hollow orb or wheel, whereby the hours may be as truly distinguished, as by any ordinary clock or watch. This wheel should be divided into several cavities, through each of which successively either sand or water must be contrived to pass; the heaviness of these bodies (being always in the ascending side of the wheel) must be counterpoised by a plummet that may be fastened about the pulley on the axis: this plummet will leisurely descend, according as the sand by running out of one cavity into the next, doth make the several parts of the wheel lighter or heavier, and so consequently there will be produced an equal and lasting motion, which may be easily applied to the distinction of hours.

3. The multitude and variety of those services for which they may be useful. Unto this kind may we refer those watches by which a man may tell not only the hour of the day, but the minute of the hour, the day of the month, the age and aspects of the moon, &c. Of this nature likewise was that larum mentioned by Walchius *, which though it were but two or three inches big, yet would both wake a man, and of itself light a candle for him at any set hour of the night. And those weights or springs which are of so great force as to turn a mill †, (as some have been contrived) may be easily applied to more various and difficult labours.

4. The littleness of their frame. *Nunquam ars magis quam in minimis nota est* (saith Aquinas.) The smallness of the engine doth much commend the skill of the artificer; to this purpose there have been watches contrived in the form and quantity of a jewel for the ear, where the striking of the minutes may constantly whisper unto us, how our lives do slide away by a swift succession. Cardan ‡ tells

---

* Fab. 9.   † Ramel. fig. 130.
‡ De Subtil. l. 2. item l. 17.

us of a smith who made a watch in the jewel of a ring, to
be worn on the finger, which did shew the hours, *(non solum sagitta, sed ictu)* not only by the hand, but by the finger too (as I may say) by pricking it every hour.

CHAP. IV.

*Of the moveable and gradient automata, representing the
motions of living creatures, various sounds, of birds, or
beasts, and some of them articulate.*

THUS much of those automata, which were said to be
fixed and stationary.

The other kind to be enquired after, are those that are
moveable and transient, which are described to be such engines as move not only according to their several parts, but
also according to their whole frames.   These are again distinguishable into two sorts:

1. Gradient.
2. Volant.

1. The gradient or ambulatory, are such as require some
basis or bottom to uphold them in their motions*.   Such
were those strange inventions (commonly attributed to
Dædalus) of self-moving statues, which (unless they were
violently detained) would of themselves run away.   Aristotle † affirms that Dædalus did this by putting quicksilver
into them.   But this would have been too gross a way for
so excellent an artificer; it is more likely that he did it
with wheels and weights.   Of this kind likewise were Vulcan's Tripodes, celebrated by Homer ‡, that were made to
move up and down the house, and fight with one another ‖.

---

* Plato in Menone. Arist. Polit. l. 1. c. 3.
† De Anima, l. 1. c. 3.   ‡ Iliad. 18.
‖ There have been also chariots driven by the force of a spring con-
trived within them.

He might as well have contrived them into journeymen statues, each of which with a hammer in his hand should have worked at the forge.

But amongst these fighting images, that in Cardan * may deserve a mention, which holding in its hand a golden apple, beautified with many costly jewels ; if any man offered to take it, the statue presently shot him to death. The touching of this apple serving to discharge several short bows, or other the like instruments that were secretly couched within the body of the image. By such a treachery was king Chennettus murdered (as Boetius relates.)

It is so common an experiment in these times to represent the persons and actions of any story by such self-moving images, that I shall not need to explain the manner how the wheels and springs are contrived within them.

Amongst these gradient automata, that iron spider mentioned in Walchius †, is more especially remarkable, which being but of an ordinary bigness, besides the outward similitude, (which was very exact) had the same kind of motions with a living spider, and did creep up and down as if it had been alive. It must needs argue a wonderful art and accurateness, to contrive all the instruments requisite for such a motion in so small a frame.

There have been also other motions contrived from magnetical qualities, which will shew the more wonderful, because there is no apparent reason of their motion, there being not the least contiguity or dependance upon any other body that may occasion it ; but it is all one as if they should move up and down in the open air. Get a glass sphere, fill it with such liquors as may be clear of the same colour, immixable, such as are oil of tartar, and spirit of wine : in which it is easy so to poise a little globe or other statue, that it shall swim in the centre. Under this glass sphere, there should be a loadstone concealed, by the mo-

---

* De Variet. Rerum, l. 12. c. 58.

† Fab. 9. There have been other inventions to move on the water. Navigium sponte mobile, ac sui remigii autorem, faciam nullo negotio, saith Scaliger, Exerc. 326.

tion of which, this statue (having a needle touched within it) will move up and down, and may be contrived to shew the hour or sign. See several inventions of this kind in *Kircher de Arte Magnetica*, 1. 2.

There have been some artificial images, which besides their several postures in walking up and down, have been made also to give several sounds, whether of birds, as larks, cuckoos, &c. or beasts, as hares, foxes. The voices of which creatures shall be rendered as clearly and distinctly by these artificial images, as they are by those natural living bodies, which they represent.

There have been some inventions also which have been able for the utterance of articulate sounds, as the speaking of certain words. Such are some of the Egyptian idols related to be. Such was the brazen head made by Friar Bacon *, and that statue, in the framing of which Albertus Magnus bestowed thirty years, broken by Aquinas, who came to see it, purposely that he might boast, how in one minute he had ruined the labour of so many years.

Now the ground and reason how these sounds were contrived, may be worth our inquiry.

First then, for those of birds or beasts, they were made from such pipes or calls, as may express the several tones of those creatures which are represented : these calls are so commonly known and used, that they need not any further explication.

But now, about articulate sounds there is much greater difficulty. Walchius † thinks it possible entirely to preserve the voice, or any words spoken, in a hollow trunk, or pipe, and that this pipe being rightly opened, the words will come out of it in the same order wherein they were spoken. Somewhat like that cold country, where the people's discourse doth freeze in the air all winter, and may be heard the next summer, or at a great thaw. But this conjecture will need no refutation.

* Cœl Rhod. Lect, Ant, 1. 2. c. 17. Maiolus Colloq.   † Fab. 9.

The more substantial way for such a discovery, is by marking how nature herself doth employ the several instruments of speech, the tongue, lips, throat, teeth, &c. To this purpose the Hebrews have assigned each letter unto its proper instrument. And besides, we should observe what inarticulate sounds do resemble any of the particular letters *. Thus we may note the trembling of water to be like the letter L, the quenching of hot things to the letter Z, the sound of strings, unto the letters N g, the jirking of a switch the letter Q, &c. By an exact observation of these particulars, it is (perhaps) possible to make a statue speak some words.

CHAP. V.

Concerning the possibility of framing an Ark for submarine navigations. The difficulties and conveniencies of such a contrivance.

IT will not be altogether impertinent unto the discourse of these gradient automata, to mention what Mersennus † doth so largely and pleasantly descant upon, concerning the making of a ship, wherein men may safely swim under the water.

That such a contrivance is feasible and may be effected, is beyond all question, because it hath been already experimented here in England by Cornelius Dreble; but how to improve it unto public use and advantage, so as to be serviceable for remote voyages, the carrying of any considerable number of men, with provisions and commodities, would be of such excellent use, as may deserve some further inquiry.

* Bacon Nat. Hist. Exper. 139. 200.
† Tract. de Magnetis Proprietatibus.

Concerning which there are two things chiefly considerable.

The many difficulties, with their remedies.
The great conveniences.

1. The difficulties are generally reducible to these three heads :

1. The letting out, or receiving in any thing, as there shall be occasion, without the admission of water. If it have not such a convenience, these kind of voyages must needs be very dangerous and uncomfortable, both by reason of many noisome, offensive things, which should be thrust out, and many other needful things which should be received in. Now herein will consist the difficulty, how to contrive the opening of this vessel so, that any thing may be put in or out, and yet the water not rush into it with much violence, as it doth usually in the leak of a ship.

In which case, this may be a proper remedy ; let there be certain leather bags made of several bignesses, which for the matter of them should be both tractable for the use and managing of them, and strong to keep out the water ; for the figure of them, being long and open at both ends. Answerable to these, let there be divers windows, or open places in the frame of the ship, round the sides of which one end of these bags may be fixed, the other end coming within the ship, being to open and shut as a purse. Now if we suppose this bag thus fastened, to be tied close about towards the window, then any thing that is to be sent out, may be safely put into that end within the ship, which being again close shut, and the other end loosened, the thing may be safely sent out without the admission of any water.

So again, when any thing is to be taken in, it must be first received into that part of the bag towards the window, which being (after the thing is within it) close tied about, the other end may then be safely opened. It is easy to conceive, how by this means any thing or person may be sent out, or received in, as there shall be occasion ; how the water, which will perhaps by degrees leak into several parts, may be emptied out again, with divers the like advantages. Though if there should be any leak at the bottom of this vessel, yet very little water would get in, because no air could get out.

2. The second difficulty in such an ark will be the motion or fixing of it according to occasion : the directing of it to several places, as the voyage shall be designed, without which, it would be very useless, if it were to remain only in one place, or were to remove only blindfold, without any certain direction : and the contrivance of this may seem very difficult, because these submarine navigators will want the usual advantages of winds and tides for motion, and the sight of the heavens for direction.

But these difficulties may be thus remedied ; as for the progressive motion of it, this may be effected by the help of several oars, which in the outward ends of them, shall be like the fins of a fish to contract and dilate. The passage where they are admitted into the ship being tied about with such leather bags (as were mentioned before) to keep out the water. It will not be convenient perhaps that the motion in these voyages should be very swift, because of those observations and discoveries to be made at the bottom of the sea, which in a little space may abundantly recompence the slowness of its progress.

If this ark be so ballast as to be of equal weight with the like magnitude of water, it will then be easily moveable in any part of it.

As for the ascent of it, this may be easily contrived, if there be some great weight at the bottom of the ship (being part of its ballast) which by some cord within may be loosened from it : as this weight is let lower, so will the ship ascend from it (if need be) to the very surface of the water ; and again, as it is pulled close to the ship, so will it descend.

For direction of this ark, the mariner's needle may be useful in respect of the latitude of places ; and the course of this ship being more regular than others, by reason it is not subject to tempests or unequal winds, may more certainly guide them in judging of the longitude of places.

3. But the greatest difficulty of all will be this, how the air may be supplied for respiration : how constant fires may be kept in it for light and the dressing of food, how those vicissitudes of rarefaction and condensation may be maintained.

It is observed, that a barrel or cap, whose cavity will contain eight cubical feet of air, will not serve a urinator or diver for respiration, above one quarter of an hour; the breath which is often sucked in and out, being so corrupted by the mixture of vapours, that nature rejects it as unserviceable. Now in an hour a man will need at least three hundred and sixty respirations, betwixt every one of which there shall be ten second minutes, and consequently a great change and supply of air will be necessary for many persons, and any long space.

And so likewise for the keeping of fire ; a close vessel containing ten cubical feet of air, will not suffer a wax candle of an ounce to burn in it above an hour before it be suffocated; though this proportion (saith Mersennus) doth not equally increase for several lights, because four flames of an equal magnitude will be kept alive the space of sixteen second minutes, though one of these flames alone in the same vessel will not last above thirty-five, or at most thirty seconds; which may be easily tried in large glass bottles, having wax candles lighted in them, and with their mouths inverted in water.

For the resolution of this difficulty; though I will not say that a man may, by custom (which in other things doth produce such strange incredible effects) be enabled to live in the open water, as the fishes do, the inspiration and expiration of water serving instead of air, this being usual with many fishes that have lungs ; yet it is certain, that long use and custom may strengthen men against many such inconveniencies of this kind, which to unexperienced persons may prove very hazardous : and so it will not perhaps be unto these so necessary, to have the air for breathing so pure and defecated, as is required for others.

But further, there are in this case these three things considerable :

1. That the vessel in itself should be of a large capacity, that as the air in it is corrupted in one part, so it may be purified and renewed in the other : or if the mere refrigeration of the air would fit it for breathing, this might be somewhat helped with bellows, which would cool it by motion.

2. It is not altogether improbable, that the lamps or fires in the middle of it, like the reflected beams in the first region, rarefying the air, and the circumambient coldness towards the sides of the vessel, like the second region, cooling and condensing of it, would make such a vicissitude and change of air, as might fit it for all its proper uses.

3. Or if neither of these conjectures will help, yet Mersennus tells us in another place *, that there is in France one Barrieus a diver, who hath lately found out another art, whereby a man might easily continue under water for six hours together ; and whereas ten cubical feet of air will not serve another diver to breathe in for half an hour, he by the help of a cavity, not above one or two foot at most, will have breath enough for six hours, and a lantern scarce above the usual size to keep a candle burning as long as a man please, which (if it be true, and were commonly known) might be a sufficient help against this greatest difficulty.

As for the many advantages and conveniencies of such a contrivance, it is not easy to recite them.

1. It is private ; a man may thus go to any coast of the world invisibly, without being discovered or prevented in his journey.

2. It is safe ; from the uncertainty of tides, and the violence of tempests, which do never move the sea above five or six paces deep. From pirates and robbers which do so infest other voyages. From ice and great frosts, which do so much endanger the passages towards the poles.

* Harmon. l. 4. prop. 6. Monit. 5.

3. It may be of very great advantage against a navy of enemies, who by this means may be undermined in the water, and blown up.

4. It may be of special use for the relief of any place that is besieged by water, to convey unto them invisible supplies; and so likewise for the surprisal of any place that is accessible by water.

5. It may be of unspeakable benefit for submarine experiments and discoveries; as,

The several proportions of swiftness betwixt the ascent of a bladder, cork, or any other light substance, in comparison to the descent of stones or lead. The deep caverns, and subterraneous passages, where the sea-water, in the course of its circulation, doth vent itself into other places, and the like. The nature and kinds of fishes, the several arts of catching them, by alluring them with lights, by placing divers nets about the sides of this vessel, shooting the greater sort of them with guns, which may be put out of the ship by the help of such bags as were mentioned before, with divers the like artifices and treacheries, which may be more successfully practised by such who live so familiarly together. These fish may serve not only for food, but for fewel likewise, in respect of that oil which may be extracted from them; the way of dressing meat by lamps, being in many respects the most convenient for such a voyage.

The many fresh springs that may probably be met with in the bottom of the sea, will serve for the supply of drink, and other occasions.

But above all, the discovery of submarine treasures is more especially considerable; not only in regard of what hath been drowned by wrecks, but the several precious things that grow there; as pearl, coral, mines; with innumerable other things of great value, which may be much more easily found out, and fetched up by the help of this, than by any other usual way of the urinators.

To which purpose, this great vessel may have some lesser cabins tied about it, at various distances; wherein several persons, as scouts, may be lodged for the taking of observations, according as the admiral shall direct them: some of them being frequently sent up to the surface of the water, as there shall be occasion.

All kind of arts and manufactures may be exercised in this vessel. The observations made by it, may be both written, and (if need were) printed here likewise. Several colonies may thus inhabit, having their children born, and bred up without the knowledge of land, who could not chuse but be amazed with strange conceits upon the discovery of this upper world.

I am not able to judge what other advantages there may be suggested, or whether experiment would fully answer to these national conjectures. But however, because the invention did unto me seem ingenious and new, being not impertinent to the present inquiry, therefore I thought it might be worth the mentioning.

CHAP. VI.

Of the volant Automata, Archytas his Dove, and Regiomontanus his Eagle. The possibility, and great usefulness of such inventions.

THE volant, or flying automata, are such mechanical contrivances as have a self-motion, whereby they are carried aloft in the open air like the flight of birds. Such was that wooden dove made by Archytas, a citizen of Tarentum, and one of Plato's acquaintance: and that wooden eagle framed by Regiomontanus at Noremberg, which, by way of triumph, did fly out of the city to meet Charles the

Fifth. This latter author is also reported to have made an iron fly, *Quæ ex artificis manu egressa, convivas circumvolitavit, tandemque veluti defessa in domini manus reversa est;* which, when he invited any of his friends, would fly to each of them round the table, and at length (as being weary) return unto its master *.

Cardan † seems to doubt the possibility of any such contrivance: his reason is, because the instruments of it must be firm and strong, and consequently they will be too heavy to be carried by their own force; but yet (saith he) if it be a little helped in the first rising, and if there be any wind to assist it in the flight, then there is nothing to hinder, but that such motions may be possible. So that he doth in effect grant as much as may be sufficient for the truth and credit of those ancient relations; and to distrust them without a stronger argument, must needs argue a blind and perverse incredibility. As for his objection concerning the heaviness of the materials in such an invention, it may be answered, that it is easy to contrive such springs, and other instruments, whose strength shall much exceed their heaviness. Nor can he shew any cause why these mechanical motions may not be as strong, (though not so lasting) as the natural strength of living creatures.

Scaliger ‡ conceives the framing of such volant automata to be very easy. *Volantis columbæ machinulam, cujus autorem Archytam tradunt, vel facillime profiteri audeo.* Those ancient motions were thought to be contrived by the force of some included air: so Gellius ||,

---

* Diog. Laer. l. 8. Pet. Crinitus de honest. discip. l. 17. c. 12. Ramus Schol. Mathem. l. 2. Dubartas 6 days, 1 W. I. Dee Preface to Euclid.

† De Variet. Rerum, lib. 12. c. 58.   ‡ Subtil. Exercit. 326.

|| Noct. Attic. l. 10. cap. 12. where he thinks it so strange an invention, that he styles it res abhorrens a fide. Athan. Kircher de Magnete. l. 2. par. 4. Proem. doth promise a large discourse concerning these kind of inventions in another treatise, which he styles Œdipus Ægyptiacus.

ita erat scilicet libramentis suspensum, et aurâ spiritus in-clusa, atque occulta consitum, &c. As if there had been some lamp, or other fire within it, which might produce such a forcible rarefaction, as should give a motion to the whole frame.

But this may be better performed by the strength of some such spring, as is commonly used in watches. This spring may be applied unto one wheel, which shall give an equal motion to both the wings; these wings having unto each of them another smaller spring, by which they may be contracted and lifted up: so that being forcibly de-pressed by the strength of the great and stronger spring, and lifted up again by the other two; according to this sup-position, it is easy to conceive how the motion of flight may be performed and continued.

The wings may be made either of several substances joined, like the feathers in ordinary fowl, as Dædalus is feigned to contrive them, according to that in the poet,

> ────*Ignotas animum dimittit in artes,*
> *Naturamque novat, nam ponit in ordine pennas*
> *A minimo cœptas longam breviore sequente,*
> *Ut clivo crevisse putes, &c* *.

Or else of one continuate substance, like those of bats. In framing of both which, the best guidance is to follow (as near as may be) the direction of nature, this being but an imitation of a natural work. Now in both these, the strength of each part is proportioned to the force of its em-ployment. But nothing in this kind can be perfectly de-termined without a particular trial.

Though the composing of such motions may be a suf-ficient reward to any one's industry in the searching after them, as being in themselves of excellent curiosity, yet there are some other inventions depend upon them of more ge-neral benefit, and greater importance. For, if there be any such artificial contrivances that can fly in the air, (as is evi-dent from the former relations, together with the grounds

* Ovid Metam. L 8.

here specified, and, I doubt not, may be easily effected by a diligent and ingenious artificer) then it will clearly follow, that it is possible also for a man to fly himself; it being easy from the same grounds, to frame an instrument wherein any one may sit, and give such a motion unto it, as shall convey him aloft through the air; than which there is not any imaginable invention, that could prove of greater benefit to the world, or glory to the author; and therefore it may justly deserve their inquiry, who have both leisure and means for such experiments.

But in these practical studies, unless a man be able to go the trial of things, he will perform but little.   In such matters,

—— *Studium sine divite venâ,*

(as the poet saith *) a general speculation, without particular experiment, may conjecture at many things, but can certainly effect nothing; and therefore I shall only propose unto the world, the theory and general grounds that may conduce to the easy and more perfect discovery of the subject in question, for the encouragement of those that have both minds and means for such experiments.   This same scholar's fate,

Res angusta domi, and
— *Curta suppellex,*

is that which hinders the promoting of learning in sundry particulars, and robs the world of many excellent inventions. We read of Aristotle, that he was allowed by his pupil Alexander eight hundred talents a year, for the payment of fishers, fowlers, and hunters, who were to bring him in several creatures, that so by his particular experience of their parts and dispositions, he might be more fitly prepared to write of their natures.   The reason why the world hath not many Aristotles, is because it hath so few Alexanders.

Amongst other impediments of any strange invention, or attempts, it is none of the meanest discouragements, that

* Horace.

they are so generally derided by common opinion; being
esteemed only as the dreams of a melancholy and distem-
pered fancy. Eusebius * speaking, with what necessity
every thing is confined by the laws of nature, and the de-
crees of providence, so that nothing can go out of that way
unto which naturally it is designed; as a fish cannot reside
on the land, nor a man in the water, or aloft in the air; infers, that therefore none will venture upon any such vain
attempt, as passing in the air, η μελαγχολιας νοσηματα αν
περιπεσοι, unless his brain be a little crazed with the humour
of melancholy; whereupon he advises that we should not in
any particular, endeavour to transgress the bounds of nature,
ὁδε απτερον εχοντα το σωμα, τα των πτηνων επι τη δευειν, and
since we are destitute of wings, not to imitate the flight of
birds. That saying of the poet,

> Demens, qui nimbos, et non imitabile, fulmen, &c †.

hath been an old censure, applied unto such as ventured
upon any strange or incredible attempt.

Hence may we conceive the reason, why there is so little
intimation in the writings of antiquity, concerning the possibility of any such invention. The ancients durst not so
much as mention the art of flying, but in a fable.

> Dædalus, ut fama est, fugiens Minoia regna,
> Præpetibus pennis ausus se credere cælo,
> Insuetum per iter gelidas enavit ad arctos, &c.

It was the custom of those former ages, in their over-
much gratitude, to advance the first authors of any useful
discovery amongst the number of their gods. And Dædalus,
being so famous amongst them for sundry mechanical inventions (especially the sails of ships) though they did not
for these place him in the heavens, yet they have promoted
him as near as they could, feigning him to fly aloft in
the air, when as he did but fly in a swift ship, as Diodorus relates the historical truth on which that fiction is
grounded ‡.

---

* Contra. Hierocl. Confut. l. 1.   † Virgil's Æneid, l. 6.
‡ So Eusebius too.

CHAP. VII.

Concerning the art of Flying. The several ways whereby this hath been, or may be attempted.

I HAVE formerly in two other discourses * mentioned the possibility of this art of flying, and intimated a farther inquiry into it, which is a kind of engagement to some fuller disquisitions and conjectures to that purpose.

There are four several ways whereby this flying in the air hath been, or may be attempted. Two of them by the strength of other things, and two of them by our own strength.

1. By spirits, or angels.
2. By the help of fowls.
3. By wings fastened immediately to the body.
4. By a flying chariot.

1. For the first, we read of divers that have passed swiftly in the air, by the help of spirits and angels † ; whether good angels, as Elias ‡ was carried unto heaven in a fiery chariot, as Philip ‖ was conveyed to Azotus, and Habakkuk from Jewry to Babylon, and back again immediately § : or by evil angels, as our Saviour was carried by the devil to the top of a high mountain, and to the pinnacle of the temple ¶. Thus witches are commonly related to pass unto their usual meetings, in some remote place ; and, as they do sell winds unto mariners **, so likewise are they sometimes hired to carry men speedily through the open air. Acosta †† affirms, that such kind of passages are usual amongst divers sorcerers with the Indians at this day.

---

* World in the Moon, cap. 14. Mercury ; or, the Secret and Swift Messenger, c. 4.

† Zanch. de Oper. part 1. l. 4.   ‡ 2 Kings, ii. 11.
‖ Acts viii. 39.   § Dan. Apoc. 39.   ¶ Luke iv.
** Erastus de Lamus.   †† Hist. Ind. l. 5. c. 26.

So Kepler, in his astronomical dream, doth fancy a witch to be conveyed unto the moon by her familiar.

Simon Magus was so eminent for miraculous sorceries, that all the people in Samaria, from the least to the greatest, did esteem him as the great power of God *. And so famous was he at Rome, that the emperor erected a statue to him with this inscription, Simoni Deo sancto †. It is storied of this magician, that having challenged Saint Peter to do miracles with him, he attempted to fly from the Capitol to the Aventine Hill; but when he was in the midst of the way, Saint Peter's prayers did overcome his sorceries, and violently bring him to the ground; in which fall having broke his thigh, within a while after he died ‡.

But none of all these relations may conduce to the discovery of this experiment, as it is here inquired after, upon natural and artificial grounds.

2. There are others, who have conjectured a possibility of being conveyed through the air by the help of fowls, to which purpose, that fiction of the ganzas is the most pleasant and probable. They are supposed to be great fowl, of a strong lasting flight, and easily tameable: divers of which may be so brought up, as to join together in the carrying the weight of a man, so as each of them shall partake his proportionable share of the burthen, and the person that is carried may by certain reins, direct and steer them in their courses. However this may seem a strange proposal, yet it is not certainly more improbable than many other arts, wherein the industry of ingenious men hath instructed these brute creatures. And I am very confident, that one whose genius doth enable him for such kind of experiments upon leisure, and the advantage of such helps as are requisite for various and frequent trials, might effect some strange things by this kind of inquiry.

---

* Acts viii. 10.   † Hegesip. l. 3. c. 2.

‡ Pol. Virgil. de Inven. Rerum, l. 8. c. 3.   Pet. Crinitus de Honesta Disciplin. l. 8. c. 1. mistrusts this relation as fabulous.   Non enim Lucas hoc omisisset.

It is reported as a custom amongst the Leucatians, that
they were wont upon a superstition, to precipitate a man
from some high cliff into the sea, tying about him with
strings at some distance, many great fowls, and fixing upon
his body divers feathers, spread to break the fall; which
(saith the learned Bacon *, if it were diligently and exactly
contrived) would be able to hold up, and carry any proportionable weight; and therefore he advises others to think
further upon this experiment, as giving some light to the
invention of the art of flying.

3. It is the more obvious and common opinion, that this
may be effected by wings fastened immediately to the body,
this coming nearest to the imitation of nature, which should
be observed in such attempts as these.   This is that way
which Fredericus Hermannus, in his little discourse *de arte
volandi*, doth only mention and insist upon ; and if we may
trust credible story, it hath been frequently attempted not
without some success †.   It is related of a certain English
monk, called Elmerus, about the Confessor's time, that he
did by such wings fly from a tower above a furlong ; and
so another from Saint Mark's steeple in Venice; another
at Norinberg; and Busbequius speaks of a Turk in Constantinople, who attempted something this way ‡.   M. Bur-
ton mentioning this quotation, doth believe that some new-
fangled wit (it is his cynical phrase) will some time or other
find out this art.   Though the truth is, most of these
artists did unfortunately miscarry by falling down, and
breaking their arms or legs, yet that may be imputed to
their want of experience, and too much fear, which must
needs possess men in such dangerous and strange attempts ‖.
Those things that seem very difficult and fearful at the first,
may grow very facil after frequent trial and exercise : and
therefore he that would effect any thing in this kind, must
be brought up to the constant practice of it from his youth;

* Nat. Hist. experim. 886   † So the ancient British Bladuds.
‡ Ernestus Burgravus in Panoplia Physico-Vulcania. Sturmius in Lat.
Linguæ Resolut.
‖ Melancholy, part 2. sect. 1. mem. 3.

trying first only to use his wings, in running on the ground,
as an ostrich or tame goose will do, touching the earth with
his toes ; and so by degrees learn to rise higher, till he
shall attain unto skill and confidence.   I have heard it from
credible testimony, that one of our own nation hath proceeded so far in this experiment, that 1 · was able by the
help of wings, in such a running pace, to step constantly ten
yards at a time.

It is not more incredible, that frequent practice and
custom should enable a man for this, than for many other
things which we see confirmed by experience. What
strange agility and activeness do our common tumblers and
dancers on the rope attain to by continual exercise ?   It is
related of certain Indians *, that they are able, when a
horse is running in his full career, to stand upright on his
back, to turn themselves round, to leap down, gathering up
any thing from the ground, and immediately to leap up
again, to shoot exactly at any mark, the horse not inter-
mitting his course : and so upon two horses together, the
man setting one of his feet upon each of them. These
things may seem impossible to others, and it would be very
dangerous for any one to attempt them, who hath not first
gradually attained to these arts by long practice and trial ;
and why may not such practice enable him as well for this
other experiment, as for these things ?

There are others, who have invented ways to walk upon
the water as regularly and firmly as upon the land. There
are some so accustomed to this element, that it hath been
almost as natural to them as to the fish ; men that could remain for above an hour together under water. Pontanus
mentions one, who could swim above a hundred miles together, from one shore to another, with great speed, and at
all times of the year. And it is storied of a certain young
man, a Sicilian by birth, and a diver by profession, who
had so continually used himself to the water, that he could
not enjoy his health out of it. If at any time he staid with

* Maffæus Hist. Ind. l. I.

his friends on the land, he should be so tormented with a pain in his stomach, that he was forced for his health to return back again to sea; wherein he kept his usual residence, and when he saw any ships, his custom was to swim to them for relief; which kind of life he continued till he was an old man, and died *.

I mention these things, to shew the great power of practice and custom, which might more probably succeed in this experiment of flying (if it were but regularly attempted) than in such strange effects as these.

It is a usual practice in these times, for our funambulones, or dancers on the rope, to attempt somewhat like to flying, when they will, with their heads forwards, slide down a long cord extended; being fastened at one end to the top of some high tower, and the other at some distance on the ground, with wings fixed to their shoulders, by the shaking of which they will break the force of their descent. It would seem that some attempts of this kind were usual amongst the Romans. To which that expression in Salvian † may refer; where, amongst other public shews of the theatre, he mentions the Petaminaria; which word (saith Jo. Brassicanus ‡) is scarce to be found in any other author, being not mentioned either in Julius Pollux, or Politian. It is probably derived from the Greek word πετασθαι, which signifies to fly, and may refer to such kind of rope dancers.

But now, because the arms extended are but weak, and easily wearied, therefore the motions by them are like to be but short and slow, answerable it may be to the flight of such domestic fowl as are most conversant on the ground, which of themselves we see are quickly weary; and therefore much more would the arm of a man, as being not naturally designed to such a motion.

It were therefore worth the inquiry, to consider whether this might not be more probably effected by the labour of the feet, which are naturally more strong and indefatigable:

* Treatise of Custom.   † De Guber. Dei, l. 6.
‡ Annot. in Salvi

in which contrivance the wings should come down from the shoulders on each side, as in the other, but the motion of them should be from the legs being thrust out, and drawn in again one after another, so as each leg should move both wings; by which means a man should (as it were) walk or climb up into the air; and then the hands and arms might be at leisure to help and direct the motion, or for any other service proportionable to their strength.   Which conjecture is not without good probability, and some special advantages above the other.

4. But the fourth and last way seems unto me altogether as probable, and much more useful than any of the rest. And that is by a flying chariot, which may be so contrived as to carry a man within it; and though the strength of a spring might perhaps be serviceable for the motion of this engine, yet it were better to have it assisted by the labour of some intelligent mover, as the heavenly orbs are supposed to be turned.   And therefore if it were made big enough to carry sundry persons together, then each of them in their several turns might successively labour in the causing of this motion; which thereby would be much more constant and lasting, than it could otherwise be, if it did wholly depend on the strength of the same person. This contrivance being as much to be preferred before any of the other, as swimming in a ship before swimming in the water.

CHAP VIII.

A resolution of the two chief difficulties that seem to oppose the possibility of a flying chariot.

THE chief difficulties against the possibility of any such contrivance may be fully removed in the resolution of these two queries.

1. Whether an engine of such capacity and weight, may be supported by so thin and light a body as the air?

2. Whether the strength of the persons within it may be sufficient for the motion of it ?

1. Concerning the first; when Callias * was required by the men of Rhodes, to take up that great helepolis, brought against them by Demetrius, (as he had done before unto some less which he himself had made) he answered that it could not be done. *Nonnulla enim sunt quæ in exemplaribus videntur similia, cum autem crescere cæperunt, dilabuntur* †. Because those things that appear probable in lesser models, when they are increased to a greater proportion, do thereby exceed the power of art. For example, though a man may make an instrument to bore a hole, an inch wide, or half an inch, and so less; yet to bore a hole of a foot wide, or two foot, is not so much as to be thought of. Thus, though the air may be able to uphold some lesser bodies, as those of birds, yet when the quantity of them is increased to any great extension, it may justly be doubted, whether they will not exceed the proportion that is naturally required unto such kind of bodies.

To this I answer, that the engine can never be too big or too heavy, if the space which it possesses in the air, and the motive-faculty in the instrument be answerable to its weight. That saying of Callias was but a groundless shift and evasion, whereby he did endeavour to palliate his own ignorance and disability. The utmost truth which seems to be implied in it, is this : that there may be some bodies of so great a bigness, and gravity, that it is very difficult to apply so much force unto any particular instrument, as shall be able to move them.

Against the example it may be affirmed and easily proved, that it is equally possible to bore a hole of any bigness, as well great as little, if we suppose the instrument, and the strength, and the application of this strength to be proportionable; but because of the difficulty of these concurrent circumstances in those greater and more unusual operations, therefore do they falsely seem to be absolutely impossible.

---

* Vitruvius Archit. l. 10. c. 22.   † So Ramus, Schol. Mathem. l. 1.

So that the chief inference from this argument and example, doth imply only thus much, that it is very difficult to contrive any such motive power, as shall be answerable to the greatness and weight of such an instrument as is here discoursed of; which doth not at all impair the truth to be maintained : for if the possibility of such a motion be yielded, we need not make any scruple of granting the difficulty of it; it is this must add a glory to the invention; and yet this will not perhaps seem so very difficult to any one who hath but diligently observed the flight of some other birds, particularly of a kite, how he will swim up and down in the air, sometimes at a great height, and presently again lower, guiding himself by his train, with his wings extended without any sensible motion of them ; and all this, when there is only some gentle breath of air stirring, without the help of any strong forcible wind. Now I say, if that very fowl (which is none of the lightest) can so easily move itself up and down in the air, without so much as stirring the wings of it, certainly then it is not improbable, but that when all the due proportions in such an engine are found out, and when men by long practice have arrived to any skill and experience, they will be able in this (as well as in many other things) to come very near unto the imitation of nature.

As it is in those bodies which are carried on the water, though they be never so big or so ponderous, (suppose equal to a city or a whole island) yet they will always swim on the top, if they be but any thing lighter than so much water as is equal to them in bigness *. So likewise is it in the bodies that are carried in the air. It is not their greatness (though never so immense) that can hinder their being supported in that light element, if we suppose them to be extended unto a proportionable space of air. And as from the former experiments, Archimedes hath composed a subtle science in his book *De insidentibus humido,* concerning the weight of any heavy body, in reference to the water

* Sen. Nat. Qu. l. 1. c. 25.

wherein it is; so from the particular trial of these other experiments, that are here inquired after, it is possible to raise a new science, concerning the extension of bodies, in comparison to the air, and motive faculties by which they are to be carried.

We see a great difference betwixt the several quantities of such bodies as are commonly upheld by the air ; not only little gnats, and flies, but also the eagle and other fowl of vaster magnitude.   Cardan and Scaliger * do unanimously affirm, that there is a bird amongst the Indians of so great a bigness, that his beak is often used to make a sheath or scabbard for a sword.   And Acosta † tells us of a fowl in Peru called candores, which will of themselves kill and eat up a whole calf at a time.   Nor is there any reason why any other body may not be supported and carried by the air, though it should as much exceed the quantity of these fowl, as they do the quantity of a fly.

Marcus Polus mentions a fowl in Madagascar, which he calls a ruck, the feathers of whose wings are twelve paces, or threescore foot long, which can with as much ease scoop up an elephant, as our kites do a mouse.   If this relation were any thing credible, it might serve as an abundant proof for the present query.   But I conceive this to be already so evident, that it needs not any fable for its further confirmation.

2. The other doubt was, whether the strength of the other persons within it, will be sufficient for the moving of this engine ?   I answer, the main difficulty and labour of it will be in the raising of it from the ground ; near unto which, the earth's attractive vigour is of greatest efficacy. But for the better effecting of this, it may be helped by the strength of winds, and by taking its first rise from some mountain or other high place.   When once it is aloft in the air, the motion of it will be easy, as it is in the flight of all kind of birds, which being at any great distance from the

* Subtil. l. 10. Exercit. 231.   † Histor. Nov. Orb. l. 4. c. 37.

earth, are able to continue their motion for a long time and way, with little labour or weariness.

It is certain from common relation and experience that many birds do cross the seas for divers hundred miles together *. Sundry of them amongst us, which are of a short wing and flight, as blackbirds, nightingales, &c. do fly from us into Germany, and other remoter countries. And mariners do commonly affirm that they have found some fowl above six hundred miles from any land. Now if we should suppose these birds to labour so much in those long journies, as they do when they fly in our sight and near the earth, it were impossible for any of them to pass so far without resting. And therefore it is probable, that they do mount unto so high a place in the air, where the natural heaviness of their bodies does prove but little or no impediment to their flight: though perhaps either hunger, or the sight of ships, or the like accident, may sometimes occasion their descending lower ; as we may guess of those birds which mariners have thus beheld, and divers others that have been drowned and cast up by the sea.

Whence it may appear, that the motion of this chariot (though it may be difficult at the first) yet will still be easier as it ascends higher, till at length it shall become utterly devoid of gravity, when the least strength will be able to bestow upon it a swift motion: as I have proved more at large in another discourse †.

But then, (may some object) if it be supposed that a man in the æthereal air does lose his own heaviness, how shall he contribute any force towards the motion of this instrument ?

I answer, the strength of any living creature in these external motions, is something really distinct from, and superadded unto its natural gravity : as common experience may shew, not only in the impression of blows or violent motions, as a river hawk will strike a fowl with a far greater force, than the mere descent or heaviness of his body could

* Plin. l. 10. c. 23.   † World in the Moon, cap. 14.

possibly perform : but also in those actions which are done without such help, as the pinching of the finger, the biting of the teeth, &c. all which are of much greater strength than can proceed from the mere heaviness of those parts.

As for the other particular doubts, concerning the extreme thinness and coldness of this æthereal air, by reason of which, it may seem to be altogether impassible, I have already resolved them in the above-cited discourse.

The uses of such a chariot may be various : besides the discoveries which might be thereby made in the lunary world, it would be serviceable also for the conveyance of a man to any remote place of this earth : as suppose to the Indies or antipodes. For when once it was elevated for some few miles, so as to be above that orb of magnetic virtue, which is carried about by the earth's diurnal revolution, it might then be very easily and speedily directed to any particular place of this great globe.

If the place which we intended were under the same parallel, why then the earth's revolution once in twenty-four hours, would bring it to be under us ; so that it would be but descending in a straight line, and we might presently be there. If it were under any other parallel, it would then only require that we should direct it in the same meridian, till we did come to that parallel ; and then (as before) a man might easily descend unto it.

It would be one great advantage in this kind of travelling, that one should be perfectly freed from all inconveniencies of ways or weather, not having any extremity of heat or cold, or tempests to molest him. This æthereal air being perpetually in an equal temper and calmness. *Pars superior mundi ordinatior est, nec in nubem cogitur, nec in tempestatem impellitur, nec versatur in turbinem, omni tumultu caret, inferiora fulminant* *. The upper parts of the world are always quiet and serene, no winds and blustering there, they are these lower cloudy regions that are so full of tempests and combustion.

* Sen de Ira, l. 3. c. 6. Pacem summa tenent. Lucan.

As for the manner how the force of a spring, or (instead of that) the strength of any living person, may be applied to the motion of these wings of the chariot, it may easily be apprehended from what was formerly delivered.

There are divers other particulars to be more fully inquired after, for the perfecting of such a flying chariot; as concerning the proportion of the wings both for the length and breadth, in comparison to the weight which is to be carried by them*; as also concerning those special contrivances, whereby the strength of these wings may be severally applied, either to ascent, descent, progressive, or a turning motion; all which, and divers the like inquiries can only be resolved by particular experiments. We know the invention of sailing in ships does continually receive some new addition from the experience of every age, and hath been a long while growing up to that perfection unto which it is now arrived. And so must it be expected for this likewise, which may at first perhaps seem perplexed with many difficulties and inconveniencies, and yet upon the experience of frequent trials, many things may be suggested to make it more facil and commodious.

He that would regularly attempt any thing to this purpose, should observe this progress in his experiments; he should first make inquiry what kind of wings would be most useful to this end; those of a bat being most easily imitable, and perhaps nature did by them purposely intend some intimation to direct us in such experiments; that creature being not properly a bird, because not amongst the *ovipara*, to imply that other kind of creatures are capable of flying as well as birds; and if any should attempt it, that would be the best pattern for imitation.

After this he may try what may be effected by the force of springs in lower models, answerable unto Archytas his dove, and Regiomontanus his eagle: in which he must be careful to observe the various proportions betwixt the

---

* As well too long as too short, too broad as too narrow, may be an impediment to the motion, by making it more difficult, slow, and flagging.

strength of the spring, the heaviness of the body, the breadth of the wings, the swiftness of the motion, &c.

From these he may by degrees ascend to some larger essays.

CHAP. IX.

Of a perpetual motion. The seeming facility and real difficulty of any such contrivance. The several ways whereby it hath been attempted, particularly by chymistry.

IT is the chief inconvenience of all the automata before-mentioned, that they need a frequent repair of new strength, the causes whence their motion does proceed being subject to fail, and come to a period ; and therefore it would be worth our inquiry, to examine whether or no there may be made any such artificial contrivance, which might have the principle of moving from itself; so that the present motion should constantly be the cause of that which succeeds.

This is that great secret in art, which, like the philosopher's stone in nature, hath been the business and study of many more refined wits, for divers ages together ; and it may well be questioned, whether either of them as yet hath ever been found out; though if this have, yet, like the other, it is not plainly treated of by any author.

Not but that there are sundry discourses concerning this subject, but they are rather conjectures than experiments. And though many inventions in this kind, may at first view bear a great shew of probability, yet they will fail, being brought to trial, and will not answer in practice what they promised in speculation. Any one who hath been versed in these experiments must needs acknowledge that he hath been often deceived in his strongest confidence ; when the imagination hath contrived the whole frame of such an in-

strument, and conceives that the event must infallibly answer its hopes, yet then does it strangely deceive in the
proof, and discovers to us some defect which we did not
before take notice of.

Hence it is, that you shall scarce talk with any one who
hath never so little smattering in these arts, but he will in-
stantly promise such a motion, as being but an easy at-
chievement, till further trial and experience hath taught
him the difficulty of it.   There being no inquiry that does
more entice with the probability, and deceive with the subtilty.   What one speaks wittily concerning the philosopher's stone, may be justly applied to this, that it is *casta
meretrix*, a chaste whore; *quia multos invitat, neminem
admittit*, because it allures many, but admits none.

I shall briefly recite the several ways whereby this hath
been attempted, or seems most likely to be effected;
thereby to contract and facilitate the inquiries of those who
are addicted to these kind of experiments; for when they
know the defects of other inventions, they may the more
easily avoid the same, or the like in their own.

The ways whereby this hath been attempted, may be
generally reduced to these three kinds :

1. By chymical extractions.
2. By magnetical virtues.
3. By the natural affection of gravity.

1. The discovery of this hath been attempted by chymistry.   Paracelsus and his followers have bragged, that by
their separations and extractions, they can make a little
world which shall have the same perpetual motions with
this microcosm, with the representation of all meteors,
thunder, snow, rain, the courses of the sea in its ebbs and
flows, and the like; but these miraculous promises would
require as great a faith to believe them, as a power to perform them : and though they often talk of such great
matters,

> *At nusquam totos inter qui talia curant,*
> *Apparet ullus, qui re miracula tanta*
> *Comprobet* ———

yet we can never see them confirmed by any real experiment; and then besides, every particular author in that art hath such a distinct language of his own, (all of them being so full of allegories and affected obscurities) that it is very hard for any one (unless he be thoroughly versed amongst them) to find out what they mean, much more to try it.

One of these ways (as I find it set down *) is this. Mix five ounces of ☿, with an equal weight of ♃, grind them together with ten ounces of sublimate, dissolve them in a cellar upon some marble for the space of four days, till they become like oil olive; distil this with fire of chaff, or driving fire, and it will sublime into a dry substance: and so by repeating of these dissolvings and distillings, there will be at length produced divers small atoms, which being put into a glass well luted, and kept dry, will have a perpetual motion.

I cannot say any thing from experience against this; but methinks it does not seem very probable, because things that are forced up to such a vigorousness and activity as these ingredients seem to be by their frequent sublimatings and distillings, are not likely to be of any duration; the more any thing is stretched beyond its usual nature, the less does it last; violence and perpetuity being no companions. And then besides, suppose it true, yet such a motion could not well be applied to any use, which must needs take much from the delight of it.

Amongst the chymical experiments to this purpose, may be reckoned up that famous motion invented by Cornelius Dreble, and made for king James †; wherein was represented the constant revolutions of the sun and moon, and that without the help either of springs or weights. Marcellus Vranckheim ‡, speaking of the means whereby it was performed, he calls it, *scintillula animæ magneticæ mundi, seu astralis et insensibilis spiritus;* being that grand

---

* Etten. Mathem. Recreat. prob. 118.
† Celebrated in an epigram by Hugo Grotius, l. 1.
‡ Epist. ad Ernestum de Lamp. Vitæ.

secret, for the discovery of which, those dictators of philosophy, Democritus, Pythagoras, Plato, did travel unto the
gymnosophists, and Indian priests. The author himself
in his discourse upon it, does not at all reveal the way how
it was performed. But there is one Thomas Tymme *,
who was a familiar acquaintance of his, and did often pry
into his works, (as he professes himself) who affirms it to
be done thus; by extracting a fiery spirit out of the mineral
matter, joining the same with his proper air, which included
in the axletree (of the first moving wheel) being hollow,
carrieth the other wheels, making a continual rotation, except issue or vent be given in this hollow axletree, whereby
the imprisoned spirit may get forth †.

What strange things may be done by such extractions, I
know not, and therefore dare not condemn this relation as
impossible; but methinks it sounds rather like a chymical
dream, than a philosophical truth. It seems this imprisoned spirit is now set at liberty, or else is grown weary,
for the instrument (as I have heard) hath stood still for
many years. It is here considerable that any force is
weakest near the centre of a wheel; and therefore though
such a spirit might of itself have an agitation, yet it is not
easily conceivable how it should have strength enough to
carry the wheels about with it. And then the absurdity of
the author's citing this, would make one mistrust his mistake; he urges it as a strong argument against Copernicus,
as if because Dreble did thus contrive in an engine the revolution of the heavens, and the immoveableness of the
earth, therefore it must needs follow that it is the heavens
which are moved, and not the earth. If his relation were
no truer than his consequence, it had not been worth the
citing.

* Epist. ad Jacobum Regem.
† Philosophical Dialogue, Confer. 2. cap. 3.

CHAP. X.

Of subterraneous lamps; divers historical relations con-
cerning their duration for many hundred years to-
gether.

UNTO this kind of chymical experiments, we may
most probably reduce those perpetual lamps, which
for many hundred years together have continued burning
without any new supply in the sepulchres of the ancients,
and might (for ought we know) have remained so for ever.
All fire, and especially flame, being of an active and stirring nature, it cannot therefore subsist without motion;
whence it may seem, that this great enquiry hath been this
way accomplished: and therefore it will be worth our examination to search further into the particulars that concern
this experiment. Though it be not so proper to the chief
purpose of this discourse, which concerns mechanical geometry, yet the subtilty and curiosity of it may abundantly
requite the impertinency.

There are sundry authors, who treat of this subject on
the by, and in some particular passages, but none that I
know of (except Fortunius Licetus *) that hath writ purposely any set and large discourse concerning it: out of
whom I shall borrow many of those relations and opinions,
which may most naturally conduce to the present enquiry.

For our fuller understanding of this, there are these particulars to be explained:

1. ὅτι, or *quod sit.*

2. διότι $\begin{cases} \textit{cur sit.} \\ \textit{quomodo sit.} \end{cases}$

1. First then, for the ὅτι, or that there have been such
lamps, it may be evident from sundry plain and undeniable
testimonies: St. Austin † mentions one of them in a temple

* Lib. de reconditis Antiquorum Lucernis.
† De Civitat. Dei, l. 21. c. 6.

dedicated to Venus, which was always exposed to the open weather, and could never be consumed or extinguished. To him assents the judicious Zanchy *. Pancyrollus † mentions a lamp found in his time, in the sepulchre of Tullia, Cicero's daughter, which had continued there for about 1550 years, but was presently extinguished upon the admission of new air.   And it is commonly related of Cedrenus, that in Justinian's time there was another burning lamp found in an old wall at Edessa ‡, which had remained so for above 500 years, there being a crucifix placed by it, whence it should seem, that they were in use also amongst some christians.

But more especially remarkable is that relation celebrated by so many authors, concerning Olybius's lamp, which had continued burning for 1500 years.   The story is thus: as a rustic was digging the ground by Padua, he found an urn or earthen pot, in which there was another urn, and in this lesser, a lamp clearly burning; on each side of it there were two other vessels, each of them full of a pure liquor; the one of gold, the other of silver.   *Ego chymiæ artis, (simodo vera potest esse ars chymia) jurare ausim elementa et materiam omnium*, (saith Maturantius, who had the possession of these things after they were taken up.) On the bigger of these urns there was this inscription:

> *Plutoni sacrum munus ne attingite fures.*
> *Ignotum est vobis hoc quod in orbe latet,*
> *Namque elementa gravi clausit digesta labore*
> *Vase sub hoc modico, Maximus Olybius.*
> *Adsit fœcundo custos sibi copia cornu,*
> *Ne tanti pretium depereat laticis.*

The lesser urn was thus inscribed:

> *Abite hinc pessimi fures,*
> *Vos quid vultis, vestris cum oculis emissitis?*
> *Abite hinc, vestro cum Mercurio*
> *Petasato caduceatoque,*
> *Donum hoc maximum, Maximus Olybius*
> *Plutoni sacrum facit.*

---

* De Operibus Dei, pars 1. l. 4. c. 12.   † De deperd. Tit. 33.
‡ Or Antioch. Licetus de Lucernis, l. 1. c. 7.

Whence we may probably conjecture that it was some chymical secret, by which this was contrived.

Baptista Porta * tells us of another lamp burning in an old marble sepulchre, belonging to some of the ancient Romans, inclosed in a glass vial, found in his time, about the year 1550, in the isle Nesis, which had been buried there before our Saviour's coming.

In the tomb of Pallas, the Arcadian who was slain by Turnus in the Trojan war, there was found another burning lamp, in the year of our Lord 1401 †. Whence it should seem, that it had continued there for above two thousand and six hundred years: and being taken out, it did remain burning, notwithstanding either wind or water, with which some did strive to quench it; nor could it be extinguished till they had spilt the liquor that was in it.

Ludovicus Vives ‡ tells us of another lamp, that did continue burning for 1050 years, which was found a little before his time.

Such a lamp is likewise related to be seen in the sepulchre of Francis Rosicrosse, as is more largely expressed in the confession of that fraternity.

There is another relation of a certain man, who upon occasion digging somewhat deep in the ground did meet with something like a door, having a wall on each hand of it ; from which having cleared the earth, he forced open this door, upon this there was discovered a fair vault, and towards the further side of it, the statue of a man in armour, sitting by a table, leaning upon his left arm, and holding a sceptre in his right hand, with a lamp burning before him ; the floor of this vault being so contrived, that upon the first step into it, the statue would erect itself from its leaning posture ; upon the second step it did lift up the scepter to strike, and before a man could approach near enough to take hold of the lamp, the statue did strike and break it to

---

* Mag. Natural. l. 12. cap. ult.

† Chron. Martin. Fort. Licet. de Lucern. l. 1. c. 11.

‡ Not. ad August. de Civit. Dei, l. 21. c. 6.

pieces: such care was there taken that it might not be stolen away, or discovered.

Our learned Cambden in his description of Yorkshire [*] speaking of the tomb of Constantius Chlorus, broken up in these later years, mentions such a lamp to be found within it.

There are sundry other relations to this purpose. *Quod ad lucernas attinet, illæ in omnibus fere monumentis inveniuntur*, (saith Gutherius [†].) In most of the ancient monuments there is some kind of lamp, (though of the ordinary sort:) but those persons who were of greatest note and wisdom, did procure such as might last without supply, for so many ages together. Pancirollus [‡] tells us, that it was usual for the nobles amongst the Romans, to take special care in their last wills, that they might have a lamp in their monuments. And to this purpose they did usually give liberty unto some of their slaves on this condition, that they should be watchful in maintaining and preserving it. From all which relations, the first particular of this enquiry, concerning the being or existence of such lamps, may sufficiently appear.

CHAP. XI.

Several opinions concerning the nature and reason of these perpetual Lamps.

THERE are two opinions to be answered, which do utterly overthrow the chief consequence from these relations.

1. Some think that these lights so often discovered in the ancient tombs, were not fire or flame, but only some of those bright bodies which do usually shine in dark places.

[*] Pag. 572.   [†] De Jure Manium, l. 2. c. 32.
[‡] De perdit. Tit. 62.

2. Others grant them to be fire, but yet think them to be then first enkindled by the admission of new air, when these sepulchres were opened.

1. There are divers bodies (saith Aristotle *) which shine in the dark, as rotten wood, the scales of some fishes, stones, the glowworm, the eyes of divers creatures.   Cardan † tells us of a bird in New Spain, called cocoyum, whose whole body is very bright, but his eyes almost equal to the light of a candle, by which alone in a dark night, one may both write and read: by these the Indians (saith he) used to eat their feasting suppers.

It is commonly related and believed, that a carbuncle does shine in the dark like a burning coal, from whence it hath its name ‡. To which purpose there is a story in Ælian ‖ of a stork, that by a certain woman was cured of a broken thigh, in gratitude to whom, this fowl afterwards flying by her, did let fall into her lap a bright carbuncle, which (saith he) would in the night time shine as clear as a lamp.   But this and the like old relations are now generally disbelieved and rejected by learned men: *doctissimorum omnium consensu, hujusmodi gemmæ non inveniuntur*, (saith Boetius de Boot §) a man very much skilled in, and inquisitive after such matters; nor is there any one of name that does from his own eye-sight or experience, affirm the real existence of any gem so qualified.

Some have thought that the light in ancient tombs hath been occasioned from some such bodies as these ¶.   For if there had been any possibility to preserve fire so long a space, it is likely then that the Israelites would have known the way, who were to keep it perpetually for their sacrifices.

But to this opinion it might be replied, that none of these noctilucæ, or night-shining bodies have been observed in any of the ancient sepulchres, and therefore this is a mere

* De Anima, l. 2. c. 7.   † Subtil. l. 9.
‡ Carlo Pyropus.   ‖ Historia Anim. l. 8.
§ De Lapid. et Gemmis, l. 2. c. 8.
¶ Vide Licet. de Lucern. l. 2.

imaginary conjecture; and then besides, some of these lamps have been taken out burning, and continued so for a considerable space afterwards. As for the supposed conveniency of them, for the perpetuating of the holy fire amongst the Jews, it may as well be feared lest these should have occasioned their idolatry, unto which that nation was so strongly addicted, upon every slight occasion; nor may it seem strange, if the providence of God should rather permit this fire sometimes to go out, that so by their earnest prayers, being again renewed from heaven, (as it sometimes was *) the people's faith might be the better stirred up and strengthened by such frequent miracles.

2. It is the opinion of Gutherius †, that these lamps have not continued burning for so long a space, as they are supposed in the former relations; but that they were then first enflamed by the admission of new air, or such other occasion, when the sepulchres were opened: as we see in those fat earthy vapours of divers sorts, which are oftentimes enkindled into a flame. And it is said, that there are some chymical ways, whereby iron may be so heated, that being closely luted in a glass, it shall constantly retain the fire for any space of time, though it were for a thousand years or more; at the end of which, if the glass be opened, and the fresh air admitted, the iron shall be as red hot as if it were newly taken out of the fire.

But for answer to this opinion, it is considerable that some urns have had inscriptions on them, expressing that the lamps within them were burning, when they were first buried. To which may be added the experience of those which have continued so for a good space afterwards; whereas the inflammation of fat and viscous vapours does presently vanish. The lamp which was found in the isle Nesis, did burn clearly while it was inclosed in the glass, but that being broken, was presently extinguished. As for that chymical relation, it may rather serve to prove that

---

* Levit. ix. 24. 2 Chron. vii. 1. 1 Kings xviii. 38.
† De Jure Manium, l. 2. c. 32.

fire may continue so many ages, without consuming any fewel.

So that notwithstanding the opposite opinions, yet it is more probable that there have been such lamps as have remained burning, without any new supply, for many hundred years together; which was the first particular to be explained.

2. Concerning the reason why the ancients were so careful in this particular, there are divers opinions. Some think it to be an expression of their belief, concerning the soul's immortality, after its departure out of the body; a lamp amongst the Egyptians being the hieroglyphic of life. And therefore they that could not procure such lamps, were yet careful to have the image and representation of them engraved on their tombs.

Others conceive them to be by way of gratitude to those infernal deities, who took the charge and custody of their dead bodies, remaining always with them in their tombs, and were therefore called *dii manes*.

Others are of opinion, that these lamps were only intended to make their sepulchres more pleasant and lightsome, that they might not seem to be imprisoned in a dismal and uncomfortable place. True indeed, the dead body cannot be sensible of this light, no more could it of its want of burial; yet the same instinct which did excite it to the desire of one, did also occasion the other.

Licetus * concludes this ancient custom to have a double end. 1. Politic, for the distinction of such as were nobly born, in whose monuments only they were used. 2. Natural, to preserve the body and soul from darkness; for it was a common opinion amongst them, that the souls also were much conversant about those places where the bodies were buried.

* De Lucernis, l. 3. c. 8.

CHAP. XII.

The most probable conjecture, how these lamps were framed.

THE greatest difficulty of this enquiry doth consist in this last particular, concerning the manner how, or by what possible means any such perpetual flame may be contrived.

For the discovery of which, there are two things to be more especially considered.

1. The snuff, or wick, which must administer unto the flame.

2. The oil, which must nourish it.

For the first, it is generally granted that there are divers substances which will retain fire without consuming: such is that mineral which they call the salamanders wool, saith our learned Bacon *. *Ipse expertus sum villos salamandræ non consumi*, saith Joachimus Fortius †. And Wecker ‡, from his own knowledge, affirms the same of plumeallum, that being formed into the likeness of a wick, will administer to the flame, and yet not consume itself. Of this nature likewise was that which the ancients did call *linum vivum* ‖, or *asbestinum:* of this they were wont to make garments, that were not destroyed, but purified by fire; and whereas the spots or foulness of other clothes are washed out, in these they were usually burnt away. The bodies of the ancient kings were wrapped in such garments, when they were put in the funeral pile, that their ashes might be therein preserved, without the mixture of any other §. The materials of them were not from any herb or vegetable, as other textiles, but from a stone called amiantus; which

---

* Nat. Hist. Exper. 774.   † Lib. Exper.
‡ De Secretis, l. 3. c. 2.
‖ Or linum carpasium.   Plutarch. de Oracul. Defectu.
§ Plin. Hist. l. 19. c. 1.

being bruised by a hammer, and its earthly nature shaken out, retains certain hairy substances, which may be spun and woven, as hemp or flax. Pliny says, that for the preciousness of it, it did almost equal the price of pearls. Pancirollus * tells us, that it was very rare, and esteemed precious in antient times, but now is scarce found or known in any places, and therefore he reckons it amongst the things that are lost. But L. Vives † affirms, that he hath often seen wicks made of it at Paris, and the same matter woven into a napkin at Lovaine, which was cleansed by being burnt in the fire.

It is probable from these various relations, that there were several sorts of it; some of a more precious, other of a baser kind, that was found in Cyprus, the deserts of India, and a certain province of Asia; this being common in some parts of Italy, but is so short and brittle, that it cannot be spun into a thread; and therefore is useful only for the wicks of perpetual lamps; saith Boetius de Boot ‡. Some of this, or very like it, I have upon enquiry lately procured and experimented; but whether it be the stone asbestus, or only plumeallum, I cannot certainly affirm; for it seems they are both so very like, as to be commonly sold for one another (saith the same author.) However, it does truly agree in this common quality ascribed unto both, of being incombustible, and not consumable by fire: but yet there is this inconvenience, that it doth contract so much fuliginous matter from the earthly parts of the oil, (though it was tried with some of the purest oil which is ordinary to be bought) that in a very few days it did choke and extinguish the flame. There may possibly be some chymical way, so to purify and defecate this oil, that it shall not spend into a sooty matter.

However, if the liquor be of a close and glutinous consistency, it may burn without any snuff, as we see in camphire, and some other bituminous substances. And it is

* De perd. Tit. 4.   † In August. de Civit. Dei, l. 21. c. 6.
‡ De Lapid. et Gemmis, l. 2. c. 204.

probable that most of the ancient lamps were of this kind, because the exactest relations (to my remembrance) do not mention any that have been found with such wicks.

But herein will consist the greatest difficulty, to find out what invention there might be for their duration: concerning which there are sundry opinions.

St. Austin * speaking of that lamp in one of the heathen temples, thinks that it might either be done by magic, (the devil thinking thereby to promote the worship and esteem of that idol to which it was dedicated) or else, that the art of man might make it of some such material, as the stone asbestus, which being once kindled, will burn without being consumed †. As others (saith he) have contrived as great a wonder in appearance, from the natural virtue of another stone, making an iron image seem to hang in the air, by reason of two loadstones, the one being placed in the ceiling, the other in the floor.

Others are of opinion, that this may be effected in a hollow vessel, exactly luted or stopped up in all the vents of it: and then, if a lamp be supposed to burn in it but for the least moment of time, it must continue so always, or else there would be a vacuum, which nature is not capable of. If you ask how it shall be nourished, it is answered, that the oil of it being turned into smoke and vapours, will again be converted into its former nature; for otherwise, if it should remain rarified in so thin a substance, then there would not be room enough for that fume which must succeed it; and so on the other side, there might be some danger of the penetration of bodies, which nature doth as much abhor. To prevent both which, as it is in the chymical circulations, where the same body is oftentimes turned from liquor into vapour, and from vapour into liquor again; so in this experiment, the same oil shall be turned into fume, and that fume shall again convert into oil. Always provided, that this oil which nourishes the lamp, be

* De Civ. Dei, l. 21. c. 6.
† Zanch. de Operibus Dei, par. 1. l. 4. c. 12.

supposed of so close and tenacious a substance, that may slowly evaporate, and so there will be the more leisure for nature to perfect these circulations. According to which contrivance, the lamp within this vessel can never fail, being always supplied with sufficient nourishment. That which was found in the isle Nesis, inclosed in a glass-vial, mentioned by Baptista Porta, is thought to be made after some such manner as this.

Others conceive it possible to extract such an oil out of some minerals, which shall for a long space serve to nourish the flame of a lamp, with very little or no expence of its own substance *. To which purpose (say they) if gold be dissolved into an unctuous humour, or if the radical moisture of that metal were separated, it might be contrived to burn (perhaps for ever, or at least) for many ages together, without being consumed. For, if gold itself (as experience shews) be so untameable by the fire, that after many meltings and violent heats, it does scarce diminish, it is probable then, that being dissolved into an oily substance, it might for many hundred years together continue burning.

There is a little chymical discourse, to prove that urim and thummim is to be made by art. The author of this treatise affirms that place, Gen. vi. 16. where God tells Noah, a window shalt thou make in the ark, to be very unfitly rendered in our translation, a window; because the original word צהר signifies properly splendour, or light : and then besides, the air being at that time so extremely darkened with the clouds of that excessive rain, a window could be but of very little use in regard of light, unless there were some other help for it. From whence he conjectures, that both this splendour, and so likewise the urim and thummim were artificial chymical preparations of light, answerable to these subterraneous lamps; or in his own phrase, it was the universal spirit fixed in a transparent body.

---

* Wolphang. Lazius, l. 3. c. 18. Camb. Brit. p 572.

It is the opinion of Licetus *, (who hath more exactly searched into the subtilties of this enquiry) that fire does not need any humour for the nourishment of it, but only to detain it from flying upwards: for, being in itself one of the chief elements (saith he out of Theophrastus) it were absurd to think that it could not subsist without something to feed it. As for that substance which is consumed by it, this cannot be said to foment or preserve the same fire, but only to generate new. For the better understanding of this, we must observe, that there may be a threefold proportion betwixt fire, and the humour, or matter of it. Either the humour does exceed the strength of the fire, or the fire does exceed the humour; and according to both these, the flame doth presently vanish. Or else lastly, they may be both equal in their virtues, (as it is betwixt the radical moisture, and natural heat in living creatures) and then neither of them can overcome, or destroy the other.

Those ancient lamps of such long duration, were of this latter kind: but now, because the qualities of heat or cold, dryness or moisture in the ambient air, may alter this equality of proportion betwixt them, and make one stronger than the other; therefore to prevent this, the ancients did hide these lamps in some caverns of the earth, or close monuments. And hence is it, that at the opening of these, the admission of new air unto the lamp does usually cause so great an inequality betwixt the flame and the oil, that it is presently extinguished.

But still, the greatest difficulty remains how to make any such exact proportion betwixt an unctuous humour, and such an active quality as the heat of fire ; or this equality being made, it is yet a further difficulty, how it may be preserved. To which purpose, Licetus thinks it possible to extract an inflammable oil from the stone asbestus, amiantus, or the metal gold; which being of the same pure and homogeneous nature with those bodies, shall be so proportioned unto the heat of fire, that it cannot be consumed by it ;

---

* De Lucernis, c. 20, 21.

but being once inflamed, should continue for many ages, without any sensible diminution.

If it be in the power of chymistry to perform such strange effects, as are commonly experimented in that which they call aurum fulminans, one scruple of which shall give a louder blow, and be of greater force in descent, than half a pound of ordinary gunpowder in ascent; why may it not be as feasible by the same art. to extract such an oil as is here enquired after? since it must needs be more difficult to make a fire, (which of its own inclination shall tend downwards) than to contrive such an unctuous liquor, wherein fire shall be maintained for many years without any new supply.

Thus have I briefly set down the relations and opinions of divers learned men, concerning these perpetual lamps; of which, though there have been so many sundry kinds, and several ways to make them, (some being able to resist any violence of weathers, others being easily extinguished by any little alteration of the air, some being inclosed round about within glass, others being open;) yet now they are all of them utterly perished amongst the other ruins of time; and those who are most versed in the search after them, have only recovered such dark conjectures, from which a man cannot clearly deduce any evident principle, that may encourage him to a particular trial.

CHAP. XIII.

Concerning several attempts of contriving a perpetual motion by magnetical virtues.

THE second way whereby the making of a perpetual motion hath been attempted, is by magnetical virtues; which are not without some strong probabilities of proving effectual to this purpose: especially when we consider, that the heavenly revolutions, (being as the first pattern imi-

tated and aimed at in these attempts) are all of them performed by the help of these qualities. This great orb of
earth, and all the other planets, being but as so many magnetical globes, endowed with such various and continual
motions, as may be most agreeable to the purposes for
which they were intended. And therefore most of the
authors *, who treat concerning this invention, do agree,
that the likeliest way to effect it, is by these kind of qualities.

It was the opinion of Pet. Peregrinus, and there is an
example pretended for it in Bettinus, (Apiar. 9. Progym. 5.
pro. 11.) that a magnetical globe, or terella, being rightly
placed upon its poles, would of itself have a constant rotation, like the diurnal motion of the earth : but this is commonly exploded, as being against all experience.

Others † think it possible, so to contrive several pieces of
steel and a loadstone, that by their continual attraction and
expulsion of one another, they may cause a perpetual revolution of a wheel. Of this opinion were Taisner ‡, Pet.
Peregrinus ||, and Cardan §, out of Antonius de Fantis. But
D. Gilbert, who was more especially versed in magnetical
experiments, concludes it to be a vain and groundless
fancy.

But amongst all these kind of inventions, that is most
likely, wherein a loadstone is so disposed, that it shall
draw unto it on a reclined plane, a bullet of steel, which
steel as it ascends near to the loadstone, may be contrived
to fall down through some hole in the plane, and so to return unto the place from whence at first it began to move;
and being there, the loadstone will again attract it upwards,
till coming to this hole, it will fall down again; and so the
motion shall be perpetual, as may be more easily conceivable by this figure.

---

* Gilbert de Magnet. Cabæus Philos. Magnet. l. 4. c. 20.

† Athanas. Kircher, de Arte Magnet. l. 1. par. 2. prop. 13. item l. 2. p. 4.

‡ Tract. de motu continuo.

|| De Rota perpetui Motus, par. 2. c. 3.

§ De Variet. Rerum, l. 9. c. 48. De Magnet. l. 2. c. 35,

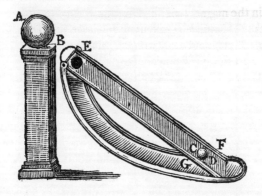

Suppose the loadstone to be represented at **A B,** which, though it have not strength enough to attract the bullet C directly from the ground, yet may do it by the help of the plane **E F.** Now, when the bullet is come to the top of this plane, its own gravity (which is supposed to exceed the strength of the loadstone) will make it fall into that hole at **E;** and the force it receives in this fall, will carry it with such a violence unto the other end of this arch, that it will open the passage which is there made for it, and by its return will again shut it; so that the bullet, (as at the first) is in the same place whence it was attracted, and consequently must move perpetually.

But however this invention may seem to be of such strong probability, yet there are sundry particulars which may prove it insufficient: for,

1. This bullet of steel must first be touched, and have its several poles, or else there can be little or no attraction of it. Suppose C in the steel to be answerable unto A in the stone, and to B; in the attraction, C D must always be directed answerable to A B, and so the motion will be more difficult, by reason there can be no rotation, or turning round of the bullet, but it must slide up with the line C D, answerable to the axis A B.

2. In its fall from E to G, which is *motus elementaris,* and proceeds from its gravity, there must needs be a rotation of it, and so it is odds but it happens wrong in the rise, the poles in the bullet being not in the same direction to

those in the magnet : and if in this reflux, it should so fall out, that D should be directed towards B, there should be rather a flight than an attraction, since those two ends do repel, and not draw one another.

3. If the loadstone A B have so much strength, that it can attract the bullet in F when it is not turned round, but does only slide upon the plane, whereas its own gravity would roll it downwards; then it is evident, the sphere of its activity and strength would be so increased when it approaches much nearer, that it would not need the assistance of the plane, but would draw it immediately to itself without that help; and so the bullet would not fall down through the hole, but ascend to the stone, and consequently cease its motion : for, if the loadstone be of force enough to draw the bullet on the plane, at the distance F B, then must the strength of it be sufficient to attract it immediately unto itself, when it is so much nearer as E B.   And if the gravity of the bullet be supposed so much to exceed the strength of the magnet, that it cannot draw it directly when it is so near, then will it not be able to attract the bullet up the plane, when it is so much further off.

So that none of all these magnetical experiments, which have been as yet discovered, are sufficient for the effecting of a perpetual motion, though these kind of qualities seem most conducible unto it, and perhaps hereafter it may be contrived from them.

CHAP. XIV.

The seeming probability of effecting a continual motion by solid weights, in a hollow wheel or sphere.

THE third way whereby the making of a perpetual motion hath been attempted, is by the natural affection of gravity; when the heaviness of several bodies is so contrived, that the same motion which they give in their descent, may be able to carry them up again.

But, (against the possibility of any such invention) it is thus objected by Cardan *. All sublunary bodies have a direct motion either of ascent, or descent; which, because it does refer to some term, therefore cannot be perpetual, but must needs cease, when it is arrived at the place unto which it naturally tends.

I answer, though this may prove that there is no natural motion of any particular heavy body, which is perpetual, yet it doth not hinder, but that it is possible from them to contrive such an artificial revolution, as shall constantly be the cause of itself.

Those bodies which may be serviceable to this purpose, are distinguishable into two kinds.

1. Solid and consistent, as weights of metal, or the like.

2. Fluid, or sliding ; as water, sand, &c.

Both these ways have been attempted by many, though with very little or no success. Other men's conjectures in this kind you may see set down by divers authors †. It would be too tedious to repeat them over, or set forth their draughts. I shall only mention two new ones, which (if I am not over-partial) seem altogether as probable as any of these kinds that have been yet invented ; and till experience had discovered their defect and insufficiency, I did certainly conclude them to be infallible.

The first of these contrivances was by solid weights being placed in some hollow wheel or sphere, unto which they should give a perpetual revolution: for (as the philosopher ‡ hath largely proved) only a circular motion can properly be perpetual.

But for the better conceiving of this invention, it is re-quisite that we rightly understand some principles in tro-chilics, or the art of wheel-instruments: as chiefly, the re-lation betwixt the parts of a wheel, and those of a balance; the several proportions in the semidiameter of a wheel,

* Subtil. l. 17. De Var. Rerum, l. 9. c. 48.
† D. Flud. Tract. 2. pars 7. l. 2. c. 4. et 7
‡ Arist. Phys l. 8. c. 12

being answerable to the sides in a balance, where the weight is multiplied according to its distance from the centre *.

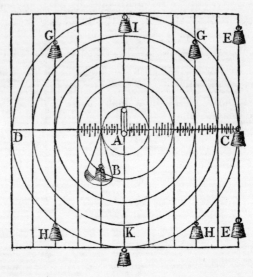

Thus, suppose the centre to be at A, and the diameter of the wheel D C to be divided into equal parts (as is here expressed) it is evident, according to the former ground, that one pound at C will equiponderate to five pound at B, because there is such a proportion betwixt their several distances from the centre. And it is not material, whether or no these several weights be placed horizontally; for though B do hang lower than C, yet this does not at all concern the heaviness; or though the plummet C were placed much higher than it is at E, or lower at F, yet would it still retain the same weight which it had at C; because these plummets (as in the nature of all heavy bodies) do tend downwards by a strait line: so that their several gravities are to be measured by that part of the horizontal semidiameter, which is directly either below or above them. Thus when the plummet C shall be moved either to G or

* Arist. Mechan. c. 2. De ratione libræ ad circulum,

ters employed for a year together, besides many other hire-
lings for carriages, and such servile works; mentions this
instrument as being instead of a pump for that vast ship;
by the help of which, one man might easily and speedily
drain out the water, though it were very deep.

Diodorus Siculus * speaking of this engine, tells us, that
Archimedes invented it when he was in Egypt, and that it
was used in that country, for the draining of those pits and
lower grounds, whence the waters of Nilus could not return. Φιλοτεχνε δ' οντος τε οργανε καθ' υπερβολην, (saith the
same author.) It being an engine so ingenious and artificial, as cannot be sufficiently expressed or commended.
And so (it should seem) the smith in Milan conceived it to
be, who having without any teaching or information found
it out, and therefore thinking himself to be the first inventor, fell mad with the mere joy of it †.

The nature and manner of making this, is more largely
handled by Vitruvius ‡.

The figure of it is after this manner :

Where you see there is a cylinder A A, and a spiral cavity or pipe twining about it, according to equal revolutions

* Biblioth. l. 1.   † Cardan. Subtil. l. 1. De Sapient. l. 5.
‡ Architect. l. 10. c. 11.

B B.   The axis and centers of its motions are at the points
C D; upon which being turned, it will so happen, that the
same part of the pipe which was now lowermost, will presently become higher, so that the water does ascend by
descending; ascending in comparison to the whole instrument, and descending in respect of its several parts.   This
being one of the strangest wonders amongst those many
wherein these mathematical arts do abound, that a heavy
body should rise by falling down, and the farther it passes
by his own natural motion of descent, by so much
higher still shall it ascend; which though it seem so evidently to contradict all reason and philosophy, yet in this
instrument it may be manifested both by demonstration
and sense.

This pipe or cavity, for the matter of it, cannot easily be
made of metal, by reason of its often turnings; but for
trial, there might be such a cavity cut in a column of wood,
and afterwards covered over with tin-plate.

For the form and manner of making this screw, Vitruvius
does prescribe these two rules:

1. That there must be an equality observed betwixt the
breadth of the pipe, and the distance of its several circumvolutions.

2. That there must be such a proportion betwixt the
length of the instrument, and its elevation, as is answerable
to the pythagorical trigon.   If the hypotenusal, or screw be
five, the perpendicular or elevation must be three, and the
basis four*.

However, (with his leave) neither of these proportions
are generally necessary, but should be varied according to
other circumstances.   As for the breadth of the pipe in
respect of its revolutions, it is left at liberty, and may be
contrived according to the quantity of water which it should
contain.   The chief thing to be considered, is the obliquity
or closeness of these circumvolutions.   For the nearer
they are unto one another, the higher may the instrument

* David Rivalt. Com. in Archim. opera exter.

be erected; there being no other guide for its true elevation but this.

And because the right understanding of this particular is one of the principal matters that concerns the use of this engine, therefore I shall endeavour with brevity and perspicuity to explain it. The first thing to be enquired after, is, what kind of inclination these helical revolutions of the cylinder have unto the horizon; which may be thus found out.

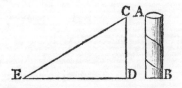

Let A B represent a cylinder with two perfect revolutions in it, unto which cylinder the perpendicular line C D is equal: the basis D E being supposed to be double unto the compass or circumference of the cylinder. Now it is certain, that the angle C E D, is the same with that by which the revolutions on the cylinder are framed, and that the line E C, in comparison to the basis E D, does shew the inclination of these revolutions unto the horizon. The grounds and demonstration of this are more fully set down by Guidus Ubaldus, in his Mechanics, and that other treatise De Cochlea, which he writ purposely for the explication of this instrument, where the subtilties of it are largely and excellently handled.

Now if this screw which was before perpendicular, be supposed to decline unto the horizon by the angle F B G, as in this second figure;

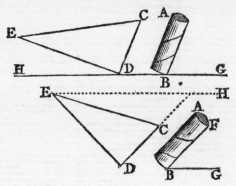

then the inclination of the revolutions in it will be increased by the angle E D H; though these revolutions will still remain in a kind of ascent, so that water cannot be turned through them.

But now, if the screw be placed so far declining, that the angle of its inclination F B G, be less than the angle E C D, in the triangle; as in this other diagram under the former; then the revolutions of it will descend to the horizon, as does the line E C; and in such a posture, if the screw be turned round, water will ascend through its cavity. Whence it is easy to conceive the certain declination, wherein any screw must be placed for its own conveyance of water upwards. Any point betwixt H and D being in descent, but yet the more the screw declines downwards towards D, by so much the more water will be carried up by it.

If you would know the just quantity of water which every revolution does contain and carry, according to any inclination of the cylinder; this may be easily found, by ascribing on it an ellipsis, parallel to the horizon; which ellipsis will shew how much of the revolution is empty, and how much full *.

The true inclination of the screw being found, together with the certain quantity of water which every helix does contain; it is further considerable, that the water by this instrument does ascend naturally of itself, without any

---

* See a further explication of this in Ubaldus de Cochlea, l. 2. prop. 25.

violence or labour ; and that the heaviness of it does lie chiefly upon the centres or axis of the cylinder, both its sides being of equal weight saith Ubaldus * : so that (it should seem) though we suppose each revolution to have an equal quantity of water, yet the screw will remain with any part upwards, (according as it shall be set) without turning itself either way. And therefore the least strength being added to either of its sides, should make it descend, according to that common maxim of Archimedes † ; any addition will make that which equiponderates with another, to tend downwards.

But now, because the weight of this instrument, and the water in it does lean wholly upon the axis, hence is it (saith Ubaldus) that the grating and rubbing of these axes against the sockets wherein they are placed, will cause some ineptitude and resistency to that rotation of the cylinder ; which would otherwise ensue upon the addition of the least weight to any one side ; but (saith the same author) any power that is greater than this resistency which does arise from the axis, will serve for the turning of it round.

These things considered together, it will hence appear, how a perpetual motion may seem easily contrivable. For if there were but such a water-wheel made on this instrument, upon which the stream that is carried up may fall in its descent, it would turn the screw round, and by that means convey as much water up as is required to move it ; so that the motion must needs be continual, since the same weight which in its fall does turn the wheel, is by the turning of the wheel carried up again.

Or if the water falling upon one wheel, would not be forcible enough for this effect, why then there might be two or three, or more, according as the length and elevation of the instrument will admit : by which means, the weight of it may be so multiplied in the fall, that it shall be equiva-

* Ubaldus de Cochlea, l. 3. prop. 4.

† De Æquipond. Suppos. 3.

lent to twice or thrice that quantity of water which ascends.
As may be more plainly discerned by this following diagram:

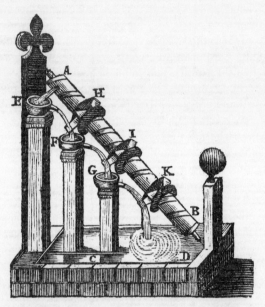

Where the figure L M, at the bottom, does represent a
wooden cylinder with helical cavities cut in it; which at
A B, is supposed to be covered over with tin-plates, and
three water-wheels upon it H I K. The lower cistern
which contains the water being C D. Now this cylinder
being turned round, all the water which from the cistern
ascends through it, will fall into the vessel at E, and from
that vessel being conveyed upon the water-wheel H, shall
consequently give a circular motion to the whole screw : or
if this alone should be too weak for the turning of it, then
the same water which falls from the wheel H, being received into the other vessel F, may from thence again descend on the wheel I; by which means the force of it will

be doubled *.   And if this be yet insufficient, then may the water which falls on the second wheel I, be received into the other vessel G, and from thence again descend on the third wheel at K : and so for as many other wheels as the instrument is capable of.   So that besides the greater distance of these three streams from the centre or axis, by which they are made so much heavier, and besides, that the fall of this outward water is forcible and violent, whereas the ascent of that within is natural; besides all this, there is thrice as much water to turn the sciew, as is carried up by it.

But on the other side, if all the water falling upon one wheel, would be able to turn it round, then half of it would serve with two wheels ; and the rest may be so disposed of in the fall, as to serve unto some other useful delightful ends.

When I first thought of this invention, I could scarce forbear with Archimedes to cry out ευρηκα, ευρηκα, it seeming so infallible a way for the effecting of a perpetual motion, that nothing could be so much as probably objected against it : but upon trial and experience I find it altogether insufficient for any such purpose, and that for these two reasons :

1. The water that ascends will not make any considerable stream in the fall.

2. This stream (though multiplied) will not be of force enough to turn about the screw.

1. The water ascends gently, and by intermissions ; but it falls continuately, and with force ; each of the three vessels being supposed full at the first, that so the weight of the water in them might add the greater strength and swiftness to the streams, that descend from them.   Now this swiftness of motion will cause so great a difference betwixt them, that one of these little streams may spend

* There is another like contrivance to this purpose in Pet. Bettin. Apiar. 4. Pogym. 1. Prop. 10. but with much less advantage than it is here proposed.

more water in the fall, than a stream six times bigger in the
ascent, though we should suppose both of them to be continuate : how much more then, when as the ascending
water is vented by fits and intermissions ; every circumvolution voiding only so much as is contained in one helix ?
and in this particular, one that is not versed in these kind
of experiments, may be easily deceived.

But secondly, though there were so great a disproportion,
yet notwithstanding, the force of these outward streams
might well enough serve for the turning of the screw ;
if it were so, that both its sides would equiponderate the
water being in them (as Ubaldus hath affirmed.)   But now,
upon farther examination, we shall find this assertion of
his to be utterly against both reason and experience.
And herein does consist the chief mistake of this contrivance : for the ascending side of the screw is made by
the water contained in it, so much heavier than the descending side, that these outward streams thus applied,
will not be of force enough to make them equiponderate,
much less to move the whole ; as may be more easily
discerned by this fig.

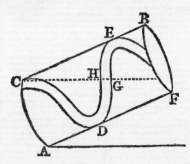

Where A B represents a screw covered over, C D E one
helix, or revolution of it, C D the ascending side, E D the
descending side, the point D the middle.   The horizontal
line C F, shewing how much of the helix is filled with water, viz. of the ascending side, from C the beginning of the
helix, to D the middle of it ; and on the descending side,

DÆDALUS; OR, MECHANICAL MOTIONS. 245

from D the middle, to the point G, where the horizontal does cut the helix. Now it is evident, that this latter part D G, is nothing near so much, and consequently not so heavy as the other D C. And thus is it in all the other revolutions ; which, as they are either more or larger, so will the difficulty of this motion be increased. Whence it will appear, that the outward streams which descend, must be of so much force, as to countervail all that weight whereby the ascending side in every one of these revolutions does exceed the other. And though this may be effected by making the water-wheels larger, yet then the motion will be so slow, that the screw will not be able to supply the outward streams.

There is another contrivance to this purpose, mentioned by Kircher de Magnete, l. 2. p. 4. depending upon the heat of the sun, and the force of winds ; but it is liable to such abundance of exceptions, that it is scarce worth the mentioning, and does by no means deserve the confidence of any ingenious artist.

Thus have I briefly explained the probabilities and defects of those subtle contrivances, whereby the making of a perpetual motion hath been attempted. I would be loth to discourage the inquiry of any ingenious artificer, by denying the possibility of effecting it with any of these mechanical helps * : but yet (I conceive) if those principles which concern the slowness of the power, in comparison to the greatness of the weight, were rightly understood, and thoroughly considered, they would make this experiment to seem (if not altogether impossible) yet much more difficult than otherwise perhaps it will appear. However, the inquiring after it cannot but deserve our endeavours, as being one of the most noble amongst all these mechanical subtleties. And (as it is in the fable of him who dug the vineyard for a hid treasure, though he did not find the money, yet he thereby made the ground more fruitful ; so) though we do not attain to the effecting of this particular, yet our

* Treated of before, l. 1. c.

searching after it may discover so many other excellent subtleties, as shall abundantly recompense the labour of our
inquiry.

And then besides, it may be another encouragement, to
consider the pleasure of such speculations which do ravish
and sublime the thoughts with more clear angelical contentments. Archimedes was generally so taken up in the delight of these mathematical studies of this familiar siren, (as
Plutarch * stiles them) that he forgot both his meat and
drink, and other necessities of nature; nay, that he neglected
the saving of his life, when that rude soldier, in the pride
and haste of victory, would not give him leisure to finish
his demonstration. What a ravishment was that, when
having found out the way to measure Hiero's crown, he
leaped out of the bath, and (as if he were suddenly pos-
sessed) ran naked up and down, crying ευρηκα, ευρηκα ! It
is storied of Thales, that in his joy and gratitude for one of
these mathematical inventions, he went presently to the
temple, and there offered up a solemn sacrifice. And Pythagoras, upon the like occasion, is related to have sa-
crificed a hundred oxen. The justice of providence having
so contrived it, that the pleasure which there is in the success of such inventions, should be proportioned to the
great difficulty and labour of their inquiry.

* Οικειας και συνοικε σειρην©ν. Plutarch. Marcell. Joan. Tzetzes, Chil. 2.
Hist. 35. Valer. Maxim, l. 8. c. 7.

ABSTRACT OF DR. WILKINS's ESSAY

TOWARDS A

REAL CHARACTER,

AND

A PHILOSOPHICAL LANGUAGE.

Which was printed by order of the Royal Society, 1668.

———

IT appears by the author's dedication to the president, council, and fellows of the royal society, that they had several times required his papers of him relating to this subject, and that in obedience to their orders, he had reduced them into method. He tells them, he was not so vain as to think he had finished this great undertaking with all the advantages of which it was capable : nor was he so diffident of his essay, but that he thought it sufficient for what it pretended to, viz. the distinct expression of all things and notions that fall under discourse. He was sensible of sundry defects in several parts of the book, and therefore desired they would appoint some of their number to consider the whole, and to offer their observations as to what they thought fit to be amended. Accordingly several of the society, as appears by the Philosophical Transactions of Monday, May 18, 1668, were appointed to answer his desire, for the furthering and facilitating the practice of what he aimed at. But what progress they made in it does not appear. Our author was sensible that his design might lie neglected as other good designs had done ; and the only expedient he could think of to prevent it, was, that it might be sent abroad with the approbation of the royal society, which might provoke at least the learned part of the world to take notice of, and encourage it, according as they should think it deserved.

The advantages proposed by this philosophical language were, the facilitating of mutual commerce among the several nations of the world; the improving of natural knowledge; and the propagation of religion : our author was also of opinion, that it might contribute much to the clearing of some modern differences in religion, by unmasking many wild errors that shelter themselves under the disguise of affected phrases: which being philosophically unfolded, and rendered according to the genuine and natural importance of words, would appear to be inconsistencies and contradictions; and several of these pretended mysterious profound notions, expressed in big swelling words, by which men set up for reputation, being this way examined, would either appear to be nonsense, or very jejune. But whatever might be the issue of this attempt, as to the establishing of a real character, and bringing it into common use among several nations of the world, of which our author had but very slender expectations, yet of this he was confident, that the reducing of all things and notions to such kind of tables as he proposed, were it as completely done as it might be, would prove the shortest and plainest way for the attainment of real knowledge, that had yet been offered to the world. To which he added, that he thought his tables, as now they are, were a much better and readier course for training up men in the knowledge of things, than any other way that he knew of. And indeed since his design of the real character is wholly neglected, that seems now to be the principal use of the book, and alone makes it truly valuable.

In his preface to the reader he gives an account how he came to engage in this work, viz. that by his converse with Dr. Seth Ward, then bishop of Salisbury, upon the various desiderata, proposed by learned men to be still wanting to the advancement of several parts of learning, he found this of an universal character, to be one of the principal and most feasible, if regularly prosecuted; but most of those who had attempted any thing like it, mistook their foundation, by proposing a character according to some particular language, without reference to the nature of things, and that common notion of them wherein mankind agrees : this suggestion gave him the first distinct apprehension of the proper course to be taken for advancing such a design.

He says it was a considerable time after this before he attempted it ; and the first occasion of it was ; his desire to assist another person in framing a real character from the natural notion of things. In order to promote that person's design, he drew up the tables of substances, or the species of natural bodies, reduced under their several heads, much the same as they are published in this Essay. But the person thinking this method of too great a compass, and conceiving that he could provide for all the chief radicals in a much shorter and easier way, he did not make use of the doctor's tables. Our author however being convinced that this was the only way to effect such a work, and being unwilling to lose so much pains, he went on with the other tables of accidents, and then attempted the reduction of all other words in the dictionary to these tables, either as they were synonimous to them, or to be defined by them; which was a true way to try the fulness of those tables ; and likewise a help to learners, who without such a direction, might not perhaps be able at first to find out the true place and notion of many words.

For the farther compleating of this work, our author found it necessary to frame such a natural grammar, as might be suited to the philosophy of speech, abstracting from many unnecessary rules belonging to instituted languages.

He takes notice of the assistance he received from his learned friends in several faculties; particularly from Mr. Francis Willoughby, as to the several species of animals ; from Mr. John Ray, as to the tables of plants ; and for the other principal difficulties from Dr. William Lloyd, than whom he knew none fitter, because of his accurate judgment in philology and philosophy ; and to him particularly

which considering the narrow compass of traffic, before the invention of the magnetic needle, must needs be but a small proportion, in comparison to the rest of the world. Some American histories say, that in every eighty miles of that country, the inhabitants speak a different language. Joseph Scaliger reckons eleven mother tongues in Europe, which have no dependance on one another; but they are so well known, that we need not insist upon them. Besides this difference of languages in their first derivation, every particular tongue has its several dialects in one and the same nation. The Hebrew is by many learned men supposed to be the first mother tongue of those now known in the world. When the Jews were captives at Babylon, their language was mixed with the Chaldean; and after the captivity, the pure Hebrew ceased to be vulgar, and remained only amongst learned men, as we find by Nehemiah, viii. 7, 8. And the pure Hebrew now in being is only that of the Old Testament; which though sufficient to express what is there intended, is not so for conversation, and therefore is guessed not to be the same which was concreated with our first parents, and spoken in paradise.

The second chapter consists of four sections. The first concerns the various changes to which all vulgar tongues are obnoxious. The second gives proofs of such changes in the English tongue in the Lord's prayer, from the year of Christ 700, to 1537. The third section determines in the affirmative, that several of the ancient languages are lost, since it is evident from the instance of our own, that in some few hundreds of years, a language may be so changed, as to be scarce intelligible. The fourth section accounts for the rise and occasion of new languages; which he says proceeds from commerce, and mixture of people by conquests, marriage of princes, or otherwise, and instances in that called the Malayan tongue, the newest in the world, and as common among the natives of the East Indies, as Latin and French in Europe. It was invented or occasioned by a concourse of fishermen from Pegu, Siam, Bengala, and other nations at Malacca, where they built the town of that name, and agreed upon a distinct language made up of the easiest words belonging to each nation.

The third chapter consists of four sections. The first treats of the original of letters and writing. Our author tells us, it is most generally agreed that Adam in process of time, upon his experience of the great necessity of letters, did first invent the ancient Hebrew character; but he rejects those particular alphabets which are by some ascribed to Adam, Enoch, and Noah; and adds, that it has been abundantly cleared by learned men, that the ancient Hebrew character has the priority before any now known. And it is none of the least arguments for the truth and divine authority of the holy scriptures, to consider the general concurrence of all manner of evidence for the antiquity of the Hebrew, and the derivation of all other letters from it. In the second section he gives us the opinion of many of the ancients, to confirm the derivation of other letters and languages from the Hebrew. In the third, he shews us that the use of letters is less ancient, and the kinds of them less numerous than the languages themselves. He proves this by several instances, that many nations do not yet understand the use of letters, and that though the German and French tongues be ancient, it is not much above four hundred years since books began to be writ in those languages; and the reason why letters are less numerous than languages, is, that several nations borrowed the use of letters from their neighbours, and adapted them to their own languages. In the fourth section, he gives us an account of the hieroglyphics of the ancients, which was a mere shift they were put to for want of letters, and was a slight and imperfect invention, suitable to those first and ruder ages. He treats also of the secret and occult ways of writing, taught by the abbot Trithemius, for which he was falsely accused of magic. He gives us some hints about letters or marks used by the ancients for brevity sake; of which nature is shorthand, so common in England. In the fifth section, he gives an account of some ancient attempts towards a real character, to signify things and notions. And in the sixth informs us, that no alphabet now in being, was invented at once, or by rules of art; but all of them, except the Hebrew, were taken up by imitation.

The fourth chapter consists of six sections. The first treats of the defects in the common alphabet, as to their true order, which is inartificial and confused, the vowels and consonants being huddled together without any distinction; whereas the vowels and consonants should be reduced into classes, according to their several kinds. In the second section, he takes notice of the redundancy and deficiency of the Hebrew alphabet, and likewise of the Greek and Latin. In the third section, he shews that they are very uncertain as to their powers and signification; of which he gives several instances in our own language. In the fourth section, he takes notice that the names of the letters in most alphabets are very improperly expressed by words of several syllables. In this respect, the Roman and English alphabet are more convenient than the rest, though not without some defects of the same nature. In the fifth section, he says their figures do not correspond sufficiently with their natures and powers, and observes that the manner of writing the oriental tongues from right to left is as unnatural as to write with light on the wrong side. In the sixth section, he takes notice of the defects of words as well as letters; some of them being equivocal, others synonimous, besides the irregularities in grammar, and the difference betwixt writing and pronouncing words. On this occasion, he takes notice of the endeavours of Sir Thomas Smith and others, to rectify our English orthography, though we still obstinately retain the errors of our ancestors.

The fifth chapter has three sections. The first maintains, that neither letters nor languages have been regularly established by rules of art: nor could it be otherwise, because grammar (by which they should be regulated) is of a much later invention than the languages themselves; as is evident from the Hebrew; which, though the oldest of all, was not reduced into order of grammar till the year 1040. In the second, he treats of the natural ground and principle of the everal ways of communication among men; where he tells us, that as they generally agree in the same principle of reason, they likewise agree in the same internal notion or apprehension of things; and those internal notions they communicate to the ear by sounds, and particularly by words, and to the eye they communicate them by motion and figure, &c. and more particularly by writing: so that if men should generally agree upon the same way of expression as they agree in the same notion, we should then be free from that curse of the confusion of tongues, and all the unhappy consequences of it. This is only to be done by some one language and character to be universally practised, and enjoined by authority; which cannot be expected without an universal monarchy; and perhaps not then: or else by some method which (without such authority) might engage men to learn it, because of its facility and usefulness, which was the design of this Essay. The third section informs us, that in order to this, the first thing to be considered, was a just enumeration and description of such things as were to have marks or names assigned them, and to be so contrived, as to be full and adequate without redundancy or defect as to their number, and regular as to their place and order. And if every thing and notion had a distinct mark, with some provision to express grammatical derivations and inflections, it would answer one great end of a real character, to signify things and not words. And if several distinct words were assigned for the names of such things, with fixed rules for such grammatical derivations and inflections as are natural and necessary, it would make a more easy and convenient language than any yet in being.

Then if these marks or notes could be so contrived, as to have such a dependance upon, and relation to one another, as might suit the nature of the things and notions they represent; and likewise, if the names of things could be so ordered, as to contain such an affinity or opposition in their letters and sounds, as might some way answer the nature of the things they signify, it would be a further advantage, by which, besides helping the memory by natural method, the understanding would be improved; and by learning the characters and names of things, we should likewise learn their natures.

Thus our author concludes the first part, and comes to the second; which contains a regular enumeration and description of all those things and notions to which names are to be assigned, and forms a system of universal philosophy. This part is divided into twelve chapters. The first contains six sections. The first section has a scheme of genus's, or more common heads of things belonging to this design. Then he shews how each of them may be subdivided by its peculiar differences, which for the better conveniency of the design, he determines for most part to the number of six, except in the numerous tribes of herbs, trees, exanguious animals, fishes, and birds, which cannot be comprehended in so narrow a compass. Then he enumerates the several species belonging to each of those differences, in such an order and dependance, as may contribute to define them, and determine their primary significations. These species he commonly joins together in pairs, for helping the memory; and so likewise are some of the genus's and differences; those things which naturally have opposites, are joined with them, according to such opposition, whether single or double; and those things that have no opposites, are commonly joined together with respect to some affinity which they have to one another, though sometimes those affinities are less proper and more remote; there being several things shifted into those places, because the author did not know how to provide for them better. The second section relates to the more general notions of things, and the difficulty of establishing those notions aright. The third treats of transcendentals general. The fourth of transcendental relations mixed. The fifth of transcendental relations of action; and the sixth of the several notions belonging to grammar or logic. But these things being digested into tables, we must refer the reader to the book itself, for a distinct idea of them.

The second chapter consists of two sections. The first

is concerning God; and the second concerning the several things and notions reducible under that collective genus of the world: which is also digested into tables.

The third chapter consists of three sections. The first is of elements and meteors; the second of stones; and the third of metals; digested also into tables.

The fourth chapter has seven sections. The first of plants; the second concerning a more general distribution of them; the third, fourth, and fifth, treat of herbs; considered according to their leaves, flowers, and seed-vessels. The sixth treats of shrubs; and the seventh of trees. All of them likewise in tables.

The fifth chapter has six sections. The first concerns animals, and the general distribution of them; the second is of exanguious animals; the third of fish; the fourth of birds; the fifth of beasts; and the sixth has a digression concerning Noah's ark: wherein he maintains the truth and authority of the scripture, against the objections of atheists and heretics, that a vessel of such dimensions could not contain so vast a multitude of animals, with the whole year's provision for them.

The sixth chapter relates to the parts of animate bodies; first, peculiar; secondly, general: and these are also digested into tables.

The seventh chapter relates to the predicament of quantity. 1. Of magnitude. 2. Of space. 3. Of measure. All digested into tables.

The eighth chapter relates to quality, and its several genus's. 1. Of natural power. 2. Of habit. 3. Of manners. 4. Of sensible quality. 5. Of diseases. With the various differences and species under each.

The ninth chapter treats of action, and its several genus's. 1. Spiritual. 2. Corporeal. 3. Motion. 4. Operation.

The tenth chapter concerns more private relation. 1. Of family relation; with the several kinds of things belonging to those in that capacity, either as possessions, or provisions.

The eleventh chapter concerns public relations; as civil, judiciary, naval, military, and ecclesiastical.

The twelfth chapter explains the design of the foregoing tables; gives particular instances of the six principal genus's of it; has some notes concerning opposites and synonymas; and an account of such things as ought not to be provided for in those tables.

The third part contains a philosophical grammar; and is divided into fourteen chapters.

The first chapter concerns the several kinds and parts of grammar. 2. Of etymology; and the more general scheme of integrals and particles. 3. Of nouns in general. 4. Of substantives common, denoting either things, actions, or persons. 5. Rules concerning nouns of action. 6. Of substantives abstracts. 7. Of adjectives, according to the true philosophical notion of them. 8. The true notion of a verb. 9. Of derived adverbs. 10. A general scheme of the forementioned derivations.

The second chapter concerns particles in general. 2. Of the copula. 3. Of pronouns more generally. 4. More particularly. 5. Of interjections more generally. 6. More particularly.

The third chapter treats of prepositions in general. 2. The particular kinds of them enumerated. 3. An explication of the four last combinations of them, relating to place or time.

The fourth chapter concerns adverbs in general. 2. The particular kinds of them. 3. Conjunctions.

The fifth chapter treats of articles. 2. Of Moods. 3. Of Tenses. 4. The most distinct way of expressing the differences of time.

The sixth chapter concerns transcendental particles, and the end and use of them. 2. The usual ways for enlarging the sense of words in instituted languages. 3. The general heads of transcendental particles.

The seventh chapter has instances of the great usefulness of those transcendental particles; with directions how they are to be applied.

The eighth chapter treats of the accidental differences of words. 1. Inflexion. 2. Derivation. 3. Composition.

The ninth chapter is of the second part of grammar, called syntax.

The tenth chapter is of orthography; and contains three sections. The first concerning letters; and the authors who have treated of this subject: of whom Dr. Wallis seems with the greatest accurateness and subtilty to have considered the philosophy of articulate sounds. The second contains a brief table of all such kinds of simple sounds, as can be framed with the mouths of men. The third contains a further explanation of this table, as to the organs of speech, and as to the letters framed by those organs.

The eleventh treats of vowels. The twelfth of consonants. The thirteenth of compound vowels and consonants. The fourteenth treats of the accidents of letters: 1. Their names. 2. Their order. 3. Affinities and oppositions. 4. Their figures; with a twofold instance of a more regular character for the letters: the latter of which may be esteemed natural. 5. Of pronunciation. 6. The several letters disused by several nations.

The fourth part contains a real character and philosophical language. This consists of six chapters: the first treats of a proposal of one kind of real character amongst many others which might be offered both for the integrals, whether genus's, differences, or species, together with the derivations and inflexions belonging to them; as likewise for all the several kinds of particles. Here our author acquaints us, that it were exceeding desirable that the names of things might consist of such sounds as should bear in them some analogy to their natures, and the figure or character of these names should bear some proper resemblance to those sounds; but he does not understand how this character can be adjusted any otherwise than by institution: and in the framing of those characters, he says, special regard must be had to these four properties. 1. That the figure be plain and easy, so as it may be made by one or at most by two strokes of the pen. 2. That they be sufficiently distinguished from one another. 3. Graceful to the eye. 4. Methodical. But we must refer to the book itself for our author's specimen.

The second chapter contains an instance of this real character in the Lord's prayer and creed.

The third shews how this character may be made affable in a distinct language, and what kind of letters or syllables may be conveniently assigned to each character.

The fourth has a comparison of the Lord's prayer and creed in this language, with 50 other languages as to the facility and euphony of it. The fifth contains directions for the more easy learning this character and language; with a brief table containing the radicals both integrals and particles, together with the character and language by which each of them are to be expressed.

The sixth is a comparison betwixt this natural philosophical grammar, and that of other instituted languages, particularly the Latin, in respect of the multitude of unnecessary rules, and of anomalisms. It treats also concerning the China character; the several attempts and proposals made by others towards a new kind of character and language, and the advantage in respect of facility which this philosophical language has above the Latin. In the last place comes an alphabetical dictionary wherein all English words according to their various significations, are either referred to their places in the philosophical tables, or explained by such words as are in those tables.

INDEX OF NAMES

(*Page numbers in italic type refer to the second volume*)

S

Sanctius 166, 172
Sarsius 241
Scaliger, Joseph . . . 34, 41, 45, 54n., 57, 167, *20, 44n., 120, 195, 207, 252*
Scheiner . . . . . 27, 29, 75, 77n.
Schickhard . . . . *27n., 49n.*
Scotus, Duns 107
Selenus, Gustav . . . *5, 22n., 24n., 25*
Seneca . . . . . . 25, 92, 131, 226, 242, 255, 258n., 260, *5, 50n., 51, 91, 142, 206n., 209n.*
Serafinus de Firmo . 16
Siculus, Diodorus . . 80
Simeon 36
Sixtus Senensis . . . 28
Socrates 104
Solinus . . . . . . 71, 121, *63n.*
Soncinus 243
Stesichorus 9
Stevin, Simon . . . 123n., *134, 139, 141n., 151*
Strabo 107, 166, 176, *171, 251*
Strada, Famianus . . *75*
Suetonius *28*
Sylenus *33*
Syracusanus 143

T

Taisner *228*
Tertullian . . . . . 108, 151, *41n.*
Theodoret . . . 176–177
Theophilact 176
Tostatus . . . . . . 7, 42, 107–108, 141, 180n.
Trigaultius *54*
Trithemius *5, 33, 50, 62, 86, 253*
Tully 256
Tycho Brahe 29, 31, 35, 39, 83, 95n., 96, 146, 198, 200, 202, 232, 254, 261
Tymme, Thomas . . *214*

U

Ubaldi, G. *94, 120, 182n., 240n., 241, 244*
Ulysses Albergettus . 37–38

V

Valerius Probus . . . *5, 42, 50*
Vallesius 159, 245n., *2n., 52*
Vatablas Sanctius . . 155.
Vegetius *5, 68, 80, 94, 154, 158*
Vincentius, St. . . . 16
Virgil *9, 76, 64, 198*
Virgilius *7, 17, 22*
Vitello 33, 53
Vitruvius 37, *94, 102n., 125n., 157, 180, 205, 237–38*
Vives, Ludovicus . . *31, 223*
Vossius . . . . . . *4–5, 20n.*
Vranckheim, Marcellus *213*

W

Walchius, Johannes . *5, 26n., 48n., 69, 175, 184, 186–87*
Ward, Seth *76n., 248*
Wecker *222*
Whaldus . . . . . . *102n.*
Willoughby, Francis . *249*
Wright, Thomas . . 19

X

Xenophanes *4, 43*
Xerxes 34

Z

Zachary 7
Zanchy . . . . . . 14, 161, *1n., 224n.*
Zeno 94
Zoncha, Vittorio . . *94*